THE SPY WHO CAME IN FROM THE CIRCUS

Inspired by his admiration for Bertram Mills Circus, Churchill produced this oil painting while Chancellor of the Exchequer in 1928. At great personal risk, Cyril Mills later collected important intelligence in Nazi Germany which reinforced Churchill's attacks on the appeasement of Hitler.

CHRISTOPHER ANDREW

THE SPY WHO CAME IN FROM THE CIRCUS

THE SECRET LIFE OF CYRIL BERTRAM MILLS

\B\b\

Biteback Publishing

First published in Great Britain in 2024 by
Biteback Publishing Ltd, London
Copyright © Christopher Andrew 2024

ISBN 978-1-78590-821-7

10 9 8 7 6 5 4 3 2 1

A CIP catalogue record for this book is available from the British Library.

Set in Minion Pro and Gill Sans

Printed and bound in Great Britain by
CPI Group (UK) Ltd, Croydon CR0 4YY

FSC
www.fsc.org
MIX
Paper | Supporting
responsible forestry
FSC® C171272

CONTENTS

LIST OF ILLUSTRATIONS

Frontispiece

Performing Elephants in the Circus Ring, 1928, Winston S. Churchill. Reproduced with permission of Curtis Brown, London on behalf of Churchill Heritage Ltd © Churchill Heritage Ltd.

Plates

Appendix

In 1933, a model of the Loch Ness monster was paraded around London on a Bertram Mills Circus lorry with the promise of a £20,000 reward for anyone who tracked it down. Courtesy of Cyril Mills Archive.

ABBREVIATIONS
AND ACRONYMS

B1a MI5's Double Agent Department
BL British Library
BSC British Security Coordination, New York
C Chief of MI6
CAB Cabinet Office files, TNA
CBM Cyril Bertram Mills
CCAC Churchill College Archives Centre, Cambridge
Cheka *Chrezvychainaya Komissiya* Extraordinary Commission for Combating Counter-Revolution and Sabotage (ancestor of KGB)
CIA US Central Intelligence Agency
CID Criminal Investigation Department, Scotland Yard
CND Campaign for Nuclear Disarmament
CPGB Communist Party of Great Britain
CUL Cambridge University Library
DG Director-General
DNI Director of Naval Intelligence
FBI US Federal Bureau of Investigation
FCO Foreign and Commonwealth Office

FO Foreign Office

GC&CS Government Code and Cypher School (predecessor of GCHQ)

GCHQ Government Communications Headquarters

GRU *Glavnoye Razvedyvatelnoye Upravlenie* (Russian/Soviet military intelligence)

HO Home Office

IB Intelligence Bureau, New Delhi

IO Intelligence Officer

IWM Imperial War Museum

JIC Joint Intelligence Committee

KGB *Komitet gosudarstvennoy bezopasnosti* (Committee for State Security, USSR)

KPG Kensington Palace Gardens

KV MI5 (Security Service) files, TNA

LCC London County Council

NAW US National Archives, Washington DC

NKVD *Narodný komissariat vnutrennih del* (People's Commissariat for Internal Affairs, USSR)

NSA US National Security Agency

ODNB *Oxford Dictionary of National Biography*

OP MI5 observation post

OSS US Office of Strategic Services

OTC Officers' Training Corps

Parl. Deb. Parliamentary Debates

PUS Permanent Under-Secretary

PWE Political Warfare Executive

RAC Royal Automobile Club

RAF Royal Air Force

RFC Royal Flying Corps (predecessor of the RAF)

RCMP Royal Canadian Mounted Police

SHAEF Supreme Headquarters Allied Expeditionary Force

SIGINT Signals Intelligence

SOE Special Operations Executive

TNA The National Archives, Kew

TUC Trades Union Congress

WO War Office files, TNA

INTRODUCTION

THE TWO LIVES OF CYRIL BERTRAM MILLS: CIRCUS AND ESPIONAGE

For almost half a century, Bertram Mills Circus, founded by Bertram Wagstaff Mills in 1920, was a household name throughout Britain, popular with both children and adults. Bertram's elder son, Cyril Bertram Mills, who became joint (in practice senior) director of the circus with his younger brother Bernard on their father's death in 1938, was one of the best-known and most influential figures in the British entertainment business.

For forty years, Cyril Mills also had a wide-ranging, top-secret career in British intelligence: obtaining the best aerial intelligence on Nazi rearmament for MI6 (Britain's foreign intelligence agency) before the Second World War, recruiting and becoming first case officer for the most successful wartime double agent, codenamed GARBO, after joining the Security Service MI5, and working part-time during the Cold War 'for MI5 or 6 or both without being paid a penny'. For fifteen years, in the middle of the Cold War, at the request of MI5's Director-General, Sir Roger Hollis, the Mills family lived in a mansion opposite the Soviet embassy so that MI5 could keep it under surveillance. Hollis and Sir Dick White, Chief of MI6, became such close family friends that the Mills children called them 'Uncle Roger' and 'Uncle Dick'.

Remarkably, not a word of Mills's secret career leaked out in public until he was over eighty.* Among the many taken aback by the belated revelation of some of his intelligence exploits was his friend, the Duke of Edinburgh.† Though, like Queen Elizabeth II, an enthusiastic patron of the Bertram Mills Circus and fascinated by British intelligence operations, Prince Philip wrote to Mills in 1985: '...I must admit that I would not have expected your involvement. I cannot imagine a better cover [than the circus]!'‡

Mills framed the letter.

During Prince Philip's lifetime, his close contacts with both MI5 and MI6 were mostly kept secret. After Philip's death in 2021 at the age of ninety-nine, however, the Chief of MI6, Sir Richard Moore, revealed that he had made 'numerous visits' to its London HQ at Vauxhall Cross, often for lunchtime discussions: 'HRH called it as he saw it with directness and wit. Visits were never dull.'§ Prince Philip had his own intelligence book collection and read the authorised centenary history of MI5 with great attention.¶ His discussions about that too – with its author, among others – were also 'never dull'.**

---

* What did leak out was often incomplete and confused. The brief references to intelligence operations in Cyril Mills's entry in the usually authoritative *Oxford Dictionary of National Biography* (*ODNB*), though revised in 2008, still includes several errors and omissions. There is, for example, no reference to any of his work for MI6. He is incorrectly described as an MI5 'secret agent' 'attached to the War Office' in the Second World War, rather than as an MI5 officer with a key role in B1a. The brief *ODNB* account of Mills's role in the Cold War surveillance of the Russian embassy is badly garbled.

† Both, like Bertram Mills, were carriage-driving enthusiasts.

‡ Unpublished letter sent to Cyril Mills by Prince Philip from Royal Yacht *Britannia* on 8 August 1985; CBM. See illustration no.27.

§ 'A Tribute to HRH the Duke of Edinburgh 1921–2021', @ChiefMI6, 7 April 2021.

¶ Christopher Andrew, *The Defence of the Realm: The Authorized History of MI5* (London: Penguin, 2010).

** Prince Philip discussed *The Defence of the Realm* with me in some detail soon after its hardback publication in 2009. In 2010 I was invited to talk to the Royal Household about the book at Buckingham Palace. Richard Eden, 'The Queen Is Amused by MI5 Inquiries at Buckingham Palace', *Sunday Telegraph*, 17 October 2010.

Prince Philip's surprise at discovering Cyril Mills's use of the circus as a cover for his intelligence work for both MI5 and MI6 reflected the lack of awareness during the Cold War of the historical links between British intelligence and the entertainment business.* Probably the earliest example of these links involved Queen Elizabeth II's oldest-known royal ancestor, King Alfred the Great (the only English monarch ever given this title). The most celebrated act of espionage in Anglo-Saxon England was King Alfred's alleged eavesdropping during his wars against Danish invaders led by Guthrum the Old. In 878, with the Danes seemingly on the brink of victory, Alfred entered Guthrum's camp disguised as a wandering minstrel. According to the great medieval historian, William of Malmesbury: 'Taking a harp in his hand, [Alfred] proceeded to the king's tent. Singing before the entrance, and at times touching the trembling strings in harmonious cadence, he was readily admitted.'† The intelligence Alfred obtained while posing as a minstrel is said to have enabled him to win the decisive Battle of Ethandun (now Edington) against the Danes – a turning point in English history.‡

Though the comparison between King Alfred's impersonation of a minstrel to deceive the Danes and his own use of the circus to deceive the Gestapo in Nazi Germany did not occur to Cyril Mills until after he began working for MI6, he grew up knowing the story of King Alfred as a spy in the Danish camp. As well as featuring in many Victorian and Edwardian children's history books, the story

---

* Christopher Andrew and Julius Green, *Stars and Spies: Intelligence Operations and the Entertainment Business* (London: Bodley Head, 2021).

† William of Malmesbury, *Gesta Regum Anglorum*, twelfth-century manuscript, Cambridge University Library (CUL) MS Ii.2.3, ff. 33v–34r. Not surprisingly, there is no surviving contemporary record to confirm William of Malmesbury's account. According to the Elizabethan historian Holinshed, Alfred 'was suffered to go into every part [of the Danish camp], and play on his instrument, as well afore the king as others, so that there was no secret, but that he understood it'.

‡ The likely consequences (short- and long-term) of a Danish victory at Ethandun were discussed in an episode of the BBC Radio 4 series *What If?*, which was recorded at the battle site (presenter: Christopher Andrew; producer: Ian Bell).

also inspired a series of widely reproduced nineteenth-century portraits of Alfred the Great holding the harp which helped save England from the Danish invaders.[*]

* * *

No leading member of the modern British entertainment industry has played such a varied and influential role as Mills in intelligence operations in both war and peace for so many years. Very little was known to Mills and his contemporaries, however, about the intermittent links between intelligence operations and the enter-tainment business during the millennium since Alfred the Great. Mills was entirely unaware, for example, that the leading French playwright at the end of the ancien régime, Pierre-Augustin Caron de Beaumarchais, used his cover as the author of the internation-ally famous Figaro plays to mastermind, against Britain, probably the most successful cloak-and-dagger operation of the eighteenth century. Without the arms that Beaumarchais secretly supplied to the American rebels at the beginning of the Revolutionary War, the Americans' victory over the British at Saratoga in 1777 – a turning point in that conflict – might have proved impossible.[†]

When Mills began his circus career in the early 1920s, he knew almost nothing about British intelligence services past or pres-ent. None of the books he read or classes he attended at Harrow School and Cambridge University made any mention of them. Well-educated Victorians and Edwardians knew far more about intelligence operations recorded in the Bible than they did about

---

[*] Joanne Parker, 'England's Darling': The Victorian Cult of Alfred the Great (Manchester: Manchester University Press, 2007), pp.108–9. The story of King Alfred's espionage may not have been included in Prince Philip's education in France, Germany and Britain before he joined the Royal Navy aged eighteen in 1939.

[†] Andrew and Green, Stars and Spies, pp.96–7.

the role of intelligence at any moment in British history. According to the Old Testament, the first major figure to emphasise the importance of good intelligence was God. Like Mills, most Victorian and Edwardian schoolchildren were taught how, at God's command, both Moses and Joshua (originally one of Moses's spies) had sent agents to 'spy out' the Promised Land; how Joseph, having become the Egyptian Pharaoh's vizier, pretended not to recognise his errant older brothers and accused them of being spies trying to identify weak points in Egypt's defences; and how Judas Iscariot, a paid agent of the high priests, betrayed Jesus days before his crucifixion.* But they could not have named any British spy more recent than Alfred the Great.

What many Edwardians knew, or thought they knew, about contemporary intelligence operations largely came from sensational spy novels, inspired by wildly exaggerated fears of German spy rings preparing an invasion of Britain. The most successful spy novelist, William Le Queux, was so popular that, at his peak, publishers paid him the same rate per thousand words as Thomas Hardy. Le Queux earned more than Hardy because he wrote more.† It is unlikely, however, that any of his novels were among Cyril's childhood reading.

The creation of the twentieth-century British intelligence community was concealed not only from the public, but also from most MPs. The founding, in 1909, by H. H. Asquith's Liberal government of the Secret Service Bureau, whose home and foreign departments became today's domestic security service MI5 and foreign intelligence agency MI6 (officially known as the Secret Intelligence

---

* Christopher Andrew, *The Secret World: A History of Intelligence* (London: Allen Lane, 2018), ch.1.
† Christopher Andrew, *The Defence of the Realm: The Authorized History of MI5* (London: Penguin, 2010), section A, introduction.

Service), was one of the best-kept secrets in British peacetime history – revealed only to a small group of senior Whitehall officials and ministers who never mentioned it to the uninitiated. Throughout Mills's lifetime, biographers of Asquith and his ministers, despite their growing access to once classified government files, remained unaware of its creation. Even the official nine-volume biography of Mills's fellow Old Harrovian and political hero, Winston Churchill, the main supporter of the Secret Service Bureau in the Asquith Cabinet, as well as the leading intelligence enthusiast in every government in which he served, makes no mention of it. Nor do any of the nine volumes mention Mills.

The first Chief of what became MI6 was a charismatic former naval officer, Sir Mansfield Cumming, in honour of whom all his successors, including the current Chief, Sir Richard Moore, have been known as 'C'. Moore still follows Cumming's practice of writing in green ink: 'so anyone getting a note in green ink knows it comes from me.'* The qualities Cumming looked for in his recruits strongly suggest he would have been happy to enlist Mills. The British spy, he wrote in his secret journal, 'should be a gentleman ... absolutely honest with considerable tact and, at the same time, force of character ... In the long run, it is only the honest man who can defeat the ruffian.'† Mills was a powerful personality with strong principles who had the remarkable tact required to recruit, in his two parallel careers, temperamental star performers for the circus and double agents for British intelligence.

Cumming would also have been impressed by Mills's role as Britain's leading circus director. He was the first head of a modern

---

*   Richard Moore, interview on BBC Radio 4 *Today* programme, 30 November 2021.

†   Alan Judd, *The Quest for C. Mansfield Cumming and the Founding of the Secret Service* (London: HarperCollins, 1999), p.470.

British intelligence agency to recruit leading members of the entertainment industry, whose unconventional creativity he much admired. Among them was Britain's most successful pre-First World
War playwright, William Somerset Maugham, four of whose plays
had recently been staged simultaneously in London's West End.
Cumming made Maugham Head of Station in revolutionary Russia,
where, after the overthrow of the Romanov monarchy in the February Revolution of 1917, he regularly entertained the head of the
provisional government, Alexander Kerensky, to convivial evenings
at Petrograd's best restaurant with the finest caviar and vodka until
Kerensky's overthrow by the Bolsheviks. As Cumming had hoped,
Maugham used his dramatic talents to persuade Kerensky 'that I
was more important than I really was.'*

The American playwright Edward Knoblock, famous for his sensational 1911 West End and Broadway hit *Kismet*, was so spellbound
by Cumming that he gave up US citizenship and became a British
national in order to work for him.† 'We all loved him to a man,'
Knoblock recalled.‡ Cumming trusted Knoblock so much that he
was one of the very few permitted to see the private photo and art
collection devoted to the naked 'female form divine', which he kept
locked in a secret drawer of his desk.§ 'C' formed an equally close
bond with the ebullient Scottish writer and entertainer Compton
Mackenzie, a member of one of Britain's leading theatrical families. Cumming made Mackenzie wartime Head of Station in Greece
and the Aegean, in which capacity he navigated the Greek islands
in a former royal yacht, dressed in a bespoke white uniform and

* Christopher Andrew, *For the President's Eyes Only: Secret Intelligence and the American Presidency from Washington to Bush* (London: HarperCollins, 1995), pp.47–8. Maugham had initially been recruited by John Wallinger of military intelligence. He found Wallinger 'a very ordinary man' and did not take to him.
† Judd, *The Quest for C*, pp.420–21.
‡ Keith Jeffery, *MI6: The History of the Secret Intelligence Service, 1909–1949* (London: Bloomsbury, 2010), p.730.
§ Judd, *The Quest for C*, p.59.

wielding a swordstick personally presented to him by Cumming. 'After the war is over,' Cumming told him, 'we'll do some amusing secret service work together. It's capital sport!'[*]

Despite Cumming's extrovert personality and A-list friends in the entertainment business, his role as first Chief of MI6 remained a closely guarded official secret. The fact that no mention of his intelligence career appeared in print until almost a decade after his death in 1923[†] was all the more remarkable because he was willing to be interviewed about his experiences as both a racing driver and a pioneer aviator. Cumming was an enthusiastic member of both the Edwardian Royal Automobile Club and Royal Aero Club. He told the *Royal Automobile Club Journal*: 'I know of nothing more exciting than skimming along at a cracking pace, especially if you are picking up on the next one ahead!'[‡] *Flight International* magazine reported in November 1913 that, at fifty-four, Cumming was 'probably the doyen of pilots': 'He does not believe in extreme youth as a necessary or even desirable qualification for the making of a successful pilot.'

Cumming was also the first major British advocate of aerial reconnaissance, later to become a key part of twentieth-century intelligence gathering. By 1913 he had drawn up detailed plans to purchase a Secret Service Bureau biplane for spy missions. The War Office, however, showed no interest in aerial reconnaissance until after the outbreak of war, when it was entrusted, not to Cumming but to the newly founded Royal Flying Corps (RFC).[§] The belated fulfilment of Cumming's plans for peacetime aerial reconnaissance by MI6 over twenty years later was chiefly due to Cyril Mills – like

---

[*]   Compton Mackenzie, *Greek Memories*, 2nd ed. (London: Chatto & Windus, 1939), p.324.
[†]   See below, p.53.
[‡]   Cumming was notorious for driving his Rolls-Royce at high speed, even through the centre of London. Christopher Andrew, *Secret Service: The Making of the British Intelligence Community* (London: Hodder & Stoughton, 1985), pp.74–5.
[§]   Judd, *The Quest for C*, pp.39–48, 251.

Cumming an adventurous aviator. Though MI6 still had no biplane of its own, Mills used his own de Havilland Hornet Moth to gather important intelligence on Nazi aerial rearmament while flying over Germany, supposedly on circus business.[*]

* * *

Long before Mills had any intention of working for MI5 or MI6, the first spies to make a deep impression on him were not British but German. Though during the First World War, both the British media and Parliament avoided all reference to spying by MI6,[†] wartime German spies, both real and imaginary, were front-page news. Britain's declaration of war on Germany on 4 August 1914 produced the most dramatic newspaper headlines seen by the then 12-year-old Cyril so far. In less than a fortnight, police arrested virtually the entire German espionage network in Britain – twenty-two agents of the naval Nachrichten-Abteilung, who had been under surveillance for several years by Vernon Kell's counter-espionage bureau (later renamed MI5) and local police.[‡]

Gustav Steinhauer, who ran the German agent network, had the unenviable task of reporting the 'wholesale round-up of our secret service agents in England' to Kaiser Wilhelm II. 'Apparently unable to believe his ears, the Kaiser raved and stormed for the better part of two hours about the incompetence of his so-called intelligence officers, bellowing: "Am I surrounded by dolts? Why was I not told? Who is responsible?" and more in the same vein.'[§]

---

[*] See below, ch.3.
[†] MI6's secret wartime designation was MI1c.
[‡] Andrew, *Defence of the Realm*, pp.50–51.
[§] Gustav Steinhauer, *Steinhauer: The Kaiser's Master Spy: The Story as Told by Himself*, ed. Sidney Felstead (London: Bodley Head, 1930), p.37.

The Home Secretary, Reginald McKenna, told the Commons on 9 October 1914 that pre-war German spies had obtained 'little valuable information' and that Germany's whole spy network in Britain had, in all probability, been 'crushed at the outbreak of the war'. Though McKenna was right, he failed to convince much of the British press and public. *The Times* claimed, absurdly, that 'in their eager absorption of the baser side of militarism, the Germans seem to have almost converted themselves into a race of spies.'[*]

Though only twelve, Cyril Mills cannot fail to have been struck by the enormous publicity given to the capture and trial of Carl Lody, the first German spy sent to Britain after the outbreak of war. A public court martial at the Westminster Guildhall sentenced Lody to death by firing squad in November 1914, the first execution at the Tower of London for over 150 years. Kell, whom Mills later got to know well, 'felt it deeply that so brave a man should have to pay the death penalty'.[†]

The dwindling number and poor quality of Lody's wartime successors, all discovered without great difficulty while spying in Britain, led some senior figures in Whitehall to wonder whether abler enemy agents with better cover were going undetected. The few officials who were informed about Cumming's foreign intelligence operations thought, like him, that German intelligence might be recruiting from sections of the entertainment business – particularly music halls and circuses. Largely ignorant of the history of British counter-espionage, they were unaware that such fears were centuries old. During the conflict with Spain in the reign of Queen Elizabeth I, at least two foreign spies were believed to have entered England 'in the guise of tumblers [acrobats]'.[‡] Foreign tumblers

---

[*]   *The Times*, 15 October 1915; Andrew, *Defence of the Realm*, pp.53–5.
[†]   Andrew, *Defence of the Realm*, pp.64–5. On Mills and Kell, see below, p.47–8, 77–8, 80.
[‡]   *Calendar of State Papers*, Elizabeth I; cited by Ward in *Beneath the Big Top*, p.44.

were thought dangerous because of their opportunities to perform at court and in noble households.

In 1916, Sir Edward Troup, the long-serving permanent secretary at the Home Office, warned all chief constables:

> ...that the German Government is endeavouring to recruit circus-riders, music-hall performers, and persons on the regular stage for purposes of espionage in this country. Two such persons, circus-riders, who were of German origin, have recently been detected endeavouring to come to this country and have been refused permission to land, and a third, who had been touring as a music-hall performer with a Dutch passport, is believed to be a German and is now in custody.* I am therefore to request that special attention may be paid to any persons belonging to these professions who may visit your area...†

Bertram Mills understood German circuses far better than the Home Office. Though he still had no intention of running a circus himself, he had got to know many leading pre-war German circus owners. As Cyril later recalled:

> ...before the war he had exhibited at most of the big horse shows on the Continent, and whenever there was a horse show it was usual for a circus to play the town at the same time, as horse lovers are always good circus customers, and on countless occasions Father had gone to the circus in the morning to watch the training of horses.‡

---

*   This was probably a reference to Leopold Vieyra, who had 'been touring as a music-hall performer with a Dutch passport' and who was 'now in custody'. Convicted of espionage in November 1916, he was the last German spy to have been discovered in the British wartime entertainment industry.
†   Sir Edward Troup to chief constables, 16 July 1916; TNA HO 45/10779.
‡   Cyril Bertram Mills, *Bertram Mills Circus: Its Story*, rev. ed. (Bath: Ashgrove Press, 1983), p.16.

Bertram Mills knew enough about leading German circuses to be convinced that none was likely to be involved in wartime espionage in Britain. Immediately after the war, he renewed and expanded his contacts with them. Ironically, however, his own interwar circus was to provide highly successful cover for his son Cyril's MI6 intelligence missions to pre-war Nazi Germany.

The First World War German spy who made the greatest impression on Cyril's then adolescent imagination was probably the Dutch exotic dancer and striptease artist Margaretha Geertruida Zelle, whose stage name Mata Hari still appears in some English dictionaries as a synonym for 'beautiful female spy'. Shot at dawn by the French in 1917 for spying for Germany after previously promising to spy for France, Zelle had shown little aptitude for intelligence operations for either side. MI5's leading interwar agent-runner, Maxwell Knight (better known as a popular BBC naturalist), whose agents penetrated both the Communist Party and fascist groups, would have nothing to do with what he called 'Mata Hari methods'. He believed that MI5 should avoid recruiting any 'woman agent who suffers from an overdose of sex'.[*]

Despite her operational incompetence, the seductive fictional image of the glamorous Mata Hari made her the best-known female spy of the twentieth century. In 1931, Greta Garbo immortalised Mata Hari on screen in the eponymous film in what was her biggest, and most erotic, box-office success as the 'temptress of the secret service'. Ironically, the Chairman of the London County Council (LCC) Licensing Committee and its Inspection of Films Sub-Committee, which approved the showing of the film in London, was none other than Bertram Mills. The LCC Licensing Committee

---

[*]   Andrew and Green, *Stars and Spies*, p.223; Andrew, *Defence of the Realm*, p.221.

possibly underestimated the film's erotic impact and it was subsequently only available in a censored version.

Mata Hari made a great impression on Cyril Mills. For the rest of his life he told his family that Greta Garbo was the greatest film actress he had ever seen.[*] As an MI5 officer in 1942, when Mills recruited the most successful double agent of the Second World War, Juan Pujol García, he gave him the codename GARBO as a tribute to his star quality. Pujol was the only male member of the British Double-Cross System to be given a female codename.[†] The proudest moment of Mills's retirement was his reunion with GARBO on the fortieth anniversary of the D-Day landings on the Normandy beaches, the greatest triumph of the Double-Cross deception.

---

[*] Mills's family believe that he met Garbo but no record survives of when and where the meeting occurred.
[†] See below, p.134.

CHAPTER I

HARROW SCHOOL AND CAMBRIDGE UNIVERSITY

The chief influence on Cyril Bertram Mills's early career was his father Bertram Wagstaff Mills, who was born in London on 11 August 1873. Bertram's father, Halford Mills, owned a successful coach-building and undertaker's business in Paddington, as well as two farms in the Home Counties. Bertram spent most of his childhood at the family farm in Chalfont St Giles, where he began a life-long passion for horses.[*] After joining his father's business in 1888, he began to compete at international as well as British horse and carriage shows, eventually becoming a leading judge. Not until after the First World War, however, did it occur to Bertram Mills that he might start a circus. But for his success in doing so, Cyril would probably never have worked for either MI5 or MI6.

Though Bertram Mills had left school before his fifteenth birthday, he was much more ambitious for his sons, Cyril and Bernard, and sent both of them to Harrow School and Cambridge University. Harrow was second only to its traditional rival, Eton College, as

---

[*] Cyril Mills wrote of his father: 'He had three loves – his family, his home and horses – and there was nothing he would not do for any of these.' Mills, *Bertram Mills Circus*, p.12.

the world's most famous school. Its former pupils include seven British Prime Ministers – more than any other school except Eton – as well as the first Prime Minister of independent India, Jawaharlal Nehru.[*] The most celebrated Old Harrovian Prime Minister, Winston Churchill, was also Cyril Mills's greatest personal hero. In 1908, aged only thirty-three, Churchill became the youngest Cabinet minister for over forty years. Two years later, he was appointed the youngest Home Secretary since his fellow Old Harrovian Sir Robert Peel in 1822.

Though Churchill has inspired some excellent biographers (himself included), none mentions Cyril Mills's extraordinary relationship with him, both public and private. The Bertram Mills Circus clowns made Churchill laugh more loudly than any other part of the entertainment industry. The secret intelligence that Mills obtained from Nazi Germany before the Second World War gave Churchill an important insight into the rise of Hitler's Luftwaffe.[†]

Throughout the course of his long career, Churchill showed greater enthusiasm for, and understanding of, intelligence than any other twentieth-century British politician. His adventures during the Boer War had included cycling in disguise through Johannesburg to carry out reconnaissance behind enemy lines. Churchill later acknowledged that, had he been caught, 'no court martial that ever sat in Europe would have had much difficulty in disposing of such a case.' He would have been shot as a spy.[‡]

During his first seven years as a Cabinet minister (1908–15), Churchill played a key role in founding all three of today's main British

---

[*] In 2005, Harrow celebrated the centenary of Nehru's admission in the presence of the Indian High Commissioner, https://timesofindia.indiatimes.com/world/rest-of-world/how-harrow-made-nehru/articleshow/1296553.cms

[†] See below, p.179.

[‡] W. S. Churchill, *My Early Life* (London: Eland, 2000 [1930]), p.372.

intelligence agencies. He was a committed supporter of both the home and foreign departments (the future MI5 and MI6) of the Secret Service Bureau founded in 1909. As Home Secretary a year later, Churchill promoted secret cooperation between police chief constables and the future MI5, which enabled the surveillance and arrest of the entire German spy network in Britain at the outbreak of war.

As First Lord of the Admiralty in 1914, Churchill presided over the secret creation of Room 40 (forerunner of today's Government Communications Headquarters (GCHQ)), Britain's first code-breaking agency since the closure of the Foreign Office Deciphering Branch after parliamentary protests seventy years earlier. British codebreakers went on to achieve major successes in breaking wartime codes and ciphers of both Britain's chief enemy, Germany, and its main ally, the United States. Churchill was right to claim a decade later:

> I have studied this information over a longer period and more attentively than probably any other minister has done. All the time I have been in office since it began in the autumn of 1914, I have read every one of these flimsies [decrypted messages] and I attach more importance to them as a means of forming a true judgement of public policy in these spheres than to any other source of knowledge at the disposal of the State.*

Cyril Mills, however, only began to learn of Churchill's key role in the creation of the modern British intelligence community when he started to work for MI5 and MI6.

Churchill himself was largely responsible for the almost total

---

* Austen Chamberlain MSS, Birmingham University Library. First cited by Andrew in *Secret Service*, p.316.

secrecy which surrounded the intelligence agencies throughout his career. As Home Secretary, in 1911, he helped to rush the Official Secrets Act through the Commons in less than an hour. Even in Parliament no reference was allowed to British intelligence operations until the 1980s, with the partial exception of those targeted against foreign espionage and subversion.

When Cyril Mills began working for British intelligence at the age of thirty-four, he did not regret having previously been kept in almost total ignorance of it. Like Churchill, Mills believed that secrecy was essential to the success of British intelligence operations. He even kept his father and his first wife in complete ignorance of his own espionage in pre-war Nazi Germany. His children, Christopher and Sandra, still vividly recall the strength of his support for the Official Secrets Act and his stern warning, when the family moved to a mansion opposite the Soviet embassy in 1960, that they should stifle all curiosity about surveillance of the embassy and other Soviet buildings from the upper floors of their house.

* * *

For rather different reasons, Cyril Mills was also unusually secretive about his years at Harrow School, which he almost never mentioned to his children. The 284 pages of Mills's partly autobiographical 1967 history of the family circus contain less than a line about his schooldays: a passing reference to spending 'four and a half years at Harrow' before going to read engineering at Cambridge in October 1920.*

Mills's memories of his schooldays were permanently scarred by the carnage of the Great War. Like many who experienced trench

---

* Mills, *Bertram Mills Circus*, p.18.

warfare, his father Bertram, who served as captain in the Royal Army Medical Corps, preferred not to talk about it afterwards. Mills followed his example.

Arriving at Harrow as a fourteen-year-old in 1916,[*] Cyril heard the Headmaster read out the names of Harrow's latest war dead at evensong every Sunday for the rest of the war. The pupil-edited newspaper, *The Harrovian*, sometimes added horrifying details about how they had died. Many were recent pupils. Almost 30 per cent of the boys who had entered Harrow in the academic year 1909/10 were killed in action, others died from wounds and illnesses contracted during military service.[†] Of the total of twenty Victoria Crosses awarded to Harrovians – more than to any other school except Eton – nine were won during the Great War.

Mills's generation of Harrovians were regularly reminded that, like Harrow's fallen heroes, they too might have to die for their country. During the last German offensive of the war in 1918, *The Harrovian* published this sombre appeal:

TO THOSE WHO 'FOLLOW UP'[‡]

You who come after the brave gone before you

You who must finish what they have begun,

Never forget, when the world goes against you,

How they were tempted—fought harder and won.

Never forget how they loved perfect freedom,

Nor how they struggled the right to maintain!

Never turned back, but gave all for their country—

---

[*] For Cyril Mills's matriculation photograph on his arrival at Harrow, see illustration no.2.

[†] Christopher Tyerman, *A History of Harrow School 1324–1991* (Oxford: Oxford University Press, 2000), ch.16.

[‡] 'Follow Up' was a reference to the most famous Harrow School song, 'Forty Years On', whose chorus repeats the phrase five times. The title of the Harrow alumni magazine is *Follow Up!*.

Surely they cannot have battled in vain?
Surely, O children, you will not forget them?
Fail to fight bravely, to finish their work?
Think, if they bitterly said to each other,
'We died but for cowards who falter and shirk!'
But, children of heroes, the enemy threatens,
He throws down the gauntlet, who dares pick it up?
Stand fast and be brave, brace yourselves for the struggle!
Then answer the challenge and cry, 'Follow Up!' [*]

Cyril Mills was determined to 'follow up' if the war continued. He joined the Harrow Officers' Training Corps (OTC) in his second term and won rapid promotion, singled out by his commanding officer, Colonel E. G. Mercer, for his 'great energy, keenness, and enterprise as Squad Commander'. Mills was also a very good shot. At the annual OTC exercises, he won his highest marks for shooting.[†] Many years later, he told his son Christopher he had expected to survive for only a few weeks if he had to 'follow up'.

Though the operations of MI5, MI6 and the future GCHQ were too secret to be mentioned in the OTC, Mills learned the importance of aerial reconnaissance, the main intelligence innovation on the Western Front at the outbreak of the First World War.[‡] When, later, Mills began reconnaissance by biplane over Nazi Germany, he probably recalled the pioneering work of his fellow Harrovian, Second Lieutenant Alan Scott Balfour, which was celebrated after his death in action early in 1918. According to *The Harrovian*, though Balfour had been 'a rather shy and retiring boy' at Harrow,

---

[*]   *The Harrovian*, 1918.
[†]   C. B. Mills file, Harrow School Archives. I owe this reference to Dr Tim Schmalz.
[‡]   Aerial reconnaissance had been attempted half a century earlier, with little success, by the Balloon Corps in the American Civil War. Andrew, *Secret World*, chs.24, 25.

he was 'devoted to a hobby which was to prove of the utmost value to his country later on'. The hobby was photography, which led to Balfour's recruitment as observer/photographer by the RFC on the Western Front. His squadron leader wrote to his father, Sir Robert Balfour, Liberal MP for Glasgow:

> Your son was on a photographic reconnaissance, and in spite of the fact that there were many enemy machines [aircraft] about, he persisted in going over to the very extreme edge of his area to start taking his photographs. The result of this very gallant conduct was that he was attacked by five hostile machines. In spite of putting up a splendid fight, your son was killed in the air...
>
> Your Son's last photographic reconnaissance, before the one on which he met his death, was so good that I brought it to the attention of the General Officer Commanding the Brigade, in which this Squadron is. He congratulated your son and told me that it was the finest photographic performance that he had ever come across.[*]

Unlike Balfour's role as an RFC observer on the Western Front, Mills's aerial reconnaissance of Nazi German airfields twenty years later was to remain secret for almost half a century.[†]

Within the Harrow OTC, Mills also learned the importance of tactical battlefield intelligence on enemy forces. *The Harrovian*'s tribute to Captain Walter Stone, the last former pupil to be awarded (posthumously) the Victoria Cross during the war, singled out the 'most conspicuous bravery' with which Stone sent intelligence reports from the Western Front:

---

[*] *The Harrovian War Supplement*, September 1918.
[†] See below, pp.73–4.

He observed the enemy massing for an attack, and afforded invaluable information to Battalion Headquarters ... Captain Stone stood on the parapet with the telephone under a tremendous bombardment, observing the enemy, and continued to send back valuable information until the wire was cut by his orders. The rearguard was eventually surrounded and cut to pieces, and Captain Stone was seen fighting to the last, till he was shot through the head. The extraordinary coolness of this heroic officer and the accuracy of his information enabled dispositions to be made just in time to save the line and avert disaster.[*]

Twenty years later, though never in as much danger as Stone, Mills also showed 'extraordinary coolness' and courage in collecting intelligence from German airfields on the rapid growth of the Luftwaffe for MI6.

At Harrow, Mills won a reputation as a (mostly modest) daredevil, which remained with him during both his circus and intelligence careers. He was also highly competitive. One of Harrow's most eccentric games was the annual scattering of thirty eggs in the large school swimming pool. Competitors dived into the pool to collect as many eggs as possible from the bottom before resurfacing to catch their breath. In 1918, Mills and Harrow's fastest competitive swimmer, J. E. Minoprio, shared first prize for collecting nine eggs each. Determined to show that he could beat Minoprio, Mills dived into the pool again and this time resurfaced with twelve eggs – a new school record that was duly recorded in *The Harrovian*.[†]

The high point of Mills's time at Harrow was the Armistice, which famously ended the Great War at the eleventh hour on the eleventh

---

[*]   *The Harrovian*, citation reprinted from the *London Gazette* of 2 February 1918.
[†]   *The Harrovian* XXXI, no.7, 14 December 1918, pp.5–6.

day of the eleventh month of 1918. *The Harrovian* probably spoke for Mills and most of his fellow pupils: 'The thought that the present generation, which so cheerfully waited its turn, should in this vast conflict have no turn to wait for brings a relief, which needs no words – were it not so deep...'

As Mills was well aware, not all of his fellow pupils had 'cheerfully waited' for their turn in the trenches. Though most tried to conceal their fear of violent death on the Western Front, the future leading fashion and royal photographer, Sir Cecil Beaton, who entered Harrow in January 1918, purchased surgical boots with metal leg splints from a Harley Street specialist and pretended to be disabled. He removed the boots before visits from his parents.[*]

Harrow on the Hill, unlike central London, held no public celebration of the Armistice. Before the eleventh hour struck, the school had been forced to close due to the 'Spanish flu' epidemic, which, globally, may have killed as many people as the Great War. In Britain there were 228,000 deaths during the epidemic. Among those who narrowly survived was Lady May Cumming. Her husband, Sir Mansfield Cumming, first Chief of MI6, wrote to a friend after her recovery: 'my wife had a very bad dose of influenza & was in bed over 4 weeks with a hospital Nurse all the time.'[†]

Though Mills won no prizes at Harrow, he did well academically, especially in natural sciences, mathematics and history. In the Harrow argot, still in use half a century later, he was a 'groize' (hard worker) and was conscious that his father expected him to do well enough to win a place at Cambridge and become the first family member with a university degree.

After leaving Harrow in the summer of 1920, Mills stuck to the

---

[*]   Hugo Vickers, *Cecil Beaton: The Authorised Biography* (London: Phoenix, 2002), ch.3.

[†]   Judd, *The Quest for C*, p.465.

unwritten rule that pupils past and present, whatever their private feelings, did not publicly criticise the school. Those who did so could expect to be ostracised. Such was the fate of the adventurous Arnold Lunn, well known to Mills (also a keen, competitive skier) as the originator of ski slalom competitions. In 1914, eight years after Lunn left Harrow, he published a novel entitled *The Harrovians*, based on his school diaries. Though not a direct attack on his old school, it was, he said later, 'a careful record of the cynicism of Harrow youth'. It caused such outrage among Old Harrovians that Lunn was forced to resign from all five of his London clubs*. He sent his son Peter (later a senior MI6 officer) to Eton.[†]

Arnold Lunn's experience helps to explain why Mills remained so reluctant to say or write anything in public about Harrow. Mills did not mention, even to his family, the ritual humiliations of school fagging, which he learned to endure with his usual stiff upper lip. The best-known school songs, composed by a Harrow director of music, John Farmer, and another master, F.W. Howson, included one in praise of fagging: 'Boy!', first sung in 1883, which Mills and his contemporaries were sometimes expected to sing a quarter of a century later.[‡] *The Harrovian* reported 'a very large audience' at the term concert attended by Mills in March 1918, 'old Harrovians being present in large numbers': 'The School songs were, as a whole, better sung than they have been for a long time … "Boy", sung by the trebles and four members of the XII [Headmaster's House], was very effective.'

Churchill later claimed that his 'first responsible office' was 'Head of the Fags' at Harrow. The unpaid menial tasks which, as a new

---

* Arnold Lunn, *The Harrovians: A Tale of Public School Life* (London: Methuen, 1914) and introduction to the posthumous 2010 edition.
† Ibid.
‡ Other Farmer and Howson songs are still sung at the annual Churchill Songs Day.

boy, Mills was expected to perform for his sixth-form 'fagmaster' were probably quite similar to those required of the actor Simon Williams over forty years later:

> As a new boy at Harrow in 1959, my morning duties were to spit and polish my prefect's shoes (even his rugby boots), to serve him tea and toast, make his bed, run his bath and fetch his paper (the *Daily Express*, for heaven's sake). It was also my duty to sit on the lavatory he intended to use after breakfast in order to warm the seat for him. 'And don't you bloody well do anything in there, Williams, I don't want you stinking the place out.'*

Mills was far less inhibited when reminiscing about his three years at Cambridge University after leaving Harrow. As he later admitted, he ceased to be a 'groize', did not 'over-exert' himself academically and enjoyed an energetic sporting and social life.

Mills's favourite recreations, like those of Sir Mansfield Cumming,† included travelling at speed – occasionally a requirement of his later spying career. The combined demands of his Cambridge degree course and the Christmas circus season at Olympia prevented him, however, from skiing for more than a fortnight each year. Nor was he able to purchase a fast car. University regulations prohibited students in residence from keeping cars within the city precincts. So, Mills bought a motorcycle and joined the fledgling University Motorcycle Club and enjoyed speeding from the city centre through the Cambridgeshire fens. He also took part in the 'grass-track' races (motorcycle scrambles) around Cambridge. One

---

* Simon Williams, '*The Archers*' Simon Williams on public school "fagging"', *Daily Telegraph*, 8 December 2017.
† See above, p.8.

such race at a Cambridge agricultural show in 1923, in which Cyril probably competed, attracted 20,000 spectators. He won a bronze medal in one of the races and bequeathed it to his daughter Sandra, who still has it. Cyril lost much of his interest in motorcycling when he left Cambridge and was forced to slow down. In 1925 the Auto-Cycle Union (ACU) banned road racing and some other competitions because of the growing number of accidents befalling both spectators and participants.

* * *

Only many years later, after he had begun working for British intelligence, did Mills realise how appropriate his choice of Cambridge college, Corpus Christi, had been. During his first year, when he had a room in the college, he passed every day the memorial in Old Court to Corpus's two greatest playwrights, Christopher Marlowe and John Fletcher, still the only monument in the college to any of its old members. Before Shakespeare began to make his reputation on the London stage in 1592, Marlowe was acknowledged as the greatest Elizabethan dramatist. Though Marlowe did not, as some have claimed, write Shakespeare's plays, it seems likely that, like Fletcher later, he did collaborate with him for a time. The current edition of *The New Oxford Shakespeare* ascribes authorship of Henry VI jointly to 'William Shakespeare and Christopher Marlowe'. At the end of his career, Shakespeare also collaborated with John Fletcher.

What makes Marlowe's precocious success as a playwright even more extraordinary is that he was also an active spy, probably recruited to Queen Elizabeth I's secret service in 1585 while studying for his master's degree at Corpus. The Corpus Christi Buttery Book, which recorded students' expenditure on food and drink, shows that from 1585, when Marlowe began his intelligence career, his presence at the college became irregular and, probably thanks to his secret service income, his expenditure while there considerably higher. Though details of Marlowe's espionage were kept secret at the time and no longer survive, in 1587 the Privy Council sent a letter to Cambridge University authorities designed to ensure that Marlowe's absences abroad on secret service did not delay the award of his master's: 'he had done her Majesty good service, & deserved to be rewarded for his faithful dealing'. Marlowe's espionage, like Mills's later, was sometimes dangerous. He was fatally stabbed in 1593 during a brawl which may have been related to the rivalries and disruption within Elizabeth I's intelligence service following the death of her spymaster, Sir Francis Walsingham.*

Mills became the most striking twentieth-century example of a leading figure in the British entertainment business who was also a major spy. But the first to combine these two professions in Britain was his fellow Corpus Christi College graduate, Christopher Marlowe.

After passing his final honours examination in engineering, Mills was awarded the BA at a traditional degree day ceremony at the Cambridge Senate House in June 1923, but he did not return to the Senate House for almost a decade to receive the MA for which he qualified, without further exams, in 1927. A convenient moment arrived in April 1932 when he brought his father's circus to Midsummer Common in Cambridge. Before receiving his MA, he was welcomed back by his former Corpus-approved landlady with whom he had lodged after moving out of his room in college. She

---

* Andrew and Green, *Stars and Spies*, ch.1. Christopher Mills believes that Cyril, who enjoyed history books as a teenager, had learned about Walsingham's career as Elizabeth's principal Secretary of State from 1573 to 1590.

now occupied a large Victorian terrace house in Maid's Causeway, overlooking Midsummer Common:

> During the [circus] build-up, she and her elderly maid, who still wore starched cuffs and a little white cap perched on top of her head, sat at a window watching our every move. I had been what she called one of her 'young gentlemen' when any of us were about, but I suspect we were referred to as 'her boys' when we were not within earshot...
>
> Every evening when work ended one of these dear ladies came over and said the other was running a hot bath and that a meal would be ready by the time I had bathed. They knew I could dine at the circus but felt they could do better and indeed they did.[*]

The circus tent was packed. As Cyril recalled over thirty years later, 'undergrads in those days had more money and less work to do than now and ... they poured into the circus'. In defiance of safety regulations, many sat on the ground between the seats and the circus ring[†] in order to be as close as possible to the animals and artistes. Cambridge's main club for gregarious, well-heeled ex-public schoolboys, the Pitt Club, was situated only a few hundred yards from Midsummer Common. The club's now most notorious member was the subversive, heavy-drinking Old Etonian Guy Burgess, who may well have been among the many students in the circus audience. Within a few years, Burgess was to join both Soviet intelligence and MI6. Though Mills did not discover it until much later, he and Burgess worked for the pre-war MI6 at the same time. In later life, he could never bring himself to mention Burgess's name.

---

[*]   Mills, *Bertram Mills Circus*, p.60. In striking contrast, Mills left no account of his return to Harrow.
[†]   Ibid., p.59.

CHAPTER 2

THE CIRCUS, ADOLF HITLER AND WINSTON CHURCHILL

The chief influence on Cyril Mills's choice of career after he left Cambridge was his father Bertram, known to his staff as 'The Guv'nor'. Lady Eleanor Smith, one of the founders of the Circus Fans' Association of Great Britain (now the Circus Friends Association), remembered him as 'a short, stocky man with a bald head, a ruddy pugnacious face, a grey moustache, and twinkling, shrewd blue eyes. His eyes were as blue as the cornflower he invariably wore in his button-hole.[*] He would have looked undressed without that cornflower.' A caricature in *The Sketch* carried the caption: 'Say It With Cornflowers! King of the circus and coaching enthusiast Bertram W. Mills, J.P., always wears a cornflower in his button-hole'. A clown is shown reaching across Mills's chest to adjust his bright blue boutonniere.[†]

---

[*] Bertram Mills was almost certainly unaware that for some years before the Anschluss, Hitler's takeover of Austria in 1938, Austrian Nazis used the blue cornflower to identify themselves to other Nazis as supporters of Hitler.

[†] Lady Eleanor Smith, *Life's a Circus* (London: Longman's, Green and Co., 1939), ch.29. Don Stacey, 'Bertram Mills'; http://www.circopedia.org/Bertram_Mills. Eleanor Smith was the daughter of F. E. Smith, 1st Earl of Birkenhead (1872–1930), Churchill's closest friend.

The main turning point in Bertram Mills's career came early in 1920 when a close friend, Sir Gilbert Greenall (later 1st Baron Daresbury), a director of the London Olympia Exhibition Hall, invited the Mills family to a performance at Olympia of *The Great Victory Circus*. When pressed over supper afterwards for his views on the performance, Bertram Mills replied, 'If I couldn't do better, I'd eat my hat!' A few days later, Olympia's managing director, Reginald Heaton, founder of the London International Horse Show, asked Mills to put on a circus during the following winter.[*]

Eighteen-year-old Cyril Mills, then about to leave Harrow School for Cambridge University, accompanied his father on a summer tour in 1920 of what seemed at the time 'all the circuses in Europe' to find the best acts for Olympia. Cyril's role was to identify those that would most appeal to 'the younger generation'. When he and his father compared notes at the end of the tour, they found that they had usually been most impressed by the same acts. By the time they returned to London, the programme for Olympia was almost complete:

> The biggest surprise I had during that tour was that Father was known to so many circus owners, but the explanation was that before the war he had exhibited at most of the big horse shows on the Continent, and wherever there was a horse show it was usual for a circus to play the town at the same time ... On countless occasions Father had gone to the circus in the morning to watch the training of horses.[†]

---

[*]   Mills, *Bertram Mills Circus*, pp.14–15. The friend, not named in the book, is identified by Christopher Mills as the future Lord Daresbury, a wealthy brewer who lost a large bet with Bertram Mills that he would be unable to put the circus on in time. Daresbury probably expected Mills to try to stage a US circus at Olympia; see below, ch.6.

[†]   Ibid., p.14.

Many of the pre-war European horse shows and circuses which Bertram Mills most admired had been German. Munich, Hamburg, Dresden, Magdeburg and Breslau each had their own circus – some of them based in the city's largest public building. Berlin had several circuses, each able to seat an audience of 5,000. All big-city circuses gave two or three performances a day for six days a week.

After the horrors of the First World War, however, Germany was widely regarded in Britain as a pariah state. In the post-war British entertainment business, Cyril later recalled, 'nobody dared present a German act or even one with a German name'. 'The first crunch came when we saw the Schumann horses in Copenhagen ... by far the best in the world.' The Schumann brothers were Danes and Swedes 'but their names sounded German so they were out'. The circus, which opened at Olympia on 17 December 1920, was billed as 'The Great International Circus', with, in very small type in the bottom right-hand corner, the words 'Organised by Bertram W. Mills'. It was an instant success. *The Times* headlined its report on the opening performance: 'The Big Circus – Enraptured Audience!'

Before the circus opened, Cyril's daredevil instincts, already evident at Harrow, made it impossible for him to resist the temptation of trying to swing on the high trapeze:

> My attempt produced more laughs than a good clown entrée and, having fallen several times, I was reduced to crawling most of the way [across the safety net] on hands and knees ... By the time I reached the ground I had resolved I was not cut out to be a performer and have ever since resisted all temptations to try to be one.

By 1921 it was possible to engage people with German (or German-sounding) names, and the first circus contract signed by

Bertram Mills was with the Schumann Brothers. Ernst Schumann brought their horses to Olympia, as he did again during the 1922–23 season, by which time his older brother Willy had taken over as Equestrian Director and Producer of the circus.*

The third Great International Circus, which opened at Olympia in December 1922, was an even bigger success than its predecessors. As Cyril recalled:

> My father had booked [the Italian-born Russian, Enrico] Rastelli, the greatest of all jugglers, and had taken me to the [United] States where we saw all the big circuses and where he booked three high-priced acts on which he had to pay return transportation across the Atlantic.

In 1922, for the first time, the name BERTRAM MILLS CIRCUS appeared prominently in capitals on circus posters.†

Cyril's growing contacts with German circuses – Europe's best as well as biggest, in both his and his father's view‡ – were later to provide excellent cover for his espionage operations for MI6 in Germany. It was also through the Zirkus Krone in Munich, the German circus with which he had the closest contact, that Mills first heard of Adolf Hitler, who remained virtually unknown in Britain. Munich was the main Nazi power base in the 1920s, where Hitler led an unsuccessful putsch in 1923. The headquarters of the Zirkus Krone, a large wooden building constructed in the centre of Munich in 1919, was also used for events organised by the Nazi Party.

No interwar British politician ever gave a major speech in a

---

*   Ibid., p.37.
†   Ibid., ch.1.
‡   Ibid, p.195.

circus arena, but Hitler did. He wrote immodestly in *Mein Kampf* of his first speech at the Zirkus Krone on 3 February 1921:

> …It was not until I had forced my way through the solid wall of people and reached the platform that I perceived the full measure of our success. The hall was before me, like a gigantic shell, packed with thousands and thousands of people. Even the arena was densely crowded. More than 5,600 tickets had been sold and, allowing for the unemployed, poor students and our own detachments of men for keeping order, a crowd of about 6,500 must have been present.
>
> …I began, and spoke for about two and a half hours. I had the feeling after the first half-hour that the meeting was going to be a big success … After the first hour, the speech was already being received by spontaneous outbreaks of applause, but after the second hour this died down to a solemn stillness which I was to experience so often later on in this same hall, and which will for ever be remembered by all those present. Nothing broke this impressive silence and only when the last word had been spoken did the meeting give vent to its feelings by singing the national anthem.[*]

The only British newspaper correspondent to interview Hitler in 1923 was Rothay Reynolds of the *Daily Mail*, which Mills read daily when at home and less regularly when he was abroad. Hitler greeted Reynolds with a 'mesmeric' stare and told him: 'If a German Mussolini is given to Germany, people would fall down on their knees and worship him more than Mussolini has ever been worshipped.' Hitler, it was clear, thought he was the 'German Mussolini',

---

[*]   Adolf Hitler, *Mein Kampf*, English translation (Delhi: Pharos Books, 2022), pp.635–6.

as indeed he later became. Reynolds, however, dismissed him as 'an odd type of unbalanced fanatic'.[*] Mills agreed. Hitler's appeal, he believed, was paradoxically magnified by the 'magnitude of the lies' he uttered in the Zirkus Krone and other venues.[†]

For most of the 1920s the Zirkus Krone remained one of Hitler's favourite venues as Nazi leader.[‡] In addition to using it for party rallies, Hitler gave seven major speeches there.[§] Unlike Cyril Mills, the future German Führer did not seem to find it odd that at other times Asian and African elephants, a hippopotamus, a rhinoceros, horses, monkeys, pigs, porcupines, goats, zebras and parrots also received enthusiastic receptions in the same circus arena.

During his dealings with Zirkus Krone, Mills cannot fail to have been struck by Munich's antisemitism. Shortly before Hitler's unsuccessful coup in November 1923, Thomas Mann, Germany's greatest novelist, called Munich 'the city of Hitler'.[¶] Mills found it difficult to grasp the hyper-inflation in post-war Germany which reached an astonishing peak in 1923. *The Times* reported in July 1923: 'It is like being caught in a typhoon. One holds on and hopes for the best. Last week we were gaping at the idea of getting a million marks for a pound, and now it is two and a half million.'[**]

Far worse was still to come. A loaf of bread in Berlin, which had cost about 160 marks at the end of 1922, cost 200 million marks by late 1923. There had never been a better moment to offer contracts to

---

[*]   Will Wainewright, *Reporting on Hitler: Rothay Reynolds and the British Press in Nazi Germany* (London: Biteback Publishing, 2017), ch.5; *Daily Mail*, 23 October 1923.

[†]   See below, p.37.

[‡]   The crew of a BBC1 documentary, which I presented on the centenary of Hitler's birth, was able to film most of the main sites in Munich associated with Hitler's early career and the failed 1923 putsch, as well as the prison at Landsberg am Lech where he was imprisoned afterwards. The main exception was the Krone Circus building, which was destroyed by Allied bombing late in the Second World War. Christopher Andrew (writer and presenter). *The Fatal Attraction of Adolf Hitler* (producer Bill Treharne Jones), first broadcast on BBC1 on 21 April 1989.

[§]   Ian Kershaw, *Hitler 1889–1936: Hubris* (London: Penguin, 2001).

[¶]   Michael Brenner, *In Hitler's Munich: Jews, the Revolution, and the Rise of Nazism* (Princeton: Princeton University Press, 2022), p.23.

[**] *The Times*, 26 July 1923.

stars of German circuses in pounds sterling. With Cyril's assistance, Bertram Mills took advantage of it, signing contracts with – among others – Baptista Schreiber, who starred at Olympia in 1923. She was, in Cyril's view, 'certainly the best'* circus equestrian in Germany.

Because of his close business dealings with the Krone Circus, Mills became aware that Munich was the 'city of Hitler' somewhat earlier than the British embassy in Berlin. Lady D'Abernon, wife of the British ambassador, noted in her diary immediately after the failed 1923 Munich coup that her husband had been woken in the middle of the night by a senior official at the German Foreign Ministry anxious for advice on how to deal with an uprising in Munich led by 'a man of low origin' named Adolf Hitler.[†]

* * *

When Mills graduated from Cambridge in 1923, he did not initially intend to make the family circus his main career. Instead, after studying oil refining in the United States, he planned to make his fortune working for Burmah Oil in the Far East, while looking out for Asian acts for his father's circus. Burma (now Myanmar), where he was based, however, struck even Cyril as dangerous, as well as offering fewer major business opportunities than the increasingly successful Bertram Mills Circus.

Rangoon [Yangon] was a beautiful city and it was always worth the journey there if only to see the huge black clouds of flying foxes [large bats] going over the golden dome of the Shwedagon Pagoda

---

* Mills, *Bertram Mills Circus*, p.25.
† Lady D'Abernon's diary: quoted by Julia Boyd, *Travellers in the Third Reich: The Rise of Fascism through the Eyes of Everyday People* (London: Elliott & Thompson, 2017), p.47.

just before sunset, but I had to spend most of my time at the refinery, as the plant we were building had to be completed before the monsoon. Life there was rather dull or, as on the two occasions when there were sizable explosions, dangerous. In one of these I was soaked in burning oil and only just managed to extinguish the flames by rolling in the dust before a well-intentioned Burman arrived with a soda-acid fire extinguisher – the last thing I wanted.[*]

The Asian act which Mills was most anxious to secure for his father's circus was the Indian rope trick, first mentioned in sacred Indian texts over two millennia earlier. While serving in India before the First World War, the future Field Marshal Earl Haig naively vouched for its authenticity. In April 1919, the *Strand Magazine* published the first ever photo of the rope trick by Lieutenant F. W. Holmes, who had won the Victoria Cross on the Western Front before being transferred to India. He described how he and several other officers had witnessed the Indian rope trick performed near Poona (now Pune) by 'an old man and his boy':

> [The old man] began by unwinding from about his waist a long rope, which he threw upwards in the air, where it remained erect. The boy climbed to the top, where he balanced himself, as seen in the photograph, which I took at that moment. He then descended, and the conjurer, holding the pole with one hand, tapped it gently with the other, when it collapsed into rope-like flexibility, and he coiled it round his waist as before. I offer no explanation. I simply relate what took place before our eyes.[†]

---

[*]   Mills, *Bertram Mills Circus*, p.31.
[†]   John Zubrzycki, *Empire of Enchantment: The Story of Indian Magic* (New York: Oxford University Press, 2018).

36

Holmes's account, though not his photograph, of the rope trick was republished in the *Daily Mail*, with which the Mills family developed close links in the early 1920s. While working as an oil engineer in Burma, however, Cyril, who had lost faith in the supernatural, became rightly sceptical about the claims made by both Haig and Holmes:

> If I have any regrets about my time in the Far East they are due to my failure to find anyone who could show me the Indian rope trick. Neither in Ceylon nor Burma did I even find anyone who had seen it, though there were countless tales of friends of friends who had, and some of these even claimed to have photographed it, but no photos were ever to be found. Some said it had been done before large audiences, but I cannot persuade myself to believe in mass hypnotism...

Though Mills's skill in mounting deceptions and illusions later played a key role in the success of both his circus programmes and the top-secret Double-Cross System of the Second World War,* he gave up hope of including the Indian rope trick in the Bertram Mills repertoire. The credulity of those who believed in it reminded Mills of the appeal of the racist fantasies promulgated by Hitler in the Krone Circus building and elsewhere in Munich: 'I am almost convinced that it is just another traveller's tale which, like Hitler's propaganda, gained credence by reason of the magnitude of the lie upon which it was based.'†

* * *

---

* See below, ch.3.
† Mills, *Bertram Mills Circus*, p.31.

During the autumn of 1924 Mills gave way, with little reluctance, to pressure from his father to leave Burmah Oil, return to London during the Olympia winter season and make a full-time career with the increasingly successful family circus.[*]

Later, Mills would also remember 1924 for the athletic triumph of his friend, Harold Abrahams; they had first met at Cambridge University, probably at the Pitt Club, and stayed in touch afterwards.[†] At the Paris Olympics in July, Abrahams won the gold medal in the 100-metre sprint, a triumph immortalised in the film *Chariots of Fire*. Both Abrahams and Mills were later to have extraordinary experiences in Hitler's Germany during the Berlin Olympics.[‡]

During the Olympia winter season of 1924/25, Mills strongly supported his father's efforts to use his expanding business and social contacts to make the circus respectable in London society: 'That going to the circus was "not done" by a great many people was one of my father's gravest anxieties, for the cost of an expensive show would only be recovered if it attracted people who could afford the expensive seats.'[§]

Bertram Mills began putting on grand pre-Christmas lunches at Olympia to attract people who had hitherto 'thought any circus beneath their dignity'. By December 1927, the annual lunch attracted about 350 guests. In his history of the circus, Cyril Mills put Winston and Clementine Churchill at the top of the guestlist.[¶]

Churchill particularly admired the elephants and painted a portrait of four of them in various poses in the circus ring.[**] He wrote nostalgically of his service in Hyderabad twenty years earlier as a major in the Queen's Own Hussars Regiment: 'It was then the

---

[*]   Cyril Mills later told Christopher Mills of the reasons for his return from the Far East.
[†]   Cyril Mills discussed his long friendship with Abrahams with Christopher Mills after seeing *Chariots of Fire*.
[‡]   See below, pp.61–2.**
[§]   Cyril Bertram Mills, *Bertram Mills Circus*, pp.20ff.
[¶]   Ibid.
[**] See frontispiece.

custom for the elephants to salute as they marched past by raising their trunks ... Later on the custom was abolished ... I mourn the elephants and their salutations...'* To Churchill's delight, in Bertram Mills Circus the elephants learned to revive their salutations.

Though the well-known politicians who accepted Bertram Mills's invitations to the pre-Christmas lunches were mostly Conservative, two had been part of Britain's first Labour-led government in 1924: Prime Minister J. Ramsay MacDonald and Colonial Secretary J. H. 'Jimmy' Thomas, General Secretary of the National Union of Railwaymen from 1916 to 1931.† At a time when Mills had established close links with German circuses, he must have been impressed by Ramsay MacDonald's acceptance of an invitation in 1928 to become the first foreigner to address the Reichstag. His speech was a great success. Lady Rumbold, the British ambassador's wife, found him 'a most attractive individual, so good-looking and distingué'.‡ MacDonald made the same impression at the annual circus lunches.

Though the popularity of the Bertram Mills Circus crossed the political spectrum, the personal sympathies of both Bertram and Cyril Mills were strongly conservative and anti-socialist. So, much more visibly, were Harrow School's. Speaking at the Harrow Luncheon Club in 1923, the Old Harrovian actor-manager and playwright Sir Gerald du Maurier, then at the height of his popularity, called for 'a sort of Klu Klux Klan of Public Schoolboys which when the Beacon flares on the [Harrow] Hill, would come down and restore England once more to law and order, and make her what she used to be and what she always should be, the pattern country in the

---

*   Churchill, *My Early Life*, p.131. I owe this reference to Dr Piers Brendon.
†   MacDonald returned to power as Labour Prime Minister in 1929 and as head of the Conservative-dominated National Government which succeeded it in 1931. Thomas was a Cabinet minister in both governments.
‡   Boyd, *Travellers in the Third Reich*, p.72.

world'. In 1924, a rare left-wing Harrow pupil, the future writer Giles Playfair, was knifed (fortunately without serious injury) by an outraged fellow pupil after writing a socialist election manifesto. The housemaster, C. W. M. Moorsom, initially threatened the culprit with severe punishment, but relented once informed of the seriousness of Playfair's political provocation.*

The *Daily Mail*, however, did more than Harrow to influence Mills's deep hostility to Soviet Russia. From the circus's first performance in 1920, it had – to quote Cyril – enjoyed 'excellent relations with the *Daily Mail* because they followed us at Olympia each year with the Ideal Home Exhibitions and we were often able to help each other'.†

The first intelligence documents ever seen by Mills were reports during the controversial negotiation in 1920–21 by the Lloyd George coalition government of the Anglo-Soviet Trade Agreement, the first de facto British recognition of the Soviet regime. Codebreakers in the recently established British SIGINT agency, the Government Code and Cypher School (GC&CS, forerunner of today's GCHQ), decrypted telegrams from the Soviet trade delegation in London to Moscow which revealed their secret payments to the socialist *Daily Herald* and to the newly founded Communist Party of Great Britain (CPGB). The payments were made possible by the sale of Tsarist jewels which the delegation had smuggled into Britain. The trade delegation and its couriers failed to realise, however, that Russian diamonds were cut in a distinctive way, which made it straightforward for London jewellers to identify them.

As the price for continuing trade negotiations with Bolshevik Russia, Lloyd George had to agree to demands from Churchill and other Cabinet ministers for public disclosure of the secret Soviet subsidies to the

---

* Tyerman, *A History of Harrow School*, ch.17.
† Mills, *Bertram Mills Circus*, p.80.

CPGB. On 18 August 1920, copies of eight top-secret decrypted Soviet telegrams recording payments to the *Daily Herald* were given to all national newspapers (except the *Daily Herald*), which published them the next day. In an attempt to protect the SIGINT source, the press was asked to say that the messages had been obtained from 'a neutral country' – in the hope that Moscow would conclude that there had been a leak from the entourage of the leading Bolshevik diplomat, Maxim Litvinov, in Copenhagen. To Lloyd George's fury, however, *The Times* gave the game away by beginning its report: 'The following wireless messages have been intercepted by the British Government.'*

Pressure rapidly built up within Whitehall to make public further intelligence reports on Soviet subversion. On 1 September, Sir Basil Thomson, head of the CID at Scotland Yard, Field Marshal Sir Henry Wilson, Chief of the Imperial General Staff and Admiral Sir Hugh Sinclair, Director of Naval Intelligence (later Chief of MI6), sent Churchill a joint memorandum which concluded:

> The presence of the Russian Trade Delegation has become in our opinion the gravest danger which this country has had to face since the Armistice. This being so, we think that the publication of the de-cyphered cables has become so imperative that we must face the risks that will be entailed.

As Prime Minister during the Second World War, Churchill would have been horrified by any action that might compromise the work of British codebreakers. But in 1920 he was 'convinced that the danger to the state which has been wrought by the intrigues of these revolutionaries and the disastrous effect which will be produced on these plans

---

* Andrew, *Secret Service*, p.268.

by the exposure of their methods outweighs all other considerations'.[*] Though the Cabinet decided against publication of further decrypts, two were leaked from an unknown Whitehall source to the *Daily Mail* and the equally right-wing *Morning Post*, which published them on 15 September. Churchill welcomed their illicit publication in the hope of further discrediting 'the foul baboonery of Bolshevism' and 'dealing a death blow to the revolutionary movement in this country'.[†] 'After conquering all the huns, tigers of the world,' Churchill declared, 'I will not submit to being beaten by the baboons!'[‡] The Mills family and their friends in the *Daily Mail* no doubt agreed.[§]

The Conservative governments which followed the fall of the Lloyd George coalition in 1922, the first since 1905, approved the publication of more top-secret evidence of Soviet subversion.[¶] In 1923, doubtless to the amusement of the Mills family, the Foreign Secretary, Lord Curzon, publicly taunted the Soviet government with Britain's success in decrypting their communications and quoted a series of decrypts in what became known as 'the Curzon Ultimatum' to the Soviet government:

> The Russian Commissariat for Foreign Affairs will no doubt recognise the following communication dated 21st February, 1923, which they received from M. Raskolnikov…[**]
>
> The Commissariat for Foreign Affairs will also doubtless recognise a communication received by them from Kabul, dated the 8th November, 1922…

---

[*] Ibid., pp.268–9.

[†] Cabinet conclusions [minutes], 15 Sept. 1920, TNA CAB 23/23. Andrew, *Secret Service*, pp.314–15.

[‡] Piers Brendon, *Churchill's Bestiary: His Life Through Animals* (London: Michael O'Mara Books, 2018), loc.446.

[§] Cabinet conclusions, 15 September 1920, TNA CAB 23/23. Andrew, *Secret Service*, pp.314–15.

[¶] Churchill lost his seat in 1922 and did not return to the Commons until 1924.

[**] Cmd. 1869 (1923). GC&CS lost the ability to decrypt Soviet telegrams after the Baldwin government publicly quoted further intercepts in 1927.

Nor will they have forgotten a communication dated the 16th March, 1923, from M. Karakhan, the Assistant Commissary for Foreign Affairs, to M. Raskolnikov...

The supply of authentic Soviet intercepts, such as those quoted in 'the Curzon Ultimatum', however, was sometimes polluted by forgeries. On 25 October 1924, four days before a British general election, a banner headline in the *Daily Mail* declared: 'CIVIL WAR PLOT BY SOCIAL-ISTS' MASTERS: MOSCOW ORDERS TO OUR REDS'. There followed the text of a sensational letter allegedly despatched by Grigory Zinoviev, Chairman of the Communist International (Comintern) to the CPGB on 15 September 1924, instructing it to 'strain every nerve' for the ratification of a recent treaty concluded by Ramsay MacDonald's Labour government with the Soviet Union, to intensify 'agitation-prop-aganda work in the armed forces' and to prepare for the coming of the British revolution. It did not occur to either the Mills family or to the great majority of the *Mail*'s other readers that, while quite similar in content to some genuine Comintern directives, the 'Zinoviev letter' was (as is now known) a forgery. Though the letter was not the main cause of the Conservative election landslide victory on 29 October, many politicians on both the left and right believed that it was.

Cyril and Bertram Mills's suspicions about covert Soviet oper-ations in Britain were strengthened by the probably well-founded belief that they were personally defrauded by Moscow, with the connivance of Soviet intelligence, in its search for scarce foreign currency. After signing a contract in 1925 with Williams Truzzi, who ran a celebrated group of circus horses in Leningrad,* Bertram Mills Circus was required to deposit a large sum with a Swiss bank

---

* Truzzi came from an Italian circus family who had founded a leading circus in Tsarist Russia.

as a guarantee that both Truzzi and the horses would return to Russia after performing at Olympia. Just before the horses were due to leave Leningrad by ship, Bertram received a cable demanding a further £1,000 (almost £60,000 in the present day) to pay for a Soviet icebreaker to clear a channel for the ship from the mouth of the River Neva on the Baltic coast. As Cyril later recalled: 'It was a lot of money, but an Olympia programme without horses was unthinkable, so it was paid at once … I have always assumed that somebody made a big profit on the deal, especially as a large convoy sailed out in the wake of the ship with [Truzzi's] horses.'*

For the rest of his life, Cyril Mills avoided further dealings with what became the Moscow State Circus and the KGB minders who accompanied its performers on their foreign travels.[†]

* * *

The event which aroused the greatest political passions in the Mills family during the 1920s was the General Strike called by the Trades Union Congress (TUC) on 3 May 1926 'in defence of miners' wages and hours'. Government propaganda during the strike was controlled by Churchill, then Chancellor of the Exchequer in the Conservative government led by his fellow Old Harrovian Stanley Baldwin.[‡] After strikes shut down most of the press, Churchill became personally responsible for editing and producing up to 2 million copies a day of an official government newssheet, the *British Gazette*, as well as overseeing its distribution. 'He simply revels in this affair', wrote the future

---

*   Mills, *Bertram Mills Circus*, pp.34–5.
†   See below, pp.218–19.
‡   Mills, like the rest of the British public, was entirely unaware that, while at Harrow, Baldwin had very nearly been expelled for sending pornography to his cousin at Eton; Simon Heffer, *Sing As We Go: Britain Between the Wars* (London: Penguin, 2023), p.165.

Prime Minister Neville Chamberlain 'which he will continually treat and talk of as if it were 1914.' The Chairman of the Conservative Party, J. C. C. Davidson, complained that Churchill 'regarded the strike as an enemy to be destroyed ... He thinks he is Napoleon.'*

Churchill welcomed the Mills family's role in circulating strike-breaking copies of the *Daily Mail* to supplement the *British Gazette*. From its first performance in 1920, the circus had – to quote Cyril – enjoyed 'excellent relations' with the *Daily Mail*.† The *Mail* printed a single-sheet daily newspaper denouncing the strike in Paris and had it flown to Kent, whence the Mills family transported it by car to be distributed in London – the first covert operation in which Cyril was involved. 'A general strike', declared the *Mail*, 'is not an industrial dispute. It is a revolutionary movement intended to inflict suffering upon the great mass of innocent persons.'‡

Cyril Mills also signed up as one of the 'special constables' recruited to keep order during the strike. Like the others, he was issued with a wooden truncheon and tin helmet. Mills's main role as a special constable was as chauffeur to a senior police officer – probably, as his family believe, the abrasive Met Commissioner, Sir William Horwood, a former Brigadier-General who much preferred the company of army officers to members of the Met. Some members of the Police Federation derisively called him the 'Chocolate Soldier' after he narrowly survived an attempt (unrelated to the strikes) to poison him with a chocolate walnut whip laced with arsenic.§

As with attacks on some London buses, some supporters of the General Strike attempted to break the windows of the car being

---

* Keith Laybourn, *The General Strike of 1926* (Manchester: Manchester University Press, 1993). Heffer, *Sing As We Go*, ch.6.
† See above, p.40.
‡ Mills, *Bertram Mills Circus*, p.80; *Daily Mail*, 6 May 1926.
§ *ODNB* William Horwood; 'The Case of the "Walnut Whip" Police Assassin', *The Independent*, 25 March 2005.

driven by Mills. Cyril later told his family of his response, no doubt with Horwood's approval, to them: '...one incident where they were surrounded by a group of strikers who were trying to attack the car. He put his foot down and drove straight through them. He didn't know whether anyone was hurt as a result of his actions.'[*]

Though Mills's motives were not mercenary, he, like other Special Constables, was paid £2 6s 3d per week, plus a food allowance. Miners had been locked out by mine owners for refusing to accept wages of only £1 11s 7½d.

The *Tatler* magazine, taken weekly by the Mills family (partly because of its high-quality photos of the circus as well as of high society),[†] featured photos of fashionable volunteers with a caption applauding:

> the magnificent response which all classes of Society made to the Government's call for volunteers in the wake of the General Strike of 1926. Here, Mr. Orbach drives cars for the Red Cross, Captain Peebles Chaplain is shown hauling coal, and a variety of aristocratic ladies work in canteens in Hyde Park and Scotland Yard for the refreshment of volunteers, special constables and transport workers.

Like Cyril Mills, many of the volunteers were Cambridge students past and present; 2,000 Cambridge undergraduates helped to run the London Underground.[‡]

The volunteers far outnumbered members of MI5. Because of drastic post-war cuts in its budget, MI5 was left with only thirty-five staff,[§] about 4 per cent of its personnel at the time of the Armistice.

---

* Information from Christopher Mills.
† Confirmed by Christopher Mills.
‡ Laybourn, *The General Strike of 1926*, p.55.
§ Evidence by Kell to Secret Service Committee, 10 March 1925, TNA FO 1093/68.

Though one of its officers, Herbert 'Con' Boddington, had succeed-ed in joining and informing on the Communist Party, Sir Vernon Kell, the long-serving head of MI5, told Whitehall's Secret Service Committee a year before the strike that, because of diminished re-sources, 'he had no "agents" in the accepted sense of the word, but only informants, though he might employ an agent for a specific purpose, if necessary[,] in which case he would consult Scotland Yard about him, if he were in doubt as to his character, or he might even borrow a man from Scotland Yard'.*

No longer possessing a permanent agent network, Kell kept a re-serve list of former MI5 officers for use in emergencies.[†] A number returned to service during the General Strike. On 12 May 1926, Kell wrote proudly to MI5 staff:

> I desire to thank all Officers and their Staffs, also the Ladies of the Office, for their splendid work and co-operation during the General Strike. The manner in which all hands have put their shoulders to the wheel shows that the ancient war-traditions of M.I.5 remained unimpaired.[‡]

The headline of Churchill's victorious final issue of the *British Gazette*, on 13 May 1926, said simply: 'GENERAL STRIKE OFF'. Harrow School sent Baldwin its congratulations.[§] Working with Kell's MI5 reserve during the strike was Mills's first experience of collaborating with intelligence officers.

---

* Secret Service Committee, minutes of 10 March 1925, TNA FO 1093/68.
† 'List of Names of Past Staff Prepared for Mobilisation as Necessary', Summary of General Strike, minutes from 1 May 1926, TNA KV4/246.
‡ Kell, letter to staff, 16 May 1926, Summary of General Strike, Appendix 4, TNA KV4/246.
§ Recent research has revealed that Baldwin had been very nearly expelled while a pupil at Harrow for sending pornography to his cousin at Eton; Heffer, *Sing As We Go*, p.165. His fellow Harrovians, Mills and Churchill, appear to have been unaware of this misadventure.

Though he usually avoided public appearances, Kell so enjoyed the Bertram Mills Circus that he took groups of female staff to performances at Olympia during the Christmas season. Catherine Morgan-Smith, later MI5 Lady Superintendent, recalled that 'Sir Vernon always gave me half-a-crown for a taxi home and I always took the bus and saved the half-crown, which was good money in those days." But, though Mills got to know him 'well',[†] the retiring Kell could not be persuaded to accept an invitation to the grand pre-Christmas lunches at Olympia put on by the Mills family for politicians and other notables.

* * *

The star lunch guest continued to be Winston Churchill. The Mills family and Churchill were right to regard each other as, in their very different fields, Britain's most successful entertainers. Competition for Commons gallery tickets when Churchill presented his third Budget as Chancellor of the Exchequer on 11 April 1927 was said to be as fierce as for a major sporting event. The Prince of Wales (the future Edward VIII) was present and Baldwin reported to King George V, 'The scene was quite sufficient to show that Mr Churchill as a star turn has a power of attraction which nobody in the House of Commons can excel.' 'It is admitted on all sides', wrote Baldwin in August 1928, 'that [Winston] has no equal in the House of Commons. His manner with the Opposition is so good-humoured that although they often interrupt him, they look forward to his speeches as the finest entertainment the House can offer.'[‡]

---

*   Andrew, *Defence of the Realm*, p.132.
†   In a letter to Nigel West on 19 November 1984 (CBM), Mills refers to 'Kell, whom I knew well'.
‡   Andrew Roberts, *Churchill: Walking with Destiny* (London: Penguin, 2019), pp.326–7.

In turn, no major politician was a more enthusiastic supporter of Bertram Mills Circus than Churchill. The key to Churchill's enthusiasm was simply how much the circus, particularly the clowns, entertained him. Throughout his long political career there are many photographs of him smiling and chuckling. The only occasions when Churchill became helpless with laughter, however, were at the circus.*

---

*   See illustration no.4: Churchill and his daughter Mary helpless with laughter watching the clowns at Bertram Mills Circus at Olympia on 22 December 1938 after being entertained to lunch by Cyril Mills and his brother Bernard. Their neighbours, though smiling, are not nearly as amused.

CHAPTER THREE

SPYING BY BIPLANE

During the 1920s, Bertram Mills Circus performed only at Olympia. In 1930 it began touring much of Britain, performing to large audiences in massive tents known as 'Big Tops'. The circus enthusiast Lady Eleanor Smith, daughter of Churchill's closest friend, W. E. Smith, 1st Earl of Birkenhead, wrote admiringly:

> The Bertram Mills Circus is like a tent-town, a canvas city where every person seems to work and play harder than in other towns where I have lived. This applies to owners, managers, artists, tent-men, musicians, blacksmiths, ring-attendants, grooms and firemen. It applies no less strongly to their wives.[*]

Bertram handed over running the travelling 'tent-town' to his two sons. Having reached his mid-fifties, he told them he was 'not well disposed towards spending a large part of his life in a caravan' on tour.[†] His growing political ambitions (scarcely mentioned in Cyril's

---

[*] Smith, *Life's a Circus*, p.178.
[†] CBM papers.

history of the circus) also made him reluctant to spend long periods away from London and the Home Counties.

From 1928 to 1938, Bertram Mills was an elected member of the LCC.* During this decade he was councillor, successively, for East Fulham and Wandsworth Clapham, representing the Municipal Reform Party, local allies of the Conservative Party, which did not stand in LCC elections.† In 1931 he became Chairman of the LCC Entertainments (Licensing) Committee (1931–34) and its Inspection of Films Sub-Committee,‡ as well as a member of the British Board of Film Censors committee of experts at a time when it approved the showing of a number of spy classics, notably those directed by Alfred Hitchcock.

What little Cyril Mills knew about MI6 before working for it later in the 1930s came largely from the entertainment business rather than from intelligence professionals. The two most successful play-wrights and writers recruited by the first MI6 Chief, Sir Mansfield Cumming, as wartime heads of station were Somerset Maugham and Compton Mackenzie.§ Both men published novels that were inspired by their work for MI6. Much of Maugham's mission to revolutionary Petrograd reappeared, thinly disguised, in his 1927 short story collection *Ashenden: Or, The British Agent*. Ashenden uses Maugham's own MI6 codename, 'Somerville', as well as his London address in Chesterfield Street, Mayfair. The British ambassador in Petrograd, Sir George Buchanan, whose welcome to Maugham in 1917 'could not have been more frigid', reappears as Sir Herbert Witherspoon, who receives Ashenden 'with a frigidity that would have sent a little

---

* LCC meeting documentation; CBM papers CBM/C.4.1.
† After losing his East Fulham seat to a Labour candidate in the 1934 LCC elections, Mills was elected Councillor for Wandsworth Clapham at a by-election a few months later.
‡ LCC/MIN/4,386; Metropolitan Archives, City of London.
§ See above, pp.6–7.

shiver down the spine of a polar bear'.* The Ashenden stories inspired Alfred Hitchcock's 1936 spy thriller, *Secret Agent*.

Compton Mackenzie's much more indiscreet *Greek Memories* (1932)† led to his prosecution under the Official Secrets Act at the Old Bailey. Mackenzie published top-secret wartime MI6 telegrams on the proposed bribery of the Greek police, identified former MI6 agents and officers and revealed wartime cover occupations still used by their interwar successors. However, some of the prosecution's claims – for example, that Mackenzie had compromised national security by revealing that the late Sir Mansfield Cumming had been Chief of MI6 – were absurd. The judge at the Old Bailey trial asked the Attorney General how recently Cumming had died. The Attorney General did not know, nor did any other member of the prosecution team. Finally, Mackenzie himself revealed that Cumming had died in 1923. Even Mackenzie, however, was unaware that Cumming's widow, Lady May Cumming, believed that since his death she had been able to talk to her late husband with the help of a medium.‡

After being persuaded by his counsel to plead guilty, Compton Mackenzie was fined £100 with £100 costs. To pay his own much greater defence costs, he wrote a comic novel entitled *Water on the Brain*, set in a fictional Directorate of Extraordinary Intelligence, whose obsession with secrecy oscillates between farce and paranoia.§

Though Mills was probably amused by *Water on the Brain*, it did not shake his conviction that the complete secrecy of intelligence

---

*   W. Somerset Maugham, *Ashenden: Or, the British Agent* (London: Mandarin, 1991).
†   Published by Cassell in London, Toronto, Melbourne and Sydney.
‡   By the time of the trial, May Cumming had moved to Gordonstoun School, to whose founder, Kurt Hahn, she had loaned 40,000 gold marks. When she died in 1938, only Hahn knew that she was the widow of the first Chief of MI6. Judd, *The Quest for C*, p.473. During the 1930s the future Prince Philip, Duke of Edinburgh, was a Gordonstoun pupil. The future King Charles III attended the school from 1962 to 1967.
§   Andrew and Green, *Stars and Spies*, pp.219–21.

operations was crucial to their success. No word of any of his own operations leaked out until after his retirement. Bertram Mills would have been astonished to discover that his son Cyril had become Britain's most successful spy in pre-war Nazi Germany – and that the circus he had founded provided wonderful cover for espionage against a notoriously hard and dangerous intelligence target.

* * *

During the early 1930s, still with no thought of working for MI6, Cyril Mills visited a series of leading Continental circuses to learn from their experience of travelling Big Tops: 'I was soon convinced that the big, well-run circuses in Germany were years ahead of those here … largely due to the German's passion for rules and regulations and his inborn willingness to accept discipline. The circuses of Sarrasani, Krone and Busch … were well run business organisations.'*

Like other German businesses, however, the entertainment industry was badly hit by the Depression which, in the short term, did more damage to the German economy than to any other in Europe. By 1932 industrial production had fallen by almost half and six million people – one third of the German labour force – were unemployed.

Cyril Mills's visits to German circuses in the early 1930s also coincided with a period of extraordinary political turmoil. At the 1928 elections, before the onset of the Depression, the Nazis only won twelve seats in the Reichstag and Hitler was widely written off. When Lord D'Abernon, the former British ambassador to Germany, published two volumes of memoirs, he mentioned Hitler only in a footnote. After referring briefly to Hitler's imprisonment after the

---

* Mills, *Bertram Mills Circus*, p.44.

failed 1923 Munich putsch, D'Abernon concluded: 'He was finally released after six months and bound over for the rest of his sentence, thereafter fading into oblivion.'[*]

The onset of the Depression rescued the Nazis from the threat of political oblivion. Cyril's contemporary at Corpus Christi College, Cambridge, the subsequently famous writer Christopher Isherwood, who moved to Berlin in 1929, wrote a year later: 'Here was the seething brew of history in the making ... The Berlin brew seethed with unemployment, malnutrition, stock market panic, hatred of the Versailles Treaty and other potent ingredients.'[†] In 1930, at the first election after the 1929 Wall Street Crash, Nazi seats in the Reichstag shot up from 12 to 107. In July 1932, at the worst moment of the German Depression, the Nazis won 37 per cent of the vote and 230 seats – more than any other party since the First World War. Hitler told a cheering audience at one of his favourite venues (well known to Mills),[‡] the Munich HQ of the Krone Circus, 'A great victory has been fought for and won!' Mills discovered from his growing contacts with the Sarrasani Circus and its owner, Hans Stosch, that Hitler also gave major speeches[§] at its Dresden headquarters. The Nazis organised a series of triumphant national rallies in the same building.[¶]

Imitating the Big Tops used by Sarrasani and its main German rivals led to Cyril Mills's first major secret operation abroad – in the interests of the family business, however, rather than of British intelligence: 'If we were to produce a modern tenting circus of the kind we planned the best thing would be to copy the equipment of

---

[*]   Viscount D'Abernon, *An Ambassador of Peace: Pages From the Diary of Viscount D'Abernon (Berlin 1920–1926)*, 2 vols (London: Hodder & Stoughton, 1929–30).

[†]   Christopher Isherwood, *Diaries: Volume One 1939–1960*, vol.1 (London: Vintage, 2011).

[‡]   See above, pp.52–3.

[§]   On 18 September 1928, 21 June 1930 and 11 December 1932.

[¶]   Sabine Hanke. 'National Identity and Cultural Difference in the British and German Circus, 1920–1945', PhD dissertation (Sheffield University, 2020).

one of Germany's best circuses. Everything demanded the utmost secrecy, as we did not want anyone [in Britain] to know our plans.'

When placing a secret order for a Big Top from the leading German tent-makers, Stonemeyer in Konstanz, Mills insisted that 'it was built to metric measurements, as feet and inches would have suggested Britain as a possible destination.'* The commercial secrecy which Mills believed was necessary to preserve a lead over rival British circuses reinforced his belief in the official secrecy required for intelligence operations.

On becoming Chancellor at the head of a coalition government on 30 January 1933, Hitler swore to uphold the German constitution and parliamentary rule. Less than two months later, on 23 March, the Enabling Act made him a dictator in all but name, able to rule without the Reichstag. Mills complained that Hans Stosch was simultaneously turning his 'superb' Sarrasani Circus, Germany's best, into a rather different kind of dictatorship:

> ...the man was a megalomaniac, for as he walked round the show every male employee was expected to raise his hat and every female to curtsey ... Male artistes had to line the ring entrance standing to attention except when they were performing and every female had to act as an usherette ... When [Stosch] entered the ring to present his elephants ... his entrance reminded me of that of a Maharajah at a Durbar.†

Mills's close connections with German circuses meant that he was one of the few foreign observers of the Nazi Third Reich to notice Hitler's growing concerns about the number of Jewish performers

---

*   Mills, *Bertram Mills Circus*, pp.44–5.
†   Ibid., pp.194–5. Sarrasani Circus posters commonly portrayed Stosch dressed as an Indian maharajah.

they employed. The Sarrasani Circus, previously favoured by the Führer, was officially labelled a 'Jüdenzirkus'. The proprietor, Hans Stosch, though not himself Jewish, took his circus to South America.[*] Stosch's son, Junior, however, returned to Germany and agreed with Hitler's Minister of Propaganda, Joseph Goebbels, on racial purification of the circus in return for a state subsidy.[†]

It did not yet occur to Mills that his regular visits to Nazi Germany on circus business would turn him into one of MI6's most productive spies. Most of his early travels to Germany had been by rail and public transport. In 1933, however, at first without telling his family, Mills began 'flying for fun' in a de Havilland Gipsy Moth biplane, taking lessons at Stag Lane, a tiny aerodrome in Edgware where 'every landing had to be just right to miss the houses during the approach and avoid running into the hedge on the far side'.[‡]

Most Gipsy Moths were owned by flying clubs rather than by individuals. The best-known private owner was the Prince of Wales (the future Edward VIII), the first royal patron of Bertram Mills's Circus, who in 1929 had purchased an early model for his personal use. One day, after a series of flying lessons at Northolt aerodrome:

> ...my instructor jumped from the airplane ... With a dramatic gesture he waved me into the air alone. Taking off, I completed without mishap two extremely lonely circuits of the field ... But I never again flew alone. Although I travelled a lot after that by air, I left the piloting to experts.[§]

---

[*]   The only foreign intelligence agency known to have analysed Hitler's attitude to the circus was the Office of Strategic Services (OSS) in the United States. Its conclusions are unconvincing: '[Hitler] is particularly pleased with tight-rope acts and trapeze artists. ... He does not much care for wild animal acts unless there is a woman in danger.' https://contingentmagazine.org/2019/03/29/the-circus-hitler-said-he-loved/
[†]   http://www.circopedia.org/Circus_Sarrasani
[‡]   Mills, *Bertram Mills Circus*, pp.76–7.
[§]   'A King's Story', Part 2, *Life*, 29 May 1950.

In 1933 Mills also purchased a Gipsy Moth for £250, though his was secondhand.[*] He had a stronger nerve than the future Edward VIII and as soon as he gained his pilot's licence in January 1934,[†] Mills flew his biplane alone:

> The family now had to be told and the news was accepted moderately well, although Mother was sure I should kill myself and was even more convinced a few days later when I landed in a small field within sight of her house, but having started in a very small aerodrome I knew what space I needed and this knowledge was useful later when I followed the circus round Britain, landing alongside the Big Top whenever the ground was large enough.

To conserve battery power for the Gipsy Moth's radio, Mills had to start the engine by hand-swinging the propeller instead of using the electric starter. He became known in the circus business as the 'Flying Director': 'When I said I was piloting my own aircraft there was amazement, for there were few private flyers then and I was the first circus man either to own or fly one.'[‡]

In the spring of 1936, Mills's father bought him a single-engine de Havilland Hornet Moth. Though the engine was usually started by its electric motor, Mills continued to occasionally swingstart the propeller to prolong battery-life.[§]

The Hornet was more comfortable, as well as safer, for long flights. Unlike the open-cockpit Gipsy Moth, it had a pilot's cabin

---

[*] See illustration no.6: Cyril Mills's first aircraft, the de Havilland Gipsy Moth, in 1934.
[†] For Mills's Aviator's Certificate, see illustration no.5.
[‡] Mills, *Bertram Mills Circus*, pp.78–9.
[§] See illustration no.7: Cyril Mills with his Hornet Moth in 1936 at a circus ground near Lympne in Ashford, Kent.

and Mills no longer needed a flying suit and goggles. He often wore a business suit instead.*

Henceforth, most of Mills's travels to Continental circuses were by air, taking off from Lympne, known as 'Kent's Garden Airfield' because of its location overlooking Hythe and Romney Marsh. His first flight abroad in the de Havilland Hornet enabled him to visit circuses in nine cities: Rotterdam, Hamburg, Copenhagen, Berlin, Düsseldorf, Cologne, Brussels, Paris and Caen in only nine days.† In Mills's view, the best circus acts were in Berlin at the Scala and Wintergarten theatres: 'Competition between them was so fierce they always had the best and most expensive acts.'‡

Mills flew to Berlin three times during 1936 and witnessed preparations for the summer Olympic Games, as well as their aftermath. With Goebbels's blessing, the racially purified Sarrasani Circus performed in Berlin during the Olympics.§ However, the 'Jews Not Welcome' signs, which Mills had previously seen throughout Nazi Germany, were removed from hotels, restaurants and public places for the duration of the Games.¶

Hitler's popularity in all the German cities visited by Mills was depressingly obvious. Before coming to power in 1933, Hitler had made no serious inroads into the working-class vote; at both elections in 1932 the combined vote of the socialists and communists was higher than ever before. Once in power, however, Hitler rapidly established his claim to be Führer of the whole nation in a series of plebiscites. In March 1936, after the reoccupation of the Rhineland,

---

*   See illustration no.9: A smartly dressed Mills boards his Hornet Moth.

†   Mills's pilot flight log book; CBM papers C.10.2.

‡   Mills, *Bertram Mills Circus*, p.84.

§   http://www.circopedia.org/Circus_Sarrasani

¶   Mills, untitled confidential memoir on his intelligence career written for his second wife Mimi and their children (undated but completed in 1984), p.1, CBM papers. Preparation for the memoir occurred after the declassification of some wartime intelligence files, beginning in the late 1970s, and the publication of the official history of British Intelligence in the Second World War by Sir F. H. Hinsley.

he won a majority of over 98 per cent. Whatever the reliability of such figures, there is little doubt that, in the words of his biographer Alan Bullock, the mood of most German people was one of 'overwhelming gratitude and approval'.

During 1936, Mills flew a total of 17,000 miles in his Hornet, concealing from both his family and circus colleagues the dangers of flying without radio over unfamiliar terrain during bad weather. He was forced to admit, however, to a narrow escape in July 1936 during his first flight to Vienna in 'a much worse thunder storm than we see in this country', when he could barely see through the windscreen:

> The only sensible thing was to get my feet on the ground as quickly as possible and wait for the storm to pass. The east side of the river [Danube] was the flatter, and therefore the most hopeful, and within half a minute I saw what I was looking for – almost praying for – a huge green field where a forced landing would be a piece of cake.

The green field, however, turned out to be growing maize, 'as high', Mills later recalled (quoting *Oklahoma*), 'as an elephant's eye'. Soon after landing, the Hornet performed a forwards somersault, leaving Mills with 'a nasty cut on the head' and lucky to escape more serious injury. With characteristic resilience, he recovered in hospital while his biplane was being repaired by the de Havilland agent in Vienna. After continuing his journey to visit circuses in Budapest, Belgrade, Sofia and Bucharest by commercial airlines, Mills had sufficiently recovered to fly his Hornet Moth from Vienna back to Lympne. Henceforth, he took particular care when flying over Germany to reconnoitre airfields along his route in case bad weather forced him to make another emergency landing.*

The Berlin Olympics and their aftermath in the summer of 1936 were a Nazi propaganda triumph. British visitors included four press barons (Lords Rothermere, Beaverbrook, Kemsley and Camrose), all much impressed. Soon after the games ended, David Lloyd George, Prime Minister at the time of Germany's defeat in 1918, arrived to take tea with the Führer at the Berghof, his mountain retreat, proclaiming Hitler 'the greatest German of the age'. He foolishly declared on his return: 'German hegemony in Europe, which was the aim and dream of the old pre-war militarism, is not even on the horizon of Nazism.'† Though Cyril Mills did not put his response in writing, it is easy to imagine his private outrage.

Mills took great pleasure, however, in his friend Harold Abrahams's role at the Berlin Olympics. Though injury had ended Abrahams's running career a year after he won gold in the 100 metres at the 1924 Paris Olympics,‡ he began a new career as a BBC athletics commentator. The BBC Controller of Programmes Cecil Graves, was initially reluctant to send him to the Berlin Olympics:

> The point about all this is, of course, that Abrahams is a Jew. He is our best commentator on athletics … We all regard the German action against Jews as quite irrational and intolerable … but should we take the line that however irrational we regard another country's attitude to be, it would be discourteous to send a Jewish commentator to a country were Jews are taboo?

---

*   Mills, untitled confidential memoir on his intelligence career (undated), CBM papers.
†   Tim Bouverie, *Appeasing Hitler: Chamberlain, Churchill and the Road to War* (London: Bodley Head, 2021).
‡   See above, p.38.

Abrahams, however, insisted on going to Berlin:

I have no delusions about the situation in Germany today; and if
I had been born in Germany, knowing myself as I do, I doubt if I
should be alive today. I still think the right thing is for us to show
the German people what Great Britain believes to be real sport ...
absolute freedom for all to participate...

Abrahams said later and must certainly have told Cyril that, while
commentating at Berlin: 'I was so close to Hitler, I could have shot
him. I wish I had.' He rejoiced at the four gold medals won by the
Black American, Jesse Owens, 'certainly the most beautiful moving
human being I have ever seen tearing down a sprint track' – and,
like Mills, at the upset they caused Hitler.[*]

During Mills's first flight on circus business from Lympne to
Berlin after the summer Olympic Games, he unexpectedly obtained
proof of Nazi Germany's secret programme of aerial rearmament in
defiance of the 1919 Treaty of Versailles:

I saw something of a kind I had never seen before. Leading away
from a very large hole on the side of a steep hill were the lines of
a miniature railway ... [which] made their ways around a huge
flat area ... clearly big enough to be an aerodrome[;] the entrance
to the hole was wide enough and high enough to allow a fighter
type aircraft to enter and I came to the conclusion that if the hole
went back far back into the hill it would be possible for an aircraft
to have nearly reached flying speed by the time it came out into
the open. On returning it would be able to taxi into a completely

---

[*]   Mark Ryan, *Running with Fire: The True Story of* Chariots of Fire *Hero Harold Abrahams* (London: Robson
Press, 2011).

bomb-proof shelter within a minute or two and what I had seen was undoubtedly a sort of underground aerodrome.

After returning to Lympne airfield, Mills told the customs officer he had seen 'something interesting' in Germany and asked him to 'put me in touch with someone who might like to hear about it'. Two days later, he was invited to a meeting at the Royal Air Force Club in Piccadilly with a man using an assumed name whom he later discovered was Frederick Winterbotham, head of the MI6 air section.*

Winterbotham had served as a scout pilot during the First World War in the Royal Flying Corps and helped to pioneer photographic reconnaissance. He had a narrow escape when he was shot down over Passchendaele in 1917. After inspecting his bullet-ridden seat cushion, the German fighter pilot responsible observed: 'just one more inch and you'd have been a soprano'. Winterbotham's family was officially told he had been killed in action and his obituary was published in a local paper. Twelve years later, by then with a law degree from Christ Church, Oxford, Winterbotham became MI6's first graduate recruit. In 1934, posing as a member of the British air staff, Winterbotham visited Germany, where he had friendly discussions with several senior Nazis and young Luftwaffe pilots, as well as being briefly received by Hitler. He returned convinced that Hitler was secretly planning to build Europe's most modern air force.†

A few days after Mills's first encounter with Winterbotham in the summer of 1936, he was invited to a second meeting at the RAF Club in Piccadilly. This time, Winterbotham was accompanied by

---

* Mills, untitled confidential memoir on his intelligence career (undated), CBM papers.
† Frederick Winterbotham, *The Nazi Connection* (London: Weidenfeld & Nicolson, 1978); Frederick Winterbotham, *The Ultra Spy: An Autobiography* (London: Macmillan, 1989); *ODNB* Frederick Winterbotham.

a high-ranking RAF officer, who also used an alias to introduce himself. Mills told them, 'I suppose you know about all the new [German] aerodromes which have been built or are now under construction?' He, however, knew much that they did not.

The next day, Mills returned to the RAF Club with maps on which he had marked the position of about thirty German aerodromes that had been built recently or were under construction. This time, a civilian was also present. He later identified himself as Dick White, a German-speaking MI5 officer who became a lifelong friend of Cyril and, in the 1950s, the only man ever to become, successively, head of both MI5 and MI6. Like Winterbotham, White was a Christ Church graduate.

After Mills's maps had been examined, White told him that: '…I could be told the truth. Over the last few days I had been very near the top of the list of suspects. The information I had produced [it was mistakenly believed] had probably been given me by the Nazis and I was a "plant" with all the makings of becoming a double agent.' Mills said later that he was still 'far too green' in intelligence matters to realise that there was 'any chance that any British subject coming forward unasked with information might be considered a plant'.[*]

Mills only discovered later that, since June 1933, MI5 had been using as its first double agent against Germany, a First World War fighter ace, Major Christopher Draper, who had become one of Europe's most daring stunt pilots. Known as the 'Mad Major', he had attracted the personal attention of Adolf Hitler, who was photographed speaking to him at a 1932 Munich airshow.[†] One of the few things on which Hitler and Mills probably agreed was admiration of Draper's skill and bravery in flying under most of London's bridges.

---

[*] Mills, untitled confidential memoir on his intelligence career (undated), pp.1–2. CBM papers.

[†] Andrew and Green, *Stars and Spies*, pp.248–50. See illustration no.10.

Draper, however, proved an unsuccessful double agent. Lacking the sophisticated interdepartmental system for assembling disinformation later developed for Britain's Double-Cross System during the Second World War,[*] MI5 began to run out of plausible falsehoods to deceive the Germans. The Abwehr increasingly expressed 'grave dissatisfaction' with the quality of Draper's inaccurate intelligence on the RAF. MI5 suspected, when it first saw Mills's aerial intelligence reports in 1936, that they were an attempt by the Abwehr to retaliate for the bogus intelligence Draper had given them.[†]

However, a joint study by Winterbotham and White of Mills's maps of German airfields convinced them that, unlike Draper, he could not be a double agent:

...I had given completely accurate information on a great many things and places which their map confirmed. I had also told them a great many things of which they had previously known nothing. I could not possibly have known how much they knew so it was obviously impossible for me to mix good with false information.

They also confessed that the names by which I knew them were false and told me their real names and who they represented ... Before I left my new friends I was asked whether I should visit Germany frequently in future and if so would I be willing to keep my eyes and ears open and report the results on my return. Of course my answers to both questions were in the affirmative although I barely realised I was allowing myself to become a spy, albeit an unpaid one.

...I must confess I was alarmed when I was told quite frankly how little the British authorities who were charged with the task

---

[*]   See below, pp.120–21.
[†]   In 1937 the Abwehr broke off contact with Draper.

knew of the build-up which was in progress in the Nazi Airforce and just felt it my duty to do all I could as by then I was convinced by what I had seen in Germany there would be war before long.[*]

Some of the corroborative intelligence which convinced Winterbotham and White that Mills's reports were genuine came from an unidentified source whom MI6 concluded must be on the staff of the commander-in-chief of the Luftwaffe, Hermann Göring, and 'either violently anti-Nazi or extremely greedy'. The source had revealed the locations and codenames of twenty-five flying schools used to train Luftwaffe pilots as well as details of a new German fighter squadron and the Stuka dive-bomber. Though no record survives of the actual amount paid to the informant, a substantial payment was left for him in a luggage locker at a Berlin station and the key to the locker posted to a cover address he had provided. Winterbotham considered it a 'copybook method of transferring payment' covertly.[†]

Mills, however, continued to provide the most important intelligence on German aerial rearmament. As a civilian pilot who ran Britain's best-known and most popular circus with strong links to those in Nazi Germany, he had the perfect cover story for intelligence operations. Among the new acts Mills introduced at Olympia in December 1936 were six baby elephants purchased from the Hagenbeck circus and zoo in a suburb of Hamburg. The owners, Lorenz and Heinrich Hagenbeck, according to Mills the biggest wild animal dealers and trainers in the world, became firm friends.[‡] The German ambassador in London, Joachim von Ribbentrop, soon to become Hitler's foreign minister, signalled his approval of

---

[*]   Mills, untitled confidential memoir on his intelligence career (undated), p.2, CBM papers.
[†]   Winterbotham, *Nazi Connection*.
[‡]   They were also the first Germans with whom Mills renewed contact after the war; Mills, *Bertram Mills Circus*, p.158.

Mills's close links to the circuses of Nazi Germany by accepting an invitation to the grand pre-Christmas circus lunch at Olympia in December 1937.[*]

Like Ribbentrop, Hermann Göring probably also welcomed the links between Bertram Mills and German circuses. He was the only major politician anywhere in Europe with a well-publicised interest in lion taming and enjoyed showing off a succession of young lions which he had trained as pets to foreign guests at his large estate. There were occasional mishaps – such as when the world-famous American aviator, Charles Lindbergh, and other lunch guests were introduced to 'Augie':

> Göring placed himself in a large armchair: 'I want you to see how nice my Augie is. Come here, Augie.' The lion bounded across the room and sprang into his lap. He put his paws on Göring's shoulders and began licking his face … Suddenly an aide laughed. The startled lion let loose a flood of yellow urine over Göring's snow white uniform![†]

Unsurprisingly, all permitted photos of Göring showed him in full control of well-behaved lions.

Mills regarded Göring's exhibitionist lion taming[‡] as further, absurd evidence of his personal vanity. The two leading European circuses outside Germany, Bertram Mills and the Moscow State Circus, both employed popular female, as well as male, professional lion tamers who must also have found Göring's antics absurd.[§]

---

[*] Ibid., pp.63, 94.
[†] Boyd, *Travellers in the Third Reich*, p.242.
[‡] As he later recalled to his stepson Frederick, CBM.
[§] In 2010, Russia issued a commemorative postage stamp to mark the centenary of the birth of Moscow State Circus's most famous female lion tamer, the Ukrainian Irina Bugrimova.

For all his pretentiousness, however, Göring remained the chief architect of the rapid growth of the Luftwaffe, the main target of Mills's espionage for MI6. Every time Mills went to Berlin to visit circuses at the Scala and Wintergarten theatres, he was reminded of the scale of Göring's ambitions by the new headquarters of the Air Ministry – the largest office buildings anywhere in Europe.

* * *

As well as having better operational cover than any other MI6 officer or agent in Germany, Mills also had a better reconnaissance aircraft than any available to the RAF. The Hornet Moth had originally been developed by de Havilland as a training aircraft for the armed services but, when the RAF showed no interest in placing an order, the biplane was put into production for the private civilian market. Production was limited: only 164 Hornet Moth aircraft came out of the factory. With an average cruising speed of 105 miles per hour and a top speed of 124 miles per hour, a ceiling of just under 15,000 feet and a range of little more than 600 miles, Mills's plane was small, slow and, of course, defenceless. But its slow speed and low ceiling enabled it to fly closer to German sites of interest than was possible for the Royal Air Force,* which also had a base at Lympne airfield but relied on large, twin-engine aircraft and paid little attention to aerial reconnaissance.

Mills knew the enormous risks he was taking in spying on German airfields from his Hornet Moth. In 1936, the year his espionage began, Nazi courts sentenced six spies – four of them British – to death by decapitation. Gustav Hoffman, who was arrested in June 1936 for

---

* I am grateful to Dr Tim Schmalz for this comparative information.

photographing forbidden areas in Magdeburg, admitted during his trial that he had been recruited by MI6. Though occasionally using a guillotine, Carl Gröpler, the official executioner, usually beheaded his victims with an axe.* The former Director of Naval Intelligence, Admiral Sir Barry Domvile, was assured during a visit to Germany that the executioners were 'very skillful with the axe'.†

While ferocious in its response to foreign espionage, Nazi Germany celebrated the First World War German spy in Britain and Ireland, Carl Lody,‡ as a national hero. A battleship, as well as streets in Berlin and his native Lübeck, were named after him. A memorial in Lübeck showed him as a knight in shining armour and every year flags flew at half-mast on the anniversary of his execution by firing squad in the Tower of London in November 1914.§ No twentieth-century British spy ever received such posthumous honours. Mills was well aware that if he was caught, the British government would refuse to even admit the existence of MI6, let alone that he was working for it.

Mills's willingness to continue solo aerial reconnaissance in his Hornet Moth was evidence of both his extraordinary nerve and the strength of his awareness of the threat from Hitler's Germany. To try to reconnoitre on the ground the new airfields Mills had identified from the air, Winterbotham chose an RAF officer, identified in MI6 archives only by the codename '479', who posed as a tourist and drove across Germany in April 1938 with 'a suitable secretary' posing as his girlfriend. It proved a difficult mission. In some cases, their view of airfields from the road was obscured by vegetation up

---

* R. T. Howard, *Spying on the Reich: The Cold War against Hitler* (Oxford: Oxford University Press, 2023), p.189. Gröpler, the last official German executioner to use an axe, retired in 1937. Thereafter, the guillotine was usually used instead.
† Boyd, *Travellers in the Third Reich*, p.198. During the Second World War, Domvile was interned as a Nazi sympathiser.
‡ See above, p.10.
§ Hans Fuchs, *Lody. Ein Weg um Ehre*, 2 vols (Hamburg: Hanseatische Verlagsanstalt, 1940).

to two hundred yards deep, 'quite unlike anything in this country' and 479 and his 'girlfriend' also made the mistake of driving a distinctive Wolseley car: 'Every time we stopped we were surrounded by small boys all anxious to know the power, speed, make and price of our Wolseley. There can be few small boys in N.W. Germany who do not remember the strange English couple and their car.'

Agent 479 reported that suspicious Nazi Brown Shirts also 'turned the car inside out' and followed the couple 'for several days', forcing them to make 'wild dashes all over the country' which either 'shook them off' or led them to lose interest.*

MI6 asked its longest-serving German agent, Otto Krüger, a naval engineer codenamed TR/16, to follow up some of Mills's intelligence leads. Like 479, he quickly aroused suspicion. In April 1938, while attempting to reconnoitre a secret airfield with underground accommodation (probably one of those identified by Mills), he was stopped and questioned by a suspicious foreman who reported his visit to the Gestapo. Krüger claimed to be an innocent naturalist who had no idea he was looking at an aerodrome and was allowed to return home. By the time the police arrived to question him at 8.15 the following morning, he had destroyed all incriminating documents.[†]

* * *

In 1937, General Stewart Menzies, deputy head of MI6 (later its wartime chief), correctly forecast to a senior French intelligence officer that Hitler would probably annex Austria and then turn on Czechoslovakia, but that neither British nor French public opinion

---

*   Jeffery, MI6, pp.298–9.
†   Judd, The Quest for C, pp.338–9.

would support military action to stop him doing so.* On 12 and 13 March 1938, as Cyril Mills put it, 'Hitler helped himself to Austria.'† All along their invasion route, German forces were welcomed by cheering crowds. On 14 March, Hitler delivered from the balcony of the Hofburg Palace in Vienna 'the greatest announcement of triumph' in his life: 'As the Führer and Chancellor of the German nation and empire, I announce ... now the entry of my homeland into the German Reich.'

Bertram Mills, meanwhile, was enjoying a much more modest triumph of his own in London. On 24 March 1938, the BBC made him the subject of the first in a new series of one-hour radio documentaries entitled *Showmen of England*. Cyril Mills remembered it as 'a magnificent programme which, using a coach horn blower and the circus band, covered the whole of my father's activities from hunting and coaching to circuses and politics'. Bertram's main ambitions were now political. After a decade as a councillor on the LCC, Cyril later recalled, Bertram was busy 'nursing a constituency as a prospective parliamentary candidate' and let it be known that, if elected, he would put on a free circus performance for his constituents.‡ By 1938 the Conservative Party Association in the now defunct Isle of Ely constituency (well known to Cyril from motorcycling at speed around the fens while at Cambridge) had officially chosen him as its candidate for the next election. Bertram Mills was clearly the favourite to defeat the Liberal incumbent in the Isle of Ely at the next election (then expected to take place in 1939 but delayed by war). Mills, however, died suddenly on 16 April 1938,

---

* Howard, *Spying on the Reich*, p.209. Mr Howard has found material on MI6 in French files that does not survive in British archives.
† Mills, *Bertram Mills Circus*, p.120.
‡ Had he done so, there would doubtless have been complaints that the free circus amounted to election bribery.

only ten days after he had ridden to hounds, one of his favourite recreations.

The most dangerous aerial reconnaissance mission entrusted by Winterbotham to Mills, a few months after his father's funeral, was to overfly for the first time the Messerschmitt factory near Regensburg in eastern Bavaria, which had officially been declared a prohibited area. The conditions at Munich Airport when he took off on 6 September 1938 would have deterred many pilots. Strong winds and driving rain descended upon the airfield as Cyril checked the gauges of his Hornet Moth biplane. At 3.55 p.m., having completed his pre-flight inspection, he received permission to attempt take off. He pulled his ignitor several times and on the third go, the roar of his four-cylinder air-cooled engine deafened the cockpit. With rain slamming into his windscreen, it was hard to even see the runway ahead. Cyril grabbed hold of the joystick tightly with both hands as he switched to maximum power. As soon as he was airborne and the rooftops of Munich grew smaller, Cyril turned southwest, heading towards the Swiss border. While his stated destination was Zürich, his target was Regensburg, where MI6 had discovered the existence of a Messerschmitt factory producing essential parts and research for Hitler's Luftwaffe.[*]

The German High Command had declared the territory around, and airspace over, Regensburg a prohibited zone. Mills's mission was to defy these restrictions and fly over at low altitude in order to obtain first-hand visual intelligence of the exact location and scope of the Messerschmitt operation:

---

[*] Mills, untitled confidential memoir on his intelligence career (undated), pp.2–3, CBM papers. See illustration no.8: Pilot flight log of Mills's mission over the Messerschmitt factory, which mistakenly refers to Regensburg as Ravensberg. I'm grateful to Dr Tim Schmalz for sharing his insights into Mills's mission.

...the weather was dreadful and cloud was down to about 500 feet ... It meant hedge-hopping or quitting so I took a chance on the former ... Fortunately, and I had taken this into consideration when deciding to have a go, the target was only about 8 minutes flying time from the Swiss border and having first started out on a course which would not take me near the area I felt I had a good chance of crossing the frontier before interception was possible.[*]

A month later, guided by what Mills had discovered during his risky aerial reconnaissance, Winterbotham sent 479 on a second mission to the Regensburg area by car. He returned with what Winterbotham considered 'very valuable' intelligence on the Messerschmitt factory,[†] which does not, however, survive in MI6 archives.

Mills's and 479's intelligence reports must have made depressing reading. In the summer of 1938, the French air force chief, General Joseph Vuillemin, was given a guided tour of a number of Luftwaffe bases by none other than Hermann Göring, who was in a genial and confident mood as he ordered the latest Messerschmitt Bf 110 fighters and Junkers Stuka dive bombers to be put through their paces. On Vuillemin's return to Paris, he and the Air Minister, Guy La Chambre, 'told anyone who would listen that, should war erupt, the French air force would be annihilated in fifteen days'.[‡]

The secret of Mills's aerial espionage over Nazi Germany has been remarkably well kept. There is no mention of it either in the still-closed archives of MI6 or in the published official history of

---

[*]   Ibid.
[†]   Jeffery, *MI6*, p.299.
[‡]   Douglas Porch, *Defeat and Division: France at War, 1939–1942* (Cambridge: Cambridge University Press, 2022), p.64; Robert J. Young, *In Command of France: French Foreign Policy and Military Planning, 1933–1940* (Cambridge, MA: Harvard University Press, 1978), p.211.

73

MI6 based on them. Winterbotham made no reference to Mills in his bestselling intelligence memoirs over thirty years later.

Mills, however, kept flight maps of his aerial espionage missions, whose existence has hitherto remained a family secret. Between the summer of 1936 and September 1938, he flew twenty-three trips across Germany and produced around thirty such maps. As always, Cyril's circus contacts provided the perfect cover story for his espionage operations. Making a record of the intelligence he collected, however, became increasingly difficult as MI6 grew and asked for drawings of the layouts of German aerodromes he saw, sometimes as many as four or five on one trip: 'Committing the details to memory was impossible and I therefore had to think of some way in which they could be put on paper without incriminating me.'

Mills disguised his plans of German aerodromes and manufacturing facilities as diagrams of his circus layouts in various German cities along the touring route, showing 'where everything was to be placed':

> ...On these drawings each unit of the circus represented something seen on an aerodrome. Thus our diesel oil or petrol store wagons represented the aircraft fuel supply source and our general office could mean the administration block and the living quarters of the staff represented barracks and the management caravans the Officers' quarters ... All this may sound easy but it was by no means so as the result still had to look like the layout of a genuine circus if examined carefully.*

A senior RAF officer who trained pilots (including Red Arrows) during the Cold War later commented:

---

* CBM papers.

What a man Cyril Mills was! ... Navigation around Europe in northern hemisphere weather is always a challenge, especially in the cooler seasons, but for a low hours pilot like Mills to be able also to mentally record his observations as well as safely map-reading to his destinations marks him out as very special.[*]

Fear of his aerial espionage being discovered by the Germans constantly worried Mills. If cornered by the German authorities and questioned about his low-level flights, his plan was to plead ignorance: '...my story would be that I just did not know what they were talking about. I had flown a great many hours over Germany and my job was to find good German acts for our circus.'[†]

* * *

In September 1938, Neville Chamberlain became the first British Prime Minister to fly (repeatedly) to Germany for negotiations designed to appease Hitler and prevent war. One anti-appeaser summed up the purpose of the Prime Minister's pioneering aerial shuttle diplomacy thus:

If at first you can't concede,
Fly, fly, fly again.

At the end of September, after the Czechs had been pressured into surrendering the German-speaking Sudetenland to Germany, Chamberlain returned from the Munich Conference to a hero's welcome

---

[*] Email to author from Squadron Leader Dennis Barber, 11 April 2023. During his long RAF career he had brief experience of flying 'a Tiger Moth which had a similar engine to the Moths of Cyril Mills'.
[†] CBM papers.

in London, brandishing a now infamous piece of paper, signed by Hitler, which he mistakenly claimed meant 'peace for our time'.

MI5 knew better. The constant refrain of its well-informed agent in the German embassy in London, the anti-Nazi diplomat, Wolfgang zu Putlitz, was that trying to 'appease' Hitler by making concessions to him made war more, not less, likely. MI5's leadership agreed. 'When Chamberlain returned from Munich waving his piece of paper', recalled the in-house MI5 historian and German expert, John 'Jack' Curry, 'we all had an acute sense of shame.'*

Like his new friend Dick White, Mills was an anti-appeaser: 'Having travelled so much in Germany I should have been blind if I had failed to notice the rate at which preparations for war were progressing, but I saw no such signs in this country.' At the time of the Munich crisis, Mills was with the circus in Glasgow. The Labour politician, Patrick Dollan (later knighted), who had just been appointed Lord Provost of Glasgow, told Mills he was unable to accept a lunch invitation before the circus opened because he was 'busy supervising the filling of sand-bags' in case of German air raids. Mills was privately scornful: 'What a way to prepare for a war that could have started next day!'†

MI6's views were in sharp contrast to those of MI5. Before and during the Munich crisis, the Chief of MI6, Admiral Sir Hugh 'Quex' Sinclair, set out to influence government policy in favour of appeasement. MI6's own policy was set out in a memorandum of 18 September entitled 'What Should We Do?', drafted by the MI6 head of political intelligence, Malcolm Woollcombe, and personally approved by Sinclair. MI6 argued strongly that the Czechs should be pressed to accept 'the inevitable' and surrender the Sudetenland.

---

* Andrew, *Defence of the Realm*, p.202.
† Mills, *Bertram Mills Circus*, p.121.

They should 'realise unequivocally that they stand alone if they refuse such a solution'. Britain, for her part, should continue with a policy of calculated appeasement. She should not wait until German grievances boil over and threaten the peace of Europe. Instead, the international community should take the initiative and decide 'what really legitimate grievances Germany has and what surgical operations are necessary to rectify them'. Some of Germany's colonies, confiscated after the last war, should be restored. If genuine cases for self-determination by German minorities remained in Europe they should be remedied:

> It may be argued that this would be giving in to Germany, strengthening Hitler's position and encouraging him to go to extremes. Better, however, that realities be faced and that wrongs, if they do exist, be righted, than leave it to Hitler to do the righting in his own way and time – particularly if, concurrently, we and the French unremittingly build up our strength and lessen Germany's potentialities for making trouble.

Britain should try to ensure 'that Germany's "style is cramped", but with the minimum of provocation'. Sir Warren Fisher, head of the civil service and Chairman of the Secret Service Committee, told Sinclair that 'What Should We Do?' was 'a most excellent document'.*

MI5 was appalled. On 7 November, Sir Vernon Kell personally delivered to the Foreign Office the first (albeit implicit) indictment

---

* Malcolm Woollcombe, 'What Should We Do?', 18 September 1938; Fisher to Sinclair (copy), 20 September, 1939, Malcolm Woollcombe MSS. A copy of 'What Should We Do?', marked 'Views of SIS [MI6]', is to be found in TNA FO 371/21659. A previous memorandum by Woollcombe, 'Germany and Colonies', 3 February 1938, had been well received by Neville Chamberlain, who added the marginal note: 'What did I say [?]' Andrew, 'Secret Intelligence and British Foreign Policy' in Christopher Andrew and Jeremy Noakes (eds), *Intelligence and International Relations, 1900–1945* (Liverpool: Liverpool University Press, 1987), p.24.

of government foreign policy ever drafted by a British intelligence agency. Kell insisted that, in view of the intelligence it had provided from 'reliable sources' (notably Putlitz) over the past few years:

> ... There is nothing surprising and nothing which could not have been foreseen in the events of this summer in connection with Czechoslovakia. These events are a logical consequence of Hitler's Nazi Weltanschauung and of his foreign policy and his views in regard to racial questions and the position of Germany in Europe.[*]

At Kell's personal insistence, Chamberlain was also privately informed that Hitler referred to him as an arsehole (*arschloch*). On this point, though Mills never used such expressions in public, it is quite possible that he agreed with Hitler.[†]

Mills did not discover Kell's extraordinary secret denunciation of government policy until he joined MI5 almost two years later. In contrast to the clubbable 'Quex' Sinclair, Kell kept the lowest of public profiles. Sinclair's surviving papers from the 1930s consist largely of elaborate menu cards from private dinners, hosted by himself and others at the Savoy and other exclusive locations. He treasured the letters of thanks he received from appreciative mandarins and service chiefs. Admiral Sir Percy Noble thanked him for 'the best dinner I have eaten in years'; Admiral Sir Arthur Bromley complimented Quex on the 'excellent' wines from his personal cellar.[‡] Kell was not invited.

---

[*] J. C. Curry, 'Note on the Aggressive Policy of Hitler and Ribbentrop: And Consequent Instructions to the Abwehr', cited by Andrew, *Defence of the Realm*, p.204. https://winstonchurchill.org/resources/speeches/1930-1938-the-wilderness/the-munich-agreement; J. C. Curry, 'Information on Hitler's Germany's Intentions in 1938 Obtained from M.I.5 sources', 5 September 1941, TNA KV4/16.

[†] Andrew, *Defence of the Realm*, p.205.

[‡] Admiral Sir Hugh Sinclair MSS, National Maritime Museum, cited by Andrew, 'Secret Intelligence and British Foreign Policy'.

Mills's views on Munich were those of his great political hero, Winston Churchill. During a Commons debate on 4 October, Churchill made his most famously prophetic peacetime speech, denouncing the Munich Agreement and the policy of appeasement to a largely unsympathetic House: 'Who pretends now that there is air parity with Germany? Who pretends now that our anti-aircraft defences were adequately manned or armed?'[*] As a committed opponent of appeasement and long-standing admirer of Churchill, Mills could not fail to have been moved by this speech – all the more so since he had recently obtained intelligence which directly supported Churchill's claims. While on the back benches during his 'wilderness years', Churchill was unofficially shown intelligence about Nazi Germany's rearmament that he was not supposed to see. It is highly likely that the intelligence included reports from Mills.[†]

Mills's last pre-war intelligence mission was probably to Prague in March 1939, prompted by reports of impending German invasion. On this occasion there is no flight record of his mission because he travelled by train rather than, as during a previous visit in August 1938, in his Hornet Moth.[‡] As during Mills's travels in Germany, he used his circus contacts as cover – among them his friend Vojtech Trubka, Europe's most famous tiger trainer, with whom he was to renew close contact after the Second World War.[§] Mills strength-

---

[*] https://winstonchurchill.org/resources/speeches/1930-1938-the-wilderness/the-munich-agreement

[†] Mills and Churchill met at the pre-Christmas circus lunch at Olympia on 22 December 1938, when Churchill was the principal guest, and perhaps on other occasions after Munich. Intelligence based on Mills's reports may also have reached Churchill via his intelligence adviser, Desmond Morton. In April 1939, Churchill accused Chamberlain in the Commons of having been blinded to good intelligence on Nazi Germany by his desire for peace. The 'good intelligence' probably included reports from Mills.

[‡] Mills's pilot's flight log records that he landed at Praha (Prague) airport on 30 August 1938 and departed on 1 September; C.10.2, CBM papers.

[§] Mills probably owed a number of his circus contacts in Prague to his long association with the Krone Circus in Munich, a third of whose artistes were Czech by 1940. See Hanuš Jordan and Veronika Štefanová, 'The Past and Present of Czech Circus' in Gillian Arrighi and Jim Davis (eds), *The Cambridge Companion to the Circus* (Cambridge: Cambridge University Press, 2021), p.81. On Trubka, see below, pp.214–15.

ened his cover while in Prague by booking 'a very good comedy act' for the next winter season at Olympia.*

By early March, intelligence from Putlitz and others led the government's Chief Diplomatic Adviser, Lord Vansittart, previously Permanent Under-Secretary (PUS) at the Foreign Office, to fear a German coup in Prague during the week of the 12th to the 19th. The current PUS, Sir Alexander Cadogan, was not convinced. On 11 March, however, the Director of MI5, Sir Vernon Kell, called at the Foreign Office 'to raise [Cadogan's] hair with tales of Germany going into Czechoslovakia in [the] next 48 hours'.†

Some of these hair-raising reports probably prompted Mills's last-minute mission to Prague. Many years later, he revealed that, probably thanks to Dick White, he had got to know Kell well before the war,‡ but kept no record of their meetings. White himself went on a dangerous mission to Munich, posing as an English teacher. He later told Mills of a rendezvous he had arranged with an informant in the innocuous surroundings of a dental surgery:

> The receptionist was polite enough to me but showed her true Nazi sympathies when a number of Jews arrived. The woman's attitude appalled me so much that I was almost tempted to say exactly what I thought. For obvious reasons I couldn't and didn't. The wretched Jews were simply put at the end of the queue.§

After dinner on 11 March 1939, Cadogan received further 'hair-raising' reports from MI6 of German plans for an invasion of Prague

---

* Mills, *Bertram Mills Circus*, p.160.
† Andrew, *Secret Service*, pp.416–17; Andrew, *Defence of the Realm*, pp.206–7.
‡ Mills to Nigel West, 19 November 1984, CBM papers.
§ Tom Bower, *The Perfect English Spy: Sir Dick White and the Secret War 1935–90* (London: Heinemann, 1995), p.32.

on the 14th.* Some of the reports came from František Moravec, who ran Czechoslovakian intelligence operations against Nazi Germany and had established a close relationship with MI6. On 14 March 1939, after being warned by his leading German agent of an impending invasion, Moravec, together with ten of his senior staff and their most important intelligence files, was secretly flown to safety in London on a plane chartered by MI6.† During his exile in Britain, Moravec became the first foreign intelligence chief to be awarded a CBE.

Mills was sent on his mission to Prague too late to make a significant contribution to British intelligence operations. From his hotel he had:

> a splendid view of the beautiful cathedral founded by the man known in our carol as 'Good King Wenceslas', but it looked as if something was wrong. People on the Platz were having urgent discussions and every newspaper was being read by five or six people at a time. It was March 13th and the Nazis were on their way in.

To try and escape from Prague before the invasion without attracting German suspicion, Mills devised a plan which he thought 'might work because it was the sort of thing which appeals to the over-methodical German mind'. Rather than attempting to avoid travelling through Germany on his return home, he took a northbound train to Dresden, the capital of Nazi Bavaria. En route to Dresden, 'the track running south was one long convoy of trains packed with troops and all the paraphernalia of war'. In Mills's

---

* Andrew, *Secret Service*, pp.416–17; Andrew, *Defence of the Realm*, pp.206–7.
† As MI6's *Official History* acknowledges, even its classified archives contain no record of this major operation. Moravec's account, however, survives, František Moravec, *Master of Spies: The Memoirs of General František Moravec* (London: Sphere Books, 1981), chs.12, 13.

first-class compartment was a Norwegian businessman who had been forced to cut short a trip to Prague to purchase expensive Czech crystal and glassware and was returning home 'loaded with Czech money which would be worthless in a few hours'. Mills told the Norwegian he would try to change the money for him at the frontier if he would carry Mills's suitcase, some of whose contents might arouse suspicion:

Luck was with us; the [Czech] bureau de change was still open and the clerk was sitting waiting for somebody to come and tell him what to do. The Nazis had been too busy doing other things to put a guard on the place, so the clerk and I were alone. The till contained dollars, pounds, francs, marks and an assortment of other currencies and rather than give anything to the invaders he gave me the lot in exchange for a handful of [now] worthless Czech notes.

As I had hoped, we were allowed to cross into Germany without any difficulty.

Before Mills continued his journey back to London, the Norwegian businessman invited him to 'the best dinner he could buy me in Dresden'.*

The first German troops entered Prague at dawn on 15 March. Hitler followed by car and, to the horror of most Czechs, spent the night in Hradčany Castle, the former residence of the kings of Bohemia, with the swastika flying from its flagpole.

It had never occurred to Mills that he might have to make such

---

* Mills, *Bertram Mills Circus*, pp.161–2. Though Mills published an account of his March 1939 journey to Prague in 1967, it was not until some years later that he revealed to his family that he had been on an intelligence mission.

a hasty exit from Prague. Even Churchill was taken aback by the speed of Hitler's takeover. He later recalled sitting with Anthony Eden in the House of Commons smoking room reading the news from Prague in the evening papers on 15 March: 'Even those like us who had no illusions and had testified earnestly were surprised at the sudden violence of this outrage. One could hardly believe that with all their secret information His Majesty's Government could be so far adrift." The problem was, however, that, unknown to Churchill, some of the secret information was badly wrong. Along with accurate reports of German designs on Prague came false alarms about a German threat to the Royal Navy. On 3 April, the Foreign Office circulated warnings from the Berlin embassy of a possible Luftwaffe attack on the Navy during the following Easter weekend when most seamen were on leave. Simultaneously, one of Vansittart's informants reported – also incorrectly – that U-boats were on patrol in the Channel and the Thames Estuary. On 4 February, the First Lord of the Admiralty, Earl Stanhope, recorded a warning to be broadcast on the BBC that he had given 'orders to man the anti-aircraft guns of the Fleet so as to be ready for anything that might happen'. Though Chamberlain stopped the broadcast, the story reached the papers and 'a fine row' followed in the Commons. 'Why do we keep exhibits like [Stanhope] in the Cabinet!' Cadogan plaintively asked his diary.

The confusion of Easter 1939 probably marked the nadir of prewar British foreign intelligence. At a Cabinet meeting on 5 April, the Foreign Secretary, Lord Halifax, discounted reports that Mussolini was about to invade Albania. Two days later, on Good Friday, while the Royal Navy was on alert against an imaginary threat from the

---

*   W. S. Churchill, *The Gathering Storm*, (New York: RosettaBooks, 2002 [1948]), p.307.

Luftwaffe, Italy occupied Albania. 'It cannot be denied', Chamberlain told his sister, 'that Mussolini has behaved to me like a sneak and a cad.'* So had Hitler.

Meanwhile, Bertram Mills Circus was at the peak of its popularity. The *Kent & Sussex Courier* enthused, shortly after Mills's unannounced hasty return from Prague:

After its triumphal [winter] season at Olympia the mammoth Bertram Mills Touring Circus is again on the road. Never in its history has such a wonderful programme been prepared and presented for the entertainment of provincial audiences.

> Sensation number one is Koringa, the only female fakir in the world. Mesmerising crocodiles and pythons appears child's play to this wonder girl of the East. Not satisfied with this, she allows herself to be buried alive for five minutes! Lady artistes are well to the fore in this assembly of internationally famous talent.[†]

After 1938, Winterbotham made no further use of Mills for aerial reconnaissance over Germany in his Hornet Moth. Mills's earlier success, however, inspired him to try and devise a secret method of high-level photo reconnaissance, which was impossible from a single-seater Hornet Moth. The French Deuxième Bureau introduced Winterbotham to F. Sidney Cotton, an Australian pilot and adventurer with business interests which gave him plausible pretexts for flying to Germany. The plane chosen for the photo reconnaissance was a two-seater American Lockheed 12A fitted with three cameras concealed behind sliding panels in the fuselage which Cotton's assistant was able to operate by pressing a button under the pilot's

---

* Andrew, *Secret Service*, p.420.
† 'Bertram Mills' Circus', *Kent & Sussex Courier*, 31 March 1939. On Koringa, see below, pp.99–100.

seat. There remained the hitherto insoluble problem of condensation and frost on the camera lens which made high-altitude photography impossible. Cotton and Winterbotham, however, discovered that the Lockheed cabin heating system could be used to keep both the windscreen and camera lens clear. 'It was as simple as that,' Winterbotham later recalled. 'I find it almost impossible to describe my elation at this chance discovery.' Cotton began photo reconnaissance in the spring of 1939. He later claimed that his greatest coup, at a German international airshow just over a month before the outbreak of war, was to persuade the Chief of the Luftwaffe General Staff, Albert Kesselring, to take the controls of his Lockheed. Cotton sat beside him as co-pilot, pressing the concealed camera button to photograph sensitive sites as they flew over them.*

After war broke out, Cotton was made Honorary Wing Commander in the RAF and head of its new Photographic Development Unit. Following a series of conflicts with senior officers, he was removed from his post in June 1940 but was later awarded an OBE. Though he was as brave and resourceful as Mills, Cotton was much more inclined to break regulations. After the post-war partition of newly independent India, he was fined £200 for gunrunning in Hyderabad.† Winterbotham later had no inhibitions in revealing Cotton's 1939 Lockheed missions for MI6 but, because Mills continued working for British intelligence, he never mentioned his espionage by biplane which helped to inspire Cotton's photographic reconnaissance on the eve of war.

* Andrew, *Secret Service*, pp.468–9; Winterbotham, *Nazi Connection*, ch.19. Interview with Winterbotham by Christopher Andrew in *The Profession of Intelligence*, Part 2, BBC Radio 4, 9 August 1981; 'Frederick Sidney Cotton', *Australian Dictionary of Biography*.

† 'Frederick Sidney Cotton', *Australian Dictionary of Biography*; 'Cotton, the Silver-Haired Man Who Struck Gold', *Times of India*, 16 September 2021.

CHAPTER 4

MI5 IN WARTIME: FROM
PRISON TO PALACE

By the time Britain declared war on Germany on Sunday 3 September 1939, Cyril Mills believed his intelligence career was over. All civilian flying in wartime was banned. Some private planes, Mills's among them, were requisitioned by the armed forces as communications and training aircraft. An inexperienced RAF pilot quickly wrote off his Hornet Moth. Mills's papers contain the brass registration plate from the aircraft marked 'Cyril Bertram Mills, Denham Aerodrome, Bucks', together with a melancholy note by Mills on the dismal fate of the biplane in which he had so successfully spied on pre-war Nazi Germany: 'This is all that was capable of salvage – given to me after the war by the man who dealt with the wreckage'.*

Despite the loss of his biplane, Mills hoped for a wartime career in the Royal Air Force. His experience of identifying secret aerodromes and reconnoitring the Messerschmitt aircraft factory, while flying solo over Germany, inspired him to try and take part in the air

---

* CBM papers.

87

war which he foresaw would be key to Hitler's plans to invade Britain. His ambition was to become a bomber pilot. Five weeks after the outbreak of war came a brutal reminder of the great risks Mills ran during his pre-war aerial espionage. On 10 October, *The Times* carried a Reuters report that MI6's longest-serving German agent, Otto Krüger, had been decapitated by axe after being 'found guilty of working against Germany in favour of foreign Powers.'[*] Among the episodes which had led to Gestapo suspicions about Krüger in 1938 was his attempt to follow up one of Mills's intelligence leads on secret Luftwaffe aerodromes for MI6.[†]

Had Mills succeeded in joining RAF Bomber Command early in the war, he would have found it deeply dispiriting. During the 'Phoney War' with Germany, which lasted until Hitler's sudden invasion of France and the Low Countries in May 1940, British bombing was strictly limited to military targets. In daylight attacks on German warships and airfields, British bombers proved easy targets for Luftwaffe fighters. During night-time raids over Germany, the RAF was permitted to drop only propaganda leaflets in a farcical attempt to undermine Hitler's position as – at the time – the most popular political leader anywhere in Europe.[‡]

* * *

Mills's priority during the Phoney War was to save the family business. For the first time, the circus winter season at Olympia had to be cancelled. Because of the wartime blackout and the threat of German

---

[*] In view of previous German decapitations of British spies (see above, pp.68–9), Mills had no reason to doubt the report. MI5 later concluded, however, that Krüger had avoided execution by committing suicide in his prison cell. Andrew, *Defence of the Realm*, pp.244–5.

[†] See above, p.70.

[‡] 'RAF Bomber Command During the Second World War'; www.iwm.org.uk

bombing raids, even though they did not materialise for another year, 'it would have been madness to have anything up to fifteen thousand people in the building at the same time, especially as it had a glass roof'. Instead, the circus moved to the stage. Mills later recalled:

Starting at New Cross we played nearly every big variety theatre from Portsmouth to Glasgow but I never want to have anything to do with a stage circus again. Running a [pre-war] tenting show and battling with mud and gales was bad, but this was infinitely worse. Horses often had to be stabled two or three miles away and walked to the theatre in the dark through traffic, rain, fog and even snow.

Some theatre stages had to be shored up to bear the weight of the circus's six elephants; 'the horses slithered about as if they were on skates until rubber pads were fitted' to their hooves.[*]

The most distressing problem faced by Cyril was the circus's 'enemy aliens'. The German and other Continental connections of some of the Bertram Mills staff and performers aroused the suspicions of the often ill-informed wartime tribunals who decided which aliens to intern. Guy Liddell, head of MI5's B Branch (counter-espionage), wrote scornfully of the tribunals: 'The proceedings were laughable ... Our records were not consulted, except to a small extent in the metropolitan area; the Chairmen had no standards and no knowledge of the political background of those who came before them; no record[s] of the proceedings were kept.'[†]

Among the tribunals' victims was the circus's Austrian elephant trainer, John Gindl, who was interned despite being, as Mills

---

[*]   Mills, *Bertram Mills Circus*, p.126.
[†]   Andrew, *Defence of the Realm*, p.222.

certified, 'as anti-Nazi as we were'. By the time a tribunal was per-suaded to release him from detention:

> Gindl could not be found. He had been put in a bus and sent
> to a camp which was full, so he was sent to another and then
> another and it was five days before he was released. In the mean-
> time his wife, Gertie, never left the elephants for more than a few
> moments, for she was the one other person they knew really well.[*]

In June 1940, after Germany had conquered France and the Low Countries in only six weeks, Cyril and his brother Bernard 'decided this really was the end' for the wartime circus: 'What had begun almost as a bet and in twenty years had been built up to Britain's biggest ever circus had been destroyed overnight.'[†]

After the circus closed, Cyril Mills mostly disappeared from public view. It was widely believed by his Continental circus con-tacts, who were impressed by his skill as a pre-war pilot, that he was now in the RAF. Mills, however, was prevented from joining Bomber Command by his age. At thirty-eight, he knew that he was officially too old to become an RAF pilot but hoped to bypass reg-ulations. Though he passed the air force medical examination, he failed to put his age on a form he was asked to sign and 'made a false declaration' during an interview:

> ...I lasted until some chair-borne officer insisted on seeing my
> birth certificate and said that I was grounded until I produced it.
> ... After an argument in which I was anything but polite to a very

---

*   Mills, *Bertram Mills Circus*, p.129.
†   Ibid., p.128.

superior officer it was agreed that as I had not signed the form I was not in the RAF and never had been.

Mills then decided to use his pre-war contacts to find a job in intelligence instead: 'My first thought was of [Dick] White.'

Though four years younger than Mills, White was now a senior MI5 counter-espionage (B Branch) officer. He had been deeply impressed by Mills during their pre-war intelligence discussions at the RAF Club, invited him to a meeting and immediately offered him a wartime job. 'You are in!', White told him. 'It is Friday [19 July]; can you start here on Monday?'[*]

* * *

Mills began work in B Branch on 22 July,[†] twelve days after the beginning of the Battle of Britain against the Luftwaffe, the first major military campaign ever fought between air forces. Intelligence on the Luftwaffe from agents and aerial reconnaissance had dramatically declined since Mills's pre-war flights over German airfields and the Messerschmitt factory at Regensburg. From June to September 1940, the Germans rapidly constructed or took over a large number of airfields along the Channel coast in France and Belgium for use during and after the Battle of Britain. Winterbotham complained in November 1940 that 'with the exception of some reports from deserters and Free Frenchmen who have managed to get across to England, reports from agents on the German Air Force in France and Belgium have been practically nil.'[‡]

---

[*] Mills, untitled confidential memoir on his intelligence career (undated), p.3; CBM papers.
[†] Ibid.
[‡] Jeffery, *MI6*, p.392.

As Mills discovered in B Branch, however, despite the shortage of information on the Luftwaffe's current airfields, wartime intelligence was being transformed by the successes of the GC&CS codebreakers at Bletchley Park in breaking the supposedly unbreakable highest-grade ciphers of the German armed forces. By an extraordinary co-incidence, what proved to be the most valuable intelligence source in British history began to operate fully less than a fortnight after Churchill became Prime Minister. On 22 May, GC&CS succeeded in breaking the Luftwaffe version of the Enigma machine cipher. From this date onwards it was able to read current German signals traffic using the air-force Enigma without a break for the remainder of the war. In the spring of 1941, Bletchley mastered the naval Enigma and, in the spring of 1942, the army Enigma. At first, the Enigma decrypts were referred to by the codeword 'Boniface' in order to suggest, if the enemy caught wind of them, that they derived from a secret agent rather than cryptanalysis. By 1941, they were known as ULTRA to the small circle of initiates, which included only six of Churchill's thirty-five ministers.* Within the Foreign Office, which was responsible for GC&CS, only Sir Alexander Cadogan, the Per-manent Under-Secretary, and Victor Cavendish-Bentinck, Chair-man of the Joint Intelligence Committee (JIC), were in the know.†

ULTRA was probably the best-kept secret in modern British histo-ry. Churchill had learned from his mistakes in the 1920s when he had repeatedly been willing to compromise GC&CS's ability to decrypt Soviet traffic by publicly revealing the contents of decrypts, culminat-ing in the cryptanalytic disaster of 1927 when Moscow adopted the

---

* ULTRA was an Allied rather than a purely British triumph, the culmination of a decade of intelligence work involving the Poles and the French, as well as GC&CS.

† Even Desmond Morton, formerly of MI6, who had advised Churchill on intelligence in the 1930s and continued to do so as his personal assistant at Number 10, almost certainly had no access to ULTRA. Bennett, *Churchill's Man of Mystery*, p.251.

almost invulnerable 'one-time-pad' cipher system.* As wartime Prime Minister, Churchill even kept his private secretaries in ignorance of the contents of the mysterious red boxes he received each day from Bletchley Park via the wartime Chief of MI6, Sir Stewart Menzies.

Cyril Mills's role as a key wartime intelligence officer thus gave him access to secrets that were even denied to most of the ministers and senior officials running the war effort and Britain's foreign relations. He and his colleagues in B Branch made extraordinary use of them. In August 1940, the 'Beavers' in B1b, who analysed decrypted Abwehr communications, gave advance warning of the imminent despatch of a new wave of German agents. Forewarned, MI5 found them 'an easy prey'.† On 8 December 1940, Guy Liddell wrote in his top-secret diary: 'Dick White has just produced another magnum opus based on the intercepted [German] messages and what we have learned from the captured agents. We are now beginning to get quite a good picture of the German espionage organisation'.‡

The lifelong friendships Mills made in MI5 were even closer than those in his long circus career. During his retirement almost forty years later, Mills privately recalled 'spending my war years among the nicest people and the best friends I have ever known'.§ Among his closest wartime friends in MI5 was the head of B Branch, Guy Liddell. In Liddell's diary, Cyril Mills was one of the few often referred to by first name rather than by surname. Even Kim Philby, during his undetected work as a Soviet spy in MI6, found it difficult to resist Liddell's mixture of intelligence, modesty and charm. Liddell, Philby later recalled, had a 'deceptively ruminative manner':

---

*   See above, p.42.
†   J. C. Masterman, *The Double-Cross System in the War of 1939 to 1945* (London: Sphere Books, 1973), p.49. Andrew, *Defence of the Realm*, p.250.
‡   Guy Liddell diary, 8 December 1940.
§   CBM papers.

He would murmur his thoughts aloud, as if groping his way towards the facts of a case, his face creased in a comfortable, innocent smile. But behind the façade of laziness, his subtle and reflective mind played over a storehouse of photographic memories. He was an ideal senior officer for a young man to learn from, always willing to put aside his work to listen and worry at a new problem.[*]

Mills agreed. As a newly recruited member of MI5, he too found Liddell 'an ideal senior officer to work with'. Liddell seems to have been equally impressed by Mills. His later decision to post Mills to Canada may well have prevented the Abwehr discovering the existence of the Double-Cross System – potentially the greatest British intelligence disaster of the war.[†]

* * *

When Mills joined MI5 in 1940, the organisation's improbable HQ was Wormwood Scrubs Prison, the only available London building large enough to house the Security Service's rapidly increasing wartime workforce.[‡] The mostly Victorian prison buildings, complained Milicent Bagot (later the model for John le Carré's fictional Connie), 'appeared never to have been ventilated since their erection and their smell was appalling.' Several cell blocks were still occupied by prisoners, whom Mills sometimes saw exercising in the yard. 'Don't go near them,' one of the warders warned Bagot and other female staff. 'Some of them ain't seen no women for years.'[§]

---

[*]   Kim Philby, *My Silent War* (London: Panther, 1969), p.74.
[†]   See below, ch.7.
[‡]   Mills, untitled confidential memoir on his intelligence career (undated), p.3; CBM papers.
[§]   Andrew, *Defence of the Realm*, p.217.

Like other MI5 officers, Mills's office was a prison cell; secretaries worked two to a cell. One of the secretaries Mills knew best, Peggy Phillips,* later recalled arriving at the Scrubs as a nineteen-year-old, fresh from secretarial college: 'I took the number 15 bus to the prison. I walked in and these great big iron gates clanged behind me. It was quite daunting. Then I was taken up an iron staircase to a cell. It was just like being in *Porridge*.'

Waiting in the cell was an MI5 officer who told her to sit down and begin taking dictation.†

The cell doors had no handles or locks on the inside. So, as one Wormwood Scrubs veteran later recalled, MI5 staff stood a good chance of being locked in by unwary visitors turning the outside door handle on leaving. 'At first there were no telephones in the cells, and with the rooms themselves soundproofed, it was possible for you to be shut in for hours before anyone noticed that you were not around.'

One wartime secretary also recalled being 'slightly taken aback by the loos which had the equivalent of steel doors with a space which revealed the legs up to the knee and from the shoulders upwards.' The working day at Wormwood Scrubs ended with the blowing of a bugle to remind staff to draw the curtains before the night-time blackout began.‡

One of Mills's first discoveries on beginning work at Wormwood Scrubs was that, six weeks earlier, Churchill had sacked General Sir Vernon Kell, Director of MI5 since its foundation in 1909 and the longest-serving head of any government department in modern British history. An in-house history of MI5 later acknowledged

---

* In 1943, Peggy Phillips married Christopher Harmer, one of Mills's MI5 colleagues and closest friends. See below, p.113.

† Peggy Harmer (née Phillips) obituary, *The Times*, 7 April 2011; Ben Macintyre, 'The Last Miss Moneypenny Recalls her War', *The Times*, 15 May 2007.

‡ Andrew, *Defence of the Realm*, pp.217–18; Helen Ouin, 'From a Prison to a Palace!', https://www.bbc.co.uk/history/ww2peopleswar/stories/84/a4427084.shtml

that, '…By the time of the fall of France [in June 1940] the organisation of the Security Service as a whole was in a state which can only be described as chaotic.'* The main blame fell on Kell. On 10 June, Sir Horace Wilson, head of the civil service, summoned Kell to his office in the Treasury and told him that 'it had been decided to make certain changes in the controlling staff of the Security Service'.† Kell wrote bitterly in his diary: 'I get the sack from Horace Wilson', added his dates of service '1909–1940' and drew a line beneath them. Then he vented his feelings on the Italians: 'Italy comes into the war against us. Dirty Dogs.'‡ Though Kell had been sacked by Wilson, Churchill had made the decision to do so. Lady Kell, then working as a wartime volunteer in the canteen, announced to staff: 'Your precious Winston has sacked the General.'§

After interim appointments, Kell was eventually succeeded as Director-General (DG) in 1941 by a sixty-year-old Scot, Sir David Petrie, former head of the Delhi Intelligence Bureau and Chairman of the Indian Public Service Commission. Mills, like most of his colleagues, found Petrie a very effective DG. His friend, Dick White, later described the new DG as 'one of the best man managers I ever met'.¶

As well as gaining access to ULTRA, Cyril Mills went on to take a leading role in running the other best-kept secret of the war: the Double-Cross System, the most successful strategic deception in the history of modern warfare. Double-Cross was made possible by the arrest, mostly unknown to the Abwehr, of all significant wartime German spies sent to Britain. Some of the ablest were turned into double agents who proved remarkably successful in feeding

---

*   *The Security Service*, p.163.
†   Sir Horace Wilson, 'Security Service', 11 June 1940, TNA Cabinet Office papers AO-2.
‡   Kell diary entry, 10 June 1940, IWM Kell papers.
§   Editorial note by Nigel West, *Guy Liddell Diaries*, vol.1, p.84.
¶   Interview with the late Sir Dick White by Christopher Andrew in 1984.

British disinformation to the Abwehr. Among the disinformation was bogus intelligence provided by fictitious sub-agents supposedly recruited by the turned Abwehr agents. Even Churchill was not told of the double agents until 1943. No postwar history of the Second World War was permitted to mention either Double-Cross or ULTRA until the 1970s.

Mills's circus career had given him greater peacetime experience of organising deception than any of his wartime colleagues in B1a, the double-agent section of MI5. More than any other part of the entertainment business, the circus in the pre-television age was based on illusions, many including wild animals. The leading theatrical weekly, *The Era*, had said of George Lockhart's elephants at the Canterbury Theatre of Varieties in 1892: 'His elephants not only polka but they waltz. They stand on their heads, too, and perform a variety of tricks with such alacrity and cheerfulness that the audience is mightily pleased. They are a happy trio of intelligent quadrupeds.'*

Half a century later, Bertram Mills audiences were equally enthralled by the circus elephants' 'tricks', now enhanced by glamorous 'elephant girl' riders. At various times, the Bertram Mills elephants were also trained to play football and cricket.†

The fantasies which were a traditional part of circus performances paved the way for more sophisticated illusions and hoaxes. The first major circus illusion devised by Cyril Mills was intended to publicise the arrival of a group of lions at the opening of the circus winter season at Olympia in December 1925. Though all the lions came from the Nouveau Cirque in Paris, Mills succeeded in persuading the press that the last to arrive had been flown directly

---

* *The Era*, 11 January 1890; David Wiles and Christine Dymkovski (eds), *Cambridge Companion to Theatre History* (Cambridge: Cambridge University Press, 2013), p.180. *The Era* was the longest running theatrical trade paper.
† Bertram Mills Circus programmes, CBM.

from Africa. Publicity organised by Mills included a photograph of a lion walking down the steps of an Imperial Airways passenger plane at Croydon Airport. As Mills later admitted, 'the temptation to wring the last drop of publicity out of the occasion had been too much' for him to resist. Though the Imperial Airways aircraft had circled the airport only once, it may well have been the first to have a lion on board. The media never discovered Mills's hoax.[*]

The illusion that wild animals had mysteriously become tame was sometimes made more exotic by using attractive female trainers who claimed to have the power to bend ferocious lions, tigers and crocodiles to their will. Top of the bill during the 1933–34 Olympia winter season was the scantily dressed French lion tamer Violette D'Argens 'and her lions'. D'Argens, however, came to a tragic end, committing suicide after being mauled by one of the lions.[†]

The British Patricia Bourne who, at the age of only twenty-two, succeeded D'Argens as Europe's most famous female lion tamer, later recalled that audiences seemed 'rather surprised because I was so small in comparison with the huge lions'. The 'ferocious roars' of one of her lions once 'cleared the better part of the front row at Bertram Mills's Circus at Olympia'.[‡] As in the case of D'Argens, the image of an attractive young woman pitting her will against ferocious animals had strong box-office appeal. The illusion spread that roars from Bourne's lions, sometimes rehearsed, were signs they might attack her.[§] As Bourne revealed in her memoirs, however: 'A lion quivers when he is contemplating villainy; ... he never roars when he is angry, but roars when he is hungry or bored.'[¶]

---

[*]   Mills, *Bertram Mills Circus*, p.36; Peta Tait, *Wild and Dangerous Performances: Animals, Emotion, Circus* (London: Palgrave Macmillan, 2011), pp.39–40.

[†]   Patricia Bourne, *Thank You, I Prefer Lions* (London: William Kimber, 1956), p.16.

[‡]   Ibid., pp.36–7.

[§]   Tait, *Wild and Dangerous Performances*, ch.2.

[¶]   Bourne, *Thank You, I Prefer Lions*, p.27.

Cyril Mills's most successful, and best-paid, circus act before the Second World War, discovered in a small French circus by a Paris antique dealer whom Mills employed as his 'private eye', was Koringa, advertised by Mills as 'the only female fakir in the world'.* Mills personally devised bogus publicity to create the illusion that Koringa was raised by fakirs in India after being orphaned at the age of three. The fakirs had supposedly taught her the sorcery and magic required to mesmerise crocodiles, walk over broken glass with bare feet and survive burial in a snake-infested sandpit unscathed. Koringa's real origins, kept secret by Mills, were much more prosaic. She was a French dancer named Renée Bernard, brought up in Bordeaux. Probably on Mills's initiative and certainly with his approval, Koringa called the largest of the crocodiles she supposedly mesmerised in the Bertram Mills Circus ring after Winston Churchill, who came to watch her perform.†

Earning more than the Prime Minister, Koringa was the circus's best-known and best-paid pre-war artiste, as well as the only one to use Churchill's name to publicise her act. From time to time, Churchill himself called both Nazis and Soviet communists 'crocodiles'. But, just as he did not object to, and was probably amused by, his name being given to Koringa's chief crocodile, so he approved the wartime decision to call a flame-throwing tank the 'Churchill Crocodile'. In 1944 he told the minister in charge of the Petroleum Warfare Department, 'I am very glad that the Churchill Crocodile Flame Thrower has justified your hopes'.‡

Mills's wartime triumphs as a leading practitioner of the

---

* Although of Muslim origin, the term fakir (or faqir) was also applied to Hindu ascetics or mystics with supposedly supernatural or mystical powers.
† Churchill saw Koringa perform with her crocodiles on at least two occasions: when she topped the bill after the pre-Christmas Olympia lunches in 1937 and 1938. See illustration no.11: Koringa with her allegedly hypnotised crocodile 'Churchill' at a Bertram Mills Circus performance in Plymouth in 1937.
‡ Brendon, *Churchill's Bestiary*, pp.101ff.

Double-Cross System derived from his ability to learn from his pre-war mistakes, as well as his successes in orchestrating the Koringa deception. During the dress rehearsal before Koringa's first performance at Olympia in 1937, Mills, as he later admitted, 'nearly came unstuck'. Unusually, he found himself without a script as Koringa began her performance and was forced to improvise:

> I took the microphone and started: 'Koringa was born in Bikan-er in the heart of India and at an early age she was given to the fakirs...' I kept going for the full five minutes, at the end of which I was in a cold sweat for I realised that I had done something for which I might have sacked anyone else...

After the rehearsal, Mills raced to his office to look at a map of India 'to see if there was a place called Bikaner'. To his immense relief, the map showed that Bikaner was a former princely capital in Rajasthan, 'although I have never known how or when I ever heard of the place'.[*]

Unlike his improvised tribute to 'the only female fakir in the world', the ingenious biographies of non-existent agents which Mills devised to deceive the Abwehr when he was a leading case officer in the Double-Cross System were always meticulously prepared. During the war, Koringa, like Mills, became involved in intelligence work, going on missions for the Free French secret service.[†] Mills's Koringa deception remained undiscovered until he revealed it after his retirement.[‡]

'In the national interest,' Dick White later admitted, 'I think we appropriated too much talent. The demand for men of ability in

---

[*]   Mills, *Bertram Mills Circus*, pp.87–9.
[†]   https://archives.shef.ac.uk/agents/people/294
[‡]   Mills, *Bertram Mills Circus*, p.89.

other [government] departments was enormous and perhaps we were a bit greedy.' What was also remarkable was the range of their abilities. Mills later quoted the claim by Guy Liddell that MI5 was 'the finest liaison of unlike minds in the history of intelligence'.* As well as recruiting six future judges, MI5 officers included extraordinary creative talents as diverse as Mills and the art historian, Anthony Blunt, whose flair for deception as a Soviet agent deceived even White and Liddell.

Mills's wartime friendships in MI5 were all the more important to him because, shortly after war broke out, his wife Elsie and their two children (eleven-year-old Rosanne and nine-year-old David) left to spend the rest of the conflict with the Canadian branch of her family in the remote but safe surroundings of Owen Sound in Georgian Bay, Ontario.† It was almost four years before Cyril saw them again. His marriage never recovered from the separation.

* * *

The Luftwaffe's night-time London Blitz, which began with a 200-bomber raid on 7 September 1940, quickly established that Wormwood Scrubs was too insecure to remain Security Service HQ. Only the ground floor of the prison was regarded as reasonably safe; during air raids three-quarters or more of the staff on the upper floors were ordered to leave their rooms. The Registry index and files were particularly vulnerable during the Blitz, following the unwise decision to house them in workshop with a glass roof which had been the prison laundry.

---

*   CBM papers.
†   Owen Sound had a reputation as the temperance capital of Ontario; the sale of alcohol was not permitted until 1972.

As MI5 night-duty officer at Wormwood Scrubs during a German incendiary attack in the early hours of 29 September, Mills 'saw through the barred windows that a great many of the filing cabinets were already red hot'. On his orders, a large wooden beam, possibly a railway sleeper, was used to break down the door in time to rescue most of MI5's files.* Marguerite Crill of MI5 later recalled arriving at the Scrubs the next morning 'to find firemen and hosepipes everywhere ... The mess was simply awful. The half-burnt files were soaking wet and there was a disgusting smell of burnt wetness.'†

Despite the mess, the sometimes singed and water-damaged files from the First World War and interwar period, saved by Mills and his helpers, were a crucially important source for the history of MI5 published almost half a century later by its official historian, Christopher Andrew. Ironically, among the oldest files saved by Mills's quick thinking were those on two of his main communist bêtes noires, Lenin and Trotsky. Trotsky's MI5 file includes an intercepted, handwritten postcard which he sent to a Russian revolutionary in London in 1916, hoping to 'meet again in the ranks of fighters for the common cause'. The postcard had been confiscated by MI5 and never reached its destination.‡ Lenin's file includes the ill-informed, handwritten comment in 1920 by a young MI5 desk officer: 'LENIN has no actual powers but serves as some kind of figure-head.' As a later head of MI5 commented when the file was eventually declassified: 'Some figure-head!'§ The maverick (and later bestselling) MI5 officer, Peter Wright, 'often examined' interwar files rescued from

---

* Mills, untitled confidential memoir on his intelligence career (undated), pp.3–4; CBM papers.
† The whole MI5 Central Card index and about 800 files were badly damaged. Though the index had been microfilmed at the suggestion of Victor Rothschild, the quality of the film was so poor that registry clerks could only work on it for a few hours at a time and the index took nine months to reconstruct. Andrew, *Defence of the Realm*.
‡ TNA KV2/502.
§ Comments by the DG, Sir Stephen Lander, at TNA conference in 2001 on 'The Missing Dimension'; https://www.mi5.gov.uk/fa/node/410.

the blaze at Wormwood Scrubs: 'It was a difficult process prizing apart the charred papers with tweezers and wooden spatulas.'[*]

In October 1940, Mills and the greater part of the Security Service moved from Wormwood Scrubs to the much safer and far more scenic surroundings of Churchill's birthplace: Blenheim Palace at Woodstock, near Oxford.[†] MI5's move was kept secret, as were Churchill's occasional weekend visits to Blenheim as the guest of his cousin, the tenth duke. Mills was struck by how the room where Churchill had been born in 1874 was being used to distribute to MI5 staff the brown envelopes containing their monthly salaries. Staff also knew that in 1908 Churchill had proposed to his future wife, Clementine Hozier, at the romantic Temple of Diana in the palace park. Persuading her to agree to his marriage proposal in the Temple was, he publicly declared, 'my most brilliant achievement'.[‡] Only a year later, Churchill became one of the key movers in the founding of MI5.

Blenheim was by far the most magnificent building ever occupied by a British intelligence service. After the spartan cells at Wormwood Scrubs and the miseries of the London Blitz, Marguerite Crill found arriving at the Palace during 'wonderful autumn weather' in 1940 a 'blissful' experience:

At Blenheim the trees were gold with autumn and the sky was blue, the palace pale yellow, really lovely. Our desks were set up under the tapestries which were still on the walls ... I swam in the lake occasionally and, when it snowed, a lot of the staff

---

[*] Peter Wright, *Spycatcher: The Candid Autobiography of a Senior Intelligence Officer* (New York: Viking, 1987), p.37.

[†] The Director (later known as the DG), some other senior officers and the counter-espionage operations officers stayed in London at the former MGM building in St James's Street whose purpose was camouflaged by a large 'To Let' sign outside. St James's Street was known as 'the town office' and Blenheim Palace as 'the country office'.

[‡] Andrew, *Defence of the Realm*, p.234; Roberts, *Churchill*, p.123.

tobogganed using the in-trays, or skated on the frozen lake to the confusion of the sentries stationed at the edge to repel intruders.[*]

Mills was more aware than most in MI5 of the historical significance of Blenheim Palace. After winning the Battle of Blenheim in 1704, the first great English land victory on the Continent since the Hundred Years' War, Churchill's ancestor, the first Duke of Marlborough, on whom he wrote a lengthy biography,[†] had been given a blank cheque to build the great Baroque palace at Woodstock named after his victory. Marlborough's passion for intelligence, which equalled Churchill's two centuries later, had helped to make his triumph at Blenheim possible.[‡]

By far the best informed of Mills's colleagues about the history and architecture of Blenheim Palace was the art historian Anthony Blunt, who was later discovered to be a Soviet agent. Helen Ouin recalled that Blunt 'used to take us around the palace giving us lectures on the contents and was a most charming man.'[§] Remarkably, though Mills and his MI5 colleagues were not suspicious of Blunt, Soviet intelligence was. Moscow could not understand why neither Blunt in MI5 nor Kim Philby in MI6 had so far identified 'a single valuable British agent either in the USSR or in the Soviet embassy in Britain'. The Centre, NKVD headquarters in Moscow, could not grasp the simple fact that there were no British agents operating against the Soviet Union for Blunt or Philby to identify.[¶] Mills, whom Blunt had identified as an MI5 officer, remained a puzzle to the NKVD. The conspiracy theorists in the Centre knew that Coco, the most popular clown, who Bertram Mills had recruited before

---

[*] Andrew, *Defence of the Realm*, p.232.
[†] W. S. Churchill, *Marlborough* (London: Harrap, 1947): originally published in four volumes, the first of which appeared in 1933.
[‡] Andrew, *Secret World*, ch.13
[§] Ouin, 'From a Prison to a Palace!'
[¶] Andrew and Mitrokhin, *Mitrokhin Archive*, pp.157–8.

the war, had begun in the Moscow State Circus but had yet to work out what Cyril Mills was up to.[*]

While Mills was stationed at Blenheim Palace, communications with MI5's London office in St James's Street were, as Guy Liddell complained, 'frightful'.[†] Mills discovered that the MI5 telephone system was less sophisticated than that of Bertram Mills Circus. The pre-war Olympia box office for circus bookings had twenty lines,[‡] ten times as many as those between Blenheim Palace and MI5's London office. Liddell noted in his diary:

> At the moment there are only two lines and one of them is not working. Whenever you ring up you are told that your name will be put on the waiting list. We have been promised five lines but quite clearly we need twenty. What seems to have been overlooked is that everyone down at Blenheim has to keep in touch with his outside contacts, and that if connection is not made those in the country will become completely isolated.[§]

Save for the telephone system, however, MI5 office circulars at Blenheim Palace reveal an attractive working environment unimaginable at the Scrubs. One circular complained that staff were picking too many flowers: 'The practice of leaving bunches of flowers in the fire buckets militates against the efficiency of our fire-fighting arrangements, and causes much extra work for the fire-fighting staff. Will all members of the staff therefore please refrain from placing their flowers in the fire bucket.'[¶]

---

[*]   See below, p.254.
[†]   Guy Liddell diary, 7 October 1940.
[‡]   Mentioned on circus posters.
[§]   Guy Liddell diary, 7 October 1940.
[¶]   Andrew, *Defence of the Realm*, p.234.

Despite the scenic surroundings, Mills found much of his early work at Blenheim Palace tedious, dealing with the aftermath of the Fifth Column scare which had swept Britain in the summer of 1940, based on conspiracy theories that enemy aliens and British fascists were making secret preparations to assist a German invasion. In July 1940, Guy Liddell described 'Fifth Column neurosis' as 'one of the greatest dangers with which we have to contend at the moment' and a damaging distraction for MI5. Shortly after being replaced as Commander-in-Chief Home Forces in that month, Field Marshal Sir Edmund (later Baron) Ironside, absurdly claimed that there were 'people quite definitely preparing aerodromes in this country' for use by the Luftwaffe.*

Though such fantasies had become far fewer by the time Mills began work at Blenheim, he complained at the amount of time he still had to waste dealing with the aftermath of 'Fifth Column neurosis'. He later recalled that, while temporary head of the department dealing with British fascists, he 'probably closed as many files as anyone has ever done in about three weeks as enquiries showed that most of the suspects were already in one of the armed services'. His experience in the entertainment business was put to better use when he was asked to investigate the case of 'a man who had been employed by [Billy] Butlin at a holiday camp on the Continent [and] had a lot of contact with a known German agent operating there'. Mills was well acquainted with Butlin, who later provided the 'big rides' for the Olympia funfair run in conjunction with the circus. After an investigation into the suspect Butlin's employee, which included three days at the holiday camp near Filey, then being turned into a wartime military training base, Mills 'typed a full report that the Butlin's employee was clean'.†

---

*   Ibid., p.223. Andrew, *Secret Service*, p.667.

†   Mills, untitled confidential memoir on his intelligence career (undated), p.4; CBM papers.

The majority of MI5's wartime staff with whom Mills worked at Blenheim Palace were women. Though mostly confined to subordinate roles as in other government departments, they included the liveliest group of female professionals he and most other male intelligence officers had ever encountered. Some probably reminded him of his circus performers, Violette D'Argens and Koringa, whose extrovert behaviour and high salaries would not have been tolerated in Whitehall or most other London offices.

Most female personnel at Blenheim Palace were lodged at Keble College, Oxford, and bussed each day to work at Blenheim. Keble's bursar complained in writing about boisterous behaviour by some of them at dinner in the college hall which, he claimed, led to far more crockery being broken than by its male undergraduates. M. B. Heywood of MI5 sent a sceptical reply: 'It is difficult to envisage that, among other things, our staff have broken 28 large coffee pots, 740 plates of [all] sorts and 104 dishes of [all] sorts unless there has been a free fight.'*

The Bertram Mills Circus company secretary at its London HQ in 1 Dorset Square, Miss A. A. Moore (never called by her first name), had little in common with the vivacious MI5 female staff who upset the bursar of Keble College. Employed by his father, Bertram Mills, as his private secretary and personal assistant soon after she left school, Cyril found her 'very prim and unsophisticated'.†

Cyril revealed little, if anything, to Miss Moore of his intelligence career. He also failed to brief her on a new secret agency, the Special Operations Executive (SOE), founded by Churchill in July 1940 in a premature attempt to rouse occupied countries to rebellion against their Nazi overlords and 'set Europe ablaze' by a campaign of sabotage. In the autumn of 1940 Miss Moore telephoned Mills to say:

---

*   Andrew, *Defence of the Realm*, p.232.
†   Mills, *Bertram Mills Circus*, p.27. One Dorset Square was owned by the Mills family.

...she had a chance to let the [Circus's] Dorset Square offices for the duration of the war, but there was something very fishy going on and she did not feel safe in going ahead. When she explained how the negotiations were being conducted I could only think it looked like S.O.E. in its best cloak and dagger style and, having made enquiries through a friend [probably Dick White] and being informed my guess was correct, I was able to give Miss Moore an assurance that the rent would be paid. Dorset Square became part of the French Underground and the jumping off place for spies and saboteurs who were dropped in France.[*]

In addition to the SOE's French F Section, mainly staffed by British personnel, there was also a French-speaking RF Section mostly composed of Free French supporters of General Charles de Gaulle. The bilingual Edward Yeo-Thomas (codenamed 'The White Rabbit'), head of Planning in Section RF, who had been brought up in France, later recalled the irony of planning dangerous operations with the Resistance in occupied France 'in rooms where Bertram Mills had contracted its [circus] clowns'.[†]

With the post-war winding-up of the SOE, Section RF headquarters once again became the head office of Bertram Mills Circus. Cyril and his family were present in June 1957 when, in Operation Croix de Lorraine, the RAF brought forty Resistance veterans to the unveiling of a memorial at 1 Dorset Square by the Queen Mother: to commemorate the deeds of men and women of the Free French Forces and their British comrades who left from this house on

---

[*] Mills, *Bertram Mills Circus*, pp.130–31. Cyril Mills's entry in the *Oxford Dictionary of National Biography* wrongly suggests that he was personally involved in the intelligence operations run from 1 Dorset Square.

[†] Bruce Marshall, *The White Rabbit : The Secret Agent the Gestapo Could Not Crack* (London: Cassell, 2000), pp.20–23.

special missions to enemy occupied territories and to honour those who did not return.[*]

Mills recalled that, after the unveiling, 'one Frenchman spotted the desk at which I still work and said he felt much easier now than when he had sat in front while briefed just before being dropped in France.'[†]

Today's occupant of 1 Dorset Square, the Alliance Française, tells those on its language courses: 'We hope you will enjoy practising your French in the old offices of SOE's RF Section, "another kind of circus"':

> Welcome to Alliance House where, by closing your eyes, you can imagine [the Resistance hero] Jean Moulin, his scarf, his smile, in what is today the library; and Pierre Brossolette say to his friend [Edward] Yeo-Thomas, perhaps while preparing their dangerous joint mission, '*la vie est un cirque, il faut savoir en rire!*' ('Life is a circus. One must know how to laugh about it!')[‡]

Even by the standards of the French Resistance, Moulin and Brossolette were among the bravest of the brave. Both are buried in the Paris Pantheon, the final resting place of almost eighty of France's greatest national heroes.

The most recent burial of a Resistance hero in the Pantheon, in December 2021, was of the American-born Josephine Baker, the celebrated former dancer and singer at the Folies Bergère, as well as the first Black woman to star in a major motion picture, the 1934

---

[*] CBM papers, C.7.1. See illustration no.12, the Queen Mother about to unveil the memorial at 1 Dorset Square.

[†] Mills, *Bertram Mills Circus*, pp.130–31.

[‡] Alliance Française de Londres, 'SOE at 1 Dorset Square'; https://alliancefrancaise.london/SOE-at-1-Dorset-Square.php

French film *Zouzou*. As well as performing in public, Baker carried out a series of secret missions for Free French intelligence, using her cover as one of France's most famous entertainers. It cannot have occurred to any of the US troops, to whom she sang 'The Star-Spangled Banner' after their landings in North Africa in late 1942, that their national anthem was being sung by an agent for the Free French intelligence. When Baker was awarded the médaille de la Résistance after the war, General de Gaulle wrote to express his personal admiration for 'the enthusiasm with which you have put your magnificent talent at the disposal of our Cause and all who have followed it'. She was later made Chevalier de l'Ordre National de la Légion d'Honneur.[*]

Though the comparison would never have occurred to Cyril Mills, he and Josephine Baker were both famous figures in the entertainment business who also had an extraordinary secret talent for intelligence operations.[†]

---

[*]   Andrew and Green, *Stars and Spies*, pp.272–6. On Operation TORCH and the North-African landings late in 1942, see below, pp.138–40.

[†]   During the First World War, one of the most successful spies to work for French military intelligence was the singer and dancer Jeanne Bourgeois, better known by her stage name Mistinguett, the star, successively, of the Moulin Rouge, Folies Bergère and the Casino de Paris. At her peak, Mistinguett was probably the best-paid female entertainer in the world. Andrew and Green, *Stars and Spies*, pp.182–4.

CHAPTER 5

DOUBLE-CROSS: MILLS'S 'LICENCE TO KILL' AND THE TRIUMPH OF GARBO

While working at Blenheim Palace in January 1941, Cyril Mills was summoned to MI5's London office in St James's Street for a meeting with Dick White and Guy Liddell, who asked whether he would be interested in a job as a case officer in B1a, MI5's double agent section. They left it to the head of B1a, Thomas Argyll ('Tar') Robertson, to explain what the job involved. As Mills later recalled, he and 'Tar' 'hit it off splendidly'.* His espionage success in pre-war Germany, many German contacts, language skills and experience in organising deception made him ideally suited for a job running German double agents. 'Tar' Robertson became a close, lifelong friend.†

Born in Sumatra in 1909 but brought up in Britain, Robertson began his career in the Seaforth Highlanders before working in the

---

*   Mills, untitled confidential memoir on his intelligence career (undated), p.4; CBM papers.
†   'Tar' was also a close friend of Liddell, who in 1942 became godfather to his daughter Belinda. Geoffrey Elliott, *Gentleman Spymaster: How Lt Col Tommy 'Tar' Robertson Double-crossed the Nazis* (London: Methuen, 2013), pp.141–2.

City in the early 1930s and joining the Security Service in 1933.[*] At MI5 headquarters he continued to wear his tartan Seaforth trousers, or 'trews', thus earning the nickname 'passion pants'.[†] 'Tar's natural air of authority did not suffer from the nickname. , an official historian of wartime intelligence, called him 'a perfect officer type, who could have been played by Ronald Colman', the epitome on stage and screen of the chivalrous English officer and gentleman.[‡]

Mills told Robertson:

> ...that whereas I would give anything to be allowed to do this kind of [double agent] work I had one condition to make. I realised immediately that this is an extremely dangerous form of warfare and that the price of a mistake is too dreadful for words. I therefore asked TAR if he would allow me to join him on the understanding that I would not have an agent to run during the first three months during which time I would do my utmost to learn how to do it by studying all he and the others were doing. He agreed...

Because Mills's department head at Blenheim Palace, Jack Curry, one of MI5's leading pre-war German experts, was determined to keep him on his staff, it took Mills another three weeks and a threat of resignation before he was able to move to B1a in London.[§]

When Mills officially transferred to MI5's St James's Street office on 21 February 1941, there were four other B1a case officers, whose numbers were later to increase. At thirty-eight, Mills was the oldest

---

[*]   Andrew, *Defence of the Realm*, p.249.
[†]   Emily Wilson, 'The War in the Dark: The Security Service and the Abwehr 1939–1944', PhD thesis (University of Cambridge, 2009), p.126.
[‡]   Thaddeus Holt, *The Deceivers: Allied Military Deception in the Second World War* (London: Weidenfeld & Nicolson, 2004), p.131.
[§]   Mills, untitled confidential memoir on his intelligence career (undated), p.4; CBM papers.

of them. Though they were all sociable, the most gregarious was the genial Glasgow industrialist William ('Billy') Luke, future Master of the London livery company, the Worshipful Company of Makers of Playing Cards; he later commissioned a set of playing cards which showed him as the Ace of Hearts.[*] Outside B1a's lengthy working hours, it was with Luke that Mills socialised the most.

Another B1a case officer, the former solicitor Christopher Harmer, also became a close, lifelong friend.[†] Harmer spent most of his free time with the B1a secretary, Peggy Phillips. For as long as possible, Phillips later recalled, they kept their affair secret:

> We were very secretive. I don't know why. I think we were embarrassed. We were well trained, you see. We didn't want people to know we were going out together, so we pretended. Funny old business.
>
> One evening, while dancing in a nightclub, 'we were spotted by someone from the office. Then everyone knew.'[‡]

Almost half a century later, Christopher Harmer and 'Tar' Robertson were the first to pay public tribute to Mills's wartime intelligence work.[§] Harmer satirically called B1a group of 'overgrown schoolboys playing games of derring-do absorbed from reading schoolboy books and adventure stories'.[¶] But Robertson had also chosen Mills because of his toughness. Though 'very kind to his agents', 'Tar' recalled, he 'was a pretty tough character in every possible way'.[**]

---

[*]   Ben Macintyre, *Double Cross: The True Story of the D-Day Spies* (London: Bloomsbury, 2012), pp.63–4.
[†]   Information from Christopher Mills.
[‡]   Ibid.
[§]   See below, p.283.
[¶]   Macintyre, *Double Cross*, p.71.
[**] See below, p.283.

Mills's reputation for toughness helps to explain why, immediately on joining B1a, Robertson made him case officer for the double agent Hans George, codenamed DRAGONFLY. Born in London of German parents, DRAGONFLY had spent much of the interwar years in Germany as a largely unsuccessful businessman. Shortly before the outbreak of war, he moved to Holland and became an Abwehr agent, leaving for England in April 1940. Once in London, he was recruited as an MI5 double agent to feed disinformation to the Abwehr. In January 1941, DRAGONFLY met his unsuspecting German controller in Portugal, returning to London with '£800, a high-class transmitting set concealed in a gramophone and secret ink in a specially made cigarette holder'. He had, noted Guy Liddell, a 'long story' to tell about his trip to Portugal,* some of which was difficult to corroborate.

No sooner had Mills begun work in B1a on 21 February than he was taken by Robertson's deputy, John Marriott, to meet DRAGONFLY at an MI5 safe house in Wembley:

> John had been running the man as a temporary measure for a few days pending my arrival but he said he was going on two weeks' leave that day and therefore TAR wanted me to start proper work at once. So much for [the] three weeks training I had been promised.

Mills introduced himself to DRAGONFLY using the cover name 'Mr Green'. He was taken aback when DRAGONFLY told him, 'I know your sister; she came to see me about two weeks ago.' On returning to St James's Street, Mills discovered that a female colleague, using the alias 'Miss Green', ran an office masquerading as

---

* Guy Liddell diary, 7 January 1941.

MI5 premises 'to which we could take agents without letting them know where our real office was'.* The identity of the real office, the former London HQ of the US Metro-Goldwyn-Mayer film studios in St James's Street, was camouflaged by a large 'To Let' notice outside.† Mills discovered that a few days before his own visit, 'Miss Green' had called on DRAGONFLY in his Wembley safe house: 'so in a way I had landed myself with a sister in M.I.5!!'‡

B1a was acutely aware of how easily the Double-Cross System could go disastrously wrong if any of its double agents revealed the deception to the Abwehr. In January 1941, a few weeks before Mills became a case officer, Gösta Caroli, a pro-Nazi Swede codenamed SUMMER, made a dramatic attempt to do so. While living under guard in a house near Cambridge, SUMMER managed to escape. He attacked the only guard on duty, claiming implausibly, 'it hurts me more than it hurts you', tied him up and then fled on a motorbike belonging to an off-duty guard. Strapped to the motorbike was a canoe in which SUMMER planned, optimistically, to paddle to the Continent across the North Sea. 'Fortunately', concluded a later report, 'the motorbike, being government property, was not very efficiently maintained' and broke down.§ The MI5 Regional Security Liaison Officer (RSLO) in Cambridge reported to Dick White that the pursuit of SUMMER was quickly over:

At the first cross roads we came to we met some roadmen who stated that they had seen a man on a motorcycle carrying a canoe turn left down the Newmarket Road. We proceeded until we got to Pampisford Station, where we met Mr F. Brown, a roadman of

---

* Mills, untitled confidential memoir on his intelligence career (undated), p.4; CBM papers.
† Andrew, *Defence of the Realm*, p.231.
‡ Mills, untitled confidential memoir on his intelligence career (undated), p.4; CBM papers.
§ Masterman, *The Double-Cross System*, p.51.

Pampisford, who said that he had seen the man on the motorcycle with the canoe – in fact he had seen a lot of him because the man on the motorcycle had fallen off just by him and he had helped the man to throw the canoe over a hedge.[*]

SUMMER was caught soon afterwards and imprisoned for the rest of the war. As comic as his plan to paddle across the North Sea was, it emphasised the danger of one successful escape undermining the whole Double-Cross System.

SUMMER had been allowed to use his own radio transmitter to communicate with the Abwehr. Mills refused to take the same risk with DRAGONFLY, whom he had begun to distrust at their first meeting. After reading further files in B1a and a second meeting in the Wembley safe house on 22 February, Mills told 'Tar' Robertson, using one of the circus metaphors which amused his MI5 colleagues, that he would not trust DRAGONFLY 'as far as I could throw an elephant'. Mills confiscated the new radio transmitter concealed in a gramophone given to DRAGONFLY by the Abwehr and handed it to a trusted 'first-class Radio "Ham" named Riesen':

I told DRAGONFLY that I was not allowing him access to the radio. I should prepare all his [message] traffic, he would translate it into German which I would approve and then Riesen would transmit it [to the Abwehr]. In fact this worked splendidly and ... [he] was still in touch with his German masters until well after 'D' Day.[†]

The recruitment of SUMMER's friend, the Danish fascist Wulf Schmidt, as a double agent codenamed TATE (because 'Tar'

---

[*]   Major Dixon (RSLO Cambridge) to Dick White, 14 January 1940, TNA KV 2/60.
[†]   Mills handed over DRAGONFLY to another B1a case officer when posted to Canada in December 1942.

Robertson thought he resembled the music hall performer Harry Tate) proved even more successful. During his interrogation at Camp 020, the MI5 London interrogation centre for captured agents, TATE was deceived into believing that SUMMER had betrayed him. According to the head of Camp 020, Robin 'Tin Eye' Stephens (so called because of the monocle which seemed glued to his right eye), TATE 'lost all his previous composure, cursed "the swine [SUMMER]" and blurted out that he would tell the whole truth. He held back little.'* After only two days' interrogation,† TATE began a career as the longest-serving of all B1a's double agents, continuously exchanging wireless messages with the Abwehr in Hamburg from October 1940 until May 1945. His German controllers called him a 'pearl' among agents, sent him large sums of money and ensured he was awarded the Iron Cross, both first and second class.‡

Among the Abwehr agents sent to take money to TATE was the Sudeten German Karel Richter, who landed by parachute in the countryside north of London early on the morning of 12 May 1941. As usual, ULTRA had already alerted MI5 to Richter's impending arrival. During interrogation at Camp 020, his identity papers in the name of Fred Snyder were quickly exposed as bogus. Curiously, Richter had also brought with him an expired Czechoslovakian passport in his real name. On 24 October, after a secret trial at the Old Bailey, he was sentenced to death by hanging.§

As Cyril told his son Christopher much later, B1a had to be tough.

---

* Oliver Hoare (ed.), *Camp 020: MI5 and the Nazi Spies. The Official History of MI5's Wartime Interrogation Centre* (London: PRO Publications, 2001), p.140. TATE later gave an alternative explanation of his reasons for becoming a double agent, which made no mention of his fury at SUMMER's 'betrayal': 'Nobody ever asked me why I changed my mind', he said after the war, 'but the reason was really very straightforward. It was simply a matter of survival. Self-preservation must be the strongest instinct in man.' Andrew, *Secret Service*, p.671.

† TNA KV 2/61.

‡ Andrew, *Defence of the Realm*, p.252.

§ TNA KV 2/30–2.

Some of the Double-Cross System was 'a dirty business'.* The case he had most in mind was probably that of Karel Richter. B1a wanted Richter's death sentence to be commuted but was even more anxious to prevent him compromising Double-Cross. In a draft appeal against his sentence, Richter said he knew that TATE was under British 'control'. Richter's veteran MI5 interrogator William Hinchley-Cooke persuaded him to remove any reference to TATE from his appeal.[†]

B1a was still fearful that the Richter case might compromise its double agents. 'Tar' wrote to Liddell on 6 November:

> I do feel that mention of RICHTER's execution in the press is going to cause the Germans to reopen interest in the case of TATE and make them look through their records with even greater care than they have done before. At this present moment from a purely B.1.A viewpoint I cannot afford to jeopardise the security of any of our agents.[‡]

The hanging, however, went ahead at Wandsworth Prison early on 10 December. In Albert Pierrepoint's twenty-five-year career as Britain's last official hangman, this was the only execution that took him longer than twenty seconds to complete after his usual early morning arrival in the condemned cell. Pierrepoint reported afterwards that Richter refused to leave his cell and during the struggle which followed: 'There were five bodies thrashing on the floor, and one of the men in blue was an accomplished judo expert.' It took seventeen minutes to subdue Richter and hang him on the scaffold

---

* Recollection of Christopher Mills.
† Guy Liddell diary, 6 November 1941. The German-educated Hinchley-Cooke had joined MI5 early in the First World War.
‡ Robertson to Liddell, 6 November 1941; TNA KV 2/32.

next door to the cell.[*] B1a was shocked by the reports it received of the hanging. Peggy Harmer (née Phillips) said later, 'we all hated it in the office [B1a]. I think it was a horrible occasion.'[†]

* * *

B1a reasonably assumed that the Abwehr must be alive to the danger that one or more of its agents in Britain might be turned into double agents. In the aftermath of Richter's execution, B1a strategy, partly devised by Mills, was not to conceal entirely its attempts to recruit double agents but rather to convince the Abwehr that these attempts were so incompetent that they would be bound to detect them and that MI5 would fail to identify most German agents sent to Britain.[‡] The key to this novel deception strategy was the arrest in September 1941 of a Belgian ship's steward, Alphons Timmerman, identified as a German agent in Abwehr wireless messages decrypted by Bletchley Park.[§]

Mills, who was put in charge of the Timmerman case, wrote later:

> Under interrogation at Camp 020 he broke down and confessed and I was offered him as a double agent. I went to see him and decided he was low class and worthless. Or at best not worth wasting a lot of time on and in any case he would be difficult or impossible to control if we allowed him to work as a merchant seaman. I gave him the cover-name SCRUFFY and suggested that he should be sent for trial and that when he had been hanged we would use him [posthumously] as a double agent.

---

*   https://josefjakobs.info/2014/05/facing-death-part-2-courage-vs.html
†   Ben Macintyre, 'The Last Miss Moneypenny Recalls her War', *The Times*, 15 May 2007
‡   Mills, untitled additions to and comments on Masterman, *The Double-Cross System* (undated but probably written in mid-1970s); CBM papers.
§   TNA KV 2/3855.

SCRUFFY, like Richter, was sentenced to death after a secret trial at the Old Bailey:

> We took steps to see that the announcement of his hanging [on 7 July 1942] was in all the English papers which were flown to Lisbon daily and read avidly by the Germans there. In the meantime I had copied his block-letter writing and was sending them low-class marine information of a kind he might pick up. As soon as they read he had been caught and hanged they [would know] his traffic was false and I therefore continued it at a very low level and making serious mistakes every few days. The purpose was to make it very clear to the enemy that we were doing their agent's work and that whoever was actually doing it had not the vaguest idea about how to run a double agent convincingly.[*]

Radio messages decrypted by Bletchley Park showed, however, to the surprise of B1a, that the Abwehr had failed to notice either the news of SCRUFFY's execution at Wandsworth Prison or the glaring errors in the intelligence reports sent by Mills in his name. Mills and B1a concluded that the Abwehr really must be as gullible as it seemed.[†]

In the summer of 1942, Guy Liddell noted that Mills's double agent 'DRAGONFLY has had quite a success in putting over a story about a possible invasion of Norway'. Abwehr and other enemy communications decrypted by Bletchley Park confirmed that the Germans had been deceived by DRAGONFLY's reports into making military preparations to meet the imaginary threat of an Allied invasion.[‡]

---

[*] Mills, untitled confidential memoir on his intelligence career (undated), p.7; CBM papers.
[†] TNA KV 2/3855. Macintyre, *Double Cross*, p.73.
[‡] Guy Liddell diary, 16 July 1942.

* * *

Though B1a was responsible for the wireless messages sent to the Abwehr by the double agents under its control, the disinformation they contained was devised by the Twenty Committee – so called because the Roman numeral for twenty (XX) is a double-cross. The Committee, chiefly composed of representatives from MI5, MI6, the War Office, the three service intelligence departments and GHQ Home Forces, began meeting in January 1941, just before Mills was appointed as DRAGONFLY's case officer. Thereafter, it met weekly for the remainder of the war. The Twenty Committee was an extraordinary historical innovation, the first committee anywhere in the world tasked with devising a credible mixture of information and disinformation that was capable of deceiving a major enemy. Such a high-level independent committee would have been unthinkable in Hitler's Germany or Stalin's Russia.

Like Mills, the Committee Chairman, the Oxford history don, J. C. Masterman (later knighted and a future Vice-Chancellor), owed his recruitment to MI5 to Dick White, who had been his pupil at Christ Church. The energetic, athletic Mills was much impressed that, as well as being an academic, Masterman was probably the best all-round games player ever to join MI5. As an undergraduate he had won an athletics blue. Between the wars he played hockey and tennis for England and, at the age of forty-six, he was still a good enough cricketer to tour Canada with the Marylebone Cricket Club (MCC). Having been interned in Germany during the First World War, Masterman was also a fluent German speaker.

Mills, however, believed that Masterman's approach to deception was too cautious:

The DG gave J.C. [Masterman] his job because he thought there should be a restraining influence having regard to the fact that everyone in B.1.a was so young. I was 38 and the eldest but fortunately TAR was a well-established regular member of MI5 and he did not allow J.C. to dominate him or any of us.

...So far as the work of B.1.a was concerned, J.C. spent most of his time twiddling his thumbs and throwing cold water on any plans which we produced.[*]

Christopher Harmer claimed that, after he became case officer for the Polish double agent BRUTUS, 'old JC' (Masterman) was 'hell bent on chopping him and intrigued behind my back'. On 5 March 1943, the day before his wedding to Peggy Phillips, Harmer found time to send Masterman 'one of the rudest letters I have ever written ... It took some time to heal the breach'. The breach was healed because Masterman knew B1a had to be adventurous and most of B1a realised Masterman had to be cautious. 'I loved the old boy,' Harmer wrote later, 'and I suppose he was only doing his job – of exercising a wise and mature restraint on the irresponsibilities of the hot-headed youngsters of those days.'[†]

In retrospect, most of B1a was less critical of Masterman than Mills. Guy Liddell wrote at the end of the war: 'Apart from his ability he is an extremely delightful personality and has been liked by us all.'[‡] Masterman preceded the first meeting of the Twenty Committee with what he later called 'a small but important decision, to wit that tea and a bun should always be provided for members':

---

[*]   Mills to Annie Luke (widow of B1a officer Billy Luke), 8 June 1990; CBM papers.
[†]   Christopher Harmer to Hugh Astor, 28 October 1992.
[‡]   Guy Liddell Report, 4 September 1945; Andrew, *Defence of the Realm*, p.256. A generation later, however, Masterman offended former B1a officers by revealing wartime successes of the Double-Cross System which they believed should have remained secret.

In days of acute shortage and of rationing, the provision of buns was no easy task, yet by hook or crook (and mostly by crook) we never failed to provide them throughout the war years. Was this simple expedient one of the reasons why attendance at the Committee was nearly always a hundred per cent?

More important than the refreshments he provided was Masterman's gift for creating consensus. At only one of the committee's 226 meetings was a disagreement pressed to a vote.[*] The Twenty Committee gradually grasped the astonishing fact, unparalleled in British intelligence history, that, in Masterman's words, thanks to the Double-Cross System, *'we actively ran and controlled the German espionage system in this country'.*[†]

The disinformation chosen to deceive the Abwehr was remarkably diverse. In the case of Mills's first double agent, DRAGONFLY, even wartime ration cards were used as a simple but ingenious method of deception. On being informed that DRAGONFLY had taken a job in a local office of the Ministry of Food which issued ration cards, the Abwehr asked him to post some of them to its cover address in Lisbon for German agents sent to England to use in the future. The cards sent to the Abwehr, however, contained a bogus ID sequence of letters. According to Mills, 'any policeman finding a man using a card with such letters would have arrested him at once.'[‡] A number of the bogus ration cards were later found in the possession of German agents sent to make contact with Arthur Owens, a Welsh electrical engineer who had begun working for the Abwehr in 1936. Unbeknown to the Abwehr, Owens had

---

[*] J. C. Masterman, *On the Chariot Wheel : An Autobiography* (Oxford: Oxford University Press, 1975), ch.21.
[†] Masterman, *The Double-Cross System*. The italics are Masterman's.
[‡] CBM papers.

been turned by MI5 and recruited as the first of its double agents, codenamed SNOW (a partial anagram of Owens), shortly after the outbreak of war.* SNOW's B1a case officers found him personally tiresome, with disagreeably plebeian habits, which included 'only wearing his false teeth when eating'.[†]

* * *

The greatest potential threat to the Double-Cross System was a German invasion of Britain, which was widely expected after the rapid conquest of France and the Low Countries. MI5, like the rest of British intelligence, was unaware that, following the failure of the Luftwaffe to win air supremacy in the Battle of Britain, Hitler postponed his invasion plans – in the end indefinitely. Churchill believed that, though invasion had become 'unlikely to material-ise' after the victory of 'the Few', the threat remained. Strong forces would therefore have to stay in Britain in case Hitler decided to go ahead. In a broadcast on 11 September 1940, Churchill described the London Blitz as 'part of Hitler's invasion plan'.[‡] Coping with an invasion would crucially require the use of MI5's double agents to feed disinformation to the Germans about the deployment of British defence forces. The danger was, however, that some double agents after the invasion would switch sides, join the German forces and compromise the whole Double-Cross System. 'Tar' Robertson wrote on 12 March 1941: 'If there is any danger of the more dangerous cases falling into enemy hands they will be liquidated forcibly'– in

---

*   Andrew, *Defence of the Realm*, pp.248–9; James Hayward, *Hitler's Spy: The True Story of Arthur Owens, Double Agent Snow* (London: Simon & Schuster, 2012), chs.1–3.

†   TNA KV2/448. SNOW's daughter Patricia, by contrast, became a glamorous post-war Hollywood film star, playing opposite – among others – Marlon Brando and James Mason.

‡   Allen Packwood, *How Churchill Waged War: The Most Challenging Decisions of the Second World War* (Barnsley: Frontline Books, 2018), pp.61, 82–3.

other words, shot. If any one of them was able to contact the enemy, it 'could blow our whole show'.*

In April 1941, preparations were made by MI5 to move all the double agents, in the event of a German invasion, to secret addresses in North Wales where they were to be kept under house arrest. Mills's reputation for 'toughness' helps to explain why he was put in charge – or, in his own words, persuaded to 'volunteer'. Though officially known later as Plan HEGIRA ('migration'),† the operation was at first satirically codenamed 'MR MILLS' CIRCUS' in his honour. The intelligence officer responsible for the Welsh end of the operation, Captain P. E. S. Finney, used circus metaphors in his correspondence with MI5 Head Office, writing from Colwyn Bay in April 1941: 'I have now completed arrangements for the accommodation of the animals, the young and their keepers, together with accommodation for Mr Mills himself.' All the double agents were to be secretly housed in hotels at Betws-y-Coed, Llanrwst and Llandudno, whose proprietors had been vetted by MI5.‡

During the CIRCUS operation, Mills was to be accompanied to Wales by an officer from Camp 020, MI5's wartime interrogation centre, who was put in charge of all the captured German agents imprisoned at the centre:

> If an invasion had been successful we two officers would stay in Wales and if the enemy approached anywhere near then all the agents were to be shot and we should have to shoot them. Had we not done so we knew that the turned agents would denounce us

---

* T. A. Robertson to Major Stephens, 12 March 1941, TNA KV 4/211.

† Mills, untitled confidential memoir on his intelligence career (undated), p.9; CBM papers. The original Hegira was in 622 CE when the prophet Muhammad left Mecca and travelled to Medina. This became the starting point of the Muslim calendar.

‡ Captain P. E. S. Finney, 're: Mills' Circus', 9 April 1941, TNA KV 4/211. Hotel details (subsequently amended) in 'Accommodation Plan', ibid.

and everyone else they had met and we should be handed over to the Gestapo for torture and death. So it was a simple question of our lives or theirs. I was provided with the papers and uniform of a Captain in the Intelligence Corps and was assured that in the event of an invasion there were plans for the names of all MI5 officers to be removed from the records, but how effective this would have been is a matter of grave doubt.[*]

Operation MR MILLS' CIRCUS remains the only known occasion on which the MI5 DG, then Sir David Petrie, authorised executions – though in the event none were carried out. Petrie's legal justification was presumably that any double agent attempting to assist an invading army would have been regarded as, in effect, an enemy combatant.[†] Mills thus became, on the direct instructions of MI5's Director-General, the first of the service's staff to be given what *James Bond* novels and films later called 'a licence to kill'. So far, as is known, no post-war MI5 officer has ever had the same licence.

The double agent of most concern to Mills among those earmarked for the MR MILLS' CIRCUS operation was TATE, whom B1a believed 'would probably attempt to escape in case of an invasion'.[‡] Petrie personally instructed TATE's escort: 'As it is of vital importance that TATE should not fall into the hands of the enemy, you must be prepared to take any step necessary to prevent this from occurring.'[§] 'Tar' Robertson had TATE particularly in mind when he warned that 'the double agent is a tricky customer and needs the most careful supervision. His every mood has to be watched.'[¶]

---

[*] Mills, untitled confidential memoir on his intelligence career (undated), p.9; CBM papers.
[†] No legal opinion by the Service legal adviser or any other lawyer appears to survive on·this controversial subject.
[‡] 'Suggestions for dealing with Double Agents in case of invasion', 1 February 1941, TNA KV 4/211.
[§] DG, 'Orders for Mr Atkinson', 3 April 1941, TNA KV 4/211.
[¶] Masterman, *The Double-Cross System*, ch.1.

MI5 believed TATE's mood needed particularly careful attention after it discovered a military intelligence officer, Colonel Alexander Scotland, exchanging blows with him while interrogating TATE at Camp 020. Scotland was head of MI19, the section of the War Office responsible for extracting information from enemy prisoners of war imprisoned in what became known as the 'London Cage', housed in several mansions in Kensington Palace Gardens. MI5 strongly disapproved of the violent interrogation methods sometimes used in the London Cage. Guy Liddell, head of B Branch, noted in his diary after a visit by Colonel Scotland to interrogate TATE at Camp 020: 'He was hitting TATE in the jaw and I think got one back for himself ... We are taking the matter up with D[irector of] M[ilitary] Intelligence and propose to say that we do not intend to have that particular military intelligence officer on the premises anymore.'*

As Mills was to demonstrate when he was later put in charge of the Double-Cross System in Canada, he had no compunction about intimidating captured spies by warning them that, if they failed to cooperate, they could be put on trial and sentenced to death for espionage. But he forbade the use of physical violence against them.

Suspecting that Colonel Scotland's attack had damaged TATE's loyalty as a double agent, Mills included special arrangements for him to be taken by car to North Wales under armed escort and kept handcuffed during the journey as part of the CIRCUS operation. Since MI5 had no handcuffs of its own, they had to be borrowed from Scotland Yard. Sir David Petrie personally instructed TATE's escort: 'As it is of vital importance that TATE should not fall into the hands of the enemy, you must be prepared to take any step necessary to prevent this from occurring.'†

---

* Guy Liddell diary, 22 September 1940.
† DG, 'Orders for Mr Atkinson', 3 April 1941, TNA KV 4/211.

Operation BARBAROSSA, Hitler's surprise attack on Russia in June 1941, however, made clear there would be no German invasion of England. Plans for Operation MR MILLS' CIRCUS were abandoned and the handcuffs intended to restrain TATE and one other double agent en route to north Wales were returned unused to Scotland Yard. TATE gave no further cause for concern, becoming the longest-serving and one of the most successful of all the double agents.[*]

* * *

Probably the most ambitious double-agent recruitment assigned to Mills by 'Tar' Robertson was of Johann 'Johnny' Jebsen, a young Abwehr officer stationed in Lisbon.[†] Neutral Lisbon was a hotbed of spies working for both Germany and the Allies. British intelligence officers on missions to the Portuguese capital at various stages of the war included Ian Fleming, Graham Greene, Kim Philby and Malcolm Muggeridge. While being driven from Madrid to Lisbon 'one brilliant spring day', Philby told an MI6 colleague, 'all a man wants on a day like this is someone like Ginger Rogers and a fast car.'[‡]

'Johnny' Jebsen, whom Mills planned to meet in Lisbon, was a wealthy playboy with the reputation of being an Anglophile, who had joined the Abwehr as a way of avoiding active service in the Wehrmacht. Before the war, he had become a devotee of P. G. Wodehouse, modelled his wardrobe on Anthony Eden's and employed as his secretary the British-born spinster Mabel Harbottle who, despite her German nationality, claimed to remain 'British at

*   See below, p.265.
†   Mills, untitled confidential memoir on his intelligence career (undated), p.6; CBM papers.
‡   Kenneth Benton, 'The ISOS Years', *Journal of Contemporary History*, vol.30, no.3 (1995), p.405.

heart'. Jebsen was reported to have lamented after being stationed in Lisbon, 'I would be willing to pay £600 for a suit of English clothes, but you cannot get them.' He regularly drove a Rolls-Royce between Lisbon and his villa at Estoril on the Portuguese Riviera.*

On 23 June 1941, the day after BARBAROSSA began, Mills flew to neutral Portugal on a commercial flight to try and make contact with Jebsen, codenamed ARTIST by MI5,[†] who had been recommended as a potential recruit by an existing double agent, his friend Duško Popov. Codenamed TRICYCLE because of his fondness for three-in-a-bed sex, Popov was made a British citizen after the war and awarded the OBE at a private ceremony in one of his favourite watering holes, the bar of the Ritz Hotel.[‡]

The Abwehr laid a number of traps for British visitors to Lisbon. Prostitutes in Abwehr-controlled brothels handed British seamen invitations: 'Madame A. cordially invites you to her home on [date] at [time] p.m. to have a jolly good time and dancing too.'[§] Though not tempted to visit Madame A., Mills was aware that the Abwehr had access to records of his pre-war travels in Germany. He therefore concealed his identity during his visit by using a false British passport in the name of Cyril Brook.[ſ] Unlike the great majority of such passports used by British intelligence personnel, Mills's survives among his private papers. It is reproduced in this book for the first time.[**]

To make the details in the passport, issued only two days before Mills flew to Lisbon, more difficult to check, his place of birth was given as the Indian city of Poona (now Pune) and his date of birth as 1904, rather than 1902. His stated profession was 'Civil Servant'.

---

* Macintyre, *Double Cross*, pp.29–31. Pujol and West, *Operation GARBO*, pp.133–5.

† Mills, untitled confidential memoir on his intelligence career (undated), p.6; CBM papers.

‡ Macintyre, *Double Cross*, p.337.

§ J. G. Beevor, *SOE: Recollections and Reflections, 1940–45* (London: Bodley Head, 1981), p.37.

ſ CBM papers, C.10.5.

** See illustration no.13: Mills's false passport in the name of Cyril Brook.

Mills was also provided with a false National Registration Identity Card in the name of Cyril Brook.[*] Surprisingly, his address was given as 1 Dorset Square, which a good London street directory would have identified as the headquarters of Bertram Mills Circus.

Mills arrived in Portugal too late to meet Jebsen. At the time, MI5 believed he had just been transferred to the new offensive on the Eastern Front. It seems more likely, however, that he had been recalled to Germany to be questioned by the Gestapo about his involvement in currency speculation. Later, Jebsen returned to Lisbon – still, MI5 believed, 'in fear of the Gestapo'. In September 1943, after Mills had moved to Canada, Jebsen was recruited as a double agent and, B1a reported, 'gave us much useful information'.[†]

In June 1941, however, believing Jebsen to have been transferred to the Eastern Front because of suspicions about his pro-British sympathies, Mills was relieved that he had arrived in Lisbon too late to meet him: 'I have always felt this was fortunate as if Jebsen had joined us his doing so would have blown TRICYCLE and any other agents in Britain whom he knew and that was likely to mean [double] agents whom we controlled.'[‡]

Though Mills failed to meet Jebsen, his visit to Lisbon unexpectedly marked an important step towards the recruitment of the man who proved to be the most important British double agent of the war: Juan Pujol García, a former Catalan chicken farmer, whose experience of the Spanish Civil War had left him with a loathing of both fascism and communism.[§] He was also, as Mills later told him, 'a great actor'.

Pujol first offered his services as a spy to the MI6 station in Madrid in January 1941 but, as Mills discovered during his trip to Lisbon, was

[*]   See illustration no.14: National Registration Identity Card in the name of Cyril Brook.
[†]   Masterman, *The Double-Cross System*, p.153.
[‡]   CBM papers.
[§]   Pujol and West, *Operation GARBO*, p.59.

turned down. He then approached the Abwehr, told them that he was travelling to England, was taken on as Agent ARABEL and given $3,000 to fund his travels, along with a bottle of secret ink and codes to use in his reports. From the outset, Pujol intended to damage German operations by sending bogus reports on the British war effort. He installed himself in a small hotel in the centre of Lisbon, from where, claiming to be in England, he despatched to the Abwehr numerous disinformation on non-existent British troop and naval movements, spiced with details of 'drunken orgies and slack morals at amusement centres' in Liverpool and the surprising revelation that Glasgow dockworkers would 'do anything for a litre of wine'. By February 1942, MI6 Section V (counter-espionage) had identified Pujol as the author of these colourful reports, which were decrypted by Bletchley Park. A month later, despite rejecting his earlier approach, they recruited him as a double agent codenamed BOVRIL.*

In March 1942, Felix Cowgill, head of MI6 Section V (counter-intelligence), told Guy Liddell that he proposed to bring Pujol to London to be debriefed at MI6 headquarters but wanted a guarantee that MI5 would then allow Pujol to return to Lisbon and be run there by MI6. Liddell was outraged:

> [Cowgill] did not wish to give [Pujol] up or to allow us to have access to him even though in all our interests it might be better that he should remain here [in Britain]. Fundamentally, his attitude is 'I do not see why I should get agents and then have them pinched by you.' The whole thing is so narrow and petty that it really makes me furious.†

---

*   , *British Intelligence in the Second World War*, vol.5: *Strategic Deception* (London: HMSO, 1990), pp.18–19. The fullest accounts of GARBO's extraordinary career are: Pujol and West, *Operation GARBO*; and Mark Seaman (ed.), *GARBO: The Spy Who Saved D-Day* (London: PRO Publications, 2004).

†   Guy Liddell diary, 26 March 1942.

Kim Philby, who worked under Cowgill in Section V, later wrote derisively: 'His intellectual endowment was slender. As an intelligence officer, he was inhibited by lack of imagination, inattention to detail and sheer ignorance of the world we were fighting in.'[*]

The far abler Liddell won the interdepartmental battle with Cowgill. Since Pujol's reports to the Abwehr claimed that he and his mythical agent network were based in Britain, it made more sense for him to be run by MI5 in London, with Mills as his case officer, than by MI6 in Lisbon.

Pujol later recalled arriving at the flying boat terminal at Mount Batten, Plymouth, on 25 April 1942:

> My first recollection of England ... as I walked down the steps of the plane, was of the terrible cold – cold outside and icy fear inside. At the bottom of the steps stood two officers from MI5, who would shape my destiny. The one who introduced himself as Mr Grey didn't speak a word of Spanish; I didn't say anything to him in my faltering English. The other, Tomás Harris, whom everyone called Tommy, spoke perfect Spanish.[†]

'Mr Grey' was Pujol's case officer, Cyril Mills of B1a. At Mills's request, 'Tommy' Harris, the bilingual son of an English father and Spanish mother who had been recruited in 1941 by B1g (Spanish counter-espionage), acted as translator.

Harris was a wealthy London art dealer, artist and socialite, recommended to MI5 early in 1941 by Anthony Blunt, with whom he shared interests in the arts. Throughout the war, Harris and his wife kept open house at their luxurious Mayfair home in Chesterfield

---

[*] Philby, *My Silent War*, pp.54–5.
[†] Pujol and West, *Operation GARBO*, p.84.

Gardens, with generous supplies (despite wartime rationing) of champagne and canapés, for friends in the intelligence and art worlds. Regular guests from MI5 included Dick White, Guy Liddell, Anthony Blunt, Victor Rothschild and – almost certainly – Cyril Mills, until he left for Canada at the end of the year. Guy Burgess, who shared a flat with Blunt, and his friend Kim Philby[*] from MI6, also came frequently. Philby later recalled his 'close and most highly prized friendship with Tommy Harris', praising him and his wife as 'inspired cooks': 'He lived surrounded by his art treasures in an atmosphere of haute cuisine and grand vin. He maintained that no really good table could be spoiled by wine stains.'[†] Harris's friendship with three leading Soviet spies – Blunt, Burgess and Philby – did not impair, though it adds piquancy to, his operational effectiveness in MI5.[‡] For a time, it seriously confused Soviet intelligence, which in the middle of the war bizarrely concluded that Blunt, Burgess and Philby were double agents working for the British.[§]

* * *

On 25 April 1942, the day after Pujol landed at Plymouth, Mills began debriefing him, with Harris as translator, at a semi-detached, late Victorian MI5 safe house at 35 Crespigny Road, Hendon, NW4, similar in appearance to many others in the area. MI5 provided a discreet housekeeper, Mrs Titoff, and, a week later, brought Pujol's wife Araceli and son Juan to live with him. For security reasons, Araceli was forbidden to make contact with the Spanish community

---

[*] Mills later recalled discussing the GARBO case with Philby, then deputy head of MI6 Section V (counter-espionage); Mills to Nigel West, 19 November 1984, CBM papers.

[†] Philby, *My Silent War*, pp.31–2, 47.

[‡] Harris's friendship with Blunt, Burgess and Philby led later to an investigation which uncovered no evidence of his own involvement in Soviet espionage.

[§] Andrew and Mitrokhin, *The Mitrokhin Archive*, pp.157–8.

in London but, probably on Mills's initiative, was provided with a nanny to help look after Juan. The debriefing continued every day until 11 May with a break on Tuesday 5 May.[*]

Pujol struck Mills as 'extremely clever', as well as brave and committed to the Allied cause. Masterman believed he was 'something of a genius'.[†] Mills was particularly impressed by Pujol's success in persuading the Abwehr, even before his actual arrival in England, that he had a network of three agents reporting to him from different parts of Britain. They were all figments of Pujol's fertile imagination, as were two couriers whom he claimed to use to send bogus intelligence to the Abwehr station in Lisbon. Mills decided, however, that one of the agents invented by Pujol, William Gerbers, supposedly a Liverpool businessman, had to be disposed of. Ships were assembling in the Mersey for an Allied invasion of North Africa. Mills realised that, after the invasion began, the Abwehr would find it very suspicious that Gerbers had sent no report of a task force easily visible in the Mersey. To pre-empt such suspicions, Mills instructed Pujol, first, to report that Gerbers had become seriously ill, then, to send a newspaper cutting of his bogus death notice, which B1a had placed in the *Liverpool Echo*. The Abwehr replied with a letter of condolence.[‡]

Mills changed Pujol's codename from BOVRIL to GARBO as a tribute to his star quality – he regarded Greta Garbo as the greatest film star of the era. His choice of codename was intended as a secret tribute to her as well as to Pujol. Her 1941 Hollywood film, *Two-Faced Woman*, was a flop – because of the direction rather than her acting. The film turned out to be her last. In 1942 her contract with MGM was cancelled by mutual consent. To the dismay of Cyril

---

[*]　Mills recorded the dates in his diary; Mills to Nigel West, 19 November 1984, CBM papers.

[†]　Masterman, *The Double-Cross System*, p.142.

[‡]　CBM papers.

Mills and Greta Garbo's many other fans, she spent the rest of her life as a semi-recluse.

Mills's papers reveal that in 1942 he personally devised an operation codenamed DREAM to persuade the Abwehr to deliver $30,000 to Pujol, double-agent GARBO, via a pro-German diplomat at the Spanish embassy in London, which had been successfully penetrated by MI5. But for Mills's persistence, Operation DREAM would never have gone ahead:

> When I produced Plan DREAM it had the enthusiastic support of TAR but J.C. [Masterman] said it was madness and would undo all we had done already, and destroy all possibility of doing anything useful in future.
>
> TAR dug his feet in and said I should show [Plan DREAM] to Guy Liddell and Dick White, which I did and both gave their approval, but with the condition that I, having produced it, should have to carry it through. The result was that we took several thousand dollars from the enemy and that money made my agent GARBO a paymaster of other [double] agents.[*]

It was probably during DREAM that Mills worked most closely with Anthony Blunt, the B Branch officer most actively concerned with the penetration of neutral embassies, particularly those most likely to assist the enemy. As Blunt informed his Soviet intelligence case officer, MI5's best agent in the Spanish embassy was a secretary, codenamed DUCK, who 'gets us cipher tape, clear versions of cipher telegrams, drafts of the ambassador's reports, private letters, notes on dinner parties and visitors, and general gossip about members of

---

[*] Mills to Annie Luke (widow of B1a officer Billy Luke), 8 June 1990; CBM papers.

the embassy.'* In January 1942,[†] and on at least two subsequent occasions,[‡] DUCK was able to walk out of the embassy with a shopping
bag containing the current Spanish diplomatic cipher tape to hand
over to an MI5 car waiting around the corner. 'Most fortunately for
us,' noted a post-war MI5 report, 'the security arrangements in the
Embassy were nil.'[§]

Because Operation DREAM involved illegal intrusion of the
Spanish embassy, Sir David Petrie decided that it would have to
be cleared with the head of the Security Executive,[⁋] Alfred Duff
Cooper. He was a prominent Conservative politician who was also
a long-standing circus enthusiast and before the war was regularly
invited to the Bertram Mills pre-Christmas lunches at Olympia. To
seek Duff Cooper's approval for DREAM, Mills was taken to his
office by Petrie's personal assistant, Richard Butler:

Having been introduced, I was asked to give details of the Plan
but within a couple of minutes I realised that Duff Cooper was
sound asleep so I asked Richard in sign language what I should
do and he said I should continue but make it short. Three or
four minutes later I came to the end and had a fit of coughing to
awaken the Minister who, as soon as he realised I had finished,
said that he was satisfied that we should go ahead with our Plan
... I am sure he never had the slightest idea what it was about but

---

*   Nigel West and Oleg Tsarev, *Crown Jewels: The British Secrets at the heart of the KGB Archives* (London: HarperCollins, 1998), p.141.
†   Guy Liddell diary, 1 January 1942.
‡   Churchill was informed by a report on 1 June 1943: 'We will now be able to read for several months the cipher telegrams sent from Madrid to the Spanish Embassy here as, through one of our agents in the Spanish Embassy here, we have for the third time, extracted, photographed and replaced the most secret diplomatic cipher tape used in Spanish official telegrams.' Third Report on Activities of Security Service, 1 June 1943. Andrew, *Defence of the Realm*, p.261 and note 110.
§   'The Story of B.1.g', [1945]; Andrew, *Defence of the Realm*, p.261.
⁋   The Security Executive was set up by Churchill in 1940 to iron out what he called the 'overlaps and underlaps' between the various agencies dealing with counter-espionage and counter-subversion'.

he had been told it had the approval of my Director General and that was good enough for him.[*]

Duff Cooper's somnolence was due to alcohol.[†] His son, John Julius Norwich, said of him: 'To those few who were immune to his intelligence and his charm he was a drinker, gambler and a shameless pursuer of beautiful women.'[‡]

Operation DREAM was a complete success. The pro-German press attaché at the Spanish embassy in London, Ángel Alcázar de Velasco, was easily deceived, handing over $30,000 sent to him by the Abwehr to a man who he believed was Pujol, but in reality was a member of MI5 selected by Mills to impersonate Pujol:

> As GARBO [Pujol] was not known to the diplomat it was quite safe for us to send someone to represent him. This money not only enabled GARBO to increase the size of his network and pay all his notional agents properly but on one or two occasions GARBO became the paymaster of other [fictional Abwehr] agents who we controlled although they were not connected with GARBO in any way.[§]

GARBO's neighbours in Crespigny Road accepted the cover story devised by Mills that he was a refugee from Franco's Spain who travelled on the Tube each day from Hendon to central London to work as a translator for the BBC. In reality, he spent every day with Mills as his case officer at a small office in Jermyn Street, close to MI5's

---

[*] Mills, untitled confidential memoir on his intelligence career (undated), p29; CBM papers.

[†] As he later admitted in his memoirs *Old Men Forget*.

[‡] These failings, however, did not prevent him becoming a successful Cabinet minister and (in the opinion of the Quai d'Orsay as well as the Foreign Office) at least an equally successful ambassador to France from 1944 to 1947. John Julius Norwich (ed.), *The Duff Cooper Diaries 1915–1951* (London: Phoenix, 2006), introduction.

[§] CBM papers.

London HQ in St James's Street, working on what became the most influential disinformation in the history of the Double-Cross System. Tommy Harris, who had no previous experience of double agents, had an increasing role in devising, as well as translating into Spanish the disinformation GARBO was to send to his Abwehr controller.

* * *

GARBO's imaginary agents became the basis for the largest bogus network in intelligence history, which eventually totalled twenty-seven members, all invented by GARBO, Mills and Harris. In Britain, they included a US Army sergeant, a Venezuelan living in Glasgow and a Welsh nationalist in Swansea leading a group of fascists called the 'Brothers of the Aryan World Order' (one of them impersonated by Mills). Other sub-agents were supposedly stationed as far afield as North America and Ceylon (now Sri Lanka).* The bogus GARBO agent network made the biggest strategic deception in the history of warfare possible.

Strategic deception was central to the first major Allied offensive of the war: Operation TORCH, the invasion of French North Africa, for which planning began in July 1942.† Two major British deception operations, OVERTHROW and SOLO I, successfully persuaded the Germans that Allied preparations for landings in, respectively, northern France and Norway but not North Africa were at an advanced stage.‡ As case officer for GARBO, the main

---

* 'THE GARBO NETWORK', TNA WO 208/4374.
† The latest study of Operation TORCH, which makes innovative use of French sources, is Porch, *Defeat and Division*, ch.10.
‡ Howard, *British Intelligence in the Second World War*, vol.5, pp.55–63. Before being duped by British deception operations, the Abwehr had correctly forecast an Allied landing in Morocco (though not Algeria and Tunisia, where there were also landings) between 15 October and 15 November 1942. 'But its chief, Admiral Wilhelm Canaris, could convince no one, least of all Hitler, that the Anglo-Americans had the ability to carry out such ambitious plans.' Porch, *Defeat and Division*, p.654, n.17.

source of the most inventive disinformation, Mills played a key role. GARBO sent the Abwehr numerous bogus reports from the fictional sub-agents invented by himself, Mills and Harris. Sub-agents in Scotland reported on mountain warfare training for Canadian, Scottish and Norwegian troops which pointed to preparations for an invasion of Norway. GARBO's contacts in the Ministry of Information were said to have revealed that officially inspired rumours of an expedition to Dakar were intended to distract attention from plans for an attack elsewhere, possibly in Norway or France. On 29 October, however, in order to maintain his credibility, GARBO reported, correctly, that a convoy had just set sail from the Clyde – but not that it was headed for North Africa.

A fortnight earlier, when Mills was Night Duty Officer at MI5's London office in St James's Street,

...a senior Police Officer came on the phone via the War Office to say that one of his men had picked up a number of maps on the main road near Beaconsfield and he did not want to describe them in detail on an open telephone. However, with a certain amount of double talk I realised that anything to do with a French coast and printed in English must mean North Africa and the area where the TORCH landings were going to take place.

There followed a frantic overnight search of the main road from London to Oxford, as well as the route from the government map office in Witney. It was discovered that the TORCH operation maps found scattered on a main road were copies given to the Americans which had fallen from the back of an open US army truck.

I think we recovered all [the maps] that were lost by about 9 a.m. and it was decided at a high level that the TORCH Operation was not blown. I was told that the Americans responsible were given a severe talking-to.[*]

To strengthen GARBO's credibility with the Abwehr after his initial reports that the Allied invasion was most likely to come in Norway or France, he sent a last-minute warning on 1 November that the latest intelligence from his (fictional) agent in the Ministry of Information pointed instead to an Allied invasion of French North Africa. Mills and B1a, however, arranged for the letters containing these reports to be delayed in the post. They did not reach GARBO's case officer in Lisbon until 7 November, a few hours before the Allied landings and after the invasion force had already been detected by the Germans. It did not occur to the Abwehr to either blame GARBO for the postal delay or to suspect the involvement of MI5. 'Your last reports are all magnificent,' they told GARBO, 'but we are very sorry they arrived late.'[†]

GARBO's productivity in the area of disinformation was extraordinary. During the last three years of the war, in addition to shorter radio messages, he and his case officers jointly composed 315 intelligence reports in secret writing, each averaging about 2,000 words and sent to an Abwehr cover address in Lisbon. German decrypts from Bletchley Park provided regular proof of how effective GARBO's disinformation was.

As a lifelong Churchill loyalist, well aware that Churchill attached more importance to intelligence than any previous Prime Minister, it must have struck Mills as extraordinary – though he did not put his views on paper – that during GARBO's first year as a double agent, Churchill was told nothing about him. MI5 files

---

[*]   CBM papers.
[†]   Howard, *British Intelligence in the Second World War*, vol.5, pp.62–3.

reveal that, despite the Prime Minister's daily diet of ULTRA decrypts, he was not informed of the Double-Cross System or any of the double agents. Unlike Sir Stewart Menzies, Chief of MI6, his MI5 counterpart, Sir David Petrie, kept his distance from the Prime Minister. Petrie was fearful that Churchill would be so excited by Double-Cross that he would try to interfere in the running of deceptions and double agents.

In March 1943, however, Petrie finally agreed that the Prime Minister could no longer be kept in the dark. For the first monthly Report on Activities of Security Service submitted to Churchill on 26 March 1943,* various sections of MI5 produced drafts that totalled almost sixteen single-spaced typed pages. Anthony Blunt prepared a précis and the final draft of about two-and-a-half pages was produced in collaboration between him and Dick White.† The first monthly report began with this summary of counter-espionage successes since the outbreak of war:

> In all 126 spies have fallen into our hands. Of these eighteen gave themselves up voluntarily; twenty-four have been found amenable and are now being used as double-cross agents. Twenty-eight have been detained at overseas stations, and eight were arrested on the high seas. In addition twelve real, and seven imaginary persons have been foisted upon the enemy as double-cross spies. Thirteen spies have been executed, and a fourteenth is under trial.

The report was an instant success with the Prime Minister.‡ Church-

---

* Arrangements were made for this and subsequent reports to be returned to the Security Service after Churchill had read them. ADB1 (White) to DG through DB, 26 March 1943, TNA KV 4/83.

† ADB1 (White) to DG through DB, 26 March 1943, TNA KV 4/83.

‡ Duff Cooper to Guy Liddell, 2 April 1943, TNA KV 4/83. Guy Liddell Diary, 3 April 1943.

ill wrote on it in red ink: 'deeply interesting'.[*] Henceforth, noted Petrie, Churchill 'took a sustained personal interest in our work'.[†]

Since Blunt continued to draft monthly reports to Churchill for the remainder of the war,[‡] it is highly probable that they went to Soviet intelligence as well – and quite possibly to Stalin personally.[§] Indeed, Moscow may well have also received the longer version before it was condensed by Blunt and thus been informed in even greater detail than Churchill on the astonishing achievements of the Double-Cross System – including the identities of Mills and the other B1a officers who had key roles in it.

The problem was that the great conspiracy theorist in the Kremlin, and his intelligence chiefs, suspected that their British agents often tried to deceive them. The Cambridge Five (Anthony Blunt, Guy Burgess, John Cairncross, Donald Maclean and Kim Philby), later acknowledged as probably the ablest group of foreign agents in KGB history, aroused deep suspicion by failing to provide any evidence of the non-existent British intelligence operations against the Soviet Union which Stalin and the Centre were convinced must be taking place. The Centre's belief that the Five were double agents was reinforced by what Blunt told his case officer about the extraordinary success of MI5's double agents against Germany. The Double-Cross System, in which Mills played a major role, was, it believed, directed against Russia as well as Germany. 'Our task', the Centre instructed its London resident, Anatoly Gorsky, 'is to

---

[*]   'Report on Activities of Security Service', with minute by Churchill of 2 April 1944, TNA KV 4/83. This report, like its successors, was returned to MI5 after being read by Churchill.

[†]   Petrie to T. L. Rowan (No.10), 23 January 1946; Andrew, *Defence of the Realm*, p.292.

[‡]   See Blunt (B1b) to DB, 13 July 1945, TNA KV 4/83.

[§]   Few details are available of how many classified British documents obtained by Soviet intelligence were passed to Stalin personally. It is known, however, that in 1935 these included over one hundred Foreign Office reports; Christopher Andrew and Julie Elkner, 'Stalin and Foreign Policy', in Harold Shukman (ed.), *Redefining Stalinism* (London: Frank Cass, 2003). The MI5 monthly reports to Churchill would probably have been of even greater interest to Stalin.

understand what disinformation our [British] rivals are planting on us.'*

In October 1942, Stalin wrote to Ivan Maisky, the Soviet ambassador in London: 'All of us in Moscow have gained the impression that Churchill is aiming at the defeat of the USSR, in order then to come to terms with the Germany of Hitler or [his predecessor] Brüning at our expense.' A year later, the Centre informed the London residency that it was now clear the Five were double agents. While pretending to work for Moscow, they were operating under orders from MI5 and MI6.† Not until 1944 did the Centre finally grasp the simple truth that the Cambridge Five were loyal and committed Soviet agents.

---

*   Andrew, *Defence of the Realm*, p.280 It is unfair to blame suspicions of the Five on personal failings of the head of the Centre's British desk, Zoya Rybkina. Her paranoid tendencies were widely shared.
†   Andrew and Mitrokhin, *Mitrokhin Archive*, pp.157–8.

CHAPTER 6

'A MAN CALLED INTREPID' AND THE SPECIAL RELATIONSHIP

Cyril Mills's first experience of an Anglo-American 'special re-lationship' (a phrase invented by Churchill in 1943)* was at the circus. At New York Horse Shows before the First World War, his father Bertram became friends with John Ringling, head of the world-famous US Ringling Bros. and Barnum & Bailey Circus, which claimed to be 'The Greatest Show on Earth'. When Bertram Mill agreed to arrange for a circus to perform at Olympia in 1920, he had originally intended Ringling to bring his circus across the Atlantic. Ringling agreed to do so but then had to refuse because of the post-war shortage of transat-lantic shipping, leading Bertram to found a circus of his own.†

Over the next two years, while Cyril was still an undergraduate at Cambridge, his father took him to the United States to see 'all the

---

* David B. Woolner, 'Churchill, the English-Speaking Peoples and the "Special Relationship"', in Allen Packwood (ed.), *The Cambridge Companion to Winston Churchill* (Cambridge: Cambridge University Press, 2023), p.263. Churchill first used the phrase 'special relationship' in public during his famous 'Iron Curtain' speech in Fulton, Missouri, in 1946.

† Mills, *Bertram Mills Circus*, p.15. Britain had lost 40 per cent of its merchant navy during the war. Bertram Mills later concluded that Ringling's two-ring circus would in any case have been difficult to fit into the single ring at Olympia.

big circuses' and book three expensive acts, which involved paying for return transport across the Atlantic. By the mid-1920s, Cyril was crossing the Atlantic 'every year or two' to sign more American acts. Like his father, he became a personal friend of John Ringling, who was also president of a railroad company. On visits to the United States, Cyril Mills travelled by train in Ringling's private coach with the circus:

> John had discovered that the president of an American railroad was, as a matter of courtesy, allowed to have his private coach hauled … on any railroad in the States and had provided himself with a magnificent affair with kitchen, complete with chef, sitting and dining rooms, four or five bedrooms and a bathroom.[*]

After John Ringling's death in 1936, Mills struck up another special relationship with his extrovert nephew and successor, John Ringling North.

The United States led the world in aerial 'thrill acts'. Some were even too thrilling for the daring Mills to try on British circus audiences:

> The sky is the limit for every thrill act and it is only reached when there is no more room for the guy wires which support the rigging. On one occasion I saw a couple do a jitterbug dance on a platform two feet square on top of a steel pole 120 feet high swaying in the wind. The first few seconds were as much as I could stomach and I did not book the act.[†]

Mills had the opportunity to bring the 'Queen of the Air', Lillian

---

[*] Mills was uncertain whether to believe the claim that John Ringling travelled by rail free of charge: 'I should hate to have to vouch for the story.' Mills, *Bertram Mills Circus*, p.62.
[†] Mills, *Bertram Mills Circus*, pp.89–90.

Leitzel, Ringling Bros. and Barnum & Bailey's greatest star, to Olympia, but decided not to offer her a contract because her act was too dangerous. Without a safety net, the German-born Leitzel, only 4 feet 9 inches tall, performed aerial acrobatics from rings and ropes 50 feet above the audience that no other circus 'aerialist' could emulate. She was fatally injured in 1931 when she fell to the floor while performing at a Copenhagen music hall.[*]

Taking risks was central to Mills's success both in managing Britain's leading pre-war circus and in helping to run the most successful double agents of the Second World War. But he was also good at risk management, refusing to take on acts as dangerous as Leitzel's or engage in wartime deceptions which risked arousing the suspicions of the Abwehr.[†]

Though Mills avoided dangerous transatlantic aerial 'thrill acts', Ringling Bros. and Barnum & Bailey Circus provided some of Bertram Mills's best-publicised pre-war wild animal acts: among them, in 1937, 'King Tuffy, the first wire-walking lion.'[‡] On the eve of war, 'King Tuffy' was followed across the Atlantic by what Mills called 'one of the most interesting side shows we ever had' in the circus menagerie: Gargantua, a 'giant gorilla'.

> Gargantua was a vegetarian and treated a case of oranges like the hors d'oeuvre to a meal, and the cost of feeding him was enormous, but it was all worth it for nobody had ever seen such a large gorilla in captivity and [anyone] who had seen one in the jungle had not lived to tell the tale ... He loved to have things to play with, but

---

[*] Kate Holmes, 'Aerial Performance', in Arrighi and Davis, *The Cambridge Companion to the Circus*, pp.xxvi, 160–61. Burt Kearns, 'The Queen of the Air Meets the Homicidal Young Man on the Flying Trapeze', 22 January 2020; https://pleasekillme.com/lillian-leitzel/

[†] See below, pp.177–8.

[‡] Mills, *Bertram Mills Circus*, p.87.

destroyed everything we gave him in seconds until he was given a giant motor lorry tyre; he could not destroy this quickly, although he crushed and twisted it as though it were kitchen paper.[*]

Circus performances continued in the United States throughout the Second World War. Convinced of their importance to public morale, President Roosevelt granted Ringling Bros. and Barnum & Bailey Circus exemption from wartime restrictions on civilian rail travel. During his first visit to New York on MI5 business in 1943, Mills made time to watch one of their performances in Madison Square Garden[†] – without revealing to John Ringling North who he was now working for.

* * *

In defiance of US neutrality, the Anglo-American intelligence 'special relationship' secretly started well before America entered the war in December 1941. Mills and his MI5 colleagues believed that both ULTRA and the Double-Cross System could only achieve their full potential in secret partnership with the United States.

Like pre-war cooperation between Bertram Mills Circus and Ringling Bros. and Barnum & Bailey's Circus, the wartime intelligence partnership grew from personal contacts. The origins of the special relationship owed much to William ('Little Bill') Stephenson. A Canadian First World War fighter ace who had become a millionaire businessman, Stephenson began part-time work for MI6 in the summer of 1939, and was appointed head of the MI6 New York

---

[*]   Ibid., p.169. Henry Ringling North with Alden Hatch, *The Circus Kings: Our Ringling Family Story* (London: Red Kestrel Books, 2019), ch.21. Mills was well known for insisting on high standards of care for his circus animals. Keeping Gargantua permanently imprisoned in a cage (as in the Ringling Bros. and Barnum & Bailey Circus) fell far short of these standards.

[†]   Mills, *Bertram Mills Circus*, p.65.

station in June 1940 – a few weeks before Mills joined MI5. To promote secret intelligence exchange with the United States, Stephenson set up British Security Coordination (BSC) on the thirty-fifth
and thirty-sixth floors of the International Building in Rockefeller
Center on New York's Fifth Avenue. Before Pearl Harbor, BSC included officers from MI6, MI5 and the Special Operations Executive
(SOE), representing all three agencies in the United States.

Like Churchill (and Mills), Stephenson was convinced that Britain could not win unless the United States entered the war. Both
Congress and public opinion, however, were opposed to doing so.
According to a Gallup poll in July 1940, only 7.7 per cent of Americans supported US intervention. Stephenson thus embarked on
a series of increasingly unscrupulous covert influence operations
designed to overcome 'isolationist' opposition. Unless the public
mood changed, President Roosevelt, though offering other support,
seemed likely to stick to the promise he made in October 1940 not
to send US soldiers 'into any foreign wars'.*

Mills believed that Stephenson was the wrong man to promote
the Special Relationship. At the end of the war, he wrote in a top-
secret MI5 report:

> The whole B.S.C. episode has been a tragic one since the day it was
> decided to appoint a Canadian to the senior position in what was
> essentially a United Kingdom organisation. At the time it may
> have been thought that such a choice would act favourably for us
> since Canadians are far more capable of seeing the US point of
> view. In fact the American reaction to the choice was rather one
> of astonishment that no suitable United Kingdom subject could

---

* Woolner, 'Churchill, the English-Speaking Peoples and the "Special Relationship."'

be found for the post. In fact it should have been obvious that a post of this kind called for the highest possible qualifications and required a man whose diplomacy was of the highest order. Furthermore it required a man whose sole interests were, and always had been, those of His Majesty's Government, and of whom it could never be hinted, however unjustly, that post-war international commercial interests might creep into the picture.[*]

Even Mills, however, never quite realised to what extent 'Little Bill' had created a bogus identity. Stephenson was probably the only person in BSC who knew that he had been born William Stanger. When he was four, his father, an impoverished labourer in Winnipeg, died from muscular dystrophy. His mother, a first-generation Icelandic immigrant, then had him adopted by another Icelandic family and left Winnipeg. Stephenson never saw her again.[†] Ashamed of his humble origins and probably traumatised by the loss of both parents in early childhood, Stephenson later created a bogus family tree in which his father was a Scottish sawmill owner 'of independent means'. Though his education had ended in elementary school at the age of twelve, Stephenson claimed to be a graduate of Exeter College, Oxford. There is no doubt, however, about Stephenson's bravery as a First World War Canadian pilot and his meteoric success as a businessman in interwar Britain. Within two years of arriving in London as a bankrupt in 1922, he was hailed by the *Daily Mail* as 'a leader of industry', as well as 'a brilliant scientist'.[‡]

---

[*]   Mills, 'Report on M.I.5 Representation in Canada and Liaison with the Federal Bureau of Investigation 1942–1945'; CBM papers.

[†]   Stephenson was an Anglicised version of Stefánsson, the name of the family that adopted him. His own family origins were revealed (but not widely publicised) in 1980 by the Icelandic-Canadian Dr George Johnson, former Minister of Health and Education in the Manitoba provincial government. Nicholas Shakespeare, *Ian Fleming: The Complete Man* (London: Harvill Secker, 2023), p.251.

[‡]   Ibid., pp.251–3.

Mills rightly believed that much of Stephenson's wartime influence as head of BSC derived from his friendship with the American First World War hero, Wall Street lawyer and fellow millionaire General William ('Big Bill') Donovan, who became the President's chief foreign intelligence adviser. In 1942, Roosevelt made Donovan head of the first civilian US foreign intelligence agency, the Office of Strategic Services (OSS). Stephenson's close relationship with Donovan, however, earned him the growing enmity of J. Edgar Hoover, Director of the Federal Bureau of Investigation (FBI) from 1924 until his death in 1972 – the longest tenure by any head of a government department or agency in US history. Mills later told his family: 'What has to be remembered is that whereas Hoover was probably the best policeman the world ever produced, neither he nor any of his people [at the outbreak of war] had any knowledge or experience of the enemy's intelligence service and he tended to regard top-class agents as common criminals…'*

Mills wrote in an MI5 report at the end of the war:

…the F.B.I., and probably Mr. Hoover in particular, has always resented the close association between B.S.C. and Colonel Donovan's O.S.S. deeply. O.S.S. has been guilty of some very stupid actions, but Colonel Donovan's ambition knows no limit and he possessed the valuable asset of being extremely close to the … President. Whilst it is not known to be the case it is suspected that Mr. Hoover hoped at one time to be given the task of organising a service to fulfil the functions of O.S.S. How well he would have been fitted for such work is a matter of speculation, but on his previous form it is safe to say that he would probably have recruited

---

* Mills, untitled confidential memoir on his intelligence career (undated), p.29; CBM papers.

more suitable types than some of the incompetent idiots who quickly found their way into important positions in O.S.S.[*]

Mainly because of 'Colonel' Donovan's close friendship with Stephenson, Mills's view of him and OSS was, uncharacteristically, ungenerous. Though Donovan's rank in the First World War had been Colonel, he was promoted to General in the Second (Brigadier-General in 1943, Major-General in 1944). He was awarded the Medal of Honor, the Distinguished Service Cross, the Distinguished Service Medal and the National Security Medal: no one else received all four. Churchill was much impressed by him, cabling Roosevelt early in 1941 to thank him for the 'magnificent work' done by Donovan during his recent tour of the Mediterranean and Middle East: 'He has carried with him throughout an animating, heart-warming flame.'[†]

Mills, however, correctly concluded that Stephenson was giving London a wildly exaggerated assessment of his own influence in Washington. Churchill's intelligence aide, Desmond Morton, was among those who were taken in:

[A] most secret fact of which the Prime Minister is aware, but not all the other persons concerned, is that to all intents and purposes U.S. Security is being run for them at the President's request by the British. A British officer [Stephenson] sits in Washington with Mr. Edgar Hoover and General Bill Donovan for this purpose and reports regularly to the President. It is of course essential that this fact should not be known in view of the furious uproar it would cause if known to the Isolationists.[‡]

---

[*] Mills, 'Report on M.I.5 Representation in Canada and Liaison with the Federal Bureau of Investigation 1942–1945'; CBM papers.

[†] Andrew, *For the President's Eyes Only*, pp.94–7.

[‡] Ibid., p.101.

Others in the British intelligence community who took at least some of Stephenson's boasts seriously before Pearl Harbor included the Director of Naval Intelligence (DNI), Admiral John Godfrey and his assistant, Lieutenant Commander Ian Fleming, future creator of the world's most famous fictional spy. 'How much I admire the wonderful set-up you have achieved in New York,' Godfrey wrote to Stephenson after visiting BSC in May 1941. '...I consider it beyond praise.' Stephenson, Fleming wrote later, had 'a magnetic personality and the quality of making anyone ready to follow him to the ends of the earth'. While watching 'Little Bill' mix 'the most powerful martinis in America', Fleming noted that they were 'shaken, not stirred' – a phrase later appropriated by James Bond.*

Mills knew and liked Fleming personally, but strongly disagreed with his assessment of 'Little Bill'. Fleming's admiration for Stephenson remained undimmed. In 1962, he wrote: 'James Bond is a highly romanticised version of a true spy. The real thing is ... William Stephenson.'†

* * *

Despite Mills's personal distrust of Stephenson, the two men had one unusual quality in common. Both knew more leading British entertainers than anyone else in MI5 or MI6. Though largely ignored in MI6's official history, its contact with the entertainment industry went back longer than MI5's. Before the First World War, the first Chief of MI6, Sir Mansfield Cumming, purchased disguises for his espionage missions from, and sometimes had himself made up by, the leading London theatrical costumier

---

* Andrew and Green, *Stars and Spies*, ch.12.
† Macintyre, *For Your Eyes Only*, p.44.

and wigmaker Willy Clarkson (telegraphic address: Wiggery, London), who supplied most London theatres. After war broke out, Cumming chose a number of leading theatricals as heads of MI6 stations abroad.[*]

Mills admired some of the equally successful entertainers who were persuaded to give their services to BSC in the Second World War. The most celebrated was Noël Coward, who recalled that at a meeting in New York in the summer of 1940, Stephenson 'gave me two strong Cuba Libres and waited politely for me to talk a great deal'. Coward then agreed to work for BSC. His proudest wartime achievement was the 1942 propaganda film *In Which We Serve*, which was inspired by the naval exploits of Lord Louis Mountbatten. As well as writing the script (with the close cooperation of Mountbatten), Coward was co-director with David Lean and played the 'Mountbatten' role of Captain Kinross. Cyril Mills regarded it as a masterpiece. The *New York Times* agreed: 'The great thing which Mr. Coward has accomplished in this film is a full and complete expression of national fortitude … Yes, this is truly a picture in which the British may take a wholesome pride and we may regard as an excellent expression of British strength.'[†]

Mills personally knew some other stars in the entertainment business who worked for Stephenson on BSC influence operations in the United States, among them the author Roald Dahl,[‡] whose later screenplays included the 1967 Bond movie *You Only Live Twice* and the 1968 film adaptation of Ian Fleming's most successful non-Bond novel, *Chitty Chitty Bang Bang*.

Both the most creative and most unscrupulous contributor to

---

[*] Andrew and Green, *Stars and Spies*, pp.162–6. See above, pp.6–8.

[†] nytimes.com/1942/12/24/archives/in-which-we-serve-depicting-cruel-realities-of-this-war-is.html.

[‡] Information from Christopher Mills.

BSC's influence operations aimed at bringing the United States into the war was Mills's Cambridge contemporary and star performer at the Cambridge Footlights, Eric Maschwitz. He and Mills had enthusiastically served together as special constables in London during the General Strike ('a little adventure', as Maschwitz remembered it). As well as working in BBC light entertainment between the wars, Maschwitz was among the most successful British lyricists of his generation, whose songs included 'These Foolish Things (Remind Me of You)' and 'A Nightingale Sang in Berkeley Square'. In 1939 he received an Oscar nomination for the screenplay of *Goodbye Mr Chips*. As head of BBC Light Entertainment, Maschwitz was involved in the first pre-war broadcasts of the Bertram Mills Circus.

Maschwitz's fame as a lyricist and his career in light entertainment, like Mills's role as Britain's leading circus director, provided wonderful intelligence cover. Unlike Mills, however, Maschwitz gave away the secret of his own extraordinary wartime operations in his memoirs, which were published in 1957[*] while he was head of BBC TV Light Entertainment – ironically, just as he was commissioning a new television series of Bertram Mills Circus.

While working for BSC early in the war, Maschwitz concluded that Stephenson was 'a genius' at devising influence operations to deceive the US public. The ingenuity of his own deception operations before Pearl Harbor is well illustrated by his use of the German-born celebrity astrologer, novelist and film scriptwriter Louis de Wohl.[†] Despite de Wohl's pretentiousness, some intelligence officers, Ian Fleming among them,[‡] were impressed by his (unfounded) claims that Hitler's strategy was influenced by astrology, as well

---

[*] Eric Maschwitz, *No Chip on My Shoulder* (London: Herbert Jenkins, 1957).
[†] MI5 report on de Wohl, 31 August 1940: TNA, KV 2/2821. The first volume of de Wohl's MI5 file, covering his early years in Britain, does not survive.
[‡] Lycett, *Ian Fleming*, p.134.

as by his ability to concoct doom-laden horoscopes for the Führer.[*] In May 1941, De Wohl was sent to the United States to conduct British Intelligence's first ever astrological propaganda campaign under the covert direction of Maschwitz in BSC. Though Maschwitz found him 'a right swindler', De Wohl's astrological disinformation campaign in the US appeared to be highly successful. In June 1941, the *New York Sun* ran a report headlined 'Seer Sees Plot to Kill Hitler'. According to an internal history of BSC:[†] 'From this triumphant beginning de Wohl went out on tour, and all the time, at public meetings and over the air, in private assemblies, in interviews, in widely syndicated articles and at an important convention of American astrologers, he declared that Hitler's doom was sealed.'[‡]

De Wohl's fraudulent horoscopes gave Maschwitz a taste for riskier methods of deceiving the American public. He complained to Stephenson that 'one thing we haven't got is a good forgery section' to manufacture bogus Nazi threats to the Americas. Stephenson agreed and made him head of a new BSC forgery section, 'Station M' (M for Maschwitz), in a Toronto suburb. His staff, Maschwitz later revealed in his memoirs, included 'two splendid ruffians who could reproduce faultlessly the imprint of any typewriter on earth. I controlled a chemical laboratory in one place, a photographic studio in another.'[§]

How much Mills knew about Station M's operations before Maschwitz published his memoirs is uncertain. But he was right to believe that Stephenson was taking unacceptable risks in his

---

[*] Paul Winter, 'Fathoming the Führer: British Intelligence, Adolf Hitler and the German High Command, 1939–1945', PhD thesis (University of Cambridge, 2009).

[†] The declassified BSC official history was published in 1998 with an introduction by Nigel West as *British Security Coordination: The Secret History of British Intelligence in the Americas* (London: St Ermin's Press).

[‡] *British Security Coordination*, pp.102–4. De Wohl returned to Britain early in 1942, following the US entry into the war.

[§] Eric Maschwitz, *No Chip on My Shoulder* (London: Herbert Jenkins, 1957). Andrew and Green, *Stars and Spies*, pp.283–4.

campaign to bring the United States into the war. Station M's most important – and risky – forgery was a map which appeared to reveal a secret Nazi master plan to take over South America. In October 1941 Stephenson sent Roosevelt, almost certainly via Donovan, a copy of the supposedly authentic map which, he claimed, had been obtained by British secret agents from a German diplomatic courier in Argentina. Both Donovan and the President were comprehensively deceived.

Roosevelt then made the forged map the centrepiece of his 'Navy and Total Defense Day' address, which was broadcast on 27 October:

> I have in my possession a secret map made in Germany by Hitler's government – by planners of the New World Order ... The geographical experts of Berlin have ruthlessly obliterated all the existing boundary lines; they have divided South America into five vassal states, bringing the whole continent under their domination. And they have also so arranged it that the territory of these new puppet states includes the Republic of Panama and our great life-line – the Panama Canal. This map, my friends, makes clear the Nazi design not only against South America but against the United States as well.[*]

The basis of Roosevelt's most outspoken attack on Nazi Germany before the Japanese attack on Pearl Harbor on 7 December 1941, three days before the US entered the war, was thus bogus intelligence foisted upon him by Maschwitz via Stephenson. Like the President, Donovan never realised he had been deceived.

Had Churchill been informed of BSC's plot to deceive the

---

[*] Andrew, *For the President's Eyes Only*, pp.102–3.

President, he would undoubtedly have forbidden it. But the Prime Minister was not told – probably the biggest act of British intelligence insubordination during the entire war – and seems never to have discovered it afterwards.

J. Edgar Hoover probably did learn of the BSC plot, as did Assistant Secretary of State for Latin American Affairs Adolf A. Berle. Early in 1942, he and Donovan had what Berle called 'no end of a row about BSC', which, Berle correctly believed, had been busy manufacturing disinformation 'to affect public opinion here': 'Though it is not possible to say so, Bill Donovan gets a good many of his ideas from the British.'* Neither Berle nor the FBI could publicly reveal that Stephenson had deceived President Roosevelt with forged documents before Pearl Harbor, because to do so would have given both the Germans and Japanese a major propaganda victory. With strong support from his friend Donovan, Stephenson remained in New York as head of BSC. Even Berle acknowledged Stephenson's immense personal charm. 'It was impossible', he said, 'not to like Bill Stephenson.'† Mills disagreed. Stephenson was the only wartime British intelligence officer whom he came to loathe.

* * *

Stephenson sometimes liked to give the impression that he had a 'licence to kill'. Grace Old, a BSC secretary, recalled a meeting at which someone suggested that an American merchant seaman who had been passing information to the Nazis should be 'dealt with': 'Stephenson took a pistol out, laid it purposely on the table and said, "I just did". Next, we read in the papers that the sailor had been

---

* Berle memo, 13 February 1942; Berle diary, Franklin D. Roosevelt Library, Hyde Park, NY.
† Andrew, *For the President's Eyes Only*, pp.128–30.

found shot dead. We assumed that Stephenson had done it, but we never heard anything more about it.'* For a few months in 1942 Mills was given a licence to kill some Abwehr agents.† Stephenson never was.

In the last resort, 'Little Bill' was able to remain at the head of BSC because he had the strong support of 'Big Bill' Donovan. Guy Liddell and MI5 had no say, though they suffered from Hoover's hostility to Stephenson. Mills later complained: 'While Stephenson represented us [in the US], the only information which we were given by the FBI was newspaper cuttings concerning espionage cases which had reached the stage of trial in public courts.'‡

BSC's influence, however, was on the wane. In October 1942, Menzies replied to Stephenson's request for more personnel with the unwelcome news that he was considering whether 'your already large staff should not be reduced rather than increased'. On 2 January 1943, Menzies bluntly instructed Stephenson 'to effect a 25% reduction in the executive staffs, and a 25% reduction in the clerical personnel' of the New York and Washington offices by 31 March. Stephenson complained of 'pettifogging charges based on malicious gossip which seemingly motivated misrepresentation of our activities' and warned that 'should B.S.C.'s position here become sufficiently weak then real danger' of gradual subordination of our established position in this ?entire hemisphere to [Hoover]'. Rather than risk subordination to Hoover, Menzies ceased to insist on drastic cuts to BSC, though a gradual reduction in Stephenson's staff continued.§

Hoover became increasingly outraged at Stephenson's attempts

---

*   Jimmy Burns, *A Faithful Spy: The Life and Times of an MI6 and MI5 Officer* (London: Chiselbury, 2023), pp.119–20.
†   See below, pp.124–7.
‡   CBM papers.
§   Jeffery, *MI6*, pp.451–3.

to block direct FBI access to MI5 with whom, concludes the FBI historian Raymond Batvinis, 'there was much to share'. In November 1942, without prior consultation, Hoover sent Special Agent Arthur Thurston to London as his liaison officer with MI5 and MI6. On 7 December 1942, the first anniversary of Pearl Harbor, Thurston had a dramatic meeting with Menzies at MI6 headquarters. The FBI, he announced, had broken off relations with BSC in New York. Stephenson had 'damaged himself irreparably and would never be able to enjoy the Bureau's confidence again'.*

Mills was delighted by Thurston's arrival in London but had closer contact with John Cimperman, who not long afterwards became FBI liaison in Britain with access to ULTRA decrypts relevant to Abwehr operations in the western hemisphere. Though Menzies tried to restrict Cimperman's access, with MI5 support he 'brazenly and nonchalantly, in full view of everyone, copied entire messages…'† Cimperman was probably the best shot in the FBI – the first to succeed in a contest set up by Hoover in which FBI agents on a carefully laid out, timed course fired sixty bullets from different angles with a six-shot revolver at a human silhouette target. On 14 May 1940, Cimperman accomplished the extraordinary feat of achieving sixty bullseyes, thus becoming the first FBI Special Agent to qualify for Hoover's curiously named 'Possible Club'.‡ During his twenty-six years in London, Cimperman became Mills's closest friend in the US intelligence community, accepting regular invitations to Bertram Mills Circus when it reopened after the war.§

---

*   Raymond J. Batvinis, 'Walking a Tightrope: FBI's John Cimperman and the ULTRA Secret', https://fbistudies.com/2022/05/30/walking-a-tightrope/
†   Raymond J. Batvinis, *Hoover's Secret War Against Axis Spies: FBI Counterespionage During World War II* (Lawrence: University Press of Kansas, 2014), p.87.
‡   Batvinis, 'Walking a Tightrope'.
§   See below, p.201.

* * *

During a secret visit to the United States and Canada in the summer of 1942, Liddell revealed to the FBI that he was planning to protect MI5's interests in North America by moving Mills across the Atlantic to assist in running double agents.[*] In December 1942, just as Thurston arrived as FBI liaison officer in London, Mills was posted to Montreal as MI5 liaison officer in Canada.[†]

Stephenson correctly interpreted Mills's posting as a threat to the influence of BSC. In February 1943, MI6's London HQ asked Mills to investigate the case of an unproductive double agent based in Canada, Hans von Kotze, codenamed SPRINGBOK.[‡] A German aristocrat with an English wife, SPRINGBOK had been recruited by the Abwehr in South America in 1941, but later contacted MI6 and agreed to become a double agent. BSC was involved in SPRINGBOK's subsequent move to Toronto. Two intelligence historians who have studied the case conclude that he 'seduced' the wife of his BSC case officer.[§] Mills's report makes no reference to a seduction but complains that SPRINGBOK's BSC and MI6 'interrogators were inexperienced and had no knowledge as to how the interrogation of an enemy agent should be conducted'.

Guy Liddell, who met SPRINGBOK in Toronto in the summer of 1942, was very impressed by his potential: 'SPRINGBOK is a mine of information and one could probably go on talking to him for a

---

[*] Guy Liddell diary, 5 July 1942.

[†] See below, ch.7.

[‡] Mills believed that Stephenson had 'stupidly' given Kotze the codename SPRINGBOK because of the amount of time he had spent in South Africa, where the Abwehr had planned to deploy him – thus breaking the rule that the codename must give no clue to the agent's real identity. Mills to Annie Luke (widow of B1a officer Billy Luke), 8 June 1990; CBM papers.

[§] Nigel West, *Historical Dictionary of World War II Intelligence* (Plymouth: Scarecrow Press, 2008); Dean Beeby, *Cargo of Lies: The True Story of a Nazi Double Agent in Canada* (Toronto: University of Toronto Press, 1996), loc.3149.

month and still obtain from him further facts.' Liddell suggested to the Anglophile Royal Canadian Mounted Police (RCMP) Commissioner, Stuart Wood, that SPRINGBOK be used as the 'beginning' of a network of 'four or five first-class double-cross agents' in Canada. Wood 'seemed pleased with the idea' but Liddell doubted 'whether he had much notion of how to set about the problem'.* At the end of the year, the problem of how to include SPRINGBOK in the Double-Cross System remained unsolved.

After meeting SPRINGBOK in Toronto in February 1943, Mills proposed to MI6 HQ that he renew contact with the Abwehr by sending a letter to its cover address in Lisbon. According to a later report to MI5 by Mills: 'This suggestion rather startled the B.S.C. representative because he did not know that SPRINGBOK had a cover address [in Lisbon], even though it was given on the first paper in the file, and the agent himself seems to have forgotten its existence.' Mills then discovered that either BSC or MI6 had lost the secret ink given to SPRINGBOK by the Abwehr to communicate with them. MI5 provided a substitute secret ink from one of its own double agents and a letter in SPRINGBOK's name was written to the Abwehr contact address in Lisbon. According to Mills:

There followed a series of tragedies and farces, for the letter was concealed in a box of scented soap and addressed to a woman. B.S.C. made themselves responsible for posting it to Lisbon, but in fact asked O.S.S. to do the job for them. The parcel was at first rejected as being unsuitable for transmission in the U.S. diplomatic pouch because it was addressed to a woman and the contents smelled of perfume. The letter contained full instructions for the

---

* Guy Liddell diary, 9 and 10 June 1942.

1.

ANNO DÑI   ÆTATIS SVÆ 21
1585

QVOD ME NVTRIT
ME DESTRVIT

2.

ABOVE Cyril Mills was the most striking modern example of a leading figure in the British entertainment business who also became a spy, but the first to combine the two professions was his fellow graduate of Corpus Christi College, Cambridge, the great Elizabethan dramatist Christopher Marlowe, of whom this is probably the only surviving portrait.

LEFT Matriculation photograph of a solemn fourteen-year-old Cyril Mills on his arrival at Harrow School in 1916. At evensong every Sunday for the rest of the war he heard the Headmaster read out the names of Harrow's latest war dead.

3.

4.

5.

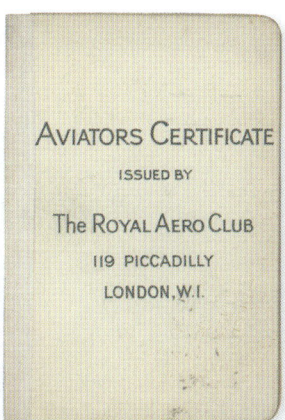

6.

OPPOSITE ABOVE Adolf Hitler at the Krone Circus arena in Munich, one of his favourite speaking venues in the 1920s. Mills's regular business visits to the Krone Circus alerted him to 'the magnitude of the lies' in Hitler's speeches.

OPPOSITE BELOW Winston Churchill with his daughter Mary watching the clowns at Bertram Mills Circus on 22 December 1938. Though Churchill often chuckled in public, the only photographs which show him helpless with laughter were taken at the circus.

TOP Mills's aviator's certificate (pilot's licence).

ABOVE Cyril Mills's first biplane, a second-hand de Havilland Gipsy Moth, in 1934: 'When I said I was piloting my own aircraft there was amazement … I was the first circus man either to own or fly one.'

7.

CIRCUS GROUND · ASHFORD
1936

ABOVE Mills's second biplane: a de Havilland Hornet Moth purchased in 1936, which he used for espionage missions as well as business travel to German circuses.

BELOW Pilot flight log of Mills's dangerous mission to reconnoitre the Messerschmitt factory at Regensburg for MI6. His log book mistakenly refers (in red capitals) to Regensburg as 'Ravensberg'.

8.

1938.							RECORD O
Date.	Aircraft.		Engines.		Journey.		
	Type.	Markings.	Type.	H.P.	From.		To.
							Brought forw
Aug. 28.	HS78.	G-ADNS.			Magdelurg		Berlin
30.					Berlin		Leipzig
Sept 1					Leipzig		Praha
2.					Praha		Budapest
					Budapest		Wien
4					Wien		Linz
6					Linz		München
					München		Zürich
							Carried forw

ABOVE British fighter ace and stunt-flyer Christopher Draper, the 'Mad Major' (*left*), meets Hitler at a Munich airshow in 1932; between them are two German pilots. Draper became MI5's first double agent against Nazi Germany.

LEFT A smartly dressed Mills boards his de Havilland Hornet Moth. Unlike the open-cockpit Gipsy Moth, it had a pilot's cabin and Mills no longer needed to wear a flying suit and goggles.

FLIGHTS.

Time of Departure.		Time of Arrival.		Time in Air.		Pilot. See Instructions (5) on flyleaf of this book.	Remarks.
Hrs.	Mins.	Hrs.	Mins.	Hrs.	Mins.		
...	...	...	...	615	05		
17	00	18	00	1	00	Self.	
16	42	17	52	1	10		
11	05	12	20	1	15		
12	40	15	20	2	40		
15	50	16	05	1	15		
11	00	12	18	1	20		
12	43	14	20	1	25		
15	55	17	58	2	05		OVER RAVENSBURG
...	...	...	...	627	15		

on the back cover

LEFT His pre-war circus gave Mills more experience of organising deceptions than anyone else at the heart of the wartime Double-Cross System. His greatest success was to turn a French dancer into 'the only female fakir in the world', brought up in India and able to mesmerise a crocodile named Churchill.

BELOW Bertram Mills Circus offices in London at 1 Dorset Square became a wartime base for secret operations in support of the French Resistance. In 1957 the Queen Mother unveiled a memorial to those sent from Dorset Square on 'special missions'. Cyril Mills stands by the French and British flags to the left of the doorway.

OPPOSITE ABOVE False passport in the name of Cyril Brook, issued to Mills after he joined MI5 in 1940. To make the details more difficult to check, his place of birth was given as Poona (now Pune) in India and his date of birth was changed from 1902 to 1904.

OPPOSITE BELOW Mills also used a false National Registration Card in the name of Cyril Brook. Surprisingly, his address was given as 1 Dorset Square, which a good London street directory would have identified as Bertram Mills Circus HQ.

13.

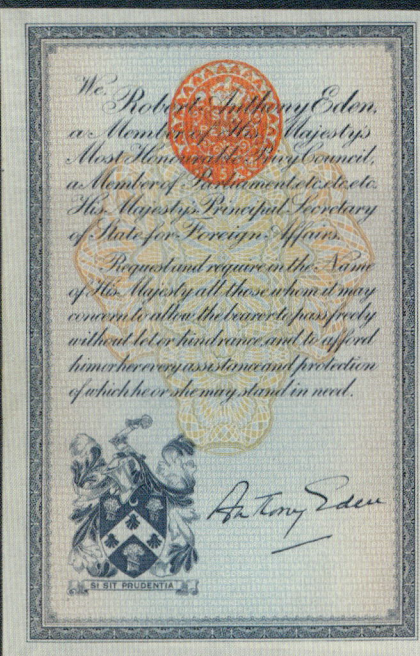

We, Robert Anthony Eden, a Member of His Majesty's Most Honourable Privy Council, a Member of Parliament etc etc etc to His Majesty's Principal Secretary of State for Foreign Affairs. Request and require in the Name of His Majesty all those whom it may concern to allow the bearer to pass freely without let or hindrance and to afford him or her every assistance and protection of which he or she may stand in need.

Anthony Eden

SI SIT PRUDENTIA

This Passport contains 32 pages.
Ce passeport contient 32 pages.

1

PASSPORT.
PASSEPORT.

UNITED KINGDOM OF GREAT BRITAIN AND NORTHERN IRELAND.
ROYAUME-UNI DE GRANDE-BRETAGNE ET D'IRLANDE DU NORD.

No. of PASSPORT } 188
No. du PASSEPORT }

NAME OF BEARER } Mr CYRIL BROOK
NOM DU TITULAIRE }

ACCOMPANIED BY HIS WIFE (Maiden name)
ACCOMPAGNÉ DE SA FEMME (Née)

and by children
et de enfants

NATIONAL STATUS   NATIONALITÉ

British Subject by birth

14.

NATIONAL REGISTRATION	NATIONAL REGISTRATION
PL. 8818	PL. 8818
BROOK, Cyril	BROOK, Cyril

1. This Identity Card must be carefully preserved. You may need it under conditions of national emergency for important purposes. You must not lose it or allow it to be stolen. If, nevertheless, it is stolen or completely lost, you must report the fact in person at any local National Registration Office.

2. You may have to show your Identity Card to persons who are authorised by law to ask you to produce it.

3. You must not allow your Identity Card to pass into the hands of unauthorised persons or strangers. Every grown up person should be responsible for the keeping of his or her Identity Card. The Identity Card of a child should be kept by the parent or guardian or person in charge of the child for the time being.

4. Anyone finding this Card must hand it in at a Police Station or National Registration Office.

51-3129   3

DO NOTHING WITH THIS PART UNTIL YOU ARE TOLD

Full Postal Address of Above Person :—

1 Dorset Square
London N.W.1.

(Signed) Cyril Brook.

Date 2.2.40.

15.

Telephone Nos.
REGENT 6050.
WHITEHALL 6789.

BOX No. 500,
PARLIAMENT STREET B.O.,
LONDON, S.W.1.

SF.50/52/7/D.G.

30th November, 1943.

My dear Mills,

    I was very glad to learn from your letters of 8th November, 1943, to myself and Butler that your first visit to the F.B.I. had passed without your having to call on us for support. As the right of escort was asserted but not exercised on the occasion of your first visit, it is less likely to be enforced on subsequent occasions.

    This is as it should be. We want a "live and let live" policy with the States and aim at nothing more than the unimpeded right to do our own business - just as we do here.

    The position, however, holds the seeds of trouble so long as Stephenson continues to think he still represents M.I.5. He definitely has ceased to do so; S.I.S. are aware of this; the F.B.I. have been told this; and I no longer hold any direct communication with him. If, therefore, he ever attempts to interfere with you, by virtue of his supposed representation of M.I.5., he must be put right about this. You can also explain the position to anyone of his staff who labours under a like delusion.

    As regards visits not taking place without the "approval" of B.S.C. (you have used this word in your letter), you will notice that Mr. Duff Cooper's memorandum contains the word "agreement." I objected to "approval" when it was suggested. All that was intended was that you should not go to Washington stealthily or behind the backs of B.S.C., which none of us has ever wished to do. The visits are thus to be made as indicated, but the business you do on them - apart from liaison with the B.S.C. - is for the F.B.I. and ourselves alone.

    It is not intended you should use this letter unless occasion arises. If it does, you can produce it as an authoritative exposition of the position, since your own notes etc., of your interview with Mr. Duff Cooper might not be accepted as conclusive.

Yours sincerely,

D. Petrie

Seen and approved.

Duff Cooper

B.S.S. (CANADA)
RECEIVED
DEC 10 1943
ACK. 10/12
BY

C.B. Mills, Esq.,
c/o Commissioner S.T. Wood,
R.C.M.P.
Ottawa.

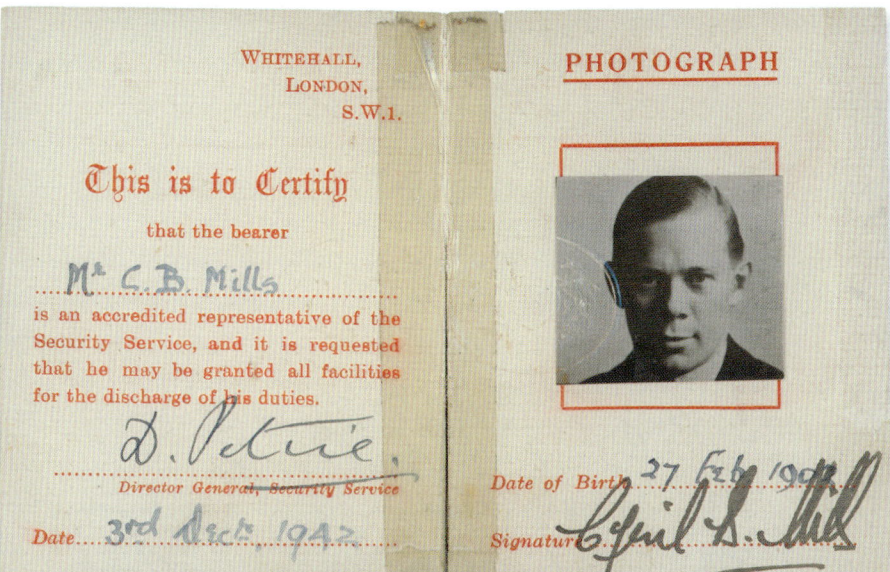

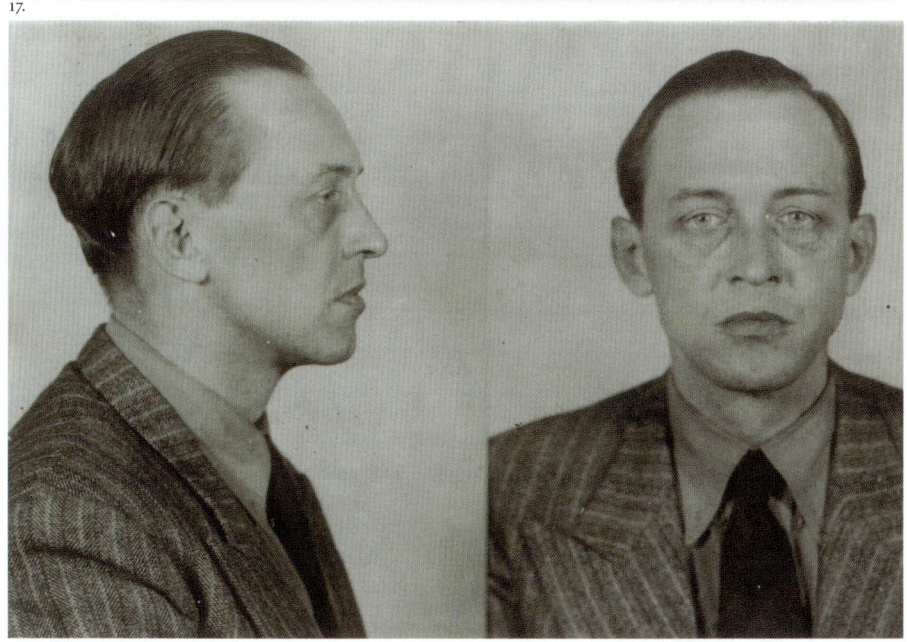

OPPOSITE Secret letter from Sir David Petrie, MI5 DG, on Mills's 1943 appointment to replace the Canadian William Stephenson, head of British Security Coordination in New York, as MI5 liaison with the FBI. Stephenson was furious; the FBI was delighted.

TOP Mills's MI5 identity card, signed by Petrie and issued for his mission to Canada late in 1942.

ABOVE Werner von Janowski, a German spy arrested in Canada. Mills told him that he was now 'the property of the British Intelligence Service'.

BOX No. 500.
PARLIAMENT STREET B.O.,
LONDON, S.W.1.

10th May, 1945.

My dear Staff,

VE-day brought us the announcement from the Prime Minister that the German war is over. With it there is an end also to the special efforts that, through its long and anxious years, the Security Service has devoted to its successful prosecution—crowned now by its triumphant conclusion. I would not care to let slip this memorable occasion without thanking you for the valuable contribution you have made—individually and collectively—to this hard-won victory.

Amid our justifiable pride and satisfaction it is worth while to cast our eyes back and to see what we have been doing and how we have been doing it. Our purpose throughout has been defence. That is to say that, apart from ensuring freedom from internal disorder, we have been labouring for the security of our information, our material and our personnel, which again means keeping the enemy from doing damage and denying to him knowledge that he might have used to his advantage and to our hurt. Throughout the war I can recall no instance of material damage suffered by any of the above major interests, certainly none that was preventable by us.

It has all along been my view that our heaviest responsibility was in its essence operational. In other words our chief task was to cut off from the enemy news of all that was going on inside our beleaguered island fortress, particularly the assembling of the great armadas that successfully sailed from these shores, carrying the men and material that smote and defeated him in Africa, Western Europe and elsewhere. In the success achieved, the element of surprise was all-important, and I feel we may fairly claim no small share in ensuring that it was complete. Had vital information of these great enterprises been passed across to the enemy, there might have been a very different story to tell to-day. The Security Service perhaps has been the most formidable of the barriers in the way of the enemy's getting at what he wanted to know. His ignorance is the measure of our success, for his efforts have been both insidious and persistent. So far as all this goes, we have played a great part in his final defeat.

ABOVE 'Message of thanks' from Petrie on 10 May 1945 (two days after VE Day) to Mills and other MI5 staff. Because the Double-Cross System remained top secret, unknown even to most of MI5, Petrie made no mention of its extraordinary success in deceiving the enemy.

Many of you have toiled through long years at what may have at times appeared dull and pointless tasks. The central purpose, now so fully attained, was not always apparent. But it was only by the doing of all these different things that we achieved what we did. The days at times were dark, the burden heavy and the road long and weary. But I believe that, looking back on the journey, each of us will share the feelings of Mr. Valiant-for-truth when his pilgrimage was ended: "And though with great difficulty I have got hither, yet now I do not repent me of all the troubles I have been at to arrive where I am."

In this message of thanks, which I offer from a full heart, I have tried to make clear the great and honourable part the Security Service, and you as a member of it, have played in the war. You have done a great job which you can remember with pride till the end of your days. For my part, I am very proud of having been the head of this organisation through these difficult years and of the loyalty, devotion and goodwill with which all of you have laboured for the security of the country through the years of its direst peril.

Yours sincerely,

D Petrie

19.

RIGHT Cyril and Mimi Mills drink champagne after their wedding in a London register office on 14 February 1950.

24   THE SPHERE   [JANUARY 1, 1949

CHRISTMASTIDE IN ENGLAND
A Survey of the Home News in Pictures

REACTIONS GRAVE AND GAY—HOW OUR STATESMEN RESPOND TO A LITTLE CHRISTMAS CLOWNING : Two pictures from the Bertram Mills Circus at Olympia where the Prime Minister, Mr. Attlee, and Britain's wartime Prime Minister, Mr. Churchill, each enjoyed himself in his own way. Mr. Attlee's concentration was noted by one critic, who declared that the Premier hardly ever took his eyes off the ring. Mr. Churchill was at the top of his form, and during the performance shook hands with Coco the Clown, whose knockabout tactics won general approval

TOP The proudest moment in Mills's circus career: a charity evening at Olympia on 18 December 1952 when Queen Elizabeth II became the first reigning British monarch to make an official visit to a public circus performance.

ABOVE Winston Churchill and Clement Attlee were the only British Prime Ministers to combine a passion for intelligence with a love of Bertram Mills Circus. Attlee met the MI5 DG more often than any other twentieth-century Prime Minister. At the circus, however, he laughed less ostentatiously than Churchill.

22.

ABOVE 17 Kensington Palace Gardens (opposite the Russian embassy) in 1960, when the Mills family moved in.

BELOW An MI5 Observation Post (OP) similar to that in 17 KPG which surveilled those entering and leaving the embassy and other Soviet buildings. A blind leaves just enough room for a long-range camera. Nearby are a blackboard with a target list and a loose-leaf binder with names and photographs to aid identification.

23.

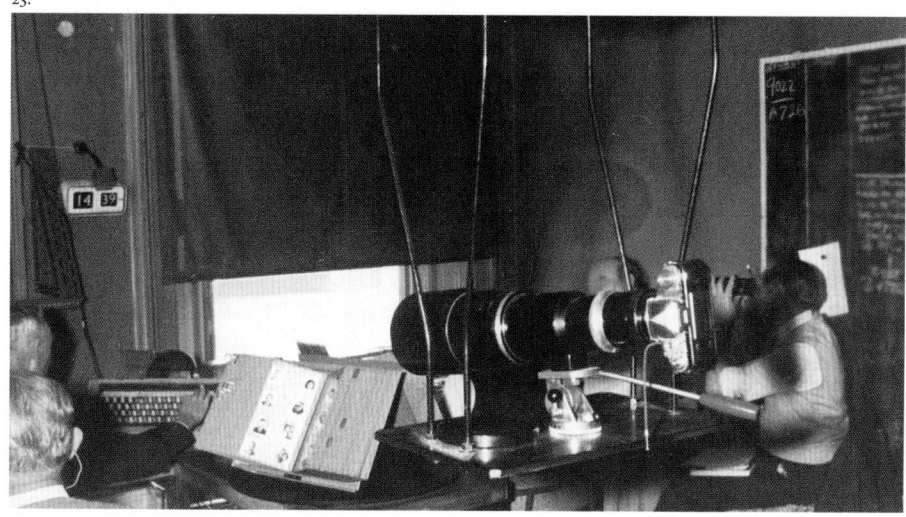

24.

25.

Christopher   Dick   C.B.M.   ROGER   HUGH
Harmer   White   HESKETH   DACRE

HUGH   Peggy   EMI-LU   TAR.   BILLY
ASTOR   Harmer   ASTOR   LUKE

26

OPPOSITE ABOVE In 1981 Mills and his ex-MI5 friends invited five leading wartime double agents, along with their former Double-Cross case officers, to a lunchtime reunion – a unique moment in British intelligence history. Mills stands in the back row, in the middle of the window.

OPPOSITE BELOW Mills, sharing a joke with his oldest friend in British intelligence, Sir Dick White (former head of both MI5 and MI6), was the only one who failed to look at the camera during the group photograph after a reunion lunch in 1985.

FROM
CYRIL B. MILLS.

51 CUMBERLAND TERRACE
LONDON NW1 4HJ
01-935 7646

5th August 1985

Your Royal Highness,

Knowing that you were interested in and kind enough to receive the Spanish Double Agent known as Garbo who took part in the Fortitude and other deception plans you may like to have the book which has been published about him.

It may interest you to read Sir on page 5 and elsewhere that it was I, who you may only have known as a Circus man in the past, who recruited Garbo and brought him to this country and acted as his first Case Officer.

It is only right to add that I had nothing to do with the writing or publication of the book.

I have the honour to be Sir,
Your Highness's most humble and obedient servant.

27

H. M. YACHT BRITANNIA

8th August 1985.

Dear Mr. Mills,

Thank you very much for sending me a copy of the book about 'Garbo'. I am particularly pleased to have it as Nigel West brought him to see me while he was in this country earlier this year. It really is a most extraordinary story and I cannot wait to read the full account.

I am no longer surprised by anything to do with clandestine operations during the war, but I must admit that I would not have expected your involvement. I cannot imagine a better cover!

Yours sincerely,

Philip

RIGHT ABOVE Letter from 83-year-old Cyril Mills to Prince Philip on 5 August 1985 revealing that 'it was I, who you may only have known as a Circus man, who recruited Garbo and brought him to this country and acted as his first Case Officer'.

RIGHT Surprised reply from Prince Philip on board Royal Yacht *Britannia*, 8 August 1985: 'I must admit that I would not have expected your involvement. I cannot imagine a better cover [than the circus]!'

28.

ABOVE Shortly before the fortieth anniversary in June 1984 of the D-Day landings, in whose success GARBO had played a key role, he was guest of honour at a reception attended by Mills and other B1a veterans. Mills kept this framed photograph of his reunion with GARBO, drinking champagne with Christopher Harmer and 'Tar' Robertson, on display at home.

BELOW Mills (*left*) reminisces in 1989 with his closest surviving MI5 friends (*left to right*: 'Tar' Robertson, Sir Dick White, Christopher Harmer) and Hugh Trevor-Roper (*right*). The photograph reflects the warmth of their long friendship.

29.

establishment of two way radio contact between SPRINGBOK
and Germany. The transmitter was installed in Montreal and a
series of transmissions was carried out over a period of about
three weeks in accordance with the detail given in the secret
letter. We failed to make contact because the parcel containing
the secret letter was still in the office of O.S.S. in Washington five
or six weeks after the transmission ended and so far as we know
has never been posted.

Mills reported to MI5 that as 'the result of B.S.C.'s incompetence',
the SPRINGBOK case had to be closed down. No further attempt
was made to use him to send disinformation to the Abwehr.[*]

Unhappiness with Stephenson and BSC went beyond Hoover
and the FBI. The RCMP Commissioner, Stuart Wood, said that his
personal relations with BSC had broken down.[†] Mills dismissed
Stephenson and BSC more colourfully as 'polished nincompoops'.[‡]
After the SPRINGBOK case, Sir David Petrie transferred Stephenson's role as MI5 representative to Mills, who was already established as MI5 Liaison Officer in Canada. Stephenson was furious,
trying to insist that he still remained the official representative of
MI5 as well as of MI6 and the SOE. Petrie warned Mills to expect
trouble '...so long as Stephenson continues to think he still repre-
sents MI5. He definitely has ceased to do so; SIS [MI6] are aware
of this; the FBI have been told this; and I no longer hold any direct
communications with him.'[§]

The FBI also refused further direct contact with BSC. Mills

---

* CBM papers.
† Batvinis, *Hoover's Secret War Against Axis Spies*, pp.91–2.
‡ CBM papers.
§ Petrie to Mills, 30 November 1943; CBM papers. The letter was approved by Duff Cooper as head of the
   Security Executive. See illustration no.15.

reported that 'Hoover did not trust Stephenson an inch and it was only when I was able to assure Hoover that we had severed all links with Stephenson that they opened all doors to me.' As Mills privately acknowledged, he had been slightly economical with the truth in the interest of MI5: 'In fact we had not severed all links with Stephenson for he was Menzies' representative in New York and Washington and therefore both the RCMP [Royal Canadian Mounted Police] and I were dependent upon him for information concerning the Western hemisphere from ULTRA.'*

MI5 had direct access only to ULTRA decrypts and other SIGINT which concerned Britain and British territory abroad. For SIGINT on enemy operations on the United States and other foreign states, MI5 was dependent on MI6.

* * *

Unlike Stephenson, Mills was able to establish what he called 'the closest and most friendly relationship' with Hoover and the FBI.[†] His own pre-war success in planting stories on topics ranging from 'the world's first female fakir'[‡] to the Loch Ness Monster[§] in the British press to promote the family circus helped him to grasp Hoover's extraordinary, if sometimes unscrupulous, flair for publicity and media manipulation – greater than that of any other western Intelligence or Security Chief before or since.

The only person ever photographed kissing Hoover in public was the world-famous child star Shirley Temple during her carefully

---

*   CBM papers.
†   Mills, 'Report on M.I.5 representation in Canada and Liaison with the Federal Bureau of Investigation 1942–1945'; CBM papers.
‡   See above, pp.99–100.
§   See below, p.290 and Appendix.

choreographed, much publicised tour of the FBI headquarters in 1938. She later recalled: 'My role models were [the aviator] Amelia Earhart and [First Lady] Eleanor Roosevelt, and my major crush was J. Edgar Hoover.'* By the time of Pearl Harbor, Hoover had established a close relationship with the film producer Louis de Rochemont, collaborating with him on *Men of the F.B.I.* (1941) and *The F.B.I. Front* (1942). Hoover wrote to him in October 1942, 'we of the FBI obviously are extremely proud of the manner in which you have portrayed our activities … It is grand to have such a friend as you.' A month later, he awarded de Rochemont the FBI Distinguished Service Cross: 'I hope it will always serve as a constant memento of our feelings toward you.' In 1945, Hoover and other FBI personnel appeared alongside Hollywood actors in the Oscar-winning film *House on 92nd Street* (1945), which was produced by de Rochemont.†

From late 1943 onwards, Hoover sent Mills regular intelligence reports on communists and foreign minority groups in the United States – 'even in places like Puerto Rico and the Philippines, which are exclusively within the American sphere of interest':

> It seems therefore that Mr. Hoover is not interested in keeping matters of this kind from the British but only from Mr. Stephenson, and that this is the case seems to be borne out by the fact that in agreeing to give us the above-mentioned summaries it was definitely stipulated that M.I.5 should not use them or the information which they contained in any way which would make it possible for them to get back into the hands of B.S.C.
>
> …That [I] should have been so well received by the F.B.I., that

---

* Shirley Temple Black, *Child Star: An Autobiography* (New York: McGraw-Hill, 1988).
† Simon Wilmetts, *In Secrecy's Shadow: The OSS and CIA in Hollywood Cinema 1941–1979* (Edinburgh: Edinburgh University Press, 2016), pp.102–4.

their files should have been opened to [me] when no such thing has ever been done with any B.S.C. representative is due to two things. First the fact that F.B.I. representatives in London [Thurston and Cimperman] have been well received and given every possible help in the way of both information and instruction and secondly that M.I.5 has carried and maintained an unimpeachable reputation for honest dealing and efficiency with the F.B.I.*

At Hoover's invitation, and no doubt much to the annoyance of Stephenson, Mills spent five days early in 1944 at the trial in Detroit of a German spy ring which had collected intelligence on local defence industries ranging from nitroglycerin plants to the Ford Company Willow Run bomber production facility. The spy ring had been hopelessly compromised in March 1942, however, by the FBI's unpublicised arrest of its organiser, Grace Buchanan-Dineen, a pro-Nazi British-Canadian socialite. Buchanan-Dineen, whose family were prominent furriers and hatters, was probably the most expensively dressed spy of the Second World War, usually wearing a mink coat, silver-fox jacket or Persian lamb coat. Until her arrest, her ostentation was good cover.

After Buchanan-Dineen's arrest, however, facing the prospect of a long prison sentence and, according to her FBI file, realising that she could no longer 'carry out the instructions of her Nazi employers', she agreed to work for the FBI as a double agent. 'No promise of immunity was made to me,' Buchanan-Dineen said later, 'but I was convinced in an hour that there was no future for me as a German agent.' The FBI installed a one-way mirror in her apartment, allowing the G-men to observe her visitors. Thereafter, Mills

---

* Mills, 'Report on M.I.5 Representation in Canada and Liaison with the Federal Bureau of Investigation 1942–1945'; CBM papers.

reported to MI5, 'the contacts she made with German American potential agents were all made under F.B.I. supervision.' The judge at Buchanan-Dineen's trial was sterner than she, and probably Mills, had expected. Despite her cooperation with the FBI, he ruled that the fact she had entered the United States 'as a Nazi spy' prevented leniency. She was sentenced to twelve years' imprisonment. 'I didn't think they would give me such a sentence,' Buchanan-Dineen complained. 'I'm very surprised.'*

* * *

Until the end of the war, Stephenson continued a devious campaign to replace Mills as the main point of contact between Hoover and the British intelligence community. On 12 December 1944, he telegraphed Petrie, the MI5 DG, to say that he would probably be bringing Hoover to London 'shortly': 'Will you send me the time you would wish to have him on anything you desire other than meetings with the Cabinet which I am arranging.' Stephenson's claim to be 'arranging meetings' between Hoover and Churchill's War Cabinet was absurd. 'Bill Stephenson', noted Guy Liddell, 'is obviously trying to impress everyone over here that he has got Hoover in his pocket.' MI5 was not impressed. Petrie sent what Stephenson called a 'rather snooty' reply, making clear that he expected to hear details of Hoover's plans to visit Britain either directly from Hoover himself or from his Chief Liaison Officer in London, Arthur Thurston, who was in close touch with MI5. Liddell suspected that Stephenson 'may merely be angling for some [invitations] from prominent people in this country in order that he can wave them in Hoover's face and

---

* Ibid., paras 110–12; https://torontoist.com/2017/04/historicist-socialite-and-nazi-spy/

suggest to him that as everybody wants to see him in London a visit should be arranged'.*

Stephenson did not give up. In February 1945, he visited London as part of a charm offensive designed to enable him to replace Mills as MI5's main intermediary with Hoover. Liddell found him 'very friendly':

> He said he was only concerned about getting Hoover over and tying him up with ourselves for all time ... He said that he thought [Hoover] would be coming in March or April ... I said that we should be very pleased to show Hoover over our establishment [MI5] and that if he would give us three or four days he could probably see quite a lot that would interest him.

Stephenson unsuccessfully recommended giving Hoover an honorary knighthood.†

'Little Bill's charm offensive failed. On 21 March, Liddell told Petrie: '...I was doubtful from what I had heard whether Hoover would come. I am quite certain that Bill Stephenson has made these elaborate plans so that before giving up his job [at the end of the war] he could show everyone that he is on friendly relations with Hoover'.‡

Hoover, however, continued to be deeply suspicious of Stephenson. His visit to London never happened and Mills remained MI5's Liaison Officer with the FBI in North America for the remainder of the war.

Stephenson, meanwhile, was still able to count on the warm support of Donovan. After the war, on Donovan's recommendation and

---

* Guy Liddell diary, 12 December 1944.
† Ibid., 16 February 1945. Hoover was, however, made an honorary KBE in 1950.
‡ Ibid., 21 March 1945.

no doubt to Mills's horror, Stephenson became the first non-American to receive the Medal for Merit, the highest U.S. civilian award, for his 'valuable assistance to America in the fields of intelligence and special operations'.* Though Stephenson was also awarded a knighthood for his wartime service, it was something of a pyrrhic victory. No role was found for him in post-war British intelligence – or for Donovan in the United States. Harry S. Truman, who had become President on the sudden death of Roosevelt in April 1945, closed down the OSS five months later with a one-sentence Executive Order. The CIA, the United States' first peacetime foreign intelligence agency, was not founded until 1947.†

Denied even a part-time intelligence career in peacetime, Stephenson increasingly took refuge in fantasies about his wartime role at BSC. Suppressing all memory of BSC's role in forcing forged intelligence on Roosevelt, Stephenson seems to have convinced himself that Churchill had made him his personal representative in the US and secret intelligence liaison with the President, with a key role in passing ULTRA to the White House.

Stephenson's final fantasy, which outraged Mills, was *A Man Called Intrepid*, a biography of him written, at his request, by the Canadian journalist, William Stevenson (no relation). Published in 1976 with Stephenson's endorsement, it quickly became the biggest-selling book ever written on intelligence history. As Mills's numerous comments on his edition demonstrate, it is also wildly inaccurate. Even the title is incorrect. Stephenson was never 'Intrepid' – a codename he claimed was personally chosen for him by Churchill but which, in reality, was merely BSC's telegraphic address in New York. In *A Man Called Intrepid*, Stephenson immodestly

---

* Andrew and Green, *Stars and Spies*, p.293.
† Andrew, *For the President's Eyes Only*, ch.5.

awarded himself the Légion d'Honneur and the Croix de Guerre with palm, as well as, even more improbably, the title of interwar world amateur lightweight boxing champion. His fantasies about the Second World War began with the frontispiece, a photograph which purported to show Churchill with Stephenson. In fact, it showed the Prime Minister with his close friend and Minister of Information, Brendan Bracken.

The publishers were eventually forced to reclassify *A Man Called Intrepid* as a work of fiction. Though Mills, as usual, was unwilling to speak publicly about intelligence matters, he felt so strongly about Stephenson's falsehoods that he gave his second wife Mimi and their children a typewritten list of the most egregious of them.[*] Honours, however, continued to be showered on Stephenson – to the dismay and incredulity of Mills and his former colleagues in MI5. In 1983, Stephenson was welcomed by 750 OSS veterans on board the aircraft carrier USS *Intrepid*, where he was presented with the William J. Donovan award and a letter of congratulations from President Ronald Reagan: 'Your career … adds up to one of the great legends. As long as Americans value courage and freedom, there will be a special place in our hearts, our minds and our history books for the Man called Intrepid.'[†]

The INTREPID myth continues to prove remarkably resilient. In 2022, the government of Manitoba celebrated his 125th birthday by naming a lake the Sir William Stephenson Lake.

---

[*] The only other book on intelligence whose contents Mills denounced in writing was Peter Wright's *Spycatcher*. See below, ch.10.
[†] David Stafford, 'A Myth Called Intrepid', *Saturday Night*, October 1989; Shakespeare, *Ian Fleming*, p.254.

CHAPTER 7

DOUBLE-CROSS IN CANADA AND ATOMIC SECRETS

Every Wednesday morning in 1941–42, Mills and his B1a colleagues met in Dick White's MI5 London office with other senior B Branch officers to discuss the progress of the Double-Cross System and counter-espionage during the previous week.* Their recurrent fear was that the Abwehr would discover that one of its agents had been turned and that this might cause the whole network of double agents to unravel.

The case which caused the greatest concern for the future of Double-Cross occurred not in Britain but across the Atlantic: the arrest in Canada of an Abwehr agent, Werner von Janowski, who landed from a U-boat on Quebec's Gaspé Peninsula early on 9 November 1942. Wearing his German naval sub-lieutenant's uniform, the 38-year-old Janowski struggled ashore carrying a bag containing a civilian suit, a wireless transmitter in a wooden box and a shovel. He changed into the suit, used the shovel to dig a hole in which to bury his uniform and threw the shovel into the sea. Janowski then

---

* CBM papers.

hitchhiked to a hotel in the nearby town of New Carlisle and tried to pay for a room with Canadian dollar bills which had been taken out of circulation in 1935. The hotel owner called the Quebec provincial police and by lunchtime Janowski was in a jail cell awaiting a visit from the RCMP. Before the RCMP arrived, Janowski persuaded the local police to take him back to his landing site, where he dug up his naval uniform and put it back on. Smartly attired in a double-breasted blue jacket with two rows of brass buttons and an Iron Cross, 1st class, he denied being a spy when questioned and claimed, implausibly, to have landed from his U-boat simply to reconnoitre local shipping and harbour lights. The RCMP was unimpressed.[*]

In Britain, all public references to the landing of German agents were strictly controlled, and usually banned, by wartime censorship. To the alarm of MI5, however, Canadian censorship lost control of the Janowski case. By 10 November, RCMP HQ was complaining to Canadian censors that press reporters were ringing with questions about the arrest of a German spy in Quebec, which was still officially secret. Poor RCMP security, however, was partly responsible for the journalists' questions. After news of the arrest (though not including Janowski's name) was published in the *Detroit Times*, US press censors discovered that the source was Detroit police officers who had been tipped off about the arrest by boastful RCMP constables at a Canadian border crossing. In Canada, probably assisted by other indiscreet Mounties, the story quickly reached the *Toronto Star*, *Toronto Telegram*, *Windsor Star*, *Le Soleil*, the *Montreal Star* and the *Montreal Standard*. The arrest was also reported in the mass-circulation US magazine, *Newsweek*.

---

[*]   Beeby, *Cargo of Lies*.

Press publicity about the Janowski case coincided with a visit to North America by MI5's counter-sabotage expert, Victor (later 3rd Baron) Rothschild, which was prompted by the arrest of German saboteurs who had landed by submarine in the United States. Rothschild's reputation had preceded him – in particular, the extraordinary bravery he showed in defusing German bombs while meticulously recording his every move by field telephone in case he was killed in the attempt. 'When Rothschild came on the scene,' Mills recalled, 'the R.C.M.P. immediately perceived that they were dealing with a man who [unlike them] was not seeing a spy for the first time in his life.' Though some junior RCMP officers were anxious to turn Janowski into a double agent, Rothschild believed they lacked the experience to do so, particularly after the publicity given to his capture.[*]

Canada had no equivalent of MI5. The office of the long-serving Canadian Prime Minister, William Lyon Mackenzie King, had concluded two years earlier that the RCMP lacked the 'capacity for intelligence work'.[†] King's diaries, released after his death, reveal that, though a shrewd politician, he himself had a deeply eccentric view of intelligence. On several occasions he used a Ouija board or crystal ball to communicate in secret with – among others – his two dead 'angel dogs', Irish Terriers Pat1 and Pat2, on affairs of state. Both, he believed, wagged their tails to indicate approval.[‡] They were not, it seems, asked about Janowski.

Mills was more concerned by the 'numerous visits and so-called interrogations' of Janowski by BSC staff sent from New York by

---

[*]   CBM papers.

[†]   Beeby, *Cargo of Lies*, loc.913. The RCMP Intelligence Branch had very few staff and only performed a liaison function. John Sawatsky, *Men in the Shadows: The RCMP Security Service* (New York: Doubleday, 1980), p.71.

[‡]   Christopher Dummitt, *Unbuttoned: A History of Mackenzie King's Secret Life* (Montreal and Kingston: McGill-Queen's University Press, 2017); Terry Reardon, *Winston Churchill and Mackenzie King: So Similar. So Different* (Toronto: Dundurn Press, 2014), pp.363–4; Charlotte Gray, 'Haunted by Weird Willie', *Literary Review of Canada*, May 2017.

'Little Bill' Stephenson, whom Mills considered woefully ignorant of counter-espionage: '...the R.C.M.P. quickly observed that these individuals had had no experience in dealing with captured agents and of interrogation, and were probably more interested in having a chance to set eyes on a live spy than anything else.'*

Mills and other B1a officers were also bemused by the RCMP questioning of Janowski. After his arrest late in 1942, his chief Canadian interrogator was Cliff Harvison, head of the RCMP Criminal Investigation Branch, who sent transcripts of the interrogation to MI5.[†] Mills later recalled:

What we read day after day had us all in fits of laughter and it was obvious to us that whoever the interrogator was he was completely ignorant of all counter-intelligence matters and that a Nazi was selling him a huge load of rubbish about the Abwehr and that he was believing it all and thought he was doing us a great favour by giving us all the information he had gathered.

Realising that Harvison was out of his depth, the RCMP Commissioner, Stuart Wood, secretly asked the MI5 DG, Sir David Petrie, to send an officer to Canada to help run the Janowski case.[‡] Probably on the advice of Guy Liddell, Petrie chose Mills[§]:

...Thinking that it would be about a three-week job, I took a small suitcase with just enough clean clothes to last that long. I flew via

---

* Mills, 'Report on M.I.5 Representation in Canada and Liaison with the Federal Bureau of Investigation 1942–1945'; CBM papers.
† On the contradictions between the account of the interrogation in Harvison's later memoirs and reports at the time, see Beeby, *Cargo of Lies*.
‡ CBM papers.
§ See illustration no.16: Mills's MI5 identity card signed by the DG, Sir David Petrie, issued for his mission to Canada.

Prestwick, Reykavik and Gander [Newfoundland] in the bomb bay of a Liberator. There were about twenty of us – all others were young RAF pilots – and we lay on wet mattresses. We were in the dark all the way and from Prestwick to Gander took 13 hours. Over the Atlantic we flew at the maximum height of which the Liberator was capable and without oxygen; most of the time [we] were just above cloud and the temperature was in the region of 50 degrees below freezing. When we tried to eat the sandwiches they splintered like thin glass and the coffee in thermos flasks was frozen. They gave us a splendid meal at Gander but three of the young RAF pilots were taken away in ambulances.[*]

After recovering from his journey, Mills 'had some sticky passages at the RCMP headquarters in Montreal as it soon became clear that Janowski had made a fool of Inspector Harvison'.[†]

Despite protests from Harvison and his staff, Mills insisted on interrogating Janowski alone and gave him the new codename WATCHDOG:

I then began the interrogation by telling the prisoner that he was now the property of the British Intelligence Service and that if he lied to me or caused me any trouble I should take him back to England where we knew how to deal with Nazi sp[ie]s which was by hanging. He was to understand that his whole fate lay in my hands. I also told him I had read the transcript of the whole interrogation and knew all that he had told the Canadians was a pack

---

[*] Mills, *Bertram Mills Circus*, pp.121–2. Since all reference to intelligence was strictly excluded from this memoir, Mills conceals the fact that he was on an MI5 mission.

[†] Mills, 'Report on M.I.5 Representation in Canada and Liaison with the Federal Bureau of Investigation 1942–1945'; CBM papers. See illustration no.17. RCMP photos of Janowski during initial interrogation by Harvison.

of lies; that I had already interrogated many of his kind and that I knew more about the Abwehr than he did. I also told him that I did not blame him for what he told the RCMP as he had quickly spotted the fact that no agent had been in their hands before and that I supposed he had done what he had done in order to serve his country and his own skin. I ended by saying that if he lied to me once and I spotted it I should give him a final warning but the second time would put a rope round his neck in England.[*]

As Mills had intended, Janowski was visibly intimidated. For the first time, he admitted that he had been a Nazi for the past ten years. Instead of being a reluctant spy, as he had told Harvison, he was a veteran of Abwehr sabotage and intelligence missions.

One of the first pieces of information he volunteered after he had answered my questions for about two days was that an important part of his mission was to prepare the way for four important agents who were to come over a little later. He offered to cooperate fully with me in the capture of these other men if I would spare his life. I knew then I was dealing with about as dirty a four letter man as possible and told him that nothing he could do would make me give him any kind of guarantee about anything and that whether he liked it or not he would do exactly what I wished him to do.

As with DRAGONFLY, Mills refused to allow WATCHDOG to operate the transmitter given him by the Abwehr and persuaded the RCMP to provide 'a top-class radio ham' to do so instead under Mills's instructions.[†]

---

[*] Ibid.
[†] Ibid.

Looking back on the case at the end of the war, Guy Liddell believed that, without Mills's intervention, the mishandling of Janowski by the RCMP might have compromised the whole Double-Cross system:

> The fact was that Cyril had been sent to deal with a very delicate double-cross case which the Canadians had bungled ... Cliff Harvison is a good chap and alright on his own job but he knew nothing about double-cross work and if Cyril had not been there and taken a strong line the most frightful bungles would have been committed and the whole of the [double agent] network in this country might have been jeopardised.[*]

Though Mills had originally expected to spend only three weeks in Canada, he stayed much longer – fearing that, in his absence, Harvison and his staff might mishandle WATCHDOG as well as the 'four important agents' expected to follow him (though, in the event, they failed to materialise) and so put in jeopardy the whole Double-Cross System. Mills's fears were confirmed when he was recalled for briefing in London in the summer of 1943:

> ...Knowing I should be away for two or three weeks, I prepared a number of messages which WATCHDOG would send to his [Abwehr] masters during my absence. These he translated into German which I approved and all the RCMP officer had to do was to check them when WATCHDOG had encyphered them. When I returned to Montreal, the first thing I spotted was that the agent had slipped the letters S.O.S. into one of the messages

---

[*] Guy Liddell diary, 27 October 1947.

and this his Canadian case officer had not seen. Of course he had tipped his masters off that he was controlled so I had to close the case and I had the man put in irons and shipped to England in a cell in the belly of a British ship. He was held in a high security prison [Camp 020] until the end of the war.[*]

* * *

Mills believed that, even if the Abwehr had failed to notice Janowski's S.O.S, the WATCHDOG case had been compromised by leaks in the Canadian press, for which he blamed ineffective official censorship.

Without informing Harvison and the RCMP, Mills decided to take personal charge of the Double-Cross System in Canada by extending the fictional GARBO agent network which he had begun in Britain. The Abwehr welcomed GARBO's proposal (drafted by Mills) that his agent MOONBEAM, supposedly a Venezuelan student currently based in Scotland, should move to Canada. GARBO forwarded a sample of MOONBEAM's handwriting personally fabricated by Mills to the Abwehr. A flow of secret-ink reports from MOONBEAM began to reach the Abwehr via GARBO soon after WATCHDOG's radio messages ceased in the autumn of 1943. As Mills later recalled:

The plan appealed to us especially because as the agent was to be purely notional, it was impossible for there to be any [Canadian] press leakage, as there would almost certainly be in the case of any [real] German agent who might be captured and turned round in Canada.[†]

---

[*] Mills, 'Report on M.I.5 Representation in Canada and Liaison with the Federal Bureau of Investigation 1942–1945'; CBM papers.
[†] Ibid.

The fictional MOONBEAM reported that he had recruited a number of (equally fictional) Canadian sub-agents as well as his own cousin in Buffalo, just across the US border in New York State. MOON-BEAM and his non-existent spy network were warmly congratulated by the Abwehr and sent at least $15,000, which was used by Mills to fund MI5 operations. As the Third Reich was approaching its end in April 1945, the Abwehr still attached so much importance to its supposedly loyal Canadian agents that it told them to divide the remaining funds between them and take all necessary measures to protect their own security.*

Mills's first six months as MI5 representative in Canada coincided with the turning point in what Churchill called the 'Battle of the Atlantic'. 'The only thing that ever really frightened me during the war', he said later, 'was the U-boat peril.' Until the spring of 1943, Germany had the advantage. As at a critical moment in the First World War in 1917, U-boats threatened to halt the flow of vital war supplies across the Atlantic. Between June 1941 and February 1943, 885 ships in Allied convoys were lost, but only 13 U-boats sunk. By contrast, from April 1943 to May 1945, 286 U-boats were sunk, as compared with 178 Allied ships.

The key intelligence breakthrough, of which Mills was unaware, was Bletchley Park's success in breaking a complex version of U-boat Enigma, codenamed SHARK.† He had no access to naval, as opposed to Abwehr, Enigma decrypts. From early 1943 onwards, British and American cryptanalysis of naval Enigma was carried out according

---

* Beeby, *Cargo of Lies*, loc.3195ff.
† The introduction, in February 1942, of the SHARK variant of the U-boat Enigma, involving the addition of a fourth rotor to the cipher machine, defeated Bletchley Park until the end of the year. In March 1943, there was another ten-day period when SHARK messages could not be decrypted. Thereafter much U-boat traffic was decrypted within hours of transmission. Though sophisticated direction-finding techniques also helped to locate U-boats, SIGINT probably made the critical difference. The use of intelligence in the war against the U-boats is told in great detail in F. H. Hinsley et al., *British Intelligence in the Second World War*, 3 vols (London: HMSO, 1979–88). For a more concise account, see the one-volume abridged edition, chs.10, 18, 34, 37.

to a single programme coordinated by Bletchley Park.[*] Communication via direct signal links between the U-boat tracking rooms in London, Washington and (from May 1943) Ottawa became so close that, according to the British official history, for the remainder of the war 'they operated virtually as a single organisation'.[†]

Mills had no contact with the Ottawa tracking room. He did, however, make a modest contribution to the final stages of the war against the U-boats by moving several of GARBO's fictitious agents from Britain to Canada in the later months of 1944. Mills gave GARBO's seaman Agent STANLEY (aka SEVEN) a job on a transatlantic steamer plying the route between Halifax, Nova Scotia and the UK. SEVEN supposedly smuggled GARBO's Agent FRED (aka FOUR) along with his wireless transmitter, on board the steamer that would cross the Atlantic to Halifax.[‡] Mills probably hoped that this intelligence, which, as usual, completely deceived the Abwehr, would help to deter U-boat attacks on merchant ships using the port of Halifax which might be carrying important German agents in the GARBO network. Though the attacks declined, they remained a threat until VE Day. U-806 sank HMCS (His Majesty's Canadian Ship) *Clayoquot* by the Halifax lightship on 24 December 1944; U-190 sank HMCS *Esquimalt* on 16 April 1945 near the same spot. In 1947, U-190 was ceremonially sunk where she had destroyed the *Esquimalt* two years before.[§]

* * *

Mills's absence in Canada meant that he only had a peripheral part

---

* Andrew, *For the President's Eyes Only*, pp.135–7.
† Hinsley et al., *British Intelligence in the Second World War*, vol.2, p.48.
‡ Mills, 'Report on M.I.5 Representation in Canada and Liaison with the Federal Bureau of Investigation 1942–1945', para 98; CBM papers.
§ https://www.thecanadianencyclopedia.ca/en/article/u-boat-operations

in one of the wartime deceptions which he most admired: Operation MINCEMEAT in 1943, which combined the expertise of the entertainment business, Mills's pre-war profession, with that of the intelligence community of which he was now a member. The Abwehr was deceived into believing that the corpse of a homeless Welshman carrying fake documents found off the Spanish coast was that of Major 'Bill' Martin, a Royal Marine officer bearing authentic top-secret plans for an Allied invasion in the Mediterranean.*

Mills later recalled being briefed on the initial planning for MINCEMEAT: 'It was first suggested by Charles Cholmondeley, the B.1.a "Ideas" man, and the original intention was to drop the body from an aircraft but [Sir] Bernard Spilsbury the pathologist said that if the Germans got hold of the body they would know it was a plant.'†

MINCEMEAT drew on skills more commonly found in film studios' scenery, props and make-up departments than in intelligence agencies. ULTRA decrypts revealed that the Germans had been comprehensively deceived by Major Martin's bogus documents. A message sent to Churchill during a visit to Washington said simply: 'MINCEMEAT swallowed whole'. Even when the Allied attack of July 1943 came in Sicily rather than Greece (the destination indicated by Martin's documents), the Germans did not doubt the authenticity of the MINCEMEAT forgeries but concluded instead that Allied plans had changed.‡

---

* Though the implementation of Operation MINCEMEAT was not MI5's responsibility, it was largely responsible for creating the corpse's fake identity. Secretaries in B Division were invited to audition for the part of Major Martin's fiancée, Pam, by submitting attractive photographs of themselves. The role was won by Jean Gerard Leslie (later Leigh) of B1b and a photograph of her in a swimsuit was placed in Martin's wallet. Peggy Harmer and other secretaries helped draft love letters from Pam, which were put in his pocket.

† CBM papers.

‡ Howard, *British Intelligence in the Second World War*, vol.5, pp.90–92. Ian Dear and M. R. D. Foot (eds), *The Oxford Companion to the Second World War* (Oxford: Oxford University Press, 1995), p.751.

What Churchill learned for the first time about the double agents during 1943 left him with the conviction that, 'in wartime, truth is so precious that she should always be attended by a bodyguard of lies'. No major military operation in British history has ever owed so much to deception as OVERLORD, the Allied invasion of occupied northern France, which began on 'D-Day', 6 June 1944. The main priority of the deception was:

> to induce the German Command to believe that the main assault and follow up will be in or east of the Pas-de-Calais area, thereby encouraging the enemy to maintain or increase the strength of his air and ground forces and his fortifications there at the expense of other areas, particularly of the Caen area [in Normandy].

The double agent who contributed the most to the success of this deception was GARBO. During the first six months of 1944, he and Tomás Harris, who had succeeded Mills as his case officer, sent more than 500 messages to the Abwehr station in Madrid, which forwarded them to Berlin, many marked 'Urgent'.

Mills's absence in Canada meant that he was unable to follow in detail all the disinformation devised by GARBO and Harris to persuade the enemy that the main D-Day target would be the Calais region rather than the Normandy beaches. But during a brief return to London in the spring of 1944, he was almost certainly briefed on the construction by Shepperton Studios (which had been founded before the war by William Stephenson)* of a huge fake oil-storage complex near Dover to supply the supposed invasion force preparing an attack on Calais. The complex was designed by Basil Spence,

---

* Shepperton Studios were originally named Sound City; Shakespeare, *Ian Fleming*, p.249.

later one of Britain's leading architects, and received official visits from King George VI, General Dwight D. Eisenhower ('Ike'), Supreme Allied Commander Europe, and General (later Field Marshal) Bernard Montgomery, Commander of Allied Ground Forces.

Before D-Day it had been expected that the fiction of a planned attack on the Pas-de-Calais could not be maintained for more than ten days after the Normandy landings began. ULTRA, however, revealed that the deception remained firmly embedded for far longer in the mindset of both Hitler and his High Command.* On 3 July, MI5 reported to Churchill that:

> It is known for a fact that the Germans intended at one time to move certain Divisions from the Pas-de-Calais area to Normandy but, in view of the possibility of a threat to the Pas-de-Calais area, these troops were either stopped on their way to Normandy and recalled or it was decided that they should not be moved at all.

Churchill was also informed that Berlin had awarded GARBO the Iron Cross and sent this example of the praise lavished on him and his imaginary sub-agents by German intelligence:

> ...I reiterate to you, as responsible chief of the service, and to all your collaborators, our total recognition of your perfect and cherished work and I beg of you to continue with us in the supreme and decisive hours of the struggle for the future of Europe.

Later in the year, GARBO became the first British agent (as opposed to intelligence officer) to be awarded the MBE. Since it was thought

---

* Holt, *The Deceivers*, p.581.

inappropriate for a double agent to meet the King, the presentation was made instead by the DG, Sir David Petrie, in a private ceremony attended by Harris and senior members of B1a. Petrie, noted Liddell, 'made a nice little speech'. Later we lunched at the Savoy when GARBO responded to the toast in halting but not too bad English. I think he was extremely pleased.* Mills, though in Canada and unable to attend, was also extremely pleased.

When Eisenhower moved from Britain to France after the success of the Allied landings in the summer of 1944, he used a trailer caravan which had a direct telephone link to the Supreme Allied Headquarters in London as his HQ. Mills was struck by the fact that 'Ike' called the caravan HQ his 'Circus wagon'.

* * *

Shortly before GARBO's apotheosis in the Savoy Hotel, the Abwehr agent, Alfred Langbein, gave himself up in Canada – the first agent to do so since Janowski two years earlier. Langbein had rowed ashore undetected from a U-boat off the coast of New Brunswick in spring 1942, some months before the arrival of Janowski. Unlike Janowski, however, he never intended to carry out his espionage mission, buried his wireless transmitter and spent two years in Montreal and Ottawa living off money given him by the Abwehr and spending some of it in brothels. Gradually running out of cash and resigned to German defeat, he handed himself in at a naval intelligence building in Ottawa on 1 November 1944, producing a fake Canadian registration certificate, supplied by the Abwehr, which gave his name as Alfred Haskins. The lead role in the interrogation

---

* Guy Liddell diary, 21 December 1944.

that followed was taken by Mills, assisted by an RCMP sergeant, Cecil Bayfield. It took only a few days for Mills to conclude that, as Langbein claimed, he had never attempted to operate as a German spy. After Langbein led his interrogators to the hidden wireless transmitter, Mills reported to MI5 that 'we were satisfied by the condition of the wrapping that it had never been used.' Mills scornfully concluded that Langbein suffered from 'cold feet', though 'all his sympathies' probably lay with Germany. 'He is a typical Hun, but not a very courageous one.'*

Both Janowski and Langbein epitomise the poor quality of many wartime Abwehr agents. Intelligence work attracted far fewer able recruits in Germany than in Britain. Only 77 of the 480 suspected wartime German spies arrested in the UK were German nationals. About 120 were turned into double agents. Unlike Churchill, Hitler had little interest in intelligence. The Holocaust, a much higher priority for Hitler, was more efficiently conducted than German foreign intelligence collection.

By the time Langbein gave himself up in Ottawa, Mills was far more concerned with the failings of Canadian security than with the threat from German espionage:

The [Army, Navy and Airforce] Directors of Intelligence have been driven time and time again almost to exasperation by the publication of information in the Canadian Press in deliberate and calculated opposition to their wishes. The Canadian Press was allowed to publish a description of the 'tank buster' which would have delighted any enemy intelligence officer, soon after it

---

*   Mills, 'Report on M.I.5 Representation in Canada and Liaison with the Federal Bureau of Investigation 1942–1945'; CBM papers.

went into production in Canada, months before it went into operation, and whilst it was still high on the list of secret equipment.*

Mills discussed his security concerns with a number of Canadian
lawyers. The most important was probably the high-flying, Brit-
ish-educated William Meredith, partner and litigation expert in a
Montreal law firm founded by his father. Mills and Meredith had
been near contemporaries at Cambridge University and probably
exchanged memories of their time as undergraduates. In 1942,
shortly before Mills was posted to Canada, Meredith was made
King's Counsel (KC), later leading the prosecution in Canada's first
espionage trial. Mills was used to discussing intelligence with leading lawyers. MI5's wartime recruits included six future judges – Patrick Barry, Edward Cussen, Helenus 'Buster' Milmo, Henry 'Toby'
Pilcher, Blanchard Stamp and John Stephenson (no relation to 'Little
Bill') – as well as a series of other able barristers and solicitors.

Meeting Meredith in Montreal proved to be a turning point in
Mills's private life. He and Meredith's wife Mimi fell, and remained,
deeply in love. They were later to marry. Mills very rarely wrote
about his private life. But, in a private handwritten note to their
children, written in retirement, Mills told them that 'every step' in
his intelligence career, from his wartime membership of MI5 to his
posting to Montreal, 'led to the point where I was able to marry the
most wonderful woman in the world'.†

* * *

By 1945, Mills's biggest fear was that the weakness of Canadian

---

*   Ibid.
†   CBM papers.

wartime censorship would give away the biggest military secret of the war – the 'Manhattan Project' to manufacture the world's first atomic bomb in a top-secret nuclear laboratory at Los Alamos in the New Mexico desert. The project was so secret that even Roosevelt's final Vice-President, Harry S. Truman, was kept in ignorance of it until he became President after FDR's sudden death on 12 April 1945. At the end of Truman's first Cabinet meeting, the Secretary of War, Henry L. Stimson, stayed behind and spoke to the new President about 'an immense project that was under way – a project that was looking to the development of a new explosive of almost unbelievable destructive power'. Truman was so stunned by the events of the day that, at first, the news did not sink in. Only when he was given more details on 13 April did he begin to grasp 'the awful power that might soon be placed in our hands'.*

As with the ULTRA secret, Mills was far better informed about the atomic bomb than Vice-President Truman had been. He was well briefed on the Anglo-Canadian atomic research laboratory in Montreal, part of the Manhattan Project, which was building a nuclear reactor at Chalk River, near Ottawa. Mines bordering Great Bear Lake in Canada's Northwest Territories were a major source of the uranium used in the construction of the atomic bomb at Los Alamos. In 1942 the Mackenzie King government took control of the Eldorado Mining Company, which owned the mines and processed uranium ore from both Great Bear Lake and the Belgian Congo.

Mills was horrified when news of the Eldorado takeover appeared in the Canadian press in 1943. He was even more shocked, a year later, by a story in the *Montreal Gazette*, quoting the Principal of Montreal's McGill University, Dr F. Cyril James, on the building

---

* Andrew, *For the President's Eyes Only*, pp.149–50.

of a radiation laboratory and experiments in 'atom smashing'. As a Canadian censor complained, 'the story pinpointed developments in Canada and to some extent indicated progress in one of the most secret of war projects'. The article included an illustration of a cyclotron used to bombard atomic nuclei with charged particles. 'This sort of thing may have gone over the heads of the Canadian public,' wrote Mills, 'but it would hardly have done so with a German Intelligence Officer, had an agent here reported it to him.' *

Mills's fear of attempts by German intelligence to penetrate Manhattan Project operations in Canada, where security was weaker than at Los Alamos, may now seem alarmist. At the time, however, it was wholly rational. Nazi Germany had entered the war with a headstart over the Manhattan Project, having begun a secret operation to build an atomic bomb in April 1939, after two German scientists had become the first to discover nuclear fission. According to the Project's Foreign Intelligence Chief, Robert Furman, it was 'built on fear': 'that the enemy had the bomb, or would have it before we could develop it. The scientists knew this to be the case because they were refugees from Germany, a large number of them, and they had studied under the Germans before the war broke out.' Not until late in the war did it become clear that, despite its early lead over the Allies, the German atomic bomb programme had failed.[†]

Unknown to Mills and MI5, or to any other Allied wartime intelligence agency, the great security threat to the Manhattan Project was not German, but Russian, penetration. Though the most successful Soviet spies, Klaus Fuchs and Ted Hall, worked at Los Alamos, the atomic research laboratory in Montreal was also penetrated. In

---

* Mills, 'Report on M.I.5 Representation in Canada and Liaison with the Federal Bureau of Investigation 1942–1945'; CBM papers.
† Bugged conversations between ten leading German scientist POWs interned at Farm Hall, Godmanchester, in the summer of 1945 finally provided proof of Germany's failure to manufacture an atomic bomb.

January 1943, the British physicist and Soviet spy Alan Nunn May began work at the laboratory. Despite the fact that Nunn May had made contact with the GRU (Soviet military intelligence) in Britain during the previous year, it took the GRU station at the Soviet embassy in Ottawa some time to grasp his importance. Nunn May's GRU case officer, Pavel Angelov, did not contact him until late in 1944. A few months later, he tasked Nunn May with obtaining samples of the Canadian uranium being used at Los Alamos.[*]

Though no evidence of Nunn May's espionage emerged until Mills was about to leave Canada at the end of the war, Mills should have been warned early in 1943 of another possible spy in Montreal nuclear research: the brilliant Italian atomic physicist, Bruno Pontecorvo. In February 1943, the FBI reported to British Security Coordination in New York that it had found communist literature in Pontecorvo's home in the United States. Stephenson, however, failed to inform MI5, which did not learn of the FBI reports until Pontecorvo unexpectedly fled to Russia in 1950. 'Nobody knows what happened to these reports', wrote Guy Liddell after his defection, 'since the records of B.S.C. have been destroyed.'[†]

Save for their scientific expertise and communist convictions, Nunn May and Pontecorvo had little in common. With pince-nez spectacles and a small moustache, Nunn May was 'a caricature of the 1940s egghead scientist'. By contrast, the vivacious Pontecorvo's exceptional good looks earned him the nickname 'Ramon Navarro', after the filmstar who had succeeded Rudolph Valentino as cinema's leading male heart-throb. Later, Mills may have been mildly amused by Pontecorvo's claim that 'I could have been in a circus'. He was good at riding his bicycle backwards up a slope. Even when

---

[*]   Andrew, *Defence of the Realm*, p.341.
[†]   Guy Liddell diary, 21 October 1950.

in Russian exile in his late seventies and suffering from Parkinson's disease, Pontecorvo still 'enjoyed playing to the crowd' by balancing an upright walking stick on his nose or foot.* During his years at the Montreal nuclear laboratory, his occasional clowning had been good intelligence cover. It did not fit any stereotype of a Russian spy.

At the end of the war Mills was pessimistic about the Mackenzie King government's understanding of security and the role of intelligence:

It is thought that there is wide scope for 'A child's guide to Intelligence work' (though not under that name) which could be issued to [Canadian] police and other organisations who by reason of their work come in contact with the British Security Service and are, from time to time, given information which has been obtained from secret sources. If the R.C.M.P. is taken as an example it may be said with truth that as an organisation it has not the background to enable it to deal with MOST SECRET [TOP SECRET] matters in a way which we would wish. It is felt that as personalities change so frequently in Police Forces it is necessary, when giving them secret information or intelligence obtained from very secret sources, to specify exactly how the information should be handled and to what extent it may be used.†

---

* Frank Close, *Half Life: The Divided Life of Bruno Pontecorvo, Physicist or Spy* (London: Oneworld, 2015).
† The Canadian Security Intelligence Service (CSIS) was not founded until 1984. Canada was, however, a key member of the post-war 'Five Eyes' SIGINT alliance, which still continues.

CHAPTER 8

COLD WAR: FROM GOUZENKO'S DEFECTION TO THE BERLIN WALL

Cyril Mills's career as MI5 representative in North America came to an end on 30 August 1945, when he vacated his office in Montreal and began preparations to return to England by sea. A signed authorisation by the DG, Sir David Petrie, copied to the RCMP, allowed Mills to take with him 'one sealed bag containing secret documents'.* For much of the Cold War, Mills's wartime intelligence work in Canada remained classified on both sides of the Atlantic. It was feared that any reference to it might reveal the top-secret post-war negotiations which led to the creation of the 'Five Eyes' SIGINT alliance between the United States, Britain, Canada, Australia and New Zealand.† In 1950, the British Secretary of State for Commonwealth Relations, Patrick Gordon Walker, told the Lord Chancellor that it was still 'particularly important to avoid saying that we have or did have security officers in Canada'.‡

---

* CBM papers.
† The existence of the Five Eyes alliance was not officially admitted until 2010. Richard Kerbaj, *The Secret History of the Five Eyes: The Untold History of the International Spy Network* (London: Blink Publishing, 2022).
‡ Patrick Gordon Walker to Lord Chancellor, 31 March 1950, TNA PREM 8/1280.

Mills left Canada convinced that the RCMP and Ministry of Justice, as well as other branches of government, still had only a feeble grasp of counter-espionage:

> If the enemy has failed to learn our secrets during the recent war it is because he failed to realize that they were so easily obtainable in Canada, but it is not to be assumed that he will repeat his mistake, or that Soviet representatives who have flooded the country during the last two years will have failed to observe the patent lack of security.[*]

Incompetent Canadian handling of the first post-war spy case seemed to prove Mills right.

On the evening of 5 September, Igor Gouzenko, a 26-year-old cipher clerk working for the GRU (Soviet military intelligence) at the Soviet embassy in Ottawa, stuffed over a hundred classified documents under his shirt and walked out of the embassy, intending to defect.[†] Though the documents revealed that a Soviet spy ring in Canada had stolen nuclear secrets, handing them over to the Canadians turned out to be much more difficult than he had expected. When Gouzenko sought help at the offices of the Ministry of Justice and the *Ottawa Journal*, he was told to return the next day. But on 6 September, both the Ministry of Justice and the *Ottawa Journal*, which failed to realise it was being offered the spy scoop of the decade, showed no more interest than on the previous evening. By the night of the 6th, the Soviet embassy realised that both Gouzenko

---

[*] Mills, 'Report on M.I.5 Representation in Canada and Liaison with the Federal Bureau of Investigation 1942–1945'; CBM papers.

[†] Gouzenko was an ideological defector, anxious that Stalin's western allies should know he had purloined their atomic secrets. Calder Walton, *Spies: The Epic Intelligence War between East and West* (New York: Simon & Schuster, 2023), pp.128–9.

and GRU documents had gone missing. While Gouzenko hid with his wife and child in a neighbour's flat, he could hear Soviet security men breaking down his door and searching his apartment. It was almost midnight before local police came to his rescue and the Gouzenko family finally found sanctuary.* 'I considered myself very lucky', Mills recalled, 'for if I had been in Montreal it is certain that I should have been given the case.'†

Mackenzie King's bafflement at the Gouzenko case added to the early confusion in handling it. Neither his spirit sources nor the RCMP had warned him of the threat from Soviet, as well as German, espionage. Writing at the desk in his Ottawa home, Laurier House, King naively informed his diary:

> As I dictate this note I think of the Russian embassy being only a few doors away and of them being a centre of intrigue. During the period of war, while Canada has been helping Russia and doing all we can to foment Canadian-Russian friendship, there has been one branch of the Russian service that has been spying on [us] … The amazing thing is how many contacts have been successfully made with people in key positions in government and industrial circles.‡

The Gouzenko case was very probably one of those which Mackenzie King discussed via mediums with the late President Roosevelt, as well as with the former Canadian Prime Minister, Wilfrid Laurier, who had died in 1919. During at least one of these discussions in the spirit world, Churchill, though still alive, was – according to

---

* Andrew, *Defence of the Realm*, pp.339–40.
† Mills, untitled confidential memoir on his intelligence career (undated), p.26; CBM papers.
‡ Andrew, *Defence of the Realm*, pp.340–41.

the medium – also present. When King mentioned his supernatural presence during a visit to London in 1946, Churchill sent him 'a most significant note' which, alas, has not survived.[*]

Avoiding involvement in the Gouzenko case spared Mills serious personal embarrassment. A key figure in the GRU spy ring identified by Gouzenko was Fred Rose, the only communist MP in Canadian history who represented a Montreal constituency. In 1946, after being found guilty of conspiring to pass secret information to Russia from a Canadian explosives expert, Rose was sentenced to six years' imprisonment and expelled from Parliament.[†] The prosecution was led by William Meredith KC, whose wife Mimi had begun a love affair with Mills soon after they met in 1943.[‡]

After Mills's death in 1991, his family found a file headed 'Notes which I treasure'[§], in which he had kept messages from Mimi, ending with one he received just before their last Christmas apart. Though Mills and his first wife, Elsie, divorced in 1946, it was another three years before Meredith agreed to a divorce from Mimi. A *decree nisi* was granted on 14 November 1949. Cyril and Mimi were married in a London registry office on 14 February 1950.[¶]

Before leaving Canada early in September 1945, Mills had discovered that, in addition to Fred Rose MP, the Soviet agents identified by Gouzenko's intelligence included a British scientist at the Anglo-Canadian nuclear research laboratory in Montreal, Alan Nunn May, the first Russian atom spy to be discovered on either side of the Atlantic. On 9 August 1945, only three days after Hiroshima, Nunn

---

[*] Reardon, *Winston Churchill and Mackenzie King*, pp.363–4. No copy of this 'most significant note' survives in the Churchill papers at CCAC. Churchill probably struggled – successfully – to keep a straight face when writing it.

[†] David Levy, *Stalin's Man in Canada: Fred Rose and Soviet Espionage* (New York: Enigma Books, 2011)

[‡] See above, p.186.

[§] CBM papers

[¶] See illustration no.19: Cyril and Mimi drink champagne after their registry office wedding.

May handed his GRU case officer, Pavel Angelov, a top-secret report on atomic research, details of the bomb dropped on Hiroshima and samples of two types of uranium: an enriched specimen of U-235 in a glass tube and a thin deposit of U-233 on a strip of platinum foil. In return, a grateful Angelov gave him 200 Canadian dollars rather oddly placed inside a whisky bottle. Next month, Nunn May returned to England.[*]

Gouzenko's top-secret documents revealed that on 8 October Nunn May was due to meet his new GRU case officer in London outside the British Museum, carrying a copy of *The Times* under his left arm to identify himself. Mills's first priority on arriving in London was to try and ensure that Nunn May was caught at the rendezvous before he could escape to Moscow. The Deputy DG of MI5, Guy Liddell, wrote in his diary on 19 September:

> Mills is back from Canada, this time for good … He is worried about Alan Nunn May getting away to Russia. I explained to him our dilemma. If we cannot get a case against May he remains a permanent menace and ultimately it will probably be impossible to prevent him going to Russia. If we follow him about before [8] October his suspicions may be roused and he may be inclined to refrain from making any contact with the Russians here.[†]

Unluckily for MI5, the head of MI6 Section IX (Soviet and communist counter-intelligence) was none other than the still undiscovered Soviet agent, Kim Philby. As one of Philby's MI6 colleagues, Robert Cecil, later concluded, his success in becoming head of Section IX 'ensured that the whole post-war [British] effort to counter

---

[*]   Andrew, *Defence of the Realm*, p.341.
[†]   Guy Liddell diary, 19 September 1945.

Communist espionage would become known in the Kremlin. The history of espionage records few, if any, comparable masterstrokes."* Thanks to a tip-off from Philby, May and his new Soviet case officer both failed to turn up outside the British Museum on 8 October.[†]

Four days later, Mills formally ended his wartime career as an MI5 officer. His official report on his years in North America ended with this extraordinary tribute to MI5 HQ staff:

> That a representative who has been overseas for more than two and a half years and who has not feared to criticize when he has felt that criticism was merited should be able to say that he has not one word of criticism to offer concerning his Headquarters is, perhaps, almost unique but it is a plain statement of fact and one which is recorded with pride and pleasure.[‡]

Though the wartime MI5 officer Victor Rothschild had no shortage of glittering peacetime careers ahead of him, he too found leaving the camaraderie of the Security Service 'painful and distressing': 'Most of the people who have been as intimately associated with it as I have been have developed an affection for the Office [MI5] as a whole and the staff in particular which I am sure is most unusual in a large Government Department.'

A post-war MI5 personnel officer told new recruits: 'One of the best things about working here is that the percentage of bastards

---

* Robert Cecil, 'The Cambridge Comintern', in Christopher Andrew and David Dilks (eds), *The Missing Dimension: Governments and Intelligence Communities in the Twentieth Century* (London: Macmillan, 1984), p.179.
† Alan Nunn May was arrested on 15 February 1946. Though the case against him was weak, skilful questioning by Commander Leonard Burt extracted a confession from him five days later. Andrew, *Defence of the Realm*, pp.345–6.
‡ Mills, 'Report on M.I.5 Representation in Canada and Liaison with the Federal Bureau of Investigation 1942–1945'; CBM papers.

is extremely low."* Mills agreed. His continuing friendships with, and admiration for, wartime colleagues who had left or remained in British intelligence explains why Mills was willing to work part-time for both MI5 and MI6 during the Cold War without payment.

His main peacetime priority after resigning from MI5, however, was to restart the family business.

* * *

Reviving the circus required Mills to renew his contacts with Continental circuses which had provided him with many of his pre-war acts. None of his contacts had any idea that he had spent most of the war as a key British intelligence officer. Most of them thought he was dead. The rumour had been spread, probably mainly to deceive the Abwehr, that he had joined the RAF and been killed during a bombing raid over Germany. Mills later recalled his first post-war visit to the Continent late in 1945:

> The morning after my arrival in Brussels I went to the Cirque Royal where the Strassburger Circus was playing. It was about noon and Karl Strassburger was exercising a dozen Friesian horses … As I walked through the main entrance and towards the ring, Karl stood still, dropped his hands and let the horses get jumbled up. Wilke, the ringmaster, pointed towards me and there was dead silence … Everybody in the circus was staring at me, so eventually I felt I had to do something and called out, 'Hello, Karl'. The spell was broken and they all came forward to shake my hand, explaining they thought they had been seeing a ghost.

---

* Andrew, *Defence of the Realm*, p.328.

The usually unemotional Mills was nearly overwhelmed by the welcome he received. He also found the trip 'one of the most fruitful I ever made', signing contracts with six-star Continental acts with which to reopen the circus in London.*

Though Bertram Mills Circus had been forced to suspend performances during the war, many bills had accumulated. Feeding the elephants alone had cost £11,000. The biggest problem faced by Cyril and his younger brother Bernard after deciding to reopen the circus shortly before Easter 1946 was finding a suitable venue. Olympia, its main pre-war base, was still being used as a government clothing store and was unavailable until just before the following Christmas. After other locations for a Big-Top circus proved impracticable, the only suitable site which remained in the London area was at Windsor. Mills never knew exactly how permission was obtained ... 'but I suspect that it may have been His Majesty, King George VI, who gave the final word of approval, for the site of the circus was just below and almost in the shadow of Windsor Castle in the Home Park.'†

As before the war, the Royal Family continued to be enthusiastic circus-goers.

Unlike his son-in-law, Prince Philip, King George VI probably knew of Cyril Mills's key role in the still top-secret wartime Double-Cross System. He had no idea, however, that the head of B1a, 'Tar' Robertson, had previously tapped his telephone during the abdication crisis. In 1944, the King had personally approved the unprecedented award of the MBE to GARBO, the most successful of all the double agents, whose codename had been chosen by Mills as his first MI5 case officer. George VI's enthusiasm for Double-Cross

---

* Mills, *Bertram Mills Circus*, p.92.
† Ibid., pp.134–7.

derived in part from the fact that before the D-Day landings in June 1944, he had personally taken part, like GARBO, in the FORTI-TUDE SOUTH deception operation designed to persuade the Germans that the main D-Day target was not the Normandy beaches but the area around Calais. The King, occasionally accompanied by Princess Elizabeth (the future Elizabeth II), visited a series of military and air force bases. Double agents sent the Abwehr accurate intelligence on the royal visits, combined with disinformation that the bases were preparing for an invasion of the Pas-de-Calais rather than the Normandy beaches.[*]

In September 1945, Mills was briefed on what Guy Liddell hoped would be 'a perfect epilogue to the whole GARBO saga' – its postwar continuation.[†] Shortly before the end of the war in Europe, Petrie had summoned Mills back to London for discussions on the future use of GARBO and his fictitious agent network on both sides of the Atlantic.[‡] After VE Day, GARBO, with help from British intelligence, succeeded in tracking down his former Abwehr case officer, Friedrich Knappe, alias Knappe-Ratey (codenamed FEDERICO) in Spain. Following the plan devised during Mills's discussions in London, GARBO told FEDERICO that, with help from his agent MOONBEAM (invented by Mills), he had escaped from Britain to Canada and thence, via Cuba and Venezuela, to Spain.[§]

GARBO reported to MI5 that FEDERICO was trying to set up a post-war neo-Nazi German secret service with him as its star agent, but that he seemed 'a very frightened man':

---

[*] Aldrich and Cormac, *Spying on the Royals*.
[†] Guy Liddell diary, 24 September 1945.
[‡] Mills, 'Report on M.I.5 Representation in Canada and Liaison with the Federal Bureau of Investigation 1942–1945'; CBM papers. Mills flew to England on 15 April and returned to Canada, also by air, on 3 May.
[§] Ibid., para 108; CBM papers.

Spain was a relatively safe country for Nazi officers to hide in, but many members of the intelligence service seemed to fear that they might be kidnapped or eliminated by their opposite numbers on the Allied side. FEDERICO was greatly saddened by Germany's defeat, so I continued to play my role of a Nazi sympathiser and told him that better times lay ahead. I offered my services and said that I would be glad to work with him. He fell for it completely...

FEDERICO took GARBO to meet his former Abwehr superior, Karl-Erich Kühlenthal, who threw his arms round GARBO's neck. Liddell gleefully noted in his diary: 'pathetic enquiries were made about GARBO's various agents and how they were going to live in the future.' There was still not the slightest suspicion that all the agents were invented by GARBO and MI5. In 1942 Mills had been personally involved in sending disinformation from the longest-serving of the imaginary agents, a Venezuelan living in the UK codenamed PEDRO, who had since become Deputy Chief of the fictitious GARBO network and a particular favourite of the Abwehr. Kühlenthal asked GARBO whether PEDRO had been 'annoyed at the repeated [Abwehr] questions about the possibility of an [Allied] attack on the south of France'. GARBO reassured him.[*]

Liddell was so pleased at GARBO's post-war deception of his war-time Abwehr case officer that he believed his role as a double agent was 'by no means over'.[†] In fact, because FEDERICO and Kühlenthal failed to set up a viable post-war neo-Nazi secret service, they found no role for GARBO. His astonishing career as Britain's greatest double agent was at an end. Mills did not see him again until 1984.[‡]

---

[*]   Guy Liddell diary, 24 September 1945. Pujol and West, *Operation GARBO*, pp.214–15.
[†]   Guy Liddell diary, 12 February 1946.
[‡]   See below, pp.273–4.

* * *

Mills's friends and former colleagues in B1a remained in close touch for the rest of their lives. 'Tar' Robertson began the tradition of an annual reunion lunch, initially at his club, the In & Out (Naval and Military), the former club of Sir Mansfield Cumming, first Chief of MI6, in St James's Square.[*] Prince Philip joined the club in 1947, later becoming its president. Among the secrets which Robertson revealed to his B1a friends, though not to Prince Philip,[†] was his role during the abdication crisis of 1936. After the Prime Minister, Stanley Baldwin, asked MI5 to check 'how the situation was moving', Robertson went to Green Park after dark to tap the telephone line to 145 Piccadilly, the London home of the Duke of York (the future George VI), in order to eavesdrop on his conversations with his older brother, Edward VIII, before the abdication on 10 December. 'Tar' thus became the first person outside the royal family to discover Edward VIII's decision.[‡] None of his B1a friends ever revealed the secret.

'Tar' Robertson's and Mills's other B1a friends were invited to annual reunions at Bertram Mills Circus after it reopened at Olympia. So was Mills's FBI friend, John Cimperman,[§] who had become so attached to his wartime posting and friendships in London that he stayed on as the Bureau's liaison officer (officially 'legal attaché') at the US embassy until 1959. Cimperman so enjoyed the company of his wartime friends in B1a that he regularly joined them for

---

[*]   CBM papers.

[†]   The abdication crisis was not mentioned during the Duke of Edinburgh's discussion of MI5 history with Christopher Andrew in 2009; see above, p.2.

[‡]   'Tar' Robertson also revealed his role in tapping the phone of the future George VI to his younger brother, Ian, an army officer who rose to the rank of Major-General. Ian Robertson's written record of 'Tar's revelations is quoted in Elliott, *Gentleman Spymaster*.

[§]   See above, p.160.

nights at the circus.* The children of B1a veterans were given ring-side seats in the Big Top when the circus went on tour. One of them recalls being shown by Mills his traditional circus wagon with its leaded-light windows.†

Apart from the royal family, the circus's most celebrated post-war patron remained Winston Churchill. Despite Labour's triumph at the 1945 general election, Churchill received a greater ovation at Olympia than his successor as Prime Minister and fellow circus-goer Clement Attlee:

> If there was one night in 1947 which none of us will ever forget, it was that on which Winston and Mrs Churchill came to Olympia. They arrived when the performance had been in progress about fifteen minutes and as they went to the box the whole audience rose and cheered. The band and even the artistes in the ring had to stop while the cheering lasted.‡

Except for the King, Churchill was almost the only person in the audience who knew of Mills's wartime role in MI5. Alfred Duff Cooper, who as head of the Security Executive had been largely responsible for the decision to brief Churchill on the Double-Cross System in 1943, was another admirer of the circus. He wrote in his diary after the pre-Christmas lunch at Olympia on 19 December 1947 that, despite rationing: 'The lunch was great fun – there was plenty of champagne – the principal article of food was sausage rolls. I thought the circus was very good.' Attlee also enjoyed the lunch. Duff Cooper noted in his diary:

---

*   Recollection of Frederick Meredith.
†   Elliott, *Gentleman Spymaster*.
‡   Mills, *Bertram Mills Circus*, p.150.

Between lunch and circus I went to relieve nature where I met the Prime Minister. While buttoning up his flies he congratulated me on the success of my mission [as Ambassador in Paris] and conveyed the thanks of H. M. Government. I while unbuttoning mine expressed my sense of the honour done to me and my gratitude to Ministers for their support and confidence.[*]

Unlike Churchill, Attlee avoided dramatic public entrances to the circus. Dame Sheila Hancock later recalled meeting Attlee, whom she much admired, while working as an usher at Bertram Mills Circus to help pay for drama school: 'The show had started and this funny little man came and stood in the corner. I said: "Can I take you to your seat?" He said: "No, I don't want to disturb people." It was our Prime Minister.' Hancock later performed as one of the 'elephant girls' who rode the circus troupe of six elephants, before beginning her dramatic career.[†]

A 1949 article in *The Sphere* on 'Christmastide in England' featured photos of Attlee and Churchill at Bertram Mills Circus, entitled 'Reactions Grave and Gay'. An unsmiling Attlee was contrasted with a beaming Churchill 'at the top of his form', shaking hands with Coco the Clown while Clemmie Churchill roars with laughter.[‡]

In fact, the usually reserved Attlee was often to be seen laughing at the circus both during and after his premiership. Like Churchill, he laughed more loudly at Bertram Mills Circus than anywhere else. Though their biographers do not mention it, Attlee and Churchill were the only Prime Ministers in British history to combine a

---

[*]   *The Duff Cooper Diaries*, p.668.
[†]   'Sheila Hancock Q&A: "I met Clement Attlee when I was working at the circus"', *New Statesman*, 8 June 2022. Sheila Hancock, *Old Rage* (London: Bloomsbury, 2022), p.142. On the role of the 'elephant girls', see Tait, *Wild and Dangerous Performances*, pp.83–5.
[‡]   See illustration no.21.

passion for intelligence with a love of the circus.* As Churchill's wartime Deputy Prime Minister, Attlee had been informed of both the ULTRA secret and the Double-Cross System. Possibly the moment when Attlee laughed loudest at the circus was when Field Marshal Viscount Montgomery, whose military operations had been greatly assisted by both ULTRA and Double-Cross, was himself deceived by Borra, the Yugoslav-born 'King of the Pickpockets'. Mills, who had played a key role in Double-Cross, must have shared Attlee's amusement when Montgomery failed to notice Borra removing his wristwatch during a performance.†

As before the war, illusion and deception were central to the circus's success. Both at Olympia and in Big-Top tours around Britain, circus audiences exceeded all of Mills's expectations: 'If the first two post-war years were good, 1948–9 was even better, for we broke all our own records and probably those of every British circus before or since.' From 1952 to 1955, Borra, who had become the world's most famous stage pickpocket, was top of the Bertram Mills Circus bill.‡

Within the circus, however, the main victim of one of Borra's deceptions was Mills himself. At a dinner party in a country hotel:

When the waiter served cocktails Borra whispered something to him. He knew I had a passion for peanuts and when the waiter returned with them he was asked the time, but his wristwatch had disappeared when the nuts were ordered. When I took a handful of nuts and took the first bite I had to splutter the lot over the floor for Borra had substituted some of his own. The business with the waiter's watch had not been to amuse him only; its real purpose

---

* The most recent biography of Attlee, the generally excellent, award-winning *Citizen Clem* (London: Riverrun, 2015) by John Bew, makes no reference to the circus and only one to MI5.
† Mills, *Bertram Mills Circus*, photo following p.130.
‡ Borra obituary, *The Independent*, 31 October 1998.

was to take my eye off the peanuts for a second or two. He had spent the whole afternoon drilling holes through peanuts, filling them with cayenne pepper and sealing the ends with butter.[*]

* * *

Mills was initially pessimistic about MI5's prospects under Attlee's Labour government. After the successful wartime DG, Sir David Petrie, retired in 1946, Mills believed that Guy Liddell, the main internal candidate, was 'cheated' of the succession due to him.[†] Attlee's initial suspicions of MI5's anti-Labour bias led instead to the appointment of the Chief Constable of Kent, Sir Percy Sillitoe. Though an effective police chief, Sillitoe had little experience of intelligence. His attempts at disguise by methods such as wearing dark glasses or walking backwards out of aeroplanes merely made him more conspicuous.[‡]

Mills privately complained that 'rot set in when Attlee appointed Sillitoe'.[§] 'Tar' Robertson resigned in 1948[¶] and amused his colleagues by applying for Sillitoe's former post as Chief Constable of Kent. Sillitoe is unlikely to have given him a strong reference. Having failed to become Chief Constable, 'Tar' turned to farming instead.[**] Robertson's and Mills's close friend Dick White said later: 'I found Sillitoe vapid and shallow and frequently wrong. I was close to leaving to try my hand at something else.' Mills believed that

---

[*] Mills, *Bertram Mills Circus*, pp.226–7.
[†] CBM papers.
[‡] Andrew, *Defence of the Realm*, p.324.
[§] CBM papers.
[¶] Unlike 'Tar' Robertson, who was a career MI5 officer, most B1a officers, like Mills, were wartime recruits who left at the end of the war and usually returned to their pre-war professions.
[**] Elliott, *Gentleman Spymaster*.

White probably stayed on in MI5 mainly 'because he didn't fancy returning to schoolmastering', his only previous profession.[*]

Attlee, however, paid far more attention to MI5 intelligence than either Mills or White had expected. He saw Sillitoe (or Liddell, who became his Deputy) far more frequently than any subsequent Prime Minister met any DG during the remainder of the twentieth century. Sillitoe's direct access to Attlee was potentially a considerable asset for the Security Service which, as Dick White later acknowledged, he and other senior officers, because of their low opinion of the DG, failed to exploit adequately. Though a committed Conservative, Mills admired Attlee personally.[†]

Sillitoe and Liddell were instructed to inform Attlee, and him alone, about any MP, irrespective of party, who was 'a proven member of a subversive organisation'.[‡] In May 1949, Sillitoe told Attlee that 'we now had quite a number of agents in the Communist Party who were well-placed and gave us good coverage.' 'The P.M.', noted Liddell, 'seemed particularly pleased about this.'[§] Ever since his landslide victory in 1945, Attlee had been worried about what he believed were 'crypto-Communists' on the Labour benches. The communist *Daily Worker* news editor, Douglas Hyde, later recalled answering the phone on the morning after the election:

> The man at the other end announced himself as the new Labour member for his constituency. He followed it with a loud guffaw and rang off. I had known him as a Communist Party man for years . . . By the time the list [of Labour MPs] was complete, we

---

[*]   CBM papers.

[†]   Christopher Mills recalls, 'My father knew Attlee and always spoke very highly of him.'

[‡]   Andrew, *Defence of the Realm*, p.322.

[§]   Guy Liddell diary, 27 May 1949.

knew that we had at least eight or nine 'cryptos' in the House of Commons in addition to our two publicly acknowledged M.P.s.*

Mills shared Attlee's suspicions that Labour benches included a number of crypto-communists. During the Attlee government, Sillitoe was a rare (perhaps unique) example of a DG who inspired greater confidence in No.10 than at MI5 headquarters.

* * *

Mills rejoiced at Churchill's return to power as peacetime Prime Minister after the Conservative election victory in October 1951, shortly before his seventy-seventh birthday and just over six years after his defeat in the 1945 election. Guy Liddell, the MI5 DDG (whom Mills believed should have been DG), noted in his diary, and probably told Mills, after his first visit to brief Churchill at No.10:

> I had to wait a little as the Prime Minister had not come down after his customary siesta. Eventually I was ushered into the Cabinet Room where he was sitting alone, contemplating some papers...
>
> He could not have been more charming and expressed his thanks for the trouble we [MI5] had taken [in vetting one of his staff]. Just as I was going away he said, 'How are you getting on over there?' I said we were getting on all right but that we were extremely pressed with work and had a really hard nut to crack, due to a large extent to the excellence of Russian security. He referred

---

* Francis Beckett's history of the Communist Party concludes that, after the 1945 election, 'About a dozen of the 393 Labour MPs were either secret CP members or were close to the CP, sharing its beliefs and enjoying the company of its leaders.' Attlee told Sillitoe in 1947 that he was 'certain' that Stephen Swingler MP was a C.P. member. Andrew, *Defence of the Realm*, p.847.

to the position which gave the Russians access to almost any part of this country, particularly to our factories.[*]

Liddell found Churchill better informed than the Foreign Secretary, Sir Anthony Eden, on the mounting evidence that Kim Philby was a Soviet spy. It was at Churchill's insistence that Philby's interrogation by MI5 was brought forward to 12 December. Though the evidence against Philby was inadequate for a successful prosecution and some of his MI6 colleagues continued to support him, MI5 had no doubt about his guilt. Mills despised him and never mentioned Philby's name to his family.

Some of the intelligence that most intrigued Churchill on his return to No.10 came, ironically, to MI5 from the Intelligence Bureau (IB) in New Delhi founded by Jawaharlal Nehru, the first Prime Minister of independent India and second only to Churchill as the world's most famous Old Harrovian politician. As Churchill was intrigued to discover, the IB had greater confidence in MI5 and in his foreign and security policy than it did in Nehru's. The first head of the IB, T. G. Sanjeevi, shared MI5's deep suspicions of the corrupt pro-Soviet Krishna Menon, Nehru's closest foreign policy adviser who went on from being first Indian High Commissioner to the United Kingdom in London to Indian representative at the UN. Fears of Menon's pro-Soviet sympathies were well-founded. On at least one occasion during his later political career in India, the KGB paid his election expenses.[†]

A steady stream of IB officials took part in MI5 training courses in London. Sanjeevi's successor, B. N. Mullik, was also an enthusiastic supporter of liaising closely with MI5. After visiting London

---

[*] Guy Liddell diary, 7 December 1951.
[†] Andrew and Mitrokhin, *The Mitrokhin Archive II*, pp.314–15, 561n20.

for a Commonwealth Security Conference, he wrote to MI5: '...In my talks and discussions, I never felt that I was dealing with any organisation which was not my own. Besides this, the hospitality and kindness which all of you showed me was also quite overwhelming.'* Had Nehru seen Mullik's letter, he would probably have been horrified.

Churchill and his Home Secretary, David Maxwell Fyfe, the minister responsible for MI5, had far greater confidence in Dick White than in Sillitoe. Resentful of his growing unpopularity among senior staff, Sillitoe resigned suddenly as DG in 1953, dramatically cutting all ties with MI5 by ordering the destruction of his official record of service. He was succeeded by White. Anthony Simkins, a future DDG, spoke for many of his senior colleagues, as well as Mills, when he said delightedly: 'We've got a professional and not a policeman in charge!'†

Though naturally clubbable, White was determined that both he and MI5 should return to the shadows as soon as possible after Sillitoe's acrimonious departure. Churchill and Maxwell Fyfe agreed with White. Churchill's bestselling war memoirs included no mention of MI5, MI6 or Bletchley Park. Officially, MI6 did not exist and Britain had no SIGINT agency. Though Sillitoe's appointment had been publicly announced, newspaper editors were asked not to publish White's name 'in the national interest'.‡ They did not do so. Mills, however, was fully briefed. 'The day Dick became DG,' Mills wrote later, 'things changed, for he knew what would be wanted of the Security Service in the face of a new and powerful enemy [Soviet Communism].'

Though Mills's paid employment by MI5 had ended in October

---

*   Andrew, *Defence of the Realm*, p.445.
†   Ibid., p.324.
‡   The request came from the Chairman of the D-Notice Committee, which advised on the publication of matters affecting national security.

1945, he continued to work part-time 'for MI5 or 6 or both without being paid a penny' until 1976, when he was seventy-four – well past the normal retirement age for full-time intelligence personnel.[*] He was very relieved that no job was found in either MI5 or MI6 for his bête noire, Sir William 'Little Bill' Stephenson, wartime head of BSC. After initial overtures by Stephenson failed, he came to Claridge's Hotel in London in 1950, accompanied by his friend, General 'Wild Bill' Donovan, Roosevelt's wartime intelligence chief, to put his case in person. After a meeting at Claridge's, Guy Liddell wrote: 'Bill Stephenson was very friendly. He evidently wants to see me again before he goes back. I suspect that he wants us to employ him in some way or another, and this, of course, would be impossible.'[†]

* * *

Post-war plans for stretching the underfunded MI6's resources included recruiting British businessmen who ran their companies without interference from a board of directors and were able to work abroad part-time for MI6 under the cover of their business.[‡] This job description fitted Cyril Mills exactly. However, renewing the oldest and closest of his pre-war German business connections – with the Zirkus Krone in Munich, once a favourite speaking venue for Adolf Hitler[§] – was made impossible by the destruction of its buildings by Allied bombing late in the war. A temporary post-war circus building in Munich was confiscated by US occupation forces

---

*   CBM papers.

†   Guy Liddell diary, 25 June 1950.

‡   'Future Organisation of the S.I.S. [MI6]', report of committee chaired by Sir Nevile Bland, October 1944. The official history of MI6 describes this report as 'a crucial document' which 'formed the basis for the organisation of the Service as it emerged after 1945'. Jeffery, *MI6*, pp.599–603.

§   See above, pp.32–4.

from the Krone family, which did not recover control of its circus until 1948.[*]

Mills's first post-war visit to Germany in 1948, to recruit new acts for the circus, was to the British occupied zone in north-western Germany, whose size and population were about half that of Britain itself. Since ex-enemy aliens were banned from employment in Britain until 1950, Mills found that 'getting permission to go to Germany was not easy'. MI6, however, persuaded the Foreign Office to allow Mills to visit resettlement camps for 'displaced persons' to recruit non-German circus performers:[†]

> I flew to Hamburg with the R.A.F. and there the F.O. provided me with a car which took me first back to the Hagenbeck Zoo at Stellingen where I was welcomed by my old friends Lorenz and Heinrich [Hagenbeck].[‡] The destruction in Hamburg and around the docks was my first sight of what real bombing means and I said to myself: 'And we thought we had been bombed!'

In one week at the end of July 1943, a firestorm caused by Allied bombing led to about 38,000 deaths. By the end of the war over half the homes in Hamburg had been destroyed.

> I soon realised that there was little talent in the resettlement camps and decided to see as many circuses as I could find, in case there were still artistes from what had been the occupied countries in them. I was the first English circus man [that German circuses] had seen for nearly ten years and, as I arrived with an

---

[*]   'Circus Krone'; www.circopedia.org.
[†]   Mills, *Bertram Mills Circus*, p.158. Mills's partly autobiographical history of the Bertram Mills Circus makes no reference to MI6, let alone to his work for it, which he later revealed to his family.
[‡]   On Mills's pre-war contacts with the Hagenbecks and their circus, see above, p.66.

army car and a corporal as my chauffeur, I think they believed I must be a very important person.

Though Mills received many dinner invitations from German circus owners, he refused all of them, fearing that, because of the serious food shortages,

> they would have to go short if I accepted their hospitality. As a search for talent the whole trip was a failure and the only act I found was that of Jolly, the Austrian [juggler] … For the rest of the Olympia programme I had to rely on Hungary, Czechoslovakia, Scandinavia, France and the Low Countries.*

MI6's failure to develop a significant role in Germany before the British occupied zone came to an end in 1949 with the founding of the (West) German Federal Republic helps to explain Mills's private criticisms of the service's Chief, Sir Stewart Menzies.† Though the MI6 station set up by Menzies in the occupied zone was easily the largest in Europe, the official history reveals that 'no initial directive has survived for the new station'. 'A perhaps apocryphal story relates that when an [MI6] secretary was asked by a male acquaintance what they did in the No.1 Planning and Evaluation Unit, she replied that "in the morning we plan and in the afternoon we evaluate what we planned in the morning".'

Though 'perhaps apocryphal', the story is sufficiently credible to appear in the MI6 official history.‡

The most active intelligence agency in the occupied zone, the

---

*   Mills, *Bertram Mills Circus*, pp.158–9.
†   See below, p.220.
‡   Jeffery, *MI6*, pp.664–5.

British Intelligence Objectives Sub-Committee (BIOS) was run not by MI6 but by the Board of Trade. BIOS sent numerous industrialists, scientists and technical experts to investigate and purloin German innovations and patents in fields ranging from ceramics to electron microscopes – an ambitious programme of industrial espionage masquerading as a quest for 'intellectual reparations'.* BIOS operations led to a number of well-publicised scandals and parliamentary questions, among them the attempt by BIOS representatives in 1946 to intimidate Maria Mühlens, the wealthy owner of the Eau de Cologne 4711 business, into handing over the secret recipe which had been used since 1799. In reality, the BIOS representatives, who claimed to be British colonels, worked for the Anglo-Dutch giant Unilever. Mühlens successfully resisted their demands.†

Mills's circus connections were of greater use to British intelligence in the Soviet Bloc under construction in Central Europe where MI6 personnel were woefully thin on the ground, than in post-war Germany. Mills's trips to Czechoslovakia and Hungary on circus business provided first-hand insights into the role of Soviet intelligence in the establishment of subservient communist one-party states. However, he no longer had the freedom he had enjoyed in his pre-war work for MI6 to fly himself to the Continent and carry out covert aerial reconnaissance: 'By 1951 a single-engined aircraft with no radio was no longer practicable, or I could not enter any of the controlled zones around airports and there were few private landing grounds, so I gave up flying…'‡

---

* Douglas M. O'Reagan, *Taking Nazi Technology: Allied Exploitation of German Science after the Second World War* (Baltimore: Johns Hopkins University Press, 2019).
† Daniel Cowling, *Don't Let's Be Beastly to the Germans: The British Occupation of Germany, 1945–49* (London: Head of Zeus, 2023), ch.15.
‡ Mills, *Bertram Mills Circus*, p.95.

Mills's first trip behind the Iron Curtain was to Czechoslovakia by commercial airliner soon after the communist seizure of power in 1948.[*] As the MI6 official history acknowledges: 'Such intelligence sources as there were had been mostly swept away, the overt collection of information was gravely impaired, and the demands on [MI6] escalated to include the most trivial details of everyday life...'[†]

From the moment Mills arrived in Prague, he was under intelligence surveillance:

...Soon after leaving Prague airport I realised I was being followed by three men who went everywhere I went with the infallibility of shadows. Having signed in at a hotel and gone to a café, I saw them sitting two tables away so told the waiter to take them some beer ... When the beer was served they all raised their glasses to me but, even if it had relieved the tension, they had orders to follow me and did not seem disturbed by the fact that I knew about it. At the circus they split up and took seats at three strategic points in case I planned to give them the slip.[‡]

Mills's main circus contact in Prague was the famous Czech wild animal trainer Vojtech Trubka,[§] whom he had known well before the war.[¶] Out of earshot of Mills's surveillance team, Trubka warned him – probably unnecessarily – that, 'I should probably be approached

---

[*] As Mills probably suspected, the first Soviet intelligence 'advisers' arrived in Prague shortly after the communist takeover in 1948. They played a crucial role in the political show-trials which accompanied the establishment of the communist one-party state. Daniela Richterova, *Watching the Jackals: Czechoslovak Spies, Terrorists and Revolutionaries* (Washington DC: Georgetown University Press, 2024).

[†] Jeffery, *MI6*, pp.655–6.

[‡] Mills, *Bertram Mills Circus*, p.99.

[§] The Prague intelligence (StB) archives contain a file on another Vojtech Trubka (a Czech communist suspected of ideological unorthodoxy) but none on the wild animal trainer of that name. There is also no file on Cyril Mills. I am grateful to Dr Daniela Richterova for this information.

[¶] See above, p.79.

by people offering valuables, including diamonds, at absurdly low prices if I paid in foreign currency; I should have nothing to do with such people as they would probably be agents provocateurs and if I were tempted I should find myself in the local cooler.'

Mills discovered that Trubka had been appointed 'some kind of commissar', in charge of running a Prague circus – despite what Mills considered his lack of managerial ability. Probably after taking advice from Mills, Trubka succeeded in escaping to the west by obtaining a lucrative contract to perform abroad with some of his tigers. 'His political bosses', Mills believed, 'were so keen to earn foreign currency that they let him go and neither he nor the tigers ever returned.'*

After Prague, Mills's next stop was Budapest, which before the war had been one of his 'favourite cities' with a successful circus as well as nightclub floor shows 'as lavish as anywhere in Europe.'† In Budapest, unlike Prague, Mills was not conscious of continuous intelligence surveillance. A possible explanation is that the new Hungarian communist security service, the AVH, closely supervised by KGB 'advisers', was devoting most of its resources to huge internal purges. About 600,000 Hungarians were deported to the Soviet gulag. One of the distinguishing characteristics of Stalinist intelligence operations during the early Cold War, as for much of the 1930s, were the conspiracy theories which led them to target imaginary enemies as well as real opponents. Stalin and the KGB interpreted the break with Moscow by Marshal Tito's communist Yugoslavia in 1948 as part of a huge imperialist conspiracy to undermine the new Soviet Bloc in Eastern and Central Europe.‡

While in Hungary on circus business, Mills was invited to dinner at Budapest's best restaurant by a friend whose circus was about to

---

*　Mills, *Bertram Mills Circus*, pp.99–100.

†　Ibid., p.99.

‡　Andrew, *Secret World*, pp.680–81.

be nationalised. The guest of honour, to whom he was warned to be 'most polite', was a Soviet 'high-ranking officer of the Secret Police who controlled the admission to Hungary of foreign performers':

> A more villainous looking character I have never seen; half Mongolian, he would have been a casting director's joy if he had been looking for a thug for a James Bond film, but if Bond had met him I think he would have decided to go out of business. He was accompanied by a twenty-year-old blonde ... probably an employee of his organisation who, when at work, was planted in the hotels used by visiting foreigners, but who in her spare time was one of his perks.*

At his secret meetings with George VI, Sir Stewart Menzies 'always tried to give [him] a good spy story'.† No record was kept of their discussions,‡ but, since Menzies knew of the King's interest in the circus, the 'spy stories' may well have included Mills's dinner with the 'villainous' Soviet adviser to Hungarian intelligence.

Mills's circus-owner friend in Budapest failed to escape the AVH purge: 'Although over sixty, [he] was sent to work in the mines, where he died after a short time.' Though Mills was too discreet to make written records of meetings with his friends and contacts in MI6, he undoubtedly kept them well informed of his encounters in the Soviet Bloc. MI6 intelligence collection in Hungary was so sparse during the post-war decade that it does not feature at all in its official history. Mills had opportunities denied to both the British embassy and its MI6 station – among them witnessing at first hand the sycophancy expected from Hungarian officials by KGB advisers.

---

* Mills, *Bertram Mills Circus*, pp.100–101.
† Smith, *The Real Special Relationship*, p.92.
‡ There is no mention of the meetings in the MI6 official history.

One of the alleged accomplices of the Hungarian Minister of the Interior, László Rajk, in the non-existent Titoist plot for which Rajk was executed in 1949, noted how, during his interrogation, officers of the Hungarian security service, the AVH, 'smiled a flattering, servile smile when the Russians spoke to them' and 'reacted to the most witless jokes of the [KGB] officers with obsequious trumpeting of immoderate laughter'.*

The British envoy in Budapest, George Wallinger, told the Joint Intelligence Committee (JIC) in 1950 that he 'could not describe the feeling of depression and frustration which surrounded the work of himself and his staff. There was very little opportunity of obtaining intelligence or of normal discussion with anybody official or otherwise'.† A year later, Wallinger told the JIC that 'Hungary had absolutely no independence at all; even in minor matters, he thought that they had often to refer back to Moscow'. In honour of Stalin's seventieth birthday in 1949, more red stars, often outsized, were affixed to historic buildings in Budapest than in any other great city outside Russia.

The circus performers most affected by the creation of the Soviet Bloc were the clowns. The role of the Cheka (forerunner of the KGB) in dealing with politically incorrect clowns after the Bolshevik Revolution thirty years earlier meant that Mills knew what to expect. The Cheka's first victims in Moscow had included Russia's two most famous clowns, Bim (Ivan Radunsky, Director of Moscow's Salamonsky Circus) and Bom (Polish-born Mieszyslaw Stanevsky), who performed as the duo Bim-Bom and dared to make fun of the Bolshevik regime. Chekists, who attended a performance at the Salamonsky Circus on 27 March 1918, were outraged by a sketch in which Bim brandished portraits of Lenin and Trotsky. On being asked by

---

* Andrew and Mitrokhin, *The Mitrokhin Archive*, pp.322–3.
† Guy Liddell diary, 14 September 1950.

Bom what he was planning to do with them, Bim replied, 'I'll hang one, and put the other up against the wall.' The Chekists in the audience leapt into the ring to halt the performance. The audience initially assumed that this was part of the act, but when the clown duo tried to escape and the Chekists began to fire their handguns into the air, the crowd panicked. Next day, Bim-Bom were interrogated by the Cheka but seem to have escaped with a warning.[*] No clown in the post-war Soviet Bloc dared to make jokes about Stalin.[†] For a decade after the Second World War, Mills made it his personal mission to prevent any performance in Britain by the world-famous Moscow State Circus:

> The Moscow State Circus was offered to us a long time before it [first] came to Britain [in 1956], but I turned it down for two reasons. In the first place, I was required to take a complete show, but was given only the vaguest indications of what it would contain. Secondly, it was not offered by the Russian Ministry of Culture, which I think would have been the proper procedure, but by a representative of a Communist front organisation and I visualised the possibility that what we were asked to pay, or at least part of it, would find its way into the pockets of the [British] Communist Party. From a purely business point of view I probably did the wrong thing, but I believe I did it for the right reasons.[‡]

Since his wartime work as an MI5 officer, Mills had been well aware that Moscow secretly sent regular subsidies to the British and other

---

[*]   Andrew and Green, *Stars and Spies*, pp.199–200.
[†]   During a visit to the Estonian State Archives of the Former Estonian KGB in Tallinn, I was shown a multi-volume file on the lengthy KGB investigation which followed the report of a disrespectful cartoon of Stalin. Though neither the cartoon nor its author (if they existed) was ever discovered, the investigation was clearly regarded as a high priority.
[‡]   Mills, *Bertram Mills Circus*, p.105.

western communist parties. He probably also knew that during the war MI5 had bugged the British Communist Party's King Street HQ in London. After the war, MI5 maintained what it called 'good coverage' of covert Soviet funding of the CPGB, monitoring by physical surveillance and bugged telephones the regular collection of Soviet cash subsidies by two members of the party's International Department.[*] Because of his belief that the proceeds of Moscow State Circus performances in Britain would find their way 'into the pockets of the Communist Party', which Mills loathed as a Soviet auxiliary during the Cold War, he used his influence after the circus's first visit in 1956 to help prevent it returning for another fifteen years.[†]

Mills also loathed the way that during tours in the west, performers in the Moscow State Circus were accompanied everywhere they went by KGB minders, whose main task was to prevent any of them defecting. After seeing a performance by the State Circus at the Cirque Royal in Brussels, Mills tried to go backstage

> ...to have a word with a few of the artistes, but the way to the dressing rooms was barred by a sentry in private clothes and after a few minutes the whole troupe was marched down the stairs and into a waiting bus by two more men in civilian clothes. When they had gone the Belgian gate-keeper told me this was the daily routine and that the ride to and from the hotel was all they ever saw of Brussels unless they went for walk accompanied by [KGB] escorts.[‡]

* * *

---

[*]   Andrew, *Defence of the Realm*, p.403.
[†]   The Moscow State Circus visited Britain twice more during the Cold War – in 1985 and 1988.
[‡]   Mills, *Bertram Mills Circus*, pp.106–8.

Mills's work for MI6 in the early Cold War had far less impact than that before the Second World War. The low-level intelligence he was able to collect during his travels in the Soviet Bloc could not compare with the high-grade intelligence on aerial rearmament he had obtained while flying solo over pre-war Nazi Germany. Stalin's Russia and, increasingly, its Soviet Bloc allies were far more difficult intelligence targets than Hitler's Germany in the 1930s. There was also a huge gap between the resources that British and Soviet intelligence had in the early Cold War. By the early 1950s, with approximately 200,000 members, the KGB[*] was by far the largest intelligence service in the world.[†] The combined strength of MI5 and MI6 was about 1 per cent that of the KGB.[‡]

The problems created for British foreign intelligence operations by inadequate resources were compounded, in Mills's view, by poor leadership. As peacetime Chief of MI6, Sir Stewart Menzies was no longer able, as in wartime, to conceal his own limitations by basking in the reflected glory of the codebreakers of Bletchley Park (for whom he had administrative, but not operational, responsibility). Mills concluded from his own experience of working for MI6 at the start of the Cold War that it was 'in a ghastly mess as a result of the stupidity and incompetence of Menzies', who remained Chief until 1952.[§] Menzies was visibly upset by a 1949 JIC review, which fairly concluded that MI6 reports on Soviet war plans were 'often unreliable and lacking in factual information'.[¶]

---

[*] Known as the MGB until 1954.

[†] Walton, *Spies*, pp.125–6. The second biggest intelligence service in the world was Soviet military intelligence, the GRU.

[‡] In the early 1950s MI5 had just over 1,000 members; see Andrew, *Defence of the Realm*, appendix 2: 'Security Service Strength, 1909–2009'. No precise figures are available for MI6.

[§] Mills later described MI6 under Menzies as 'corrupt from end to end' – probably a reference to Soviet penetration rather than financial irregularities; CBM papers. Cyril's daughter, Sandra Menzies, believes that probably the only occasion upon which he met Menzies was at her wedding to Menzies' nephew.

[¶] Michael S. Goodman, *The Official History of the Joint Intelligence Committee*, vol.1 (London: Routledge, 2014), p.252.

Most MI6 agent networks in the Soviet Bloc were penetrated by the KGB and its allies – as was MI6 itself, notably in the person of the talented Kim Philby, whom some thought of as a future succes-sor to Menzies. When Philby published his memoirs in 1968 (five years after fleeing to Moscow), Mills was not surprised by his con-descending comments on Menzies as an ideal Chief from his and the KGB's point of view:

> I look back on the Chief with enduring affection ... His intellectu-al equipment was unimpressive, and his knowledge of the world and views about it were just what one would expect from a fairly cloistered son of the upper levels of the British Establishment. In my own field, counter-espionage, his attitudes were schoolboyish – bars, beards and blondes.*

Philby was equally condescending about General Sir John 'Sinbad' Sinclair, who succeeded Menzies as Chief in 1952 and who, unlike Dick White, refused to credit persuasive evidence that Philby was a long-standing Soviet spy: 'Sinclair, though not overloaded with mental gifts (he would not have claimed them) was humane, en-ergetic and so obviously upright that it was impossible to withhold admiration ... It was distasteful to lie in my teeth to the honest Sinclair.'†

Though Philby was forced to leave MI6 after being discredited by the flight to Moscow of his friend and former lodger Guy Burgess in 1951, another major Soviet spy, George Blake, remained in MI6. 'I liked being an intelligence officer', Blake later recalled. 'I loved the romantic side of the job.' Among the biggest secrets betrayed

---

*   Philby, *My Silent War*, pp.104–5.
†   Ibid., pp.105, 171.

by Blake was Operation GOLD, one of the most ingenious US–UK intelligence operations of the Cold War: the secret construction of a 500-metre-long, 2-metre-high underground tunnel from West to East Berlin to intercept landline communications to and from Soviet military and intelligence headquarters at Karlshorst in the East Berlin suburbs.* In the year before the KGB staged an 'accidental' discovery of the tunnel in April 1956, Operation GOLD generated over 50,000 reels of magnetic tape recording intercepted Soviet and East German communications. East Germany turned its end of the tunnel into a major tourist attraction with long queues, especially at weekends.†

Four years later, Mills was to allow a miniature eavesdropping tunnel, targeted on the Russian embassy in London, to be constructed underneath his own garden lawn.‡ It did not compare, however, to the far more sophisticated tunnel on public display in East Berlin.

Mills's confidence in MI6 greatly improved when Dick White was moved from MI5 to replace the discredited Sinclair as its Chief in 1956. He was less happy that White was succeeded as DG of MI5 by his former Deputy, Roger Hollis. Though Hollis was a friend, Mills doubted whether he had the leadership qualities required of a successful DG. White later came to the same conclusion, writing in a sympathetic obituary that, though respected within the Security Service during his nine years as DG, Hollis 'did not enjoy easy personal relations with its ordinary members who tended to find him reserved and aloof'. Some, probably many, did not meet him at all.

---

* Roger Hermiston, *The Greatest Traitor: The Secret Lives of Agent George Blake* (London: Aurum Press, 2013); Andrew, *Defence of the Realm*, pp.488–90.
† Steve Vogel, *Betrayal in Berlin: George Blake, the Berlin Tunnel and the Greatest Conspiracy of the Cold War* (London: John Murray, 2020).
‡ See below, p.231.

One staff member, who encountered Hollis in the lift and failed to recognise him, said: 'Oh, we haven't met. What section are you?' 'I am the DG,' replied Hollis.* Walter Bell, Hollis's Private Secretary during his first year as DG, found his style of leadership plodding.†

As Mills later acknowledged, he was 'none too keen' on using his circus connections to travel to East Berlin, which contained the largest KGB station outside Moscow, as well as the HQ of its ally, the East German Stasi. Possibly after being persuaded by White, he did so for the first time in 1959. A highly successful 'wild animal act' at a circus in East Berlin gave Mills a plausible reason to cross into the Soviet sector. No doubt on MI6 advice, he posed as a German for the only time during his Continental travels. The daughter of a German with whom Cyril had done 'a lot' of pre-war circus business, agreed to drive him from the British to the Soviet sector of Berlin. '…But there were conditions. I should go hatless, as an English hat would be spotted; I should wear her husband's German raincoat, keep my mouth shut and let her do the talking, if any.'

The 'commissar' of the circus he visited in the Soviet sector, a former German circus owner, pretended to be pro-communist. But, as Mills discovered, the supposedly communist commissar and a colleague were secretly planning an epic escape to the west with some of their circus animals across the East German frontier '…Some months later, having routed a small "state circus" along the … frontier through small towns, they succeeded – elephants and all. They must have had good friends among the [frontier] guards who probably went with them. If they did not, I expect they would have been shot.'

Before leaving the Soviet sector, Mills had personally arranged

---

* Andrew, *Defence of the Realm*, p.326.
† Burns, *A Faithful Spy*, p.293.

for a circus artiste with 'a new and very interesting act' to escape to London:

> I must keep repeating the word artiste, for a mention of the name or even the sex might still result in repercussions on parents or relatives … From East Berlin the artiste would take the U-Bahn (Underground) to the British sector and then be flown in a British plane to Hamburg … The plot took some time to hatch but it worked like a Swiss watch; a highly talented artiste was freed and the success of the act in London made all the trouble worthwhile.[*]

Mills kept the secret, never revealing the identity of the 'highly talented artiste' from East Berlin even to his children. A possible clue, however, is that the only performer whose national origins were not mentioned in the Bertram Mills programme for Olympia late in 1959 used the name 'Atilana'.[†] According to the circus programme: 'She has been universally acclaimed as the greatest girl wire walker of our time – no mean praise for a girl of 24. Her act is climaxed by a somersault on the wire without any balancing aid whatsoever.'[‡] The identification of Atilana as the 'highly talented artiste' whom Mills helped to escape in 1959 is not, however, conclusive. It is possible that the artistes at Olympia included an East German who sought to conceal their identity by falsifying their nationality.[§]

Mills's ability to attract more Atilanas to his circus ended with the construction, in 1961, of the heavily fortified Berlin Wall, which

---

[*] Mills, *Bertram Mills Circus*, pp.132–3. Curiously, there is almost no mention of circuses, despite their popularity, in the best recent histories of East and West Germany during the Cold War: Frank Trentmann, *Out of the Darkness: The Germans 1922–2022* (London: Allen Lane, 2023); Katya Hoyer, *Beyond the Wall: East Germany 1949–1990* (London: Allen Lane, 2023).

[†] I am grateful to Sandra Menzies for this information.

[‡] CBM papers.

[§] Atilana later claimed to be Spanish.

divided East from West Berlin, and the strengthening of the much lengthier frontier between East and West Germany. Most (but not all) further escapes were prevented for almost thirty years. At least 140 people died or were killed trying to cross the Wall. Cyril's family vividly recall his rejoicings when the Wall was finally toppled in 1989.

CHAPTER 9

THE RUSSIAN EMBASSY, MILLS AND OPERATION FOOT

Throughout Harold Macmillan's Conservative government (1957–63), Cyril Mills remained in closer touch with the Security Service than either most ministers or the Labour front bench. When the Labour leadership decided to seek MI5's help in investigating alleged secret communists within the Parliamentary Labour Party (PLP) in 1961, it did not know how to do so. With the approval of the Party Leader, Hugh Gaitskell, the Deputy Leader, George Brown, approached the journalist Chapman Pincher who supplied him with contact details for both Sir Roger Hollis and the MI6 Chief, Sir Dick White. MI5 was given a handwritten list on Commons notepaper of sixteen Labour MPs who 'were in effect members of the CPGB pretending to be Labour members or men under Communist Party direction' and nine 'possible' additional crypto-communists. Hollis thought the Labour leadership's fears of communist penetration of the PLP somewhat alarmist.*

---

* The handwritten list by the former (and future) Labour Cabinet minister Patrick Gordon Walker given to MI5 survives in MI5 files. It is reproduced in Andrew, *Defence of the Realm*, pp.411–13. The KGB was less effective than its Czechoslovak ally, the StB, in targeting MPs. During the 1950s and 1960s, Czechoslovakia had more embassies than the Soviet Union in both the west and the developing world; Richterova, *Watching the Jackals*.

As Home Secretary for most of the Macmillan government, R. A. ('Rab') Butler was the minister responsible for MI5. At his first meeting with Hollis in 1957, Butler said he 'knew already that the Security Service was doing a very good job, and promised us all the support he could give us.' In reality, Butler knew so little about MI5 that he did not even know where it was based. When Hollis told him its headquarters were at Leconfield House in Curzon Street, Mayfair, he seemed surprised 'as he imagined we operated under cover' – apparently believing MI5 hid its staff in safe houses around London rather than accommodating most of them in a conventional office building.[*] London bus conductors, usually happy to point out MI5 HQ to their passengers, were better informed than the Home Secretary.

Butler accepted an invitation from Hollis to see Leconfield House for himself.[†] What probably struck him most was its shabbiness. When the future MI5 DG, Stella Rimington, began work at Leconfield House in 1969, she found it still 'dreadfully run down'. 'The inside had not been painted for an age, the windows were dirty and everything about it was dark and gloomy.'[‡] Since 1960, Mills, by contrast, had been installed by MI5 in one of London's most expensive mansions to help the service monitor Soviet diplomats and intelligence personnel.

Most Soviet intelligence officers in London operated under either diplomatic or other official cover. The basis of MI5 counterespionage against KGB and GRU operations was the wearisome surveillance by various means of the Soviet embassy, the nearby KGB and GRU intelligence 'residencies' and the Trade Delegation.

---

[*] Andrew, *Defence of the Realm*, p.483.
[†] Ibid.
[‡] Stella Rimington, *Open Secret: The Autobiography of the Former Director-General of MI5* (London: Hutchinson, 2001), p.107. MI5 left Leconfield House in 1977.

It is unlikely that either Butler or Macmillan was aware that Hollis had given Cyril Mills a key role in expanding this surveillance. Though Macmillan liked and respected Sir Dick White, he called the less sociable Hollis 'insignificant' and inept.[*]

Mills's private papers reveal that, early in 1960, Richard Butler (no relation to Rab), a senior MI5 officer whom he had first met almost twenty years earlier when Butler was Sir David Petrie's wartime personal assistant,[†] brought him a top-secret request from his friend Roger Hollis. Mills was asked by the DG if he 'would do something very important in connection with Security':

A few days later I met Hollis and he told me what he wanted me to do. We were to move into [17] K[ensington] P[alace] G[ardens] and allow M.I.5 to occupy and use the attics for the installation of bugging equipment which would be used to listen to what was going on in the Soviet Embassy on the other side of the road, the offices of the Service Attachés at No.16 and the so-called Ministry of Culture at No.18.

I said I could not possibly afford the staff which would be necessary for running a house with 34 rooms and I was told that if I let them know what my living expenses were in Stanhope Terrace [the Mills family home in Paddington] M.I.5 would make up the difference … On the other hand I should not be paid a salary or expenses unless the latter were incurred in helping them do the work they had in mind.

Mills agreed.[‡]

---

[*] Andrew, *Defence of the Realm*, p.483.
[†] See above, p.136.
[‡] CBM papers.

Popularly known as 'Millionaires [later Billionaires] Row', Kensington Palace Gardens (KPG), whose freehold is owned by the Crown Estate, was London's most expensive street. In recent versions of the traditional boardgame Monopoly, KPG replaces Mayfair as the most valuable property. Stretching half a mile from Bayswater Road in the north to Kensington High Street in the south, each end is guarded by gates and checkpoints manned by Diplomatic Protection Group police officers because of the presence of Russian and other diplomatic buildings. Though pedestrian access is unrestricted, vehicles require a security pass.

Some of Mills's new neighbours in 'Millionaires Row' believed that the arrival of a circus family lowered the tone of their exclusive street. Among them was Lady Seligman who had been born at 17 KPG when it was owned by her millionaire father, Sir Isaac Seligman. According to the *Daily Sketch*:

> Lady Seligman is 81 – and very annoyed.
> Subject of her wrath circus owner Mr Cyril Mills ... :
> 'I am sure Mr Mills is not the sort of man to appreciate a fine house like that. It is tragic to see it fall into the wrong hands.'
> A high-handed comment?
> We thought so.
> And Mrs [Mimi] Mills said so.*

In reality, the 'fine house' fondly remembered from childhood by Lady Seligman had become badly run down. Mills complained that it was 'filthy beyond description'. The previous leaseholder, Lady Grace Dance, a former professional dancer who died early in 1960 at the age

---

* *Daily Sketch*, 22 July 1960.

of eighty-three, had lived alone in growing squalor for some years after the death of her wealthy husband. Before the Mills family moved into 17 KPG, MI5 agreed to pay for complete redecoration inside and out:

> When the decorators visited the house they said they would not allow their men to enter until the whole of the basement had been cleaned under their supervision by labourers from the Labour Exchange.

Once redecoration was complete, MI5 told Mills

> ...they wanted to dig a tunnel under the lawn to run cables to a house in the road behind ours which was exactly behind the house in which were the [Soviet] Service Attachés. While they dug the tunnel all the earth which came out of it had to be stored in the garage and when they put it back they were unable to pack it very tight with the result that its path across the lawn sank a few inches every few months and therefore the turf had to be lifted and a little earth placed beneath it.*

Mills's move to 17 KPG attracted colourful headlines such as 'Circus Man Moves Into Spy Street.' But it did not occur to anyone in the media or almost anyone in Whitehall, that for almost a quarter of a century, Britain's best-known 'Circus Man' had been a spy himself (part-time or full-time). When told by a journalist that the Soviet buildings next door contained Russian spies as well as diplomats, Mills managed to keep a straight face: 'Spies on either side of me? Oh goodness gracious!' His family, he explained, had moved to

---

* '17 Kensington Palace Gardens'; CBM papers, S.1.1.

KPG simply because their existing house in Paddington was 'far too small for us', as well as having no garden for the children: 'Take it from me. I have no feelings whatever about having Soviet Embassy officials as my neighbours.'*

As a wartime MI5 officer, Mills had known far more about SIGINT – including the ULTRA Secret – than most of Churchill's ministers and senior diplomats.[†] He was doubtless aware when he agreed to move to KPG in 1960 to facilitate 'listening in' to Soviet diplomatic buildings, that Hollis's earliest plans to bug the embassy went back to the Second World War.[‡] Mills was unaware, however, that, thanks chiefly to Kim Philby, the plans were also known to Soviet intelligence. In 1944, a decade after Philby's recruitment as a Soviet agent, his case officer in London, Boris Krötenschield, had reported to the Centre (KGB Moscow headquarters): 'STANLEY [Philby] informed me of a plan to bug simultaneously all the telephone conversations of all staff in Soviet [embassy] in England. STANLEY is an exceptionally valuable source.'[§]

The PUS at the Foreign Office, Sir William Strang, concluded in 1953, 'Sigint is our best source of intelligence about the Soviet Union and Satellites. In war it would again of course be vital.'[¶] But the ULTRA era was long gone. 'We are not at present reading any Russian cyphers…,' Strang noted regretfully. The majority of Soviet SIGINT came from unencrypted communications and 'traffic

---

*   Ibid.

†   See above, pp.91–3.

‡   Declassified GCHQ files reveal that in June 1943 Hollis and John Curry of MI5 met Alastair Denniston (former head of Bletchley Park, currently director of a diplomatic SIGINT unit) and Colonel Ted Maltby (Radio Security Service) to discuss 'the interception of certain apparently illicit transmission from this country which have been "DF-ed" [traced by direction-finding] to the Soviet embassy'. Aldrich, *GCHQ*, p.75.

§   Genrikh Borovik, *The Philby Files* (London: Little, Brown, 1994).

¶   John Ferris, *Behind the Enigma: The Authorised History of GCHQ, Britain's Secret Cyber-Intelligence Agency* (London: Bloomsbury, 2020), loc.5710.

analysis', the study (computerised from 1955) of patterns of communication in encrypted messages.*

The case for secretly monitoring the low-level signals traffic of the Soviet embassy in London was strengthened in 1956 by GCHQ's discovery of the TEMPEST phenomenon, which enabled emissions from electronic equipment to be intercepted from several hundred yards away.† In 1957 Cyril's friend, Sir Dick White, Chief of MI6 and Hollis's predecessor as DG of MI5, persuaded the Chiefs of Staff to back TEMPEST operations to intercept the communications of Soviet official premises in London. 'Orthodox methods of obtaining intelligence were particularly ineffective against totalitarian states', White argued, because of the difficulty of running well-placed human agents in Moscow and the Soviet Bloc.‡ Eavesdropping from 17 KPG on the Soviet embassy and neighbouring buildings was part of White's proposed alternative to agent recruitment in Moscow and was strongly supported by Hollis.

Soviet success in bugging foreign embassies in Moscow, which comfortably exceeded that of Britain and the United States in London and Washington, helps to explain the decision to run TEMPEST and other surveillance operations from 17 KPG. Remarkably, most published studies of US–Soviet relations continue to take no account of the haemorrhage of diplomatic secrets from the US embassy in Moscow for more than thirty years. The American embassy was penetrated almost continuously from when Soviet–American diplomatic relations began in 1933 until after the 1962 Missile Crisis. Just as Hollis began drawing up plans to bug the Soviet embassy in London in 1944, a long-overdue electronic sweep of the US embassy

---

*   Ibid.
†   Ibid., loc.12824. David Easter, 'The Impact of "Tempest" on Anglo-American Communications Security and Intelligence, 1943–1970', *Intelligence and National Security*, vol.36, no.1 (2021).
‡   Aldrich, *GCHQ*, pp.174–5.

in Moscow by an FBI expert discovered 120 hidden microphones in 24 hours.[*]

On 26 May 1960, only two months before Mills moved into 17 KPG, the United States publicly revealed for the first time one of the most remarkable successes achieved by Soviet intelligence in bugging its Moscow embassy. Henry Cabot Lodge Jr, US representative at the United Nations in New York, displayed to a Security Council meeting the eavesdropping device concealed in a wooden replica of the Great Seal of the United States presented by Soviet schoolchildren which hung above the Ambassador's desk until the device was discovered in 1952.[†] Cabot Lodge was unaware, however, that US embassy security in Moscow was still seriously compromised. At about the same time he made his speech to the Security Council, a team from the KGB headed by Nikolai Andreev was awarded the Lenin Prize for decrypting communications between the embassy and Washington.[‡]

Soviet intelligence took public revenge for Cabot Lodge's speech to the Security Council. At a 1961 press conference in Moscow, two defectors from the National Security Agency (NSA), the US SIGINT agency, Bernon F. Mitchell and William Hamilton Martin, declared that: 'The United States Government is as unscrupulous as it has accused the Soviet Government of being. Our main dissatisfaction concerned some of the practices the United States uses in gathering intelligence information ... intercepting and deciphering the secret communications of its own allies.' Among them, said Martin, were 'Italy, Turkey, France, Yugoslavia, the United Arab

---

[*]   Andrew, *Secret World*, p.662.

[†]   Christopher Andrew and Oleg Gordievsky, *KGB: The Inside Story of Its Foreign Operations from Lenin to Gorbachev* (London: Sceptre, 1991), pp.454–6.

[‡]   David Easter, 'State Department Cipher Machines and Communications Security in the Early Cold War, 1944–1965', *Intelligence and National Security*, vol.38 (2023), p.7.

Republic, Indonesia, Uruguay – that's enough to give a general picture, I guess."*

Plans for TEMPEST and other surveillance operations against the Soviet embassy in London from 17 KPG in 1960 were stimulated by the belated discovery of KGB bugging of the British embassy in Moscow. In October 1959 microphones were found in rooms that had been used as the embassy registry and for cipher communications. The Foreign Office believed there was 'a distinct possibility' that 'the Russians had ... been able to read our telegrams or pick `up information of value'.† Macmillan wearily concluded that bugging embassies by both the Soviet Union and, on a smaller scale, by some NATO members, was now part of diplomatic life: 'In every Embassy in the world there were listening devices in the walls, or the ink stands, or the telephones.'‡

On his appointment as Ambassador in Moscow in 1960, Sir Frank Roberts, one of the ablest diplomats of his generation, believed that at least his own office in the embassy was secure. This illusion was dispelled soon afterwards, however, when a technical expert from London arrived to make the first electronic sweep of the Ambassador's office. Roberts told the expert that he was wasting his time but would be allowed twenty minutes to complete his check. By the time the twenty minutes was up, the expert, who later became an MI6 officer, had discovered three listening devices. Just as he was withdrawing the third from behind the skirting board in the Ambassador's office, Roberts said, 'Give me that!', took it from him and began shouting into the device in Russian. Such experiences led to

---

* Andrew, *Secret World*, pp.674–5.
† Trevor Barnes, *Dead Doubles: The Extraordinary Worldwide Hunt for One of the Cold War's Most Notorious Spy Rings* (London: Weidenfeld & Nicolson, 2020), p.167.
‡ David Easter, 'Soviet Bloc and Western Bugging of Opponents' Diplomatic Premises during the Early Cold War', *Intelligence and National Security*, vol.31, no.1 (2016), p.47.

the construction of special rooms in British embassies which were believed to be proof against all eavesdropping attempts.[*] Eavesdropping, however, continued unabated in diplomats' living quarters.[†]

Aware that their penetration of the British, American and other Moscow embassies had been partly detected, the Russians increased the security of their own embassies and intelligence posts in London and other foreign capitals at the end of the 1950s. GCHQ ruefully acknowledged that 'in general their awareness of the need for the greatest possible precautions in the use of radio, and the need for complete security is outstanding'.[‡] By the time the Mills family moved into their KPG mansion there was no longer the prospect that TEMPEST or other electronic operations could obtain high-level intelligence from the neighbouring Soviet embassy and intelligence residencies. Less sophisticated forms of surveillance to collect lower-level intelligence, as well as to identify and monitor the growing number of Soviet intelligence and diplomatic personnel in London, were nonetheless a high priority. The total SIGINT budget was far higher than it had ever been in British peacetime history. By 1962, as Professor Richard J. Aldrich has shown, Britain was spending as much on SIGINT as on the whole of the Foreign Office and all its overseas embassies, legations and diplomats.[§]

* * *

*   Interview by Christopher Andrew with 'David', a former MI6 officer, in November 2012. Christopher Andrew, 'Remembering the Cuban Missile Crisis', in Len Scott, David Gioe and Christopher Andrew (eds), *An International History of the Cuban Missile Crisis: A 50-year retrospective* (London: Routledge, 2015).

†   During his first diplomatic posting in Moscow in 1962–64, Brian Crowe complained that 'You couldn't talk in your own flat without being overheard'. He also resisted a series of KGB honeytraps – unlike an Australian colleague who, he claimed, 'had a great time with Russian girls'. Sir Brian Crowe obituary, *The Times*, 9 April 2020.

‡   Evidence by Arthur Bonsall (GCHQ) to Romer Enquiry, 11 May 1961; TNA CAB 301/253. Barnes, *Dead Doubles*, p.215.

§   Walton, *Spies*, pp.246–7.

The Mills family's move to 17 KPG came during the most fraught period in the history of British–Soviet relations. There were entirely rational fears, which reached a climax during the Cuban Missile Crisis of October 1962, that the Cold War might end in a thermo-nuclear Armageddon.

In 1957, a government white paper had publicly admitted for the first time that there was 'no means of providing adequate protection for the people of this country against the consequences of an attack by nuclear weapons'.* The Campaign for Nuclear Disarmament (CND), founded in London in the same year, claimed to be Europe's largest single-issue peace movement. CND's most publicised demand was for unilateral British nuclear disarmament. Every Easter weekend during the late 1950s and the 1960s its 'Ban the Bomb' protest marches from the UK Atomic Weapons Research Establishment at Aldermaston to Trafalgar Square in central London attracted tens of thousands of demonstrators.

Many CND supporters were also outraged by Nikita Khrushchev's boast to the 22nd Congress of the Communist Party of the Soviet Union in October 1960 that a test of a 50-megaton Soviet hydrogen bomb (nicknamed Tsar Bomba), three thousand times more powerful than the bombs dropped by the Americans on Hiroshima and Nagasaki in 1945, would take place on 30 October.† On Saturday 21 October, prevented from demonstrating directly outside the Soviet embassy by the closure of KPG, several thousand protesters gathered in Bayswater Road as close as possible to the police checkpoint at the end of the street. Over 350 of them were arrested. Hundreds more staged a sit-down protest in Bayswater Road in defiance of police orders.

---

* Andrew, *Defence of the Realm*, p.848.
† Gerard J. DeGroot, *The Bomb: A Life* (Cambridge MA: Harvard University Press, 2005).

The Mills family were taken by surprise at the size and noise of the demonstration. With Cyril at work, Mimi out socialising with friends and Christopher boarding at prep school, only five-year-old Sandra and her nanny were at home.* Up in her bedroom on the second floor, Sandra heard a commotion at the end of the street. She remembers the cacophony growing louder and louder, and leant out of her window overlooking KPG, but most of her view of the police checkpoint and Bayswater Road was blocked by trees. Eager to investigate, Sandra raced downstairs to the front door. There, Nanny stood next to the cloakroom, peering outside and holding back Sandra at the threshold, before letting her into the front garden. Outside, what seemed to be hundreds of police officers in helmets and dark-blue tunics were assembling in the street.

Sandra still remembers feeling unnerved by the volume of the protestors' chants, as well as the sheer number of bodies pushing up against the gates at the end of KPG, which acted as a bulwark between the mansions with their manicured gardens and the masses of impassioned demonstrators. Throughout the day, the Mills household staff served tea and sandwiches made in their basement kitchen to policemen who were assembled outside in case protestors broke down the KPG gates.

After the angry demonstration on 21 October, Sandra began to take a greater interest in the surveillance from 17 KPG of the Soviet embassy, against which the protests had been directed. When Christopher returned from prep school, they both went round the outside of the house identifying the windows of rooms to which they were not allowed access. The Observation Post (OP) with its half-open window and partly closed curtain was easy to spot. Once

---

*   Frederick Meredith, Mimi's son from her first marriage, then spent much of the year with his father in Canada.

Cyril realised what they were up to, he gave them a severe talking to which they never forgot. Later, in a private note to Mimi, he wrote: 'Although Frederick, Christopher and Sandra were never asked to sign the Official Secrets Act they have always understood that … they would never mention to anyone' surveillance of the Soviet embassy.[*] At the time Cyril put such emphasis on the Official Secrets Act that, in some mysterious way, Christopher and Sandra believed that they had actually signed it.

For several years Sandra's parents rarely allowed her to leave KPG unaccompanied. The family chauffeur drove her to most destinations, usually with Nanny at her side. Sandra pleaded with her father to allow her to go on a bus ride with a friend instead of Nanny. Cyril finally permitted her to board the bus just outside the KPG gates and ride to the first stop – provided she promised to get off there and walk straight back home with her friend. Sandra kept her promise.[†]

* * *

During the Cuban Missile Crisis in 1962, almost exactly a year after the London demonstration against 'Tsar Bomba', the world came closer to thermonuclear warfare than ever before or since. The crisis began when an American U-2 spy plane secretly photographed the construction of Soviet missile bases in Cuba – the most momentous discovery in the entire history of aerial espionage. At a crisis meeting with his chief advisers on the morning of Tuesday 16 October, President John F. Kennedy insisted that for the time being the existence of the bases must be kept secret. In the words of Theodore

---

*   CBM papers.
†   Recollection of Sandra Menzies.

'Ted' Sorensen, Kennedy's special counsel, 'we had to be sure of what we were facing … Any premature disclosure could precipitate a Soviet move or panic the American public.'[*]

Kennedy's broadcast at 7 p.m. (EST) on Monday 22 October, revealing the construction of the missile sites on Cuba, was the most terrifying speech by an American during the Cold War:

> Good evening, my fellow citizens. This Government, as promised, has maintained the closest surveillance of the Soviet military build-up on the island of Cuba. Within the past week, unmistakable evidence has established the fact that a series of offensive missile sites is now in preparation on that imprisoned island. The purpose of these bases can be none other than to provide a nuclear strike capability against the Western Hemisphere.

The impact of the speech in Britain was heightened by a BBC television broadcast, ahead of any US channel, showing previously highly classified U-2 photographs of the missile bases under construction. The aim was to overcome public scepticism about the reality of the bases.[†] For Mills, the photos had a special significance. A quarter of a century earlier, he had begun his espionage career by flying solo over Nazi German airfields and the Messerschmitt factory to obtain vital intelligence on the expansion of Hitler's Luftwaffe. Mills must have imagined himself in the position of the lone U-2 pilot making even more sensational discoveries in Cuba.

---

[*] As far as it is known, the only member of EXCOMM to disobey the President's insistence on secrecy was his Vice-President, Lyndon B. Johnson. Soon after the first meeting of EXCOMM, without telling Kennedy, Johnson passed on the news of the missile bases by phone to one of the people the President was most anxious should not know: Senator Richard Russell, Chairman of the Senate Armed Services Committee and a leading Congressional hawk, whom Kennedy regarded as chief of the 'war party' as well as an unrepentant racist. Andrew, 'Remembering the Cuban Missile Crisis'.

[†] Because of a mix-up, the photos, which Kennedy had intended to be released simultaneously in Britain and the United States, were broadcast first on the BBC. Andrew, *For the President's Eyes Only*, p.296.

Kennedy's repeated charges of 'deliberate deception' by the Soviet Union underlined the gravity of the crisis. He declared a 'strict quarantine' to be enforced by the US Navy 'on all offensive military equipment under shipment to Cuba'. Neither the President nor his British allies had any idea whether the Russians would accept or challenge the blockade. Nor did it occur to them that the crisis might be peacefully resolved within a week. Kennedy expected a long drawn-out, highly dangerous crisis. He warned the American people: 'Many months of sacrifice and self-discipline lie ahead."[*]

Had the crisis worsened, as seemed entirely possible, the Prime Minister, Harold Macmillan, would have authorised the move to a 'precautionary stage' in the countdown to thermonuclear war. He and the War Cabinet, together with senior defence and intelligence staff (Hollis and White among them), would then have taken up residence in the large top-secret underground bunker, codenamed TURNSTILE, near Corsham in the Cotswolds, whose existence – though known to Mills – was not publicly revealed for another fifty years. TURNSTILE contained miles of underground tunnels with names such as NorthWest Ring Road. Transport was provided by electrically powered trolleys. By each chair in the large telephone exchange were Rolodexes of telephone numbers on the surface which no doubt included 17 KPG. Macmillan had directed that TURNSTILE should 'act as the seat of government' in what he optimistically described as 'the period of survival and reconstruction' following a nuclear attack.[†] More realistically, in a third world war, the bunker would probably have provided no more than a short-lived underground refuge for the remnants of the British government

---

[*]   Andrew, *For the President's Eyes Only*, p.294.
[†]   Andrew, *Defence of the Realm*, p.492. I was able to visit TURNSTILE while writing this history of MI5.

and its defence and intelligence leadership while the country was obliterated above them.

At a time when surveillance of the Soviet embassy and its neighbouring intelligence 'residencies' from 17 KPG was at its peak, Cyril and Mimi were faced with the terrible dilemma of what to tell their children about a crisis which might bring both their lives and British history to an end. The paediatrician whom British and North American parents most often turned to when worried about their children (especially small children) was Dr Benjamin Spock, whose *The Common Sense Book of Baby and Child Care* was translated into thirty-nine languages. During the 1950s and 1960s it was a global bestseller with sales second only to those of the Bible. Spock published his advice to parents at the height of the missile crisis under the headline, 'Don't Panic on Cuba Crisis, Children Feel Your Fears'. 'And remember,' Spock added, 'you can reassure your child by your manner ever so much more than you can by words.' If a child raised fears about the threat of nuclear warfare, however, parents should respond honestly – but 'on the child's level'.* Cyril instinctively followed Spock's advice to remain calm – as he always did in times of crisis. He and Mimi did not, however, speak to Christopher and Sandra about the missile crisis 'at the child's level'. Instead, they successfully concealed from both children that there was a crisis at all.

On 28 October, Khrushchev brought the crisis to a sudden and unexpected end by giving in to US demands to dismantle the Cuban missile bases. Subsequently, Mills never mentioned the crisis to his children or made any reference to it in his papers.

* * *

---

*   Andrew, 'Remembering the Cuban Missile Crisis'.

Though able to eavesdrop on some Russian phone calls and conversations, MI5 had no prospect of placing listening devices inside the Soviet embassy in London as it had in the headquarters of the British Communist Party ever since the Second World War. The transcription of intercepted telephone calls and the product of eavesdropping operations such as those in Kensington Palace Gardens was carried out on the sixth floor of Leconfield House in section A2A, which was off limits to most members of MI5. The intensification of operations against Soviet Bloc targets helps to explain the jump in A2A staff, from 94 in 1964 to 140 in 1966. Russian transcribers came mostly from White Russian émigré families. To Peter Wright, they seemed to have turned their sixth-floor hideaway into 'a tiny piece of Tsarist Russia … Some even installed icons in their rooms.' By contrast the threat from Arab terrorism still seemed so remote that until 1970 A2A only had one Arab linguist.[*]

Peter Wright's provocative claim after his retirement that he and some of his MI5 colleagues had 'bugged and burgled our way across London at the state's behest' was broadly accurate. Most of these operations, secretly authorised by the Permanent Under-Secretary at the Home Office, were against communist and Soviet Bloc targets. The contemporary belief in both the Home Office and MI5 that bugging and burglary in defence of the realm were covered by the royal prerogative was mistaken. There was no legal authority for these operations until the passage of the Security Service Act in 1989.[†]

Eavesdropping from 17 KPG was supplemented by an MI5 OP which visually surveilled those entering and leaving the embassy and other Soviet buildings. A rare photograph in the MI5 archives of another OP targeting Soviet Bloc officials gives a good indication of

---

[*]   Andrew, *Defence of the Realm*, pp.354–5.
[†]   Ibid., pp.335–6.

what it was like. A blind covers most of the partly open OP window, leaving just enough room at the bottom for a long-range camera to take photographs outside. Near to the camera is a blackboard with a target list chalked on it and a loose-leaf binder with names and photographs to aid identification.[*]

Unknown to Mills, the Soviet intelligence 'residencies' being monitored from 17 KPG, as well as – probably – the ambassador, knew about his long-standing links to MI5. Their original source was the well-known art historian and Surveyor of the Queen's Pictures Anthony Blunt, who had joined MI5 as a wartime officer in 1940, three years after he became a committed Soviet agent. His charm offensive quickly won over most of his colleagues. As Dick White later recalled:

> He made a general assault on key people to see that they liked him. I was interested in art and he always used to sit down next to me in the canteen and chat. And he betrayed us all. He was a very nice and civilised man and I enjoyed talking to him. You cannot imagine how it feels to be betrayed by someone you have worked side by side with unless you have been through it yourself.[1]

After Blunt was publicly exposed as a Soviet agent by Margaret Thatcher in 1979, he boasted to 'Tar' Robertson, 'it has given me great pleasure to pass on the names of every MI5 officer to the Russians.'[‡] Mills was among them.

As well as knowing their new neighbour's long involvement with

---

[*] See illustration no.23. Unsurprisingly, there is no photo of the OP at 17 KPG.

[†] Barrie Penrose and Simon Freeman, *Conspiracy of Silence: The Secret Life of Anthony Blunt* (London: Grafton, 1986), p.251.

[‡] 'Tar' revealed Blunt's boast to Chapman Pincher as well as, almost certainly, to Mills and the other B1a veterans; Chapman Pincher, 'The Blunt Truth about Britain's Wicked Traitor' *Daily Express*, 24 July 2009.

MI5, the KGB and GRU residencies quickly discovered that his house at 17 KPG was being used to spy on them. Mills told 'Tar':

> One room on the first floor had a camera so near the window that it could almost be seen from the Marble Arch with field glasses. When Watchers were installed on the top floor they sat by an open window, and when standing in the drive in front of the house we could hear all their telephone conversations with Watchers at the end of the road. On more than one occasion we saw Russians look up at the window and give the Watchers the two finger Harvey Smith [V-sign] salute.[*]

Mills later informed Sheldon, the MI5 legal adviser, that 'a great many Office [MI5] people' (not including Peter Wright) visited 17 KPG during his fifteen years there.[†] Visitors also included some from MI6. Hollis and White were such frequent visitors that the Mills children called them 'Uncle Roger' and 'Uncle Dick'. Sandra Menzies remembers being brought down from the nursery by her nanny to say good night to these and other honorary uncles.

The continued priority attached to bugging and surveillance operations from 17 KPG by senior British intelligence officers reflected their concern at the growth in Soviet intelligence operations from the nearby residencies. According to a later MI5 report: 'The steady and alarming increase in Soviet official representation in the UK during the 1950s (from 138 in 1950 to 249 in 1960), accompanied as it was by a proportional increase in the number of Russian intelligence officers (IOs) threatened to swamp our then meagre resources.'

Largely to cope with this 'alarming' growth of Soviet IOs, MI5

---

[*] CBM papers.
[†] CBM papers.

was authorised in 1962 to recruit an additional 50 officers, 150 'other ranks' and 100 in secretarial and clerical grades.* The shortage of experienced MI5 staff probably explains the early lapses in security at 17 KPG. Mills later complained to his friend 'Tar' Robertson: 'Some of the things done were a sick joke; when they were digging the tunnel two dozen bottles of beer were delivered to the doorstep of the chauffeur's flat every day.'†

Surviving MI5 records suggest that no major Soviet secrets were discovered at 17 KPG by either bugging operations or the OP. A good deal of information, however, was gathered on the behaviour and sometimes extravagant lifestyle of Soviet diplomats and intelligence officers in London. On one occasion, Provotorov, a Soviet Trade Delegation official, was overheard discussing with Kaplin, head of the Soviet fur-trading organisation, where to have dinner. According to a report by A2A staff who transcribed the discussion: 'Provotorov suggests the Savoy Grill. Kaplin thinks it would be too crowded ... Provotorov sings the praises of the Mirabelle – it is downstairs, wealthy, fresh, has a fountain [and is] comfortable.'‡ In the 1960s, Mirabelle was probably London's leading celebrity restaurant. Few customers suspected that it was also highly thought of by Soviet spies and officials.

Among the biggest Russian spenders at exclusive restaurants was the KGB officer (and later successful spy novelist) Mikhail Lyubimov, who from 1961 to 1965 operated undercover in London as a press attaché. One of Mills's favourite journalists, Peregrine Worsthorne, *Daily Telegraph* leader writer and subsequently editor of the *Sunday Telegraph*, knighted by Margaret Thatcher, later recalled:

---

*   Andrew, *Defence of the Realm*, p.565.

†   CBM papers.

‡   Andrew, *Defence of the Realm*, pp.483–4.

Lyubimov would give me luxurious lunches at the Ecu de France in Jermyn Street where, over the aperitifs, he would go through the motions of asking abstruse questions about NATO weaponry. Rather than lose face by admitting I had no inside information on this subject I would trot out whatever I had read in the previous week's *Economist*. Then, both our duties done, we would have a jolly lunch.[*]

From time to time Worsthorne probably reported his lunchtime conversations with Lyubimov to an MI5 contact.

Lyubimov was declared *persona non grata* in 1965 after a botched attempt to recruit a British agent. Most KGB and GRU personnel in London were more discreet. Though often of minor importance in themselves, their overheard conversations, as well as the comings and goings in KPG observed by OPs, were essential in distinguishing Soviet intelligence personnel operating under diplomatic cover from the genuine diplomats, service attachés and their staff. In turn, that information was central to MI5's attempts to persuade successive governments that the threat posed by the rapidly growing KGB and GRU presence in London could only be met by mass expulsion.

The KGB resident (Head of Station) when Mills moved into 17 KPG was the pompous but shrewd Nikolai Borisovich Rodin (alias Korovin), who was later discovered to have recruited George Blake, second only to Philby as the most important Cold War Soviet agent inside MI6. Monitoring Rodin's movements and contacts revealed little about KGB operations but much about his personality and relations with his staff. Whereas the Soviet ambassador was at his desk promptly at 8.30 a.m., Rodin usually arrived at lunchtime, driven by

---

[*] Peregrine Worsthorne, *Tricks of Memory: An Autobiography* (London: Weidenfeld & Nicolson, 1993), p.218.

the KGB operational driver, whom he had turned into his personal chauffeur, to be greeted by sycophantic subordinates. Yuri Modin, the main post-war controller of the Cambridge Five, used Rodin as a case study in how not to run a KGB residency in classified lectures at the KGB's Andropov Institute.[*]

* * *

The British politician most frequently observed by the 17 KPG OP was probably Julius Silverman, the long-serving Labour MP for several Birmingham constituencies. According to an MI5 report: 'He has, for a long time, had extremely close relations with the Soviet Embassy, and may well be considered a useful source of Parliamentary information, if nothing more.'[†]

Other callers at the Soviet embassy kept under surveillance by the OP included the senior British Communist Party official, Betty Reid, who was responsible for testing members' loyalty and identifying those who failed to follow the party line. Even a sympathetic history of the CPGB describes her as 'the party's witchfinder general'. Reid also had a weakness for cream cakes, which was regularly indulged by her main contact in the embassy, Nikolay Timofeev, whom she called her 'cream cake pal'.[‡]

The most colourful Soviet intelligence officer under MI5 surveillance during Mills's early years at 17 KPG was Yevgeny 'Eugene' Ivanov of the GRU, who operated undercover as Assistant Soviet naval attaché based at No.16. The British Director of Naval Intelligence reported to MI5 that Ivanov's 'character weaknesses are

---

[*] Information to Christopher Andrew from Oleg Gordievsky, who was present at Modin's lecture on this topic to the KGB Andropov Institute in the early 1980s.

[†] Ibid..

[‡] Andrew, *Defence of the Realm*, p.493.

apparent when under the influence of alcohol, notably his lack of discretion and loss of personal control, his thirst for women and his tactless bluster.' According to other reports in his MI5 file, Ivanov 'got drunk at parties and enjoyed "propositioning, pinching and dancing with women"'. His file also contains a handwritten note by Ivanov giving his address at 16 KPG (the GRU London residency). It was written with the pink lipstick of a woman he was probably trying to seduce.* The note was probably shown to Mills, who lived next door.

MI5's surveillance of Ivanov led to an attempt to turn him into a double agent. In February 1961, an MI5 agent codenamed CAT BURGLAR told Ivanov that the Admiralty was so concerned by his 'misbehaviour' that he 'might be kicked out' of Britain. The implication was that if Ivanov passed information to CAT BURGLAR, he would be allowed to remain. Though Ivanov remained in touch with CAT BURGLAR, the recruitment pitch failed.[†]

Ivanov had a highly publicised role, however, at the centre of the Profumo Affair, which reached its climax in 1963 with the resignation of John Profumo, Secretary of State for War, after he admitted lying to the Commons about his affair with the Soho showgirl Christine Keeler. Ivanov also had a brief affair with Keeler and was summoned back to Moscow in early 1963 to remove him from public view.

Both Profumo and Ivanov first met the nineteen-year-old Keeler at a party around the swimming pool on the Cliveden estate of Lord ('Bill') Astor on 8 July 1961. Three days later, Profumo and his wife attended a reception at the Russian embassy in honour of the first cosmonaut, Yuri Gagarin. Profumo later told his son that during

---

*   Ibid., illustration no. 54.
†   MI5 report, 'Evgeni N. Ivanov', 16 February 1961; released to TNA in KV 2 file series in October 2022. Caroline Davies, 'Profumo Spy Had Weakness for Women and Drink, Archives Reveal', *The Guardian*, 11 October 2022.

the reception 'Ivanov came up to me and asked if we remembered him from Cliveden and asked if he could get me a glass of vodka.'* Since it was easier to eavesdrop on receptions than most other events at the embassy, the conversation was probably overheard from 17 KPG. But there was nothing about the exchange to attract MI5's attention. Ivanov already had a reputation as an enthusiastic, heavy-drinking party-goer and there was no mention of Christine Keeler. Though Cyril and Mimi Mills were quite frequently invited to parties at Cliveden, they were not present on 8 July 1961.[†]

MI5 did not discover that Profumo had slept with Keeler until 28 January 1963, almost eighteen months after their first meeting at Cliveden. At that point, though rumours were circulating around Fleet Street and Westminster, there was still some reason to believe that Keeler would not publicise their affair. On 6 February, F4 (counter-subversion agent-running) informed the DG that 'our newspaper source' had reported that 'the courtesan, Christine Keeler, has told source that she has no intention of putting her name to anything that would embarrass Mr Profumo.' It was not long before she changed her mind.[‡] Conspiracy theorists in the media and Westminster wrongly claimed that Ivanov had passed on to the GRU British defence secrets which Keeler had extracted from Profumo.[§] In a personal statement to the Commons on 22 March, Profumo admitted to being 'on friendly terms' with Keeler but claimed there was 'no impropriety whatsoever' in their relationship: 'I shall not hesitate to issue writs for libel and slander if scandalous allegations are made or repeated outside the House.' On 5 June, however,

---

*   David Profumo, *Bringing the House Down: A Family Memoir* (London: John Murray, 2006), p.162.
†   CBM papers.
‡   Andrew, *Defence of the Realm*, pp.497–8.
§   In some versions of the conspiracy theory, the secrets allegedly obtained by Keeler from Profumo were passed to Ivanov through the intermediary of Stephen Ward, a society osteopath and portrait painter with whom Keeler lived in Wimpole Mews.

he admitted lying to the Commons about his relations with Keeler and announced his resignation from the government.

Through his contacts with Hollis at the time of the Profumo Affair, Mills was aware of the DG's involvement in a unique moment in parliamentary history, which went unreported by the media and has gone unnoticed by subsequent historians. Harold Wilson, then Leader of the Opposition, declared the Commons debate on the Profumo Affair on 17 June 'without precedent in the annals of this House'. By convention, MI5, like MI6 and GCHQ, was never mentioned in debates or parliamentary questions. But the allegations against Ivanov made it impossible for Macmillan, to his annoyance, to avoid revealing some of what he had been told by MI5. Though he did not identify Hollis by name, the Prime Minister told the House that 'the head of the security service' was satisfied, after investigation, 'that the indirect contact between Ivanov and Mr. Profumo had not involved any breach of security'. But Macmillan said twice during his speech that he thought it 'very unfortunate' that MI5 had not warned him earlier of its investigation and 'strongly' regretted that it had not done so.*

Unknown to almost everyone in the Commons, except the Prime Minister and Home Secretary, Hollis was in the public gallery to witness this first ever official public criticism of MI5 and its DG by the Prime Minister. Hardly any MP even knew Hollis's name, which was officially secret, let alone recognised him by sight. Chapman Pincher, probably the only journalist able to identify the DG during the debate, watched Hollis sit 'expressionless and hunched in his seat' in the public gallery.† This was probably the only time that a

---

* HC *Parl Deb*, 17 June 1963, vol 679.

† Chapman Pincher, *Their Trade Is Treachery* (London: Biteback Publishing, 2014), loc.1526. Despite Pincher's conspiracy theories about Hollis and others, his accounts of whom he met or personally observed are mostly reliable. MI5 files reveal that when the Labour Party leadership decided to approach MI5 in 1961 for help in identifying secret communists on their back benches, they approached Pincher who supplied Hollis's name and contact details. Andrew, *Defence of the Realm*, p.412.

British intelligence chief attended a twentieth-century Commons debate.

An MI5 investigation plausibly concluded that it must have been obvious to Ivanov from the outset that Keeler had no information of significant value for him. It added condescendingly: 'Although undoubtedly attractive, Keeler was vacuous and untruthful. Ivanov had no need to sleep with her to discover that.' She remembered Ivanov as 'a huge bear of a man, all vodka and hugs'. In her partly ghostwritten memoirs, she fantasised that Roger Hollis, Anthony Blunt and the society osteopath Stephen Ward, in whose house she lived, were all involved with Ivanov in passing secrets to Moscow.[*] Ivanov's Russian memoirs also later fancifully claimed that Profumo's wife, the actress Valerie Hobson, had allowed him into Profumo's study and left him alone while he photographed top-secret documents with a Minox miniature camera.[†]

During the Profumo Affair it did not occur to the media that Mills could have revealed a sensational story about Profumo's earlier involvement with a glamorous female Nazi spy which would have been front-page news. The weekly wartime meetings to discuss German espionage in MI5's B Branch (counter-espionage),[‡] chaired by Dick White and attended by Mills, had considered the case of Gisela Klein (later Winegard), a German fashion and photographer's model with whom Profumo had an affair while a student at Oxford in the 1930s. He remained in touch with her intermittently for over twenty years.

During the war, Klein ran a secret Nazi information service in occupied Paris and had a child with a high-ranking German officer.

---

[*] Christine Keeler and Douglas Thompson, *The Truth at Last: My Story* (London: Sidgwick & Jackson, 2001).
[†] Yevgeny Ivanov and Gennady Sokolov, *The Naked Spy* (London: Blake Publishing Ltd, 1992).
[‡] See above, chapters 4 and 5.

She was imprisoned for espionage after the liberation of Paris in 1944. In 1941, Profumo, then Britain's youngest MP as well as an army officer, visited MI5's London office to pass on what he knew of Klein's movements since she left Oxford. As well as downplaying his own past relationship with her, he reported – probably misleadingly – that 'she always claimed to be anti-Nazi'. In 1942, Klein sent Profumo a letter from Switzerland which began, 'JACK darling, I found it very difficult to write this letter. I can't get used to the idea that I am free to write to you without a censor.' Klein claimed to be happy but 'not nearly as happy' as when she had known Profumo in Oxford. Contact resumed after the war. According to her MI5 file, Klein's husband, Edward Winegard, said in 1950 that 'his wife had left him because he had discovered that she had been receiving endearing letters from John Dennis Profumo. The letters were written on House of Commons notepaper.'*

The Mills family's early years in KPG coincided with the publication of the first books by John Cornwell, far better known by his pen-name John le Carré, whom Mills – like many others – believed to be the greatest of all spy novelists. Though forbidden to mention his own intelligence career, le Carré was the first spy novelist to have served in both MI5 and MI6; he knew that Mills had also worked for both. In le Carré's novels and films, beginning with *Call for the Dead* in 1961, MI5 and MI6 were amalgamated into a single fictional secret service, 'the Circus' – a name possibly somewhat inspired by Mills's circus career. Le Carré's 1963 global bestseller, *The Spy Who Came in from the Cold*, and the even more successful film version two years later, brought 'the Circus' to an enthusiastic

---

* MI5 Gisela Klein file, TNA KV6/146.

global audience. Apart from le Carré, Mills was the only reader to be struck by the connection with his own career.

* * *

As at previous peacetime stages of his intelligence career, the family circus provided Mills with wonderfully effective cover, further strengthened by support from the Royal Family. In the twenty years since the Second World War, he hosted almost fifty royal visits. One of the most publicised visits was to the Royal Charity Performance at Olympia on 21 December 1961 by the Queen, Duke of Edinburgh, Prince Charles and Princess Anne. No other circus received similar royal patronage.

In 1963 Coco the Clown (Nikolai Poliakoff), a star of Bertram Mills Circus since his first appearance in 1929, became the first clown in British history to be awarded the OBE.* Born in 1900 in Latvia (then part of the Russian Empire), he had performed in the Moscow State Circus during the 1920s and was thus regarded by the Russian embassy in KPG as a defector.

Despite its royal patronage, the financial fortunes of the Bertram Mills Circus rapidly declined in the mid-1960s. The main problem, as with other leading areas of the entertainment industry was growing competition from television. The number of London variety theatres fell from twenty-one in 1950 to only four a decade later and in 1960 cinema audiences were only 37 per cent of those in 1950.† The last season of Bertram Mills Circus was at Olympia in the winter

---

* Poliakov (or Poliakoff) was awarded the OBE at least partly for giving road safety lessons to children while dressed as Coco the Clown.
† Spectator sports and dance halls, however, continued to flourish. Peter Michael Scott, 'Not Going Out: Television's Impacts on Britain's Commercial Entertainment Industries and Popular Leisure during the 1950s', *Social History*, vol.48, no.4 (2023), pp.475–500.

of 1965–66. The final charity performance was honoured with what one journalist called 'a royal straight flush': the Queen, the Duke of Edinburgh, Prince Charles, Princess Anne, Princess Margaret, the Earl of Snowdon, Princess Alexandra and her husband Angus Ogilvy.*

* * *

During the 1960s the British embassy in Moscow was much more successfully penetrated than the Soviet embassy in London. For several years the most successful KGB penetration agent was the Ambassador's strikingly attractive blonde chambermaid, Galya Ivanova. While on an official visit to Moscow as Foreign Secretary in 1967, the notoriously bibulous George Brown took an immediate fancy to her while she was serving him coffee and brandy at a reception in the British embassy attended by John Miller, long-serving Moscow correspondent for the *Daily Telegraph* (Mills's favourite newspaper during the Cold War): 'Leaping to his feet, George gave Galya a big hug, and then a kiss, saying "That's a lot better. I've always wanted to do that to a Russian lass." I thought at the time that the ambassador [Sir Geoffrey Harrison] was giving the Foreign Secretary a funny look.'

Not long afterwards, Galya succeeded in seducing the Ambassador. In 1968, following its usual practice in 'honeytraps', the KGB sent Sir Geoffrey Harrison explicit photographs of their liaison and he was forced to resign. John Miller learned from a credible Russian contact that Galya Ivanova, who lost her job as the Ambassador's chambermaid, was the sister of 'Eugene' Ivanov, a chief surveillance

---

*   Mills, *Bertram Mills Circus*, p.258.

target earlier in the decade whose affair with Christine Keeler had been at the centre of the Profumo Affair.[*]

The main importance of the eavesdropping and surveillance operations run from and around 17 KPG during the 1960s was that they provided proof of the record growth in Soviet intelligence personnel as well as information about some of their British contacts. The first major success of the MI5 campaign to 'educate' Whitehall on the growing threat from Soviet espionage was the decision by Harold Wilson's government in 1968 to allow no further increase in the Soviet embassy's size. The KGB and GRU, whose residencies were already the largest in the world outside the United States, managed to circumvent this ceiling by sending 'working wives' to the embassy and stationing more undercover intelligence officers in other Soviet offices in London, particularly in the Trade Delegation.[†]

If, as was widely expected, Harold Wilson had won the June 1970 general election, there would have been no mass expulsion of Soviet intelligence personnel from London. Instead, Wilson would have accepted an official invitation to visit Moscow extended to him earlier in the year by Mikhail Smirnovsky, Soviet Ambassador in London since 1967. Discussions on possible dates for the visit had already begun.[‡] The Conservative victory at the June 1970 general election boosted MI5's counter-espionage campaign within Whitehall. The incoming Prime Minister, Edward Heath, and his Foreign Secretary, Sir Alec Douglas-Home, were convinced that the size of the Soviet intelligence presence in London had become 'a real threat to our national security'. The Home Secretary, Reginald Maudling, took

---

[*]   John Miller, *All Them Cornfields and Ballet in the Evening* (London: Hodgson Press, 2010) pp.260–61. Simon Freeman and Barrie Penrose, 'My KGB Chambermaid by British Envoy', *Sunday Times*, 22 February 1981.

[†]   Andrew, *Defence of the Realm*, pp.565–6.

[‡]   TNA FCO 28/1111.

longer to convince but was eventually impressed by MI5's ability 'to identify so many Russian I[intelligence] O[fficer]s'. In a joint memo to Heath on 30 July 1971, Maudling and Douglas-Home argued that the numbers of KGB and GRU officers were 'more than the Security Service can be expected to contain'. Based on the Service's estimate of 130 Soviet intelligence officers in London, the Foreign & Commonwealth Office (FCO) agreed on a target of 100 expulsions.

The most important case of physical surveillance by the OP at 17 KPG during Mills's tenancy was that of the KGB officer Oleg Lyalin, whom MI5 was encouraging to defect. During secret meetings with MI5 beginning in April 1971, as well as revealing or confirming the identities of other Soviet intelligence personnel, Lyalin disclosed that he was personally responsible for preparing sabotage operations in Britain (including plans for landing KGB saboteurs on the North Yorkshire coast) to be implemented in time of war or serious international crisis. Lyalin's defection on 9 September was the prelude to Operation FOOT, the mass expulsion of Soviet intelligence personnel from London. On 24 September 1971, the PUS at the FCO, Sir Denis Greenhill, summoned the Soviet chargé d'affaires, Ivan Ippolitov, and informed him that ninety KGB and GRU officers stationed in Britain under official cover were to be expelled. Another fifteen then on leave in the Soviet Union would not be allowed to return, making a grand total of 105 expulsions. The OP at 17 KPG reported seeing a military intelligence officer sprinting over the road to the embassy from the GRU residency at No.16, no doubt summoned by telephone to an urgent briefing on the impending expulsions after Ippolitov's return from the FCO.

That evening there was a celebration party at MI5 headquarters. A guest from the Foreign Office was initially concerned by the lack of alcohol: 'Then one of them opened a vast imposing safe. It was chock-a-bloc with bottles.'* Mills was probably invited.† Congratulations (some almost certainly passed on to Mills by Dick White) flooded in from Britain's intelligence allies after Operation FOOT. The long-serving and often irascible J. Edgar Hoover, whom Mills had met while a wartime MI5 officer, expressed 'delight' and rewarded MI5's liaison officer, Cecil Shipp, in Washington with a record two-hour audience. Equally remarkably, Shipp reported to London, the meeting did not turn into 'a monologue' by Hoover.‡

The 'Centre', KGB headquarters, chose as its chief scapegoat Yuri Nikolayevich Voronin, its London resident from 1967 to 1971, who was accused of having covered up Lyalin's misdeeds in order to avoid a scandal in the residency. Despite the fact that only a few months earlier, Voronin had been promoted to head the Third Department of the First Chief Directorate, which ran foreign intelligence operations in the UK, Ireland, Scandinavia and Australasia, he was dismissed from the KGB.§ His disgrace demonstrated the Centre's shock at what it saw as a major humiliation.

MI5 had wisely excluded the inexperienced and rather bungling security officer at the Trade Delegation, Yevgeni Lazebny from the Soviet intelligence personnel selected for expulsion. When the OP at 17 KPG reported that Lazebny was coming to the embassy every day, it was clear that, following Voronin's expulsion, he had been made an acting KGB resident. Though out of his depth when running intelligence operations in the wake of Operation FOOT, during his fourteen months as acting resident, Lazebny insisted on time-consuming

---

*   Andrew, *Defence of the Realm*, pp.571–2.

†   No guest list survives, but Mills is likely to have been on it. In the decade before Operation FOOT, many MI5 staff had visited 17 KPG. Though Hollis's successor as DG from 1965 to 1972, Sir Martin Furnival Jones ('FJ'), did not become a personal friend, Mills was on good terms with him. He later recalled 'no problems at all' with FJ over MI5 use of 17 KPG; Mills to 'Tar' Robertson, 3 October 1987, CBM papers.

‡   Andrew, *Defence of the Realm*, section E, ch.1.

§   Ibid., p.574.

security procedures which further complicated the life of the deplet-
ed and demoralised residency. The precautions clearly indicated that
Lazebny had a greatly exaggerated view of the degree to which MI5
had succeeded in penetrating the embassy. No one was allowed to
enter the residency wearing an overcoat for fear that it might be used
to conceal material being smuggled in or out. Briefcases, bags and
packages were also forbidden, and the shoes of operations officers
were X-rayed for bugs and hidden compartments.[*]

After Operation FOOT, the main KGB and GRU agents run by
the London residencies had either to be put on ice or handed over
to other Soviet Bloc intelligence services and their Cuban ally. Geoffrey Prime of GCHQ, the KGB's most productive British agent for
much of the 1970s, was run exclusively outside the UK and therefore
unaffected by the London expulsions. Operation FOOT marked the
high point of Mills's fifteen years in Kensington Palace Gardens – a
turning point in KGB and GRU operations in Britain. According
to MI5 files, the number of their personnel did not return to pre-
FOOT levels until after the Cold War.[†]

The success of FOOT led Sir Michael Hanley, who became DG in
1972, to draw up plans to intensify surveillance of the Russian embassy from 17 KPG. Hanley was a large, powerfully built man with
a forceful personality who had acquired the nickname 'Jumbo' early
in his career. The Prime Minister, Edward Heath, initially wondered
if Hanley might prove 'a little heavy-footed' as DG but changed his
mind.[‡] Mills, however, found Hanley's attempt to increase surveillance from 17 KPG distinctly 'heavy-footed':

---

[*]   MITN 1/7 CCAC; Andrew and Mitrokhin, *Mitrokhin Archive*, pp.546–7.
[†]   Andrew, *Defence of the Realm*, pp.573–8.
[‡]   Hanley's supporters within MI5 included the future DG, Stella Rimington, whose 'kindly interest' when she
      returned from maternity leave in 1971 'was unusual in those days when personal contact between directors
      and junior staff was rare'. Ibid., p.548.

He wanted to make a change which would have made the place uninhabitable so far as we were concerned and I told his representative that I could not agree it. He asked me to visit him which I did and when he realised I was not willing to be pushed around, he started shouting at me and I told him that this was not the kind of thing I expected from the D.G. and I would not tolerate it. He had to give in…

In Mills's view, Hanley 'tried to make amends' when he left 17 KPG in 1975 by giving a lunch for him and Mimi at MI5 HQ.[*]

Unknown to Mills, as well as to the great majority of other British intelligence personnel, in late 1974, MI6 had recruited its best-ever agent inside the KGB, Oleg Gordievsky, then operating in Denmark. From 1975 onwards, MI6 copied all Gordievsky's intelligence to the counter-espionage branch of MI5, which contributed to the assessment of it. In 1982, to the secret delight of both MI5 and MI6, he was posted to the KGB residency in Kensington Palace Gardens. A year later, Gordievsky was promoted to its head of political intelligence. In 1985 he was named resident-designate, in charge of the whole residency.[†]

* * *

Since the Mills family left 17 KPG, the mansion has had a curious history. In 2009 it was purchased, allegedly for £90 million, by the billionaire Russian oligarch, Roman Abramovich, former owner of Chelsea Football Club and former close associate of Vladimir Putin. It is now on the market again.

---

[*]   Mills to 'Tar' Robertson, 3 October 1987, CBM papers.
[†]   Andrew, *Defence of the Realm*, pp.674, 679, 708–9.

CHAPTER 10

MILLS UNMASKED

The British entertainment industry's most novel success during the Cold War, with some help from Hollywood, was to create the most popular fictional spy in world history. James Bond is still far better known than any real secret agent alive or dead. By the time that Cyril and his brother Bernard took the painful decision to close the Bertram Mills Circus, Bond had become a global superstar.

While Mills's children were growing up, their father's intelligence career, both past and present, was strictly off limits to them. Christopher and Sandra had powerfully impressed upon them the supreme importance of the Official Secrets Act.* Mills and Billy Luke, his closest friend since their years in MI5, also had personal reasons for keeping secret even their wartime intelligence careers: 'At that time Double-Cross was regarded as a dirty word and, as Billy and I were still in business, we did not like the idea of our friends, shareholders or business associates knowing we had been in such a dirty game during the war.'†

Mills did, however, occasionally mention spy fiction, especially

---

* See above, pp.18, 236.
† Mills to Annie Luke, 8 January 1990; CBM papers.

the *James Bond* stories, to his children. After taking ten-year-old Christopher to see the first Bond film, *Dr. No*, in 1962, he laughed as they left the cinema and said he knew 'a real James Bond', but gave no clues to his identity.*

Several years later, Ian Fleming revealed that the 'real James Bond' was a wealthy American ornithologist after whom he had named his fictional spy hero. The real James (or 'Jim') Bond, it turned out, had been at both Harrow School and Cambridge University at the same time as Mills. Because knife crime at Harrow was so rare during the First World War, Mills was probably aware of one episode recounted by Bond's first biographer:

> The English boys mocked his American accent, all the while insisting that America was a savage and uncouth land filled with wild Indians and the dregs of European society. The worst of the teasing stopped only after Jim became so enraged that he grabbed a penknife and stabbed one of his tormentors in the arm. From then on most of the boys respected him for standing up and fighting back.†

When writing a reference for Bond to Trinity College, Cambridge, his Harrow housemaster decided not to prejudice his prospects of admission by mentioning the stabbing: 'Bond is a virtuous boy, American by parentage, of no particular ability. He will never give any trouble.'‡ The now virtuous Bond duly graduated from Cambridge without causing any trouble, but with only a third-class ordinary degree, in 1922 (a year before Mills graduated with honours).

---

* Recollection of Christopher Mills.

† David R. Contosta, *The Private Life of James Bond* (Lititz, PA: Sutter House, 1993); https://trinitycollegelibrary cambridge.wordpress.com/2021/10/08/james-bond-at-trinity

‡ The brief handwritten reference is reproduced in https://trinitycollegelibrarycambridge.wordpress. com/2021/10/08/james-bond-at-trinity

After a tedious few years as a banker in the United States, James Bond spent the next decade much more enjoyably, using his inherited wealth to explore Caribbean islands – and particularly their bird life. The main product of his explorations was a classic, profusely illustrated field guide, *Birds of the West Indies*, first published in 1936. Ian Fleming kept a copy at Goldeneye, his winter home in Jamaica. After inviting Bond to lunch at Goldeneye in 1964, Fleming gave him a copy of his latest novel, *You Only Live Twice*, the last one published during his lifetime, with a handwritten dedication: 'To the real James Bond from the thief of his identity, Ian Fleming, Feb. 5, 1964 (a great day!).' *

Mills mostly enjoyed Bond films. He was particularly intrigued by *Octopussy* (1983), the only film in which Bond – like Mills for much of his career – used the circus as cover for intelligence operations. The owner of the circus was Octopussy, a glamorous international jewel smuggler. Bond dramatically boards Octopussy's circus train in communist East Germany from a car driven along the railway track. The train scenes were filmed much closer to home on the Nene Valley steam railway, which Mills had first seen sixty years earlier as an undergraduate racing around Cambridgeshire on his motorbike.† The village station at Wansford was given an expensive makeover to turn it, improbably, but realistically, into the East German Karl-Marx-Stadt.

Bond later disguises himself as a clown to enter Octopussy's Big Top at a NATO base in West Germany where her circus is performing. Having (with some difficulty) drawn the attention of both Octopussy and the base's Commanding Officer to a nuclear bomb

---

* Mary Wickham Bond (Mrs James Bond), *How 007 Got His Name* (London: Collins, 1966); Contosta, *The Private Life of James Bond*.
† The Nene Valley railway officially closed in 1972 but a 7.5 mile track reopened to steam trains in 1977.

hidden inside the Human Cannonball's cannon, Bond successfully defuses it. Back in her boudoir, Octopussy offers Bond a job in her circus. He refuses and they tumble into bed instead. Maud Allen, who played Octopussy, later revealed that during the tumbling she accidentally kneed Moore painfully in the groin. The scene had to be reshot.[*] Mills dismissed the Octopussy plot as fantasy but enjoyed the circus sequences, which he thought were mostly realistic and well performed.[†] The later MI5 DG and keen amateur actor, Stella Rimington, told a literary festival after her retirement that the role she would most like to have played in a Bond film was that of Octopussy.[‡]

*　*　*

Mills's eventual willingness to acknowledge some of his own wartime (but not peacetime) intelligence career stemmed from the gradual declassification during the late 1970s and early 1980s of the extraordinary successes of the Double-Cross System. The revelations about wartime deception operations were among the chief topics discussed at the annual lunches and other gatherings of B1a veterans and Sir Dick White, who had been Mills's closest friends ever since the Second World War. They were, Mills told his family, 'the nicest people and the best friends I have ever known'.[§] Theirs were the first known discussions of major intelligence triumphs

---

[*]　'Octopussy star Maud Adams Injured Roger Moore's "Sensitive Region" on James Bond Set', *Daily Express*, 6 June 2023.

[†]　Recollection of Christopher Mills, who watched *Octopussy* with his father.

[‡]　Rimington revealed her fantasy of playing Octopussy at a book festival in 2011: telegraph.co.uk/culture/books/ways-with-words/8628803/Ways-with-Words-I-would-rather-have-been-a-Bond-girl-says-Dame-Stella-Rimington.html.

[§]　See above, p.93.

forty years after the events by some of those largely responsible for them.*

In October 1981, Mills and his ex-MI5 friends invited five of their leading wartime double agents to the annual B1a lunch – a unique moment in British intelligence history. Celebratory lunches for individual star agents were not uncommon, but a lunch for five with their former case officers was unheard of.

Though the hosts would have liked to invite Mills's most important recruit, Juan Pujol García (GARBO), whom all regarded as the star of the Double-Cross System, he had gone to ground in South America and did not re-emerge for another three years.† The 1981 lunch guests did, however, include the longest-serving of all the double agents, Wulf Schmidt (TATE), who had transmitted disinformation to the Abwehr in Hamburg from October 1940 until less than twenty-four hours before the city fell to British forces in one of the last battles of the war.‡ TATE was still unaware that Mills, standing next to him in the back row of the lunch photograph,§ had been ordered to shoot him in 1941 if he tried to escape.⁵

Also at the lunch was the former Polish fighter pilot, Roman Garby-Czerniawski, whose role as a double agent in the deception operations before D-Day was second only to GARBO's.** His case officer, Christopher Harmer, gave him the codename BRUTUS: 'Roman Czerniawski had been turned by the Germans and returned by us, so I thought "Et tu, Brute?"'†† Before eventually decid-

---

*   No minutes were kept at the meetings.

†   Until GARBO's reappearance in 1984, Mills thought he was dead; see below, pp.272–3.

‡   Masterman, *The Double-Cross System*, pp.52–3. Also present at the lunch was Malcolm Frost, who had been one of TATE's first interrogators in 1940.

§   See illustration no.24: B1a lunch October 1981.

⁵   See above, pp.126–7. In the group photo, Mills is to the right of TATE; Mills's close friend, Bill Luke, is to the left.

**   See above, pp.182–4.

††   Macintyre, *Double Cross*, p.110.

ing to recruit him in 1942, BRUTUS's MI5 interrogators had found him 'intensely dramatic and egotistical'.* Characteristically, in the group photograph taken after the B1a lunch almost forty years later, BRUTUS succeeded in sitting in the centre of the front row, holding up a book (probably his memoir, *The Big Network*).†

Also in the front row of the photograph,‡ to the right of BRUTUS, were the Norwegian double agents, John 'Helge' Moe (MUTT)§ and Tor Glad (JEFF)§, for whom Harmer had also been case officer. The codenames MUTT and JEFF were taken from the well-known characters in a long-running American strip cartoon, which generated numerous film and stage adaptations. Like MUTT, Moe was short and stout; Glad, like JEFF, was tall and lanky. JEFF's career as a double agent was quickly compromised by his own indiscretions and MI5's doubts about his loyalty. He was interned in August 1941 for the remainder of the war, though B1a, with help from MUTT, continued to send the Abwehr misleading radio messages in his name. The much more reliable, British-born MUTT, son of the opera singer Ida Wade, was one of the few double agents permitted to undertake sabotage operations in order to enhance his credibility with the Abwehr: among them a staged explosion in 1943 at a Suffolk power station.**

Less prominently positioned in the back row of the photograph was Eddie Chapman (ZIGZAG), a pre-war British career criminal who was so successful as a wartime double agent that in 1943 he

---

* Andrew, *Defence of the Realm*, p.298.
† Roman Garby-Czerniawski, *The Big Network* (London: George Ronald, 1961). The cover of the book is indistinct in the group photograph. An alternative possibility is that he is holding a recent intelligence history, mentioning him, by Nigel West.
‡ See illustration no.24.
§ TNA, KV 2/1067.
§ TNA, KV 2/1068.
** Tony Insall, *Secret Alliances: Special Operations and Intelligence in Norway 1940–1945* (London: Biteback Publishing, 2019), pp.133–5.

became the first British subject to be awarded the German Iron Cross in recognition of what the Abwehr praised as his 'outstanding zeal and success'. But for Mills's posting to Canada in December 1942, he would probably have become ZIGZAG's case officer.[*] Like MUTT, though on a much larger scale, ZIGZAG carried out bogus sabotage operations that completely deceived the Abwehr. His German case officer, Stephan von Gröning, then stationed in a chateau in occupied France, celebrated the news of ZIGZAG's supposed destruction of the bulk of a de Havilland aircraft factory by ordering 'champagne all round'.[†]

In the summer of 1944, however, Masterman decided that ZIGZAG had 'developed a dangerous tendency to talk about his work and his achievements, and it therefore became necessary to terminate the case.'[‡] The final straw probably came late in October, when he was found discussing the publication of a book of his experiences with a convicted pre-war Soviet agent, Wilfred Macartney.[§] Early in November, ZIGZAG was abruptly dismissed by MI5.[¶] Having ceased to be Agent ZIGZAG, Chapman later published three sets of memoirs: *The Eddie Chapman Story* (1953), *Free Agent: Being the Further Adventures of Eddie Chapman* (1955) and *The Real Eddie Chapman Story* (1966), whose colourful contents help to explain his lunch invitation from the B1a veterans.[**]

The most distinguished wartime MI5 officer among the lunch

---

* Mills, untitled confidential memoir on his intelligence career (undated), p.10; CBM papers.
† Macintyre, *Agent Zigzag*. Chapman's lengthy MI5 file is TNA KV2/455–63.
‡ Masterman, *The Double-Cross System*, pp.172–3.
§ Guy Liddell diary, 31 October 1944. Oddly, this episode does not appear in Macintyre's excellent biography.
¶ Report by Michael Ryde, 24 October 1944, TNA KV 2/460; Macintyre, *Agent Zigzag*, p.305.
** Other lunch guests included Bill Kenyon-Jones, who, while in Security Intelligence Middle East (SIME), had helped to run Renato Levi, codenamed CHEESE, probably the most important MI6 double agent of the war. Disinformation from CHEESE in Cairo (or sent to the Abwehr in his name) helped prevent the Germans from taking Cairo and the Suez Canal, contributed to their loss of Tobruk and helped to starve Rommel's Afrika Korps of fuel. Nigel West, *Double Cross in Cairo: The True Story of the Spy Who Turned the Tide of the War in the Middle East* (London: Biteback Publishing, 2015). Kenyon-Jones is standing on the far left of the photo; his wife, seated next to him, was a former secretary of Sir Vernon Kell.

guests was Herbert Hart, one of the twentieth century's most eminent legal philosophers who had become successively Professor of Jurisprudence at Oxford University and Principal of Brasenose College. While working in B1b during the war he had derived intelligence from Abwehr decrypts which helped B1a to recruit some of the double agents present at the lunch.[*] Mills probably knew that, while stationed at Blenheim Palace, Hart had shared an office with Anthony Blunt; he later wondered, as no doubt, did Mills, which of the top-secret papers on his desk Blunt had managed to pass on to his Soviet case officers.[†]

In 1983, however, probably to the surprise of Mills and the B1a veterans, Herbert Hart became involved in a public controversy about his wife Jenifer's links with Soviet intelligence. Jenifer Hart (née Fischer Williams) had joined the CPGB while a student at Oxford and was still a member when she became a civil servant in the pre-war Home Office and married Herbert. In an interview for a special edition of the BBC television programme *Timewatch*,[‡] she described for the first time how, while in the Home Office, she had had several secret meetings with Arnold Deutsch, NKVD recruiter of the Cambridge Five, but said that she had refused to become a Soviet spy. The interview and the controversy which followed generated media publicity that cannot fail to have been discussed by the B1a veterans, Dick White and some of their guests. The *Sunday Times* claimed Jenifer Hart had been a Soviet spy. Jenifer Hart threatened to sue, Herbert Hart had a nervous breakdown and the *Sunday Times* was forced to apologise.

Though Herbert Hart recovered from his breakdown, he came to

---

[*]   Andrew, *Defence of the Realm*, p.249.

[†]   Nicola Lacey, *A Life of H. L. A. Hart: The Nightmare and the Noble Dream* (Oxford: Oxford University Press, 2004).

[‡]   I was the *Timewatch* interviewer and presenter.

no further B1a lunches and discussions. By the early 1980s, however, two wartime intelligence officers from outside MI5 regularly took part in both: Roger Fleetwood-Hesketh and Hugh Trevor-Roper (ennobled by Margaret Thatcher in 1979 as Baron Dacre of Glanton). Hesketh was an Old Etonian lawyer and Oxford graduate who had served as a Lieutenant-Colonel in the deception section of the Supreme Headquarters Allied Expeditionary Force (SHAEF) which helped plan Operation FORTITUDE before D-Day. His post-war interrogation of German officers and research in German intelligence files provided further proof of the extent of the deception. Hesketh was commissioned to write an official history of deception in western Europe during the final two years of the war. Though not officially declassified until 1997 (a decade after Hesketh's death), bootleg copies were available to Mills and his B1a friends.*

Hugh Trevor-Roper, one of Britain's best-known historians, had been a wartime member of MI6. Like Mills, he took a dim view of its Chief, Sir Stewart Menzies: 'a bad judge of men' who 'drew his personal advisers from a painfully limited social circle' and 'never really understood the war in which he was engaged'. Though Trevor-Roper had a low opinion of most of his MI6 colleagues, he admired Dick White and 'Tar' Robertson of MI5, both of whom became close friends. 'Tar' was probably the only intelligence officer whom Trevor-Roper ever described as a 'genius'.†

Trevor-Roper became Regius Professor of Modern History at Oxford from 1957 to 1980, when he was elected Master of Peterhouse, Cambridge's oldest college. In 1981, at an Oxford dinner in his honour, he was presented with a Festschrift of essays by colleagues, friends and former students. Michael Howard, his successor

---

* I was also given a copy in the 1980s.
† Elliott, *Gentleman Spymaster*, p.1.

as Regius Professor, revealed at the dinner that his own essay for the Festschrift on GARBO, the most successful of Mills's wartime double-agent recruits, had been officially banned because it made use of intelligence files. Howard reasonably called the ban absurd, given the official approval of previous publications on GARBO and handed Trevor-Roper a copy of his essay, inscribed 'Confidential Annex, Top Secret Ultra'. The Oxford University Chancellor and former Prime Minister Harold Macmillan rose to his feet to denounce Howard's allegedly frivolous attitude to official secrecy.*

Sir Dick White, who was present at the Festschrift dinner, agreed with Howard. So did Mills and the B1a veterans who, probably at White's suggestion, invited Trevor-Roper to join their discussions on wartime intelligence.† The invitation remained so confidential that it has never previously been revealed. With a degree of satirical understatement, Trevor-Roper admitted that he had 'sometimes shown mild irreverence towards some sacred cows'‡ in MI6, most recently in interviews on the BBC's first documentary series on British intelligence history, *The Profession of Intelligence*.§ He and Mills shared a deep dislike of both Peter Wright and Victor Rothschild. As Trevor-Roper wrote to Mills: 'It is curious that [Victor Rothschild] is the only person in that [intelligence] world whom Wright praises without qualification. Wright's statement that V. R. ought to

---

* Richard Davenport-Hines and Adam Sisman (eds), *One Hundred Letters from Hugh Trevor-Roper* (Oxford: Oxford University Press, 2014), pp.256–8.

† In September 1945, Dick White, then head of counter-intelligence in the British sector of occupied Berlin, instructed Trevor-Roper to investigate the evidence for Hitler's suicide in order to refute Soviet disinformation that Hitler was still alive and living in the west. In only two months White produced a masterly report demolishing most of the disinformation and proving that Hitler had died by his own hand in his Berlin bunker. Largely under White's initiative and despite opposition from Menzies, the report was cleared for publication in 1947 as *The Last Days of Hitler*. Trevor-Roper dedicated it to White, 'both the first parent and the ultimate midwife of this book'.

‡ Davenport-Hines and Sisman (eds), *One Hundred Letters from Hugh Trevor-Roper*, pp.256–8; Sisman, *Hugh Trevor-Roper*, p.465.

§ Written and presented by Christopher Andrew; producer Peter Everett, originally a three-part series broadcast on BBC Radio 4 and the World Service, later extended to five parts.

have been DG of MI5 and that it would have been "a brilliant and popular choice" is surely bizarre.*

Like Trevor-Roper, Mills and the B1a veterans found the contradictions in government policy on revealing the intelligence successes of the Second World War ridiculous. In 1979 Her Majesty's Stationery Office began publication of Professor Sir F. H. Hinsley's magisterial (and severely academic) three-volume official history of the 'part played by British intelligence in allied strategy and operations in the Second World War', but was refused permission to publish Professor Sir Michael Howard's official history of the role of deception in the same strategy and operations.[†] Dick White told Trevor-Roper, and doubtless Mills, that current government policy on revealing wartime intelligence successes was being undermined by 'idiot secrecy'.[‡]

Trevor-Roper had the lead role in the Radio 4 documentary broadcast on the fiftieth anniversary of Hitler's appointment as German Chancellor on 30 January 1933, probably heard by most of the B1a veterans.[§] A few months later, they were startled by a quite different pronouncement on Hitler by Trevor-Roper. In a front-page article in *The Times* on 23 April, he announced the sensational discovery, in Germany, of an 'archive of great historical significance': 'It is Hitler's private diary, kept by him, in his own hand, throughout almost all of his reign...' Within twenty-four hours, however, he began to realise that he had been deceived. Final proof that the diaries were forged was provided by chemical tests showing that the paper on

---

* Trevor-Roper to Mills, 21 October 1987, CBM papers.
† Wartime German intercepts of the early 1940s were released to TNA, but peacetime Soviet intercepts of the early 1920s remained classified, despite the fact that some had already appeared in print and others were publicly available in the House of Lords Record Office; Andrew, *Secret Service*, pp.505–6. Mills had read some of the Soviet intercepts leaked to the press while he was still at university in the early 1920s; see above, pp.40–42.
‡ Davenport-Hines and Sisman (eds), *One Hundred Letters from Hugh Trevor-Roper*, p.258.
§ *The Night of the Miracle*, Radio 4, 30 January 1983. Written and presented by Christopher Andrew, producer, Peter Everett.

which they were written was manufactured post-war. Trevor-Roper was mocked in *Private Eye* as 'Hugh Very-Ropey', 'Lord Facre' and 'Lord Lucre of Claptout'.

In the company of friends such as White and Mills, despite the public humiliation of the Hitler diaries, Trevor-Roper remained good company and capable of self-irony.* The previously unpublished photograph of a B1a lunch, to which Trevor-Roper and Hesketh were invited,† captures the relaxed conviviality of their regular reunions. All, except the 63-year-old Peggy Harmer (née Phillips), were in their eighties. 'I hate to say it but I found the war really exciting,' she recalled. 'There was a wonderful atmosphere; such camaraderie. We all had a common enemy. That made a huge difference.'‡

For those at the lunch, the most welcome surprise of the past few years had been the re-emergence of double agent GARBO (Juan Pujol García), who had been recruited by Mills in 1942. In the summer of 1984, Mills wrote in a confidential memoir for Mimi and their children:

> ...Garbo has just come back from the dead. Many years ago he feared some Nazis in South America might try to take their revenge and he asked his wife to write to Tommy Harris [his second case officer] and say he had died. Just before Tommy died in a car crash [in 1964] I asked him if he had heard from Garbo recently and he told me he was dead. Therefore when I was asked to meet

---

* Among friends, as at the B1a gatherings, Trevor-Roper could also be wittily unpretentious. Some of his most engaging correspondence during the 1980s was with Alasdair Palmer, a Cambridge graduate student whom he first encountered on a train journey from London. Davenport-Hines and Sisman (eds), *One Hundred Letters from Hugh Trevor-Roper*, pp.295–8, 303–26.

† See illustration no.25: B1a lunch, with Roger Hesketh and Hugh Trevor-Roper as guests, hosted by Hugh and Emi[ly]-Lu[cy] Astor at the idyllic Folly Farm, their Lutyens-designed home in the Kennet Valley, Berkshire, on 9 June 1985.

‡ Peggy Harmer obituary, *The Times*, 7 April 2011.

him a few days ago I was prepared in case the man I was asked to meet was an imposter. As I entered the room where he was, he saw me, rushed across and threw his arms around me saying 'Dear Mr Grey'. That was the name by which he had known me and it was his way of expressing his gratitude for the fact that I brought him to this country and set him up as a double agent although S.I.S. [MI6] in Madrid and Lisbon had refused to have anything to do with him on three occasions when he had offered himself and all he knew to them.[*]

GARBO's sudden reappearance and return to London were chiefly due to the intelligence historian Nigel West, who, after a sometimes frustrating ten-year hunt, had finally tracked him down in South America.[†]

To mark the fortieth anniversary, in June 1984, of the D-Day landings, in whose success GARBO had played a key role, he was invited to Buckingham Palace to be personally congratulated by the Duke of Edinburgh, made guest of honour at a reception at the Special Forces Club on 31 May, which was attended by Mills and other B1a veterans, then taken on a guided tour of the Normandy beaches.[‡] Mills kept a framed photograph of his reunion with GARBO on display at home.[§]

A year later, the 83-year-old Mills sent the Duke of Edinburgh a copy of the newly published *Operation Garbo*, co-written by GARBO and Nigel West: 'It may interest you to read, Sir, on page 5 and elsewhere that it was I, who you may only have known as a

---

[*] Mills, untitled confidential memoir on his intelligence career shown to Mimi and their children (undated but completed in 1984), p.17; CBM papers. Though previously turning Pujol down, in March 1942 MI6 had recruited him as double agent BOVRIL; see above, p.131.

[†] Pujol and West, *Operation Garbo*, introduction.

[‡] Ibid. GARBO died in 1988.

[§] See illustration no.28: GARBO and Mills drinking champagne to celebrate the 40th anniversary of D-Day.

Circus man, who recruited Garbo and brought him to this country and acted as his first Case Officer.'

It is only right to add that I had nothing to do with the writing or publication of the book.[*]

The revelation of Mills's role as GARBO's recruiter and first MI5 case officer, however, attracted little public interest. Because he had left for Canada at the end of 1942 and his continuing central role in the Double-Cross System had yet to be revealed, media attention focused instead on GARBO's work with his second case officer, Tommy Harris. Mills was delighted that his own intelligence career, which he had not wanted to publicise, remained in the shadows. Almost forty years later, the bestselling (and otherwise excellent) history of Double Cross and D-Day included only a misleading half-sentence reference to Mills as 'a part-time circus impresario' in B1a.[†]

* * *

The best-publicised Soviet spy case during Margaret Thatcher's early years in power was that of Mills's former wartime colleague in MI5, Anthony Blunt. Mills had met him frequently after Blunt became Guy Liddell's assistant early in 1941. When Guy Burgess defected to Moscow in 1951, however, Mills became suspicious of Blunt's loyalties, privately describing the wartime flat near Oxford Street, which he had shared with the promiscuous Burgess, as 'little more than a homosexual brothel'.[‡]

In November 1979, six months after Thatcher became Prime Minister, she named Blunt in the Commons as a former Soviet spy, after

---

* See illustration no.26: Mills to Duke of Edinburgh, 5 August 1985.

† Macintyre, *Double Cross*, p.70.

‡ Mills to 'Tar' Robertson, October 1987, CBM papers.

strong hints of his treachery had appeared in the press.* Though Mills welcomed Blunt's public exposure as the Fourth Man in the Cambridge 'Ring of Five', he regarded the ensuing sensationalist media hunt for more British traitors in the service of the KGB as ridiculous. Imaginary moles multiplied rapidly in print: among them Donald Beves, Frank Birch, Andrew Gow, Sir Roger Hollis, Guy Liddell, Graham Mitchell and Arthur Pigou (all dead), Sir Rudolf Peierls (who denied claims that he too was dead and sued successfully for libel), Lord (Victor) Rothschild (the target, during his lifetime, of innuendo rather than open allegation in case he also sued) and Wilfrid Mann (who did not sue but wrote a book to prove his innocence).[†]

Though MI5 knew that none of the imaginary moles had ever worked for Moscow, it was not until August 1982 that intelligence from a major MI6 agent inside the KGB, Oleg Gordievsky, secretly identified John Cairncross as the real Fifth Man in the Cambridge 'Magnificent Five' recruited by pre-war Soviet intelligence. In the decade after his recruitment in 1937, Cairncross had worked as a Soviet agent in, successively, the Foreign Office, the Treasury, the private office of one of Churchill's ministers, Bletchley Park and MI6. Only in 1990, however, did Gordievsky make the identification public.[‡] Mills watched the sensational Granada TV documentary *The Fifth Man: The Secrets of the Ring of Five*,[§] in which Gordievsky, disguised with a false moustache and ill-fitting wig, identified Cairncross as the Fifth Man.

During the 1980s the main target of mole-hunting conspiracy theorists was not Cairncross, but the entirely innocent former MI5

---

* In 1963 Blunt had made a secret confession in return for a promise of immunity from prosecution.
† Andrew, *Defence of the Realm*, p.706.
‡ Though Cairncross had secretly confessed to espionage in 1964, MI5 had failed to realise how highly the KGB rated him.
§ Producer: Michael Beckham; presenter: Christopher Andrew: bfi.org.uk/films-tv-people/4ce2b830d30df.

DG and friend of Mills, Sir Roger Hollis, who had died in 1973. Mills was particularly outraged by the attacks on Hollis by Chapman Pincher, then Britain's best-known espionage writer. Pincher's 1981 bestseller, *Their Trade Is Treachery*, claimed that Hollis was a 'supermole' who had played a key role in handing over Britain's intelligence community to Soviet control: 'The view of the loyal MI5 officers who uncovered the evidence [against Hollis] is that the Russians penetrated both the security and intelligence services [MI5 and MI6] so deeply and for so long that they not only neutralised them but effectively ran them.'*

If Hollis had been a Soviet mole, it followed that Mills had been personally duped by him into hosting at his home in 17 Kensington Palace Gardens a fifteen-year surveillance operation against the neighbouring Russian embassy and intelligence residencies which, in reality, was an elaborate KGB deception.

Mills applauded Margaret Thatcher's unprecedented public rubbishing of Pincher's *Their Trade Is Treachery* in the Commons on 26 March 1981. Though she did not, of course, mention the surveillance conducted from 17 KPG against the Soviet embassy and intelligence residencies before Operation FOOT, Thatcher declared that 'the expulsion of members of the Russian intelligence service from this country in 1971 would hardly have been achieved if the Security Service had been penetrated'. She also contradicted Pincher's woefully inaccurate account of the 1974 inquiry by the former Cabinet Secretary, Lord Trend, into the allegations that Hollis was a Soviet mole:

Mr Pincher's account of Lord Trend's conclusions is wrong. The book asserts that Lord Trend 'concluded that there was a strong

---

* Pincher, *Their Trade Is Treachery*, loc.160.

prima facie case that MI5 had been deeply penetrated over many years by someone who was not Blunt', and that he 'named Hollis as the likeliest suspect'. Lord Trend said neither of those things, and nothing resembling them.*

Thatcher could have said much more to discredit Chapman Pincher's conspiracy theories had she been willing to quote directly from MI5 files. As Mills was probably aware, far from attempting to cover up Blunt's treachery, Hollis was probably the first at the end of the war to express suspicions about him. Philby later recalled that 'Hollis was always vaguely unhappy about him.' When Blunt secretly confessed to working as a Soviet agent in 1964, he told his MI5 interrogators, Peter Wright and Arthur Martin, 'I believe [Hollis] disliked me – I believe he slightly suspected me'. Blunt recalled one particularly dramatic example of Hollis's suspicions. After Igor Gouzenko revealed the existence of an unidentified Soviet agent codenamed ELLI in 1945, Hollis turned to Blunt and said, 'Isn't that so, ELLI?'[†] It was sadly ironic that Wright and Martin, the most damaging conspiracy theorists in the history of MI5, should later persuade themselves that the unidentified Soviet agent was Hollis himself.

On 16 July 1984, Pincher's chief informant, the maverick former MI5 officer Peter Wright, starred in a Granada *World in Action* television documentary devoted to his allegations that Hollis was a Soviet spy. Mills was appalled. What *World in Action* did not reveal was that, as Wright later admitted, his conspiracy theories had made him deeply unpopular among present members of MI5 as well as retirees such as Mills: 'There was talk of the Gestapo. Younger officers began to avoid me in the canteen. Casual conversation with many

---

*   *Parl. Deb.* (Commons), 26 March 1981.
†   Andrew, *Defence of the Realm*, p.282.

of my colleagues became a rarity." The future DG, Stella Rimington, was among those who believed Wright had become 'paranoid': 'By the time I knew him well he was quite clearly a man with an obsession and was regarded by many of the newer arrivals in the Service and even by some of the older hands as quite mad and certainly dangerous'.[†]

* * *

Press reports after *World in Action*'s claim that Hollis had been a Soviet agent revealed that, in retirement in Australia, Wright was writing a sensational memoir, eventually entitled *Spycatcher*, about his MI5 career.[‡] In 1985 the Attorney General, in the name of the British government, began proceedings against Wright and his publisher in Australia, seeking an injunction to prevent publication on the grounds that Wright was in breach of his duty of confidentiality to the Crown. The *Spycatcher* trial, which was to last five weeks, opened in Sydney in November 1986 and attracted a level of global publicity unequalled by any other book since the Macmillan government's equally ill-fated attempt to ban the publication of *Lady Chatterley's Lover* on the grounds of obscenity a quarter of a century earlier. 'It was an enormous lark', recalled Wright's counsel, the 32-year-old future Australian Prime Minister Malcolm Turnbull, 'and I enjoyed every minute of it.'

Mills, by contrast, found daily newspaper reports of the trial and the repetition of Wright's claim that Hollis was a traitor deeply depressing. The Thatcher government, unsurprisingly, lost its case in

---

* Wright, *Spycatcher*, p.224.
† Rimington, *Open Secret*, pp.115, 130.
‡ Wright's ghostwriter was the *World in Action* producer Paul Greenglass.

the New South Wales Supreme Court. It continued, however, to try and prevent *Spycatcher* being published in Britain – despite the fact that it was top of the bestseller list in the United States. The Labour MP David Winnick facetiously asked the Attorney General whether Wright had 'expressed his gratitude to the British government for helping to boost the sales and publicity of his book'. The Law Lords accepted the government argument that the book constituted a serious breach of confidentiality but concluded that, since it had already been published abroad, publication in Britain would cause no further damage to national security. *Spycatcher* quickly became – and remains – the greatest global bestseller in the entire history of intelligence (alleged) non-fiction.*

When *Spycatcher* was published, Mills told his family that the real 'traitor' was not Hollis but Wright. A secret internal MI5 inquiry concluded a year after *Spycatcher*'s publication that Wright was so dishonest that he 'did not scruple to invent evidence where none existed' in order to attack Hollis.† Though Mills did not see this report, he independently came to the same conclusion.

Mills also took deep personal offence at Wright's references to his own intelligence career. *Spycatcher* revealed that from 1960 onwards MI5 had installed Mills in 17 KPG, to use it as a base for eavesdropping and surveillance operations against the nearby Soviet embassy and intelligence 'residencies' (stations). Wright, however, embroidered his account with colourful inventions:

Mills operated his circus business from the house for many years, and every time [MI5] needed to deliver staff or equipment to the

---

* Andrew, *Defence of the Realm*, pp.763–5.
† Ibid., pp.518–20.

house, or remove debris from the [eavesdropping] tunnel, we used a garishly painted Mills Circus van.[*]

Mills commented angrily:

1. I never did Circus or any other business at the [KPG] house.
2. No Circus vehicle ever went to the house. [MI5] had their own plain van.[†]

According to *Spycatcher*:

The secret of the Mills [KPG] house remained intact … until one night the alarm systems detected two Soviet diplomats climbing onto the roof. They broke a skylight, but before they could enter the roof space, the housekeeper frightened them off. Cyril Mills made a formal protest to the Soviet embassy…[‡]

In reality, 17 KPG had no skylight, there were never any Russians on the roof and Cyril never spoke to any of his Soviet neighbours. Nor was there any housekeeper. Having discovered that the housekeeper originally installed by MI5 had accepted an invitation to drinks with some of his Russian neighbours, Mills sacked him from 17 KPG as soon as he took up residence.[§]

Mills informed MI5's legal adviser, Bernard Sheldon, after the publication of *Spycatcher* in 1987, that he was 'shocked beyond measure' by what Wright had published about his intelligence career – particularly at 17 KPG. He told Mimi that, now his role at the house

---

[*]   Wright, *Spycatcher*, pp.104–5.
[†]   CBM papers.
[‡]   Wright, *Spycatcher*, pp.104–5.
[§]   CBM papers.

had been revealed by Wright's bestseller, he was determined to set the record straight:

> There is one subject which I had decided I would never write about and although Frederick [Mimi's son from her first marriage], Christopher and Sandra were never asked to sign the Official Secrets Act they have always understood that it is one which they would never mention to anyone.
>
> However, during this year 1987, things have changed as the result of a book entitled SPYCATCHER written by a traitor named Wright … He has revealed that we were installed in Kensington Palace Gardens by MI5. In these circumstances I have every right to record the truth which does not always correspond with what Wright or his ghostwriter wrote.*

An internal MI5 inquiry later discovered that Wright had deliberately distorted some of the intelligence obtained from the surveillance from 17 KPG of the KGB resident (Head of Station), Nikolai Borisovich Rodin (alias Korovin), in order to cast suspicion on Hollis:

> Wright has quoted an incident in 1961 when the KGB Resident Korovin [Rodin] was said to have been watching television [news] on the evening of the day when [the Soviet spies] Lonsdale and the Krogers etc were arrested – and showed no emotion. This is quite untrue. Korovin was having a party with his two deputies and they were not watching television or listening to the radio.

---

* CBM papers.

Wright's aim in distorting intelligence obtained from the surveillance of Rodin was to imply that he registered no surprise at the arrest of Soviet spies because he had been tipped off, presumably by Hollis – further evidence that, as the MI5 inquiry concluded, Wright 'did not scruple to invent evidence where none existed'.[*]

In the Granada documentary, *The Fifth Man: The Secrets of the Ring of Five*, Oleg Gordievsky revealed that some of his senior colleagues in the KGB regarded Wright's allegation against Hollis as such nonsense that they suspected it might be part of a bizarre British plot to discredit Soviet intelligence.

The *Spycatcher* saga changed the attitude of Mills and his former B1a colleagues to talking about their wartime intelligence careers. In the 1970s they had all strongly opposed the publication of Masterman's *Double-Cross System*. Mills had threatened to sue Masterman if he was mentioned in it.[†] The public embarrassment created by Peter Wright, however, left most members of the Security Service, past and present, with the conviction that things could not go on as before. MI5 must be more open about both its past history and current role. The Master of the Rolls, Sir John Donaldson, said, when giving judgement in an action against British newspapers that had published extracts from *Spycatcher*, 'It may be that the time has come when Parliament should regularise the position of the Security Service', which had no basis in either statute or common law. MI5 agreed. Its classified *Annual Report* for 1987–88 concluded: 'There is complete acceptance among staff of the desirability of legislation for the Security Service.' The DG, Sir Antony Duff, persuaded the Home Secretary, Douglas Hurd, hitherto opposed to legislation, that 'the time had passed when the Security Service could successfully operate on the basis that it did not exist.

---

*   Andrew, *Defence of the Realm*, p.520.
†   Mills to Annie Luke, 8 January 1990; CBM papers.

The pretence had worn threadbare, making it increasingly difficult to recruit and train men and women of quality for the Service.*

On 22 November 1988, it was announced in the Queen's Speech that 'a Bill will be introduced to put the Security Service on a statutory basis under the Secretary of State.' The Security Service Act of 1989 at last placed MI5 on a statutory footing, sidestepping the contentious issue of the previous legal basis for MI5 operations by use of the equivocal formula: 'There shall continue to be a Security Service.'

For the first time, Mills was persuaded to talk briefly in public about some of his own wartime (but not Cold War) intelligence career, notably his role in the Double-Cross System. The occasion was a programme in the popular long-running Thames Television series, *This Is Your Life*, which lured celebrities into a studio where they unexpectedly encountered friends, family and former colleagues who helped to tell the story of their lives on TV. To celebrate Mills's career, luminaries of the circus world were joined by his friends and former MI5 colleagues, 'Tar' Robertson and Christopher Harmer. 'We double-crossed you!' they gleefully told the initially dumbfounded Mills.

Robertson told viewers that, as a wartime spymaster: 'Cyril was a marvellous operator. He was a pretty tough character in every possible way but he was very kind to his [double] agents. He was known by us, with no ill feeling, as 'the old dog'. He had under his control the best agent we ever had – GARBO.'† Mills was probably the only person in the studio who had first appeared on television over fifty years earlier. In 1937, a year after regular TV broadcasts began, he had stood in for the well-known (but temporarily indisposed) BBC

---

* Andrew, *Defence of the Realm*, section 3, ch.11.
† youtube.com/watch?v=-0FCG2K4sFo. Billy Luke, who would otherwise have taken part in the programme, died before it was made.

commentator Freddie Grisewood during a circus performance at Olympia.* He revealed to a much larger TV audience in 1989, two years before his death, that his circus career had provided cover for intelligence operations. Even Mills's first TV performance for half a century, however, failed to disclose most of his extraordinary intelligence career. It is revealed in this book for the first time.

* * *

At a summit meeting in Malta in December 1989, Mikhail Gorbachev and US President George H. W. Bush (a former head of the CIA) jointly declared the end of the Cold War. Mills had no doubt that the West had won. Throughout the Cold War, he loathed both Communism and the Soviet system. So did Coco the Clown OBE and the other performers and animal trainers from the Soviet Bloc who Cyril had signed up to work for Bertram Mills Circus.

Mills lacked a detailed understanding of the Soviet Union, the only major European country he never visited. But, unlike many western international relations experts, he grasped the central role of the KGB, which was barely mentioned by any scholarly studies of Soviet foreign policy published during and immediately after the Cold War. The bibliography of an academic history of Russian foreign relations from 1917 to 1991, published in 1998 and praised by a British authority on the subject as 'easily the best general history of Soviet foreign policy', includes – apart from a biography of Stalin's most fearsome intelligence Chief, Lavrentiy Beria – not a single work on Soviet intelligence among its 120 titles.†

During the final years of his life, Mills continued to follow the

---

* Mills, *Bertram Mills Circus*, pp.206–7.
† Caroline Kennedy-Pipe, *Russia and the World, 1917–1991* (London: Arnold, 1998).

fortunes of foreign circuses closely. He must have been surprised that in the later 1980s, when the Soviet system was in existential crisis, the Moscow State Circus was at the peak of its popularity.* Annually, there were more than a thousand auditions for the seventy places available at the prestigious and demanding Moscow Circus School.†

The KGB was well aware, however, that among young Russians, western popular music had a far bigger following than the Soviet circus. In Dnipropetrovsk Oblast, where the Soviet leader, Leonid Brezhnev, had begun his career as a party apparatchik, the local KGB calculated, after opening young people's correspondence, that almost 80 per cent of 15- to 20-year-olds 'systematically listened to broadcasts from Western radio stations', especially popular music, and showed other alarming signs of interest in western pop stars, such as asking for their autographs: 'Even listening to musical programmes gave young people a distorted idea of Soviet reality, and led to incidents of a treasonable nature. Infatuation with trendy Western popular music, musical groups and performers falling under their influence leads to the possibility of these young people embarking on a hostile path.'‡

During the later Cold War, many in the KGB domestic security directorates believed that western pop stars were doing more to undermine the Soviet Union than western spies.

Cyril Mills died, aged eighty-nine, on 20 July 1991§, just over five months before the final disintegration of the Soviet Union. Stella Rimington, who was shortly to become MI5's DG, visited

---

* Among the packed, enthusiastic audience at a performance in December 1985 were Christopher and Jenny Andrew with their three children.
† Miriam Birch, *Inside the Soviet Circus*, National Geographic film, 1988.
‡ CCAC, GBR/0014/MITN; Andrew and Mitrokhin, *The Mitrokhin Archive*, p.712.
§ The death certificate records that Mills died of bronchopneumonia.

Moscow in December 1991: 'I thought the Cold War would last for my lifetime, yet there I was in the British ambassador's Rolls-Royce with the Union Jack flying on the bonnet, driving through a snowy Moscow night to have dinner with the KGB.' Rimington found it 'difficult to avoid the feeling that we had somehow slipped into a James Bond film.'[*]

B1a veterans probably had the same feeling. By 1994 only three of them remained: 'Tar' Robertson, Christopher Harmer and Hugh Astor[†], who planned what was to be the last B1a lunch on 19 June, to celebrate the fiftieth anniversary of the FORTITUDE deceptions and D-Day landings with Stella Rimington as their guest. 'Tar', however, died on 10 May soon after returning from holiday in Portugal. His widow, Rachel Robertson, decided that the lunch should go ahead, as planned, at the Astors' Folly Farm. Christopher Harmer, however, was too ill to attend either the lunch or the memorial service for 'Tar' Robertson at Pershore Abbey the next day. Harmer's address at the service, read for him in his absence by a step-grand-son, praised 'Tar' for having created in B1a half a century earlier 'the happiest and most united environment in which I ever worked': 'We all remained firm friends for the rest of our lives.'[‡] In his private papers, Cyril Mills recorded the same memory of 'spending my war years among the nicest people and the best friends I have ever known.'[§] Unlike Philby, who betrayed numerous British agents and was distrusted by many in the KGB, Mills was truly 'a spy among friends'.

---

[*] Rimington, *Open Secret*, ch.19; Stella Rimington interview, December 2018: bigissue.com/interviews/stella-rimington-kgb-saw-us-as-extraordinary-creatures-from-another-world.

[†] Sir Dick White died in February 1993.

[‡] Elliott, *Gentleman Spymaster*, pp.312–15. Mimi Mills was among those at 'Tar''s memorial service; recollection of Christopher Mills.

[§] CBM papers.

THE SPY WHO CAME IN FROM THE CIRCUS

Cyril Mills's two professions – the entertainment industry and secret intelligence – appear to have little in common. Entertainers spend as much time in the spotlight as possible. Spies avoid it altogether. A famous spy is either a failed spy or an ex-spy.* But, as Prince Philip, Duke of Edinburgh, told Mills, it was because running a circus is such an improbable occupation for a spy that it proved to be such wonderful cover.† Even Bertram Mills never suspected that his son Cyril used the family circus as cover for espionage in Nazi Germany. Nor, happily, did the Gestapo.

The circus provided Cyril with intelligence opportunities as well as operational cover. Even when he was in his early twenties, with no thoughts of working for either MI5 or MI6, Bertram Mills Circus brought him into personal contact with both the Zirkus Krone in Munich, Hitler's favourite speaking venue at the start of his political career, and Mills's fellow Harrovian Winston Churchill, later Hitler's

---

*   Andrew and Green, *Stars and Spies*, introduction.
†   See above, p.2.

leading British opponent and already the circus's most enthusiastic supporter in the House of Commons.

The family circus also taught Cyril some of the skills which were later central to his work for MI5 and MI6. Among the most remarkable was the ability to hold his nerve in terrifying situations. He later recalled, for example, one evening in the Big Top at Devonport in 1933:

> I was standing inside the main entrance watching the last few members of the audience arrive. I turned and saw three tigers walking towards me and they were all fully grown ones. The cage door was wide open. For some reason which I have never understood the one thing I did not feel was fear.

Because Mills remained calm, so did the audience, which 'seemed to regard tigers walking about in their midst as a perfectly normal thing.' The tigers were eventually returned to their cage, though one woman 'received a nasty scratch and had to go to hospital.'*

Mills showed the same bravery in his first major intelligence operations: flying dangerous reconnaissance missions for MI6 over secret airfields and the Messerschmitt factory in pre-war Nazi Germany. A crashlanding when his Hornet Moth turned a somersault during torrential rain might well have proved fatal. Mills also knew that, like several other British spies, he ran the risk of being caught by the Gestapo and executed, probably by decapitation.†

Mills's main wartime intelligence success was to recruit and run double agents against the Abwehr in the Double-Cross System. His

---

* Mills modestly, but inaccurately, denied that he was brave: 'Bravery can be ruled right out, for it involves the capacity to recognise danger and to overcome the fear which it produces.' Mills, *Bertram Mills Circus*, pp.70–71. Lady Eleanor Smith, a great admirer of Mills, was present at the performance when the tigers escaped. Smith, *Life's a Circus*, ch.31.
† See above, ch.3.

B1a colleague and close friend, Christopher Harmer, later said of him: 'Cyril was tailor-made for this activity. He had no difficulty in coping with the odd characters – some very odd – we were dealing with.' Before the war, Mills had recruited and employed some even odder characters for the circus and its sideshows: among them lion tamers, wire walkers, snake charmers and sword swallowers. The oddest re-cruits included Zaro Agha a Turk who claimed to be the world's oldest man. Mills put Agha's passport on public display, 'which proved the man was entitled to celebrate his 156th birthday when he was with us on the 19th of August 1931.'* The pre-war circus had also given Mills more experience of devising and organising deceptions and illusions than anyone else at the heart of the Double-Cross System, probably the most successful strategic deception in the history of warfare. In a pre-television era when few families went further afield for their holi-days than Blackpool or Margate, the circus was Britain's most magical environment with a unique mix of performing wild animals, clowns and thrilling aerial acrobatics. It was, as Mills discovered, the natural home of illusion and deception. He quickly learned how popular and convincing some illusions were. While working in Burma early in his career, Mills identified as a fraud the Indian rope trick, which he had hoped to include in the circus. Britain's most senior soldier, Field Marshal Earl Haig, however, vouched for its authenticity. The ease with which Haig was taken in must have strengthened Mills's later belief in the gullibility of the Abwehr.

Mills's most successful, and best-paid, circus performer before the Second World War was a dancer from Bordeaux, Renée Bernard, whom he helped to masquerade as an Indian called Koringa, 'the only female fakir in the world', able to mesmerise crocodiles and survive

---

* 'Even so', wrote Mills, 'I still wonder just what kind of records were kept in Turkey in 1775.' Mills, *Bertram Mills Circus*, p.171.

burial in a snake-infested pit. Improbable though the masquerade now appears, Koringa's real identity remained undiscovered until Mills himself gave away the secret after his retirement thirty years later.

Occasional echoes still linger, even today, of Mills's interwar hoaxes and deceptions. No one did more to promote the myth of the Loch Ness Monster than Bertram Mills Circus. After Bertram telephoned his friend, the editor of the *Daily Mail*, a headline in the newspaper announced on 13 December 1933: 'Bertram Mills Offers £20,000 for Loch Ness Monster' – about £1.5 million today.* The original aim was to generate sensational publicity for the circus's winter season, which was due to open at Olympia on 21 December. Photographs of a model of the Monster being paraded around London on a circus lorry were widely printed in the press.[†]

Cyril Mills arranged insurance for £20,000 to be paid to the circus to fund its promised reward if the Monster put in an appearance before the end of the Olympia winter season. Though no monster emerged from Loch Ness, the myth was now firmly established. Two books on the Monster appeared in 1934, as well as a film, *The Secret of the Loch*, edited by a young David Lean. The Chairman of Eagle Star Insurance appointed twenty official 'Watchers Of The Monster', all equipped with notebooks, binoculars and cameras, and promised each of them a bonus of a guinea for every sighting. Within a short time there were twenty sightings but no satisfactory photograph. The imaginary monster still remains a firm favourite with the Scottish tourist board.[‡]

---

[*]   Ibid., p.80; the date given by Mills for the *Daily Mail* headline is incorrect.

[†]   See Appendix.

[‡]   The insurance policy taken out by Mills defined the monster as 'an animal and/or reptile and/or fish either hitherto unknown or believed to be extinct, measuring not less than twenty feet in length or weighing not less than one thousand pounds.' Gareth Williams, *A Monstrous Commotion: The Mysteries of Loch Ness* (London: Orion, 2015).

* * *

At the age of sixty-five, shortly after the end of his career in the entertainment industry, Mills published a personal history of Bertram Mills Circus, which carefully avoided any reference to the forty years he had spent working full-time or part-time for MI5 and MI6. At this point, he expected his intelligence career to remain secret indefinitely. Even the existence of MI6 was not officially admitted until a year after he died. Professor Sir Michael Howard, the official historian of Second World War strategic deception, wrote in 1985: 'So far as official government policy is concerned, the British security and intelligence services do not exist. Enemy agents are found under gooseberry bushes and intelligence is brought by the storks.*

Until almost the end of the Cold War, both Conservative and Labour governments refused to countenance any parliamentary discussion of the intelligence services. Harold Macmillan warned the Commons after Philby's defection in 1963: 'It is dangerous and bad for our general national interest to discuss these matters.' Harold Wilson quoted Macmillan's dictum with approval in his attempted distillation of the constitutional wisdom of the ages, *The Governance of Britain*. The chapter entitled 'The Prime Minister and National Security' is barely a page long and concludes thus: 'The Prime Minister is occasionally questioned on security matters. His answers may be regarded as uniformly uninformative. There is no further information that can usefully or properly be added before bringing this chapter to an end.'†

Though no admirer of Harold Wilson, Mills agreed with him on the secrecy of 'security matters'.

---

*   Andrew, *Defence of the Realm*, p.753.
†   Harold Wilson, *The Governance of Britain* (London: Weidenfeld & Nicolson, 1976).

It was the circus, however, not espionage, which first introduced Mills to secret operations. Running Britain's best circus involved identifying and signing the best Continental acts ahead of the competition. To do so, Mills sometimes used agents, whom he called his 'private eyes' – among them a Paris antiques dealer who discovered Koringa. As during his later work in MI5, the subterfuges devised by Mills for the family circus paid great attention to detail. In the last three years before the Second World War, Mills's business contacts with Continental circuses overlapped with espionage for MI6. He ingeniously disguised plans of German aerodromes and aircraft factories as diagrams of circus layouts in German cities along his route.

The secret of Mills's reconnaissance by biplane of Hitler's pre-war aerial rearmament lasted even longer than the ULTRA Secret and the Double-Cross System; there was no mention of it in the official centenary history of MI6 published in 2010. Few, if any, wartime intelligence officers were as successful as Mills in keeping their careers secret. Despite the fact that he had recruited GARBO, the most successful of all the double agents, and devised his codename, Mills's name still barely featured in major studies of Double-Cross published twenty years after his death. What would have horrified Mills, however, was the continued circulation of sometimes garbled versions of Peter Wright's discredited conspiracy theories. Taking *Spycatcher* as its inspiration, the usually dependable *Oxford Dictionary of National Biography* continues to suggest that Mills 'was recruited to carry out surveillance activities on the Russians during the Suez Canal crisis', using his circus business as a cover: 'As a tenant in a flat sandwiched between a cluster of Soviet diplomatic buildings in Kensington Palace Gardens, he intercepted signals between these buildings in London and Moscow." In reality, the cramped flat was one of London's most expensive mansions and Mills himself intercepted no signals.

* * *

'In the national interest', Sir Dick White later admitted, 'I think we [British wartime intelligence] appropriated too much talent. The demand for men of ability in other [government] departments was enormous and perhaps we were a bit greedy.' What was also remarkable was the range of abilities. Mills later quoted the claim by Guy Liddell that wartime MI5 was 'the finest liaison of unlike minds in the history of intelligence'.[†] As well as recruiting six future judges, MI5 officers included extraordinary creative talents as diverse as Mills and the art historian Anthony Blunt, whose flair for deception as a Soviet agent deceived even White and Liddell. Neither Hitler nor Stalin would have tolerated either such a range of creative talents within their intelligence services or the freedom with which they expressed themselves. Hitler rather despised the profession of intelligence. In 1942, he declared over lunch with Heinrich Himmler, head of the SS and the most powerful of his intelligence chiefs, 'it's difficult to conceive that a genuine officer can be a sneaking spy'.[‡]

By contrast, espionage was at the heart of Soviet foreign policy. There was a huge gulf, however, between the sometimes spectacular successes of Soviet intelligence collection, greatly assisted by

---

[*] *ODNB* Cyril Mills; text as revised in 2008. Mill and his family moved into 17 KPG not in 1956 but in 1960.
[†] CBM papers.
[‡] Hugh Trevor-Roper (ed.), *Hitler's Table Talk, 1941–1944* (London: Weidenfeld and Nicolson, 1953), 17 February 1942. The transcript of Hitler's lunchtime monologue records that Himmler was present as a 'special guest'.

western ideological recruits such as the Cambridge 'Magnificent Five', and Moscow's serious limitations in interpreting their remarkable reports. The well-founded warnings by Stalin's German agents, Arvid Harnack, Harro Schulze-Boysen and Richard Sorge, in June 1941 of impending German invasion of the Soviet Union were brushed aside as disinformation. Even more than in most one-party states, intelligence analysis in Moscow was distorted by the demands of ideological orthodoxy. Soviet intelligence personnel who failed to subscribe to Stalin's conspiracy theories with sufficient enthusiasm put at risk not merely their career prospects but also their life expectancy.[*]

Stalin claimed to want only 'factual' intelligence reports. He was apt to dismiss intelligence analysis as 'dangerous guesswork'. Churchill, by contrast, encouraged it. During his pre-war 'wilderness years' on the backbenches, he was unofficially shown intelligence on Germany (probably including Mills's) which he used to challenge the Chamberlain government's policy on appeasement. On 17 May 1940, only a week after becoming Prime Minister, Churchill gave the Joint Intelligence Committee (JIC) enhanced status as the central body responsible for producing operational intelligence 'appreciations'. It was told to take the initiative, whenever it saw fit, 'at any time of day or night' to submit appreciations directly to the Prime Minister as well as to the War Cabinet and Chiefs of Staff.[†]

While Mills was in B1a, however, MI5's leadership feared that Churchill would find the Double-Cross System so exciting that he might interfere in the running of it. The concern was well-founded. At the time of the 1944 D-Day Normandy landings, GARBO sent the Abwehr a bogus Political Warfare Executive (PWE) directive on the

---

[*]   Andrew and Elkner, 'Stalin and Foreign Intelligence', p.75.
[†]   Andrew, *Secret World*, pp.617–18.

need to avoid any public reference to 'further attacks and diversions'. Churchill, however, announced to the Commons that D-Day was the first of a 'series of landings in force upon the European continent' which were still to take place. At 8 p.m. on D-Day, GARBO felt forced to send a wireless message to his Abwehr case officer, reporting that he had spoken personally to the PWE Director, who was dismayed that Churchill had ignored his directive. The Prime Minister, claimed GARBO rather lamely, had felt obliged not to distort the facts when announcing the Normandy invasion to the Commons and to the country. To B1a's relief, the Abwehr did not challenge this unconvincing explanation.[*] Mills and his colleagues rightly believed that Churchill's unprecedented success in integrating intelligence into the war effort greatly outweighed his occasional lapses.

Churchill also played a key role in promoting Mills's public reputation as, in succession to his father, Britain's leading circus proprietor in an era when the circus was a central and enormously popular part of the British entertainment industry. For over thirty years Churchill was the principal guest at the annual Bertram Mills pre-Christmas lunch at Olympia. Because he enjoyed the circus so much, he laughed more loudly in public there than anywhere else. One of Mills's proudest post-war moments was when Churchill, then Leader of the Opposition, returned to the reopened circus in 1947 – an occasion 'none of us will ever forget' when 'the whole audience rose and cheered'.[†] Like Churchill, Mills was a lifelong monarchist, proud of the royal patronage that 'gave the circus a kind of prestige which nothing else could give it'.[‡] In the twenty years after the Second World War, there were almost fifty royal visits. Queen

---

[*] Andrew, *Defence of the Realm*, p.308. David Stafford, *Ten Days to D-Day: Countdown to the Liberation of Europe* (London: Little, Brown, 2004), pp.308–9.
[†] See above, p.202.
[‡] Mills, *Bertram Mills Circus*, p.220.

Elizabeth II's award of the OBE to Coco the Clown was a unique moment in circus history.

Though Mills only worked part-time for British intelligence during the Cold War, he had a major role in facilitating surveillance operations against the Soviet embassy and intelligence residencies in London. Despite his secret wartime membership of MI5, Mills's peacetime career as one of the best-known figures in the entertainment industry, famous for organising Royal Command performances, provided perfect cover. His wealth and status prevented any suspicion in the media that the leasehold to 17 Kensington Palace Gardens opposite the Soviet embassy had been paid for by MI5 from public funds. Covert surveillance conducted from and around 17 KPG played an important part in collecting the evidence required to persuade the government to approve Operation FOOT: the unprecedented expulsion of over one hundred Soviet intelligence personnel from Britain in 1971. Continued surveillance after 1971 confirmed that FOOT had been the single most damaging blow against KGB and GRU operations in Britain during the Cold War. Most Soviet agents had to be put on ice for some years. The KGB was forced to ask Soviet Bloc and Cuban intelligence stations in London to help plug the gap.*

* * *

The Mills family's departure from Kensington Palace Gardens in 1975 brought an end to Cyril's almost forty-year career in British intelligence. Remarkably, there had so far been no public reference to it. Revelation of the two greatest intelligence secrets of the British

---

* Andrew, *Defence of the Realm*, p.576.

war effort – Double-Cross and ULTRA – had, however, begun a few years earlier. In 1972, to the fury of Mills and the B1a veterans, as well as the current MI5 leadership, J. C. Masterman succeeded in publishing his still-classified history of the Double-Cross System in the United States.* The main omission in the published version was any reference to the ULTRA decrypts which enabled B1a and others to follow Abwehr communications with its agents. The first major revelation of Bletchley Park's codebreaking successes came with the publication, in 1974, of *The Ultra Secret* by F. W. Winterbotham, Mills's main pre-war MI6 contact. ULTRA and other wartime SIGINT was discussed in much greater detail in Sir F. H. Hinsley's official history of British Intelligence in the Second World War, whose first volume was published in 1979.

'To write the history of the war without mentioning [intelligence]', wrote Professor , 'was like writing *Hamlet* without the Ghost.'† Mills, his B1a friends and Sir Dick White agreed. But Mills made it clear at their discussions that he would prefer his own career to be left out of the new intelligence histories.

Mills's longest friendship in the intelligence community was with Sir Dick White, the only man ever to become head of both MI5 and MI6 and subsequently the first holder of the new post of Intelligence Coordinator in the Cabinet Office. In 1936 he had been the first person to inform Mills of the importance of the intelligence he was collecting in Nazi Germany. In 1940 White recruited Mills to MI5. The warmth of their lifelong friendship is reflected in photographs of them together when both were in their eighties.‡ White knew, however, that Mills still wished to keep his intelligence career

---

*   Masterman, *The Double-Cross System*.
†   Paul Winter, *Defeating Hitler: Whitehall's Secret Report on Why Hitler Lost the War* (London: Continuum, 2012).
‡   See illustration no.29: Cyril Mills, 'Tar' Robertson, Sir Dick White, Christopher Harmer and Hugh Trevor-Roper reminisce in 1985.

as secret as possible and never mentioned it to the uninitiated. A 426-page biography of White, which draws on many discussions with him, includes his memories of Mills's close friends in B1a, Christopher Harmer and 'Tar' Robertson, but makes no reference to Mills.*

After the passage of the Security Service Act of 1989, celebrated by a party at MI5 headquarters, which was attended by both Margaret Thatcher and the Lord Chancellor, Lord Mackay,† Mills became more relaxed about acknowledging his own past membership of the Security Service. He was persuaded, for the first time, to talk briefly in public about some of his own wartime (but not Cold War) intelligence career on the Thames Television series *This Is Your Life*.‡ Even Mills's first TV performance for half a century, however, failed to disclose more than a small fraction of his extraordinary intelligence career. Most of it is revealed in this book for the first time.

Cyril Mills lived through the greatest eras in the history of British intelligence and of the British circus. Only he had a key role in both.

---

* Bower, *The Perfect English Spy*.
† Andrew, *Defence of the Realm*, pp.767–8.
‡ Mills's final TV appearance came in 1990, also on *This Is Your Life*, to pay tribute to his last circus ringmaster, Norman Barrett.

BIBLIOGRAPHY

Richard Aldrich, *The Hidden Hand: Britain, America and Cold War Secret Intelligence* (London: John Murray, 2001)

Richard Aldrich, *GCHQ: The Uncensored Story of Britain's Most Secret Intelligence Agency*, revised edition (London: William Collins, 2019)

Richard Aldrich and Rory Cormac, *The Secret Royals: Spying and the Crown, from Victoria to Diana* (London: Atlantic, 2021)

Christopher Andrew, *What If?* A BBC Radio 4 Alternative History (Audible audiobook, 2021): 34 episodes first broadcast 1991–2004 (producer: Ian Bell)

Christopher Andrew, *The Profession of Intelligence*, three-part Intelligence History series, BBC Radio 4; first broadcast August 1981; expanded into five-part series in 1982 (producer: Peter Everett)

Christopher Andrew (writer and presenter), *The Fatal Attraction of Adolf Hitler*, BBC 1, 21 April 1989 [television programme]

Christopher Andrew (writer and presenter), *The Fifth Man: The Secrets of the Ring of Five*, Granada TV documentary first broadcast October 1990 (producer: Michael Beckham)

Christopher Andrew, *Secret Service: The Making of the British Intelligence Community* (London: Heinemann, 1985)

Christopher Andrew (ed.), *Codebreaking and Signals Intelligence* (London: Frank Cass, 1986)

Christopher Andrew, *For the President's Eyes Only: Secret Intelligence and the American Presidency from Washington to Bush* (London: HarperCollins, 1995)

Christopher Andrew, *The Defence of the Realm: The Authorized History of MI5*, paperback edition (London: Penguin, 2010)

Christopher Andrew, *The Secret World: A History of Intelligence* (London: Allen Lane, 2018)

Christopher Andrew and David Dilks (eds), *The Missing Dimension: Governments and Intelligence Communities in the Twentieth Century* (London: Macmillan, 1984)

Christopher Andrew and Julie Elkner, 'Stalin and Foreign Policy', in Harold Shukman (ed.), *Redefining Stalinism* (London: Frank Cass, 2003)

Christopher Andrew and Oleg Gordievsky (eds), *Instructions from the Centre: Top Secret Files on KGB Foreign Operations, 1975–1985* (London: Hodder and Stoughton, 1991)

Christopher Andrew and Oleg Gordievsky, *KGB: The Inside Story of Its Foreign Operations from Lenin to Gorbachev* (London: Sceptre, 1991)

Christopher Andrew and Julius Green, *Stars and Spies: Intelligence Operations and the Entertainment Business* (London: Bodley Head, 2021)

Christopher Andrew and Vasili Mitrokhin, *The Mitrokhin Archive: The KGB in Europe and the West* (London: Penguin, 2000)

Christopher Andrew, 'Secret Intelligence and British Foreign Policy', in Christopher Andrew and Jeremy Noakes (eds), *Intelligence And International Relations, 1900–1945* (Liverpool: Liverpool University Press, 1987)

Christopher Andrew, 'Remembering the Cuban Missile Crisis', in David Gioe, Len Scott and Christopher Andrew (eds), *An International History of the Cuban Missile Crisis: A 50-year Retrospective* (London: Routledge, 2015)

Gillian Arrighi and Jim Davis (eds), *The Cambridge Companion to the Circus* (Cambridge: Cambridge University Press, 2021)

Australian Dictionary of Biography

Trevor Barnes, *Dead Doubles: The Extraordinary Worldwide Hunt for One of the Cold War's Most Notorious Spy Rings* (London: Weidenfeld & Nicolson, 2020)

Raymond J. Batvinis, *Hoover's Secret War Against Axis Spies: FBI Counterespionage During World War II* (Lawrence: University Press of Kansas, 2014)

Raymond J. Batvinis, 'Walking a Tightrope: FBI's John Cimperman and the ULTRA Secret', FBI Studies, 30 May 2022, https://fbistudies.com/2022/05/30/walking-a-tightrope/

Dean Beeby, *Cargo of Lies: The True Story of a Nazi Double Agent in Canada* (Toronto: University of Toronto Press, 1996)

J. G. Beevor, *SOE: Recollections and Reflections, 1940–45* (London: Bodley Head, 1981)

Gill Bennett, *Churchill's Man of Mystery: Desmond Morton and the World of Intelligence* (London: Routledge, 2009)

Kenneth Benton, 'The ISOS Years: Madrid 1941– 3', *Journal of Contemporary History*, vol.30, no.3 (1995)

John Bew, *Citizen Clem* (London: Riverrun, 2016)

Mary Wickham Bond (Mrs James Bond), *How 007 Got His Name* (London: Collins, 1966)

Genrikh Borovik, *The Philby Files* (London: Little, Brown, 1994)

Patricia Bourne, *Thank You, I Prefer Lions* (London: William Kimber, 1956)

Tim Bouverie, *Appeasing Hitler: Chamberlain, Churchill and the Road to War* (London: Bodley Head, 2020)

Tom Bower, *The Perfect English Spy: Sir Dick White and the Secret War 1935–90* (London: Heinemann, 1995)

Julia Boyd, *Travellers in the Third Reich: The Rise of Fascism through the Eyes of Everyday People* (London: Elliott & Thompson, 2017)

Piers Brendon, *Churchill's Bestiary: His Life Through Animals* (London: Michael O'Mara Books, 2018)

Michael Brenner, *In Hitler's Munich: Jews, the Revolution, and the Rise of Nazism* (Princeton: Princeton University Press, 2022)

British Security Coordination: The Secret History of British Intelligence in the Americas, with introduction by Nigel West (London: Little, Brown & Company, 1998)

Jimmy Burns, *A Faithful Spy: The Life and Times of an MI6 and MI5 Officer* (London: Chiselbury, 2023)

J. P. T. Bury, *The College of Corpus Christi and of the Blessed Virgin Mary from 1822 to 1952* (Cambridge: Corpus Christi College, 1952)

Robert Cecil, 'The Cambridge Comintern', in Christopher Andrew and David Dilks (eds), *The Missing Dimension: Governments and Intelligence Communities in the Twentieth Century* (London: Macmillan, 1984)

W. S. Churchill, *My Early Life* (London: Eland, 2000 [1930])

W. S. Churchill, *Marlborough: His Life and Times* Volumes 1 and 2 (London: Harrap, 1947)

W. S. Churchill, *The Gathering Storm* (New York: RosettaBooks, 2002 [1948])

Frank Close, *Half Life: The Divided Life of Bruno Pontecorvo, Physicist or Spy* (London: Oneworld, 2015)

David R. Contosta, *The Private Life of James Bond* (Lititz, PA: Sutter House, 1993)

Daniel Cowling, *Don't Let's Be Beastly to the Germans: The British Occupation of Germany, 1945–49* (London: Head of Zeus, 2023)

Viscount D'Abernon, *An Ambassador of Peace: Pages from the Diary of Viscount D'Abernon* (Berlin 1920–1926) (London: Hodder & Stoughton, 1929)

Richard Davenport-Hines and Adam Sisman (eds), *One Hundred Letters from Hugh Trevor-Roper* (Oxford: Oxford University Press, 2014)

Gerard J. DeGroot, *The Bomb: A Life* (Cambridge, MA: Harvard University Press, 2005)

Christopher Draper, *The Mad Major* (London: Air Review, 1962)

Christopher Dummitt, *Unbuttoned: A History of Mackenzie King's Secret Life* (Montreal and Kingston: McGill-Queen's University Press, 2017)

David Easter, 'Soviet Bloc and Western Bugging of Opponents' Diplomatic Premises during the Early Cold War', *Intelligence and National Security*, vol.31, no.1 (2016)

David Easter, 'The Impact of "Tempest" on Anglo-American Communications Security and Intelligence, 1943–1970', *Intelligence and National Security*, vol.36, no.1 (2021)

David Easter, 'State Department Cipher Machines and Communications Security in the Early Cold War, 1944–1965', *Intelligence and National Security*, vol.38, no.4 (2023)

Richard Eden, 'The Queen Is Amused by MI5 Inquiries at Buckingham Palace', *Sunday Telegraph*, 17 October 2010.

Geoffrey Elliott, *Gentleman Spymaster: How Lt Col. Tommy 'Tar' Robertson Double-crossed the Nazis* (London: Methuen, 2011)

John Ferris, *Behind the Enigma: The Authorised History of GCHQ, Britain's Secret Cyber-Intelligence Agency* (London: Bloomsbury, 2020)

Simon Freeman and Barrie Penrose, 'My KGB Chambermaid by British Envoy', *Sunday Times*, 22 February 1981

Hans Fuchs, *Lody. Ein Weg um Ehre* 2 vols (Hamburg: Hanseatische Verlagsanstalt, 1940)

Roman Garby-Czerniawski, *The Big Network* (London: George Ronald, 1961)

Martin Gilbert, *Winston S. Churchill*, 8 vols. (London: Heinemann, 1966–88)

David Gioe, 'The Anglo-American Special Intelligence Relationship: Wartime Causes and Cold War Consequences, 1940–63', PhD thesis (University of Cambridge, 2014)

David Gioe, Len Scott and Christopher Andrew (eds), *An International History of the Cuban Missile Crisis: A 50-year retrospective* (London: Routledge, 2015)

Michael S. Goodman, *The Official History of the Joint Intelligence Committee: From the Approach of the Second World War to the Suez Crisis,* 2 vols (London: Routledge, 2014–17)

Charlotte Gray, 'Haunted by Weird Willie', *Literary Review of Canada,* May 2017.

Sheila Hancock, *Old Rage* (London: Bloomsbury, 2022)

'Sheila Hancock Q&A: "I met Clement Attlee when I was working at the circus"', *New Statesman,* 8 June 2022

Sabine Hanke, 'National Identity and Cultural Difference in the British and German Circus, 1920–1945', PhD dissertation (Sheffield University, 2020)

James Hayward, *Double Agent Snow: The True Story of Arthur Owens, Hitler's Chief Spy in England* (London: Simon & Schuster, 2012)

Simon Heffer, *Sing As We Go: Britain Between the Wars* (London: Hutchinson Heinemann, 2023)

Henry Hemming, *Our Man in New York: The British Plot to Bring America into the Second World War* (London: Quercus, 2019)

Roger Hermiston, *The Greatest Traitor: The Secret Lives of Agent George Blake* (London: Aurum Press, 2013)

Sir F. H. Hinsley et al., *British Intelligence in the Second World War: Its Influence on Strategy and Operations,* vols. 1, 2, 3i, 3ii, 4 (London: HMSO, 1979–90)

Adolf Hitler, *Mein Kampf,* English translation (Delhi: Pharos Books, 2022)

Oliver Hoare (ed.), *Camp 020: MI5 and the Nazi Spies. The Official History of MI5's Wartime Interrogation Centre* (London: Public Record Office Publications, 2001)

Kate Holmes, 'Aerial Performance', in Gillian Arrighi and Jim Davis (eds), *The Cambridge Companion to the Circus* (Cambridge: Cambridge University Press, 2021)

Thaddeus Holt, *The Deceivers: Allied Military Deception in the Second World War* (London: Weidenfeld & Nicolson, 2004)

Sir Michael Howard, *British Intelligence in the Second World War*: Volume 5, *Strategic Deception* (London: HMSO, 1990)

R. T. Howard, *Spying on the Reich: The Cold War against Hitler* (Oxford: Oxford University Press, 2023)

Tony Insall, *Secret Alliances: Special Operations and Intelligence in Norway 1940–1945* (London: Biteback Publishing, 2019)

Christopher Isherwood, *Diaries, Volume One: 1939–1960* (London: Vintage, 2011)

Yevgeny Ivanov and Gennady Sokolov, *The Naked Spy* (London: Blake Publishing, 1992)

Keith Jeffery, *MI6: The History of the Secret Intelligence Service, 1909–1949* (London: Bloomsbury, 2010)

Hanuš Jordan, Veronika Štefanová and David Konečný, 'The Past and Present of Czech Circus' in Gillian Arrighi and Jim Davis (eds), *The Cambridge Companion to the Circus* (Cambridge: Cambridge University Press, 2021)

Alan Judd, *The Quest for C: Mansfield Cumming and the Founding of the Secret Service* (London: HarperCollins, 1999)

Christine Keeler and Douglas Thompson, *The Truth at Last: My Story* (London: Sidgwick & Jackson, 2001)

Caroline Kennedy-Pipe, *Russia and the World, 1917 –1991* (London: Arnold, 1998)

Richard Kerbaj, *The Secret History of the Five Eyes: The Untold Story of the International Spy Network* (London: John Blake Publishing, 2022)

Ian Kershaw, *Hitler 1889–1936: Hubris* (London: Penguin, 2001)

Nicola Lacey, *A Life of H. L. A. Hart: The Nightmare and the Noble Dream* (Oxford: Oxford University Press, 2004)

Keith Laybourn, *The General Strike of 1926* (Stroud: Sutton Publishing, 1999)

David Levy, *Stalin's Man in Canada: Fred Rose and Soviet Espionage* (New York: Enigma Books, 2011)

Guy Liddell Diaries 1939–53: the originals, with some redactions on security grounds, are in TNA KV 4/185–196 and KV 4/470–475. Most of the text has also been published in six volumes edited by Nigel West (London: Routledge)

Arnold Lunn, *The Harrovians: A Tale of Public School Life* (London: Methuen, 1914)

Arnold Lunn, 'Introduction', *The Harrovians: A Tale of Public School Life* (South Carolina: CreateSpace, 2010)

Andrew Lycett, *Ian Fleming* (London: Weidenfeld and Nicolson, 1995)

Ben Macintyre, *Double Cross: The True Story of the D-Day Spies* (London: Bloomsbury, 2012)

Ben Macintyre, 'The Last Miss Moneypenny Recalls her War', *The Times*, 15 May 2007

Compton Mackenzie, *Greek Memories*, 2nd edn (London: Chatto & Windus, 1939)

Compton Mackenzie, *Greek Memories*, unexpurgated edition (London: Biteback Publishing, 2017)

William of Malmesbury, *Gesta Regum Anglorum*, Cambridge University Library MS Ii.2.3

Bruce Marshall, *The White Rabbit: The Secret Agent the Gestapo Could Not Crack* (London: Cassell, 2000)

Peter Martland, *Lost Generation: The Lives of Those Members of the College of Corpus Christi and of the Blessed Virgin Mary, Cambridge who Died Undertaking Military Service during the First World War, 1914 to 1919* (Cambridge: Corpus Christi College, 2023)

Eric Maschwitz, *No Chip on My Shoulder* (London: Herbert Jenkins, 1957)

J. C. Masterman, *The Double-Cross System 1939–1945* (London: Sphere Books, 1973)

J. C. Masterman, *On the Chariot Wheel: An Autobiography* (Oxford: Oxford University Press, 1975)

W. Somerset Maugham, *Ashenden: Or, the British Agent* (London: Mandarin, 1991)

John Miller, *All Them Cornfields and Ballet in the Evening* (London: Hodgson Press, 2010)

Cyril Bertram Mills, *Bertram Mills Circus: Its Story*, rev. ed. (Bath: Ashgrove Press, 1983)

František Moravec, *The Master of Spies: The Memoirs of General František Moravec* (London: Sphere, 1981)

Timothy J. Naftali, 'Intrepid's Last Deception: Documenting the Career of Sir William Stephenson', *Intelligence and National Security*, vol.8, no.3 (1993)

Henry Ringling North with Alden Hatch, *The Circus Kings: Our Ringling Family Story* (London: Red Kestrel Books, 2019)

John Julius Norwich (ed.), *The Duff Cooper Diaries 1915–1951* (London: Phoenix, 2006)

Eunan O'Halpin, 'The Liddell Diaries and British Intelligence History', *Intelligence and National Security*, vol.20, no.4 (2005)

Helen Ouin, 'From a Prison to a Palace!', BBC History, 11 July 2005, https://www.bbc.co.uk/history/ww2peopleswar/stories/84/a4427084.shtml

Oxford Dictionary of National Biography

Allen Packwood, *How Churchill Waged War: The Most Challenging Decisions of the Second World War* (Barnsley: Frontline Books, 2018)

Joanne Parker, *'England's Darling': The Victorian Cult of Alfred the Great* (Manchester: Manchester University Press, 2007)

Barrie Penrose and Simon Freeman, *Conspiracy of Silence: The Secret Life of Anthony Blunt* (London: Grafton, 1986)

Kim Philby, *My Silent War* (London: Panther 1969)

Chapman Pincher, *Their Trade Is Treachery* (London: Biteback Publishing, 2014)

Chapman Pincher, 'The Blunt Truth about Britain's Wicked Traitor', *Daily Express*, 24 July 2009.

Douglas Porch, *Defeat and Division: France at War, 1939–1942* (Cambridge: Cambridge University Press, 2022)

David Profumo, *Bringing the House Down: A Family Memoir* (London: John Murray, 2006)

Douglas M. O'Reagan, *Taking Nazi Technology: Allied Exploitation of German Science after the Second World War* (Baltimore: Johns Hopkins University Press, 2019)

Terry Reardon, *Winston Churchill and Mackenzie King: So Similar, So Different* (Toronto: Dundurn Press, 2014)

Daniela Richterova, *Watching the Jackals: Czechoslovak Spies, Terrorists and Revolutionaries* (Washington DC: Georgetown University Press, 2024)

Stella Rimington, *Open Secret: The Autobiography of the Former Director-General of MI5* (London: Hutchinson, 2001)

Andrew Roberts, *Churchill: Walking with Destiny* (London: Penguin, 2019)

Mark Ryan, *Running with Fire: The True Story of* Chariots of Fire *Hero Harold Abrahams* (London: Robson Press, 2011)

John Sawatsky, *Men in the Shadows: The RCMP Security Service* (New York: Doubleday, 1980)

Peter Michael Scott, 'Not Going Out: Television's Impacts on Britain's Commercial Entertainment Industries and Popular Leisure during the 1950s', *Social History*, vol.48, no.4 (2023)

Secret History Files, *GARBO: The Spy Who Saved D-Day* (London: PRO Publications, 2004)

Nicholas Shakespeare, *Ian Fleming: The Complete Man* (London: Harvill Secker, 2023)

Harold Shukman (ed.), *Redefining Stalinism* (London: Frank Cass, 2003)

Adam Sisman, *Hugh Trevor-Roper: The Biography* (London: Phoenix, 2011)

Lady Eleanor Smith, *Life's a Circus* (London: Longman's, Green and Co., 1939)

Michael Smith, *The Real Special Relationship: The True Story of How the British and US Secret Services Work Together* (London: Simon & Schuster, 2022)

David Stafford, *Ten Days to D-Day: Countdown to the Liberation of Europe* (London: Little, Brown, 2003)

David Stafford, 'A Myth Called Intrepid', *Saturday Night*, October 1989

Gustav Steinhauer, *Steinhauer: The Kaiser's Master Spy: The Story as Told By Himself*, ed. Sidney Felstead (London: Bodley Head, 1930)

William Stevenson, *A Man Called Intrepid* (New York: Harcourt Brace Jovanovich, 1976)

Peta Tait, *Wild and Dangerous Performances: Animals, Emotion, Circus* (London: Palgrave Macmillan, 2011)

Shirley Temple Black, *Child Star: An Autobiography* (New York: McGraw-Hill, 1988)

Frank Trentmann, *Out of the Darkness: The Germans 1922–2022* (London: Allen Lane, 2023)

Hugh Trevor-Roper (ed.), *Hitler's Table Talk, 1941–1944: His Private Conversations* (London: Weidenfeld and Nicolson, 1953)

Hugh Trevor-Roper, *The Last Days of Hitler*, 7th edition (London: Pan Books, 1995)

Christopher Tyerman, *A History of Harrow School 1324–1991* (Oxford: Oxford University Press, 2000)

Peter Verney, *Here Comes the Circus* (London: Paddington Press, 1978)

Hugo Vickers, *Cecil Beaton: The Authorised Biography* (London: Phoenix, 2002)

Steve Vogel, *Betrayal in Berlin: George Blake, the Berlin Tunnel and the Greatest Conspiracy of the Cold War* (London: John Murray, 2020)

Boris Volodarsky, *The Birth of the Soviet Secret Police: Lenin and History's Greatest Heist* (Barnsley: Frontline Books, 2023)

Will Wainewright, *Reporting on Hitler: Rothay Reynolds and the British Press in Nazi Germany* (London: Biteback Publishing, 2017)

Calder Walton, *Spies: The Epic Intelligence War between East and West* (New York: Simon & Schuster, 2023)

Nigel West, *Historical Dictionary of World War II Intelligence* (Plymouth: Scarecrow Press, 2007)

Nigel West, *Double Cross in Cairo: The True Story of the Spy Who Turned the Tide of War in the Middle East* (London: Biteback Publishing, 2015)

Nigel West and Oleg Tsarev, *Crown Jewels: The British Secrets at the Heart of the KGB Archives* (London: HarperCollins, 1998)

David Wiles and Christine Dymkovski (eds), *Cambridge Companion to Theatre History* (Cambridge: Cambridge University Press, 2012)

Gareth Williams, *A Monstrous Commotion: The Mysteries of Loch Ness* (London: Orion, 2015)

Simon Wilmetts, *In Secrecy's Shadow: The OSS and CIA in Hollywood Cinema 1941–1979* (Edinburgh: Edinburgh University Press, 2016)

Emily Wilson, 'The War in the Dark: The Security Service and the Abwehr 1939–1944', PhD thesis (University of Cambridge, 2009)

Harold Wilson, *The Governance of Britain* (London: Weidenfeld & Nicolson, 1976)

Paul Winter, 'Fathoming the Führer: British Intelligence, Adolf Hitler and the German High Command, 1939–1945', PhD thesis (University of Cambridge, 2009)

Frederick Winterbotham, *The Nazi Connection* (London: Weidenfeld & Nicolson, 1978)

Frederick Winterbotham, *The Ultra Spy: An Autobiography* (London: Macmillan, 1989)

David B. Woolner, 'Churchill, the English-Speaking Peoples and the "Special Relationship"', in Allen Packwood (ed.), *The Cambridge Companion to Winston Churchill* (Cambridge: Cambridge University Press, 2023)

Peregrine Worsthorne, *Tricks of Memory: An Autobiography* (London: Weidenfeld & Nicolson, 1993)

Peter Wright, *Spycatcher: The Candid Autobiography of a Senior Intelligence Officer* (New York: Viking, 1987)

Robert J. Young, *In Command of France: French Foreign Policy and Military Planning, 1933–1940* (Cambridge, MA: Harvard University Press, 1978)

John Zubrzycki, *Empire of Enchantment: The Story of Indian Magic* (New York: Oxford University Press, 2018)

Even in the twenty-first century, there are occasional echoes of the interwar deceptions devised by Mills which preceded the wartime Double-Cross System. He did much to promote the still popular myth of the Loch Ness Monster. In 1933 a model of the monster was paraded around London on a Bertram Mills Circus lorry with the promise of a £20,000 reward for anyone who tracked it down.

ACKNOWLEDGEMENTS

The Spy Who Came in from the Circus has been made possible by Cyril Bertram Mills's son, Christopher, who generously allowed me access to his father's papers without attempting to influence my interpretation of Cyril's career. I share Christopher Mills's view that, after all that has been officially disclosed about British intelligence operations against Nazi Germany and at the height of the Cold War with the Soviet Union, recognition of Cyril Bertram Mills's usually forgotten key role is long overdue.

I am also grateful for the support of Cyril Mills's daughter, Sandra Menzies, whose childhood memories fill an important gap in the written record. Also essential to the project has been the expertise, dedication and commitment of Christopher Mills's colleague, Jenny Manstead, Managing Director of UniPress Books.

Like Cyril Mills, I am fortunate to be a graduate of Corpus Christi College, Cambridge. Unlike Mills, however, I have spent most of my career at Corpus. I am grateful to the Master and Fellows for permission to reproduce what is widely believed to be the only contemporary portrait of Christopher Marlowe, the first Corpus graduate to be recruited as a spy while, like Cyril Mills in the twentieth century, a leading figure in the entertainment business.

Since the creation of the Cambridge University Intelligence Seminar in 2000, its convenors have often met for tea beneath Marlowe's portrait in the Corpus Senior Combination Room. My current co-convenors, Dr Dan Larsen, Dr John Ranelagh, Dr Daniela Richterova and Professor Calder Walton, have provided leads to valuable sources on both sides of the Atlantic. Dr Tim Schmalz also catalogued many of the Cyril Mills papers before leaving Cambridge to become head of history at Radley College.

For almost twenty years I had the good fortune to serve on the committee of the Churchill College Cambridge Archives Centre, an indispensable research centre for both modern British politics and intelligence operations which includes the Churchill papers. The current Archives Director, Allen Packwood, and his predecessor, Piers Brendon, have provided crucial guidance on Churchill's little studied links with Bertram Mills Circus.

My literary agent, Bill Hamilton of A. M. Heath, with whom I have enjoyed working for over thirty years, has skilfully represented both Christopher Mills and myself. Thanks also to my editor at Biteback, Lisa Goodrum. By a happy coincidence described in the introduction, almost a millennium ago a leading member of her family, then known as Guthrum, was centrally involved in the first known intelligence operation by an English entertainer against a foreign invader.

INDEX

Cyril Mills is CM throughout.

315

The Truth About God's Grace

The Truth About God's Grace

Vinny Smith

iUniverse, Inc.
Bloomington

The Truth About God's Grace

iUniverse books may be ordered through booksellers or by contacting:

iUniverse
1663 Liberty Drive
Bloomington, IN 47403
www.iuniverse.com
1-800-Authors (1-800-288-4677)

ISBN: 978-1-4759-4010-7 (sc)
ISBN: 978-1-4759-4011-4 (e)

Printed in the United States of America

iUniverse rev. date: 07/24/2012

Introduction

Grace is a precept that really must be studied in depth. Most people I hear talk about grace say that "grace" is "God's unmerited favor." This sounds good, but is it what God's grace truly is? In order to get a true understanding of any precept, it is important to look up the definition of the word in the Hebrew and/or Greek Concordance and then review each scripture and let the scriptures define what that precept means. The word grace is mentioned 159 times in the scriptures; 37 times in the Old Testament, and 122 times in the New Testament. In this book, we are going to look only at scriptures in the New Testament. When we look up the word "grace" in the Greek, we will see that it is "the divine influence upon the heart, and its reflection in the life." In each chapter of this book, we will see why God divinely influences our hearts and how it should be reflected in our lives.

Note: As we read through this book, when we see a word followed by (" "), the Hebrew or Greek word or definition for the English words will be located within the parentheses. For example:

Church ("Christian community of members on earth")

Church is the English word and "Christian community of members on earth" is the Greek definition of Church.

These Hebrew and Greek definitions come from "The New Strong's Exhaustive Concordance of the Bible."

Chapter 1:

cwc

Grace comes through / by Jesus

1. John 1:6-18 ⁶There was a man sent from God, whose name was John. ⁷The same came for a witness, to bear witness of the Light, that all men through him might believe. ⁸He was not that Light, but was sent to bear witness of that Light. ⁹That was the true Light, which lighteth every man that cometh into the world. ¹⁰He was in the world, and the world was made by him, and the world knew him not. ¹¹He came unto his own, and his own received him not. ¹²But as many as received him, to them gave he power to become the sons of God, even to them that believe on his name: ¹³Which were born, not of blood, nor of the will of the flesh, nor of the will of man, but of God. ¹⁴And the Word was made flesh, and dwelt among us, (and we beheld his glory, the glory as of the only begotten of the Father,) full of **grace** and truth. ¹⁵John bare witness of him, and cried, saying, This was he of whom I spake, He that cometh after me is preferred before me: for he was before me. ¹⁶And of his fullness have all we received, and **grace** for **grace**. ¹⁷For the law was given by Moses, but **grace** and truth came by Jesus Christ. ¹⁸No man hath seen God at any time, the only begotten Son, which is in the bosom of the Father, he hath declared him.

In this chapter, we will not go in depth on each passage of scripture. Our main goal with these scriptures is to recognize that grace comes through/ by Jesus. Verse 17 says, "… grace and truth came by Jesus Christ."

* * * * *

2. Romans 5:1-2 ¹Therefore being justified by faith, we have peace with God through our Lord Jesus Christ: ²By whom also we have access by faith into this **grace** wherein we stand, and rejoice in hope of the glory of God.

Verses 1 and 2 say, "... we have peace with God through our Lord Jesus Christ: By whom also we have access by faith into this grace wherein we stand..."

* * * * *

3. Romans 5:12-17 ¹²Wherefore, as by one man sin entered into the world, and death by sin; and so death passed upon all men, for that all have sinned: ¹³(For until the law sin was in the world: but sin is not imputed when there is no law. ¹⁴Nevertheless death reigned from Adam to Moses, even over them that had not sinned after the similitude of Adam's transgression, who is the figure of him that was to come. ¹⁵But not as the offence, so also is the free gift. For if through the offence of one many be dead, much more the **grace** of God, and the gift by **grace**, which is by one man, Jesus Christ, hath abounded unto many. ¹⁶And not as it was by one that sinned, so is the gift: for the judgment was by one to condemnation, but the free gift is of many offences unto justification. ¹⁷For if by one man's offence death reigned by one; much more they which receive abundance of **grace** and of the gift of righteousness shall reign in life by one, Jesus Christ.)

Verse 17 says, ". . . much more they which receive abundance of grace and of the gift of righteousness shall reign in life by one, Jesus Christ."

* * * * *

4. 1 Corinthians 1:1-8 ¹Paul called to be an apostle of Jesus Christ through the will of God, and Sosthenes our brother, ²Unto the church of God which is at Corinth, to them that are sanctified in Christ Jesus, called to be saints, with all that in every place call upon the name of Jesus Christ our

Lord, both their's and our's: ³**Grace** be unto you, and peace, from God our Father, and from the Lord Jesus Christ. ⁴I thank my God always on your behalf, for the **grace** of God which is given you by Jesus Christ; 5That in every thing ye are enriched by him, in all utterance, and in all knowledge; ⁶Even as the testimony of Christ was confirmed in you: ⁷So that ye come behind in no gift; waiting for the coming of our Lord Jesus Christ: ⁸Who shall also confirm you unto the end, that ye may be blameless in the day of our Lord Jesus Christ.

Verse 4 says, "I thank my God always on your behalf, for the grace of God which is given you by Jesus Christ."

* * * * *

5. Hebrews 2:6-10 ⁶But one in a certain place testified, saying, What is man, that thou art mindful of him? or the son of man that thou visitest him? ⁷Thou madest him a little lower than the angels; thou crownedst him with glory and honour, and didst set him over the works of thy hands: ⁸Thou hast put all things in subjection under his feet. For in that he put all in subjection under him, he left nothing that is not put under him. But now we see not yet all things put under him. ⁹But we see Jesus, who was made a little lower than the angels for the suffering of death, crowned with glory and honour; that he by the **grace** of God should taste death for every man. ¹⁰For it became him, for whom are all things, and by whom are all things, in bringing many sons unto glory, to make the captain of their salvation perfect through sufferings.

Verse 9 says, "But we see Jesus, who was made a little lower than the angels for the suffering of death, crowned with glory and honour; that he by the grace of God should taste death for every man."

Chapter 2:

Grace is given to do God's
Work / Good Works

1. Acts 14:1-3 [1]And it came to pass in Iconium, that they went both together into the synagogue of the Jews, and so spake, that a great multitude both of the Jews and also of the Greeks believed. [2]But the unbelieving Jews stirred up the Gentiles, and made their minds evil affected against the brethren. [3]Long time therefore abode they speaking boldly in the Lord, which gave testimony unto the word of his **grace**, and granted signs and wonders to be done by their hands.

When we see "they" mentioned in this passage, it is speaking of Paul and Barnabas (see Acts 13:46-52). When Paul and Barnabas spoke boldly in the Lord, this was a testimony to the word of His grace. Also, because of God's grace, they were granted signs and wonders to be done by their hands. It is by God's grace, the divine influence upon Paul and Barnabas' heart, that enabled them to speak boldly in the Lord and that signs and wonders would be done by their hands. The signs and wonders are how the divine influence upon the heart was reflected in Paul and Barnabas' life. The same is true for us today. Through God's grace, signs and wonders should be done by our hands and we should speak boldly in the Lord.

Acts 5:12-29 says, "[12]And by the hands of the apostles were many signs and wonders wrought among the people; (and they were all with one accord in Solomon's porch. ¹³And of the rest durst no man join himself to them: but the people magnified them. ¹⁴And believers were the more added to the Lord, multitudes both of men and women.) ¹⁵Insomuch that they brought forth the sick into the streets, and laid them on beds and couches, that at the least the shadow of Peter passing by might overshadow some of them. ¹⁶There came also a multitude out of the cities round about unto Jerusalem, bringing sick folks, and them which were vexed with unclean spirits: and they were healed every one. ¹⁷Then the high priest rose up, and all they that were with him, (which is the sect of the Sadducees,) and were filled with indignation, ¹⁸And laid their hands on the apostles, and put them in the common prison. ¹⁹But the angel of the Lord by night opened the prison doors, and brought them forth, and said, ²⁰Go, stand and speak in the temple to the people all the words of this life. ²¹And when they heard that, they entered into the temple early in the morning, and taught. But the high priest came, and they that were with him, and called the council together, and all the senate of the children of Israel, and sent to the prison to have them brought. ²²But when the officers came, and found them not in the prison, they returned and told, ²³Saying, The prison truly found we shut with all safety, and the keepers standing without before the doors: but when we had opened, we found no man within. ²⁴Now when the high priest and the captain of the temple and the chief priests heard these things, they doubted of them whereunto this would grow. ²⁵Then came one and told them, saying, Behold, the men whom ye put in prison are standing in the temple, and teaching the people. ²⁶Then went the captain with the officers, and brought them without violence: for they feared the people, lest they should have been stoned. ²⁷And when they had brought them, they set them before the council: and the high priest asked them, ²⁸Saying, Did not we straitly command you that ye should not teach in this name? and, behold, ye have filled Jerusalem with your doctrine, and intend to bring this man's blood upon us. ²⁹Then Peter and the other apostles answered and said, We ought to obey God rather than men." In verse 12 we see that many signs and wonders were performed amongst the people by the hands of the apostles. In verse 20, the angel of the Lord instructs the apostles to go speak to the people in the temple all the words of this life. When the high priest questioned the apostles because they were previously commanded not to teach in the name of Jesus, Paul and the other apostles responded, "We ought to obey God rather than men." As disciples ("a learner, i.e. pupil" - basically a student of God's word), we must do likewise.

Mark 16:14-18 says, "[14]Afterward he appeared unto the eleven as they sat at meat, and upbraided them with their unbelief and hardness of heart, because they believed not them which had seen him after he was risen. [15]And he said unto them, Go ye into all the world, and preach the gospel to every creature. [16]He that believeth and is baptized shall be saved; but he that believeth not shall be damned. [17]And these signs shall follow them that believe; In my name shall they cast out devils; they shall speak with new tongues; [18]They shall take up serpents; and if they drink any deadly thing, it shall not hurt them; they shall lay hands on the sick, and they shall recover." Here Jesus is speaking to His eleven apostles and the instruction He gives to them is the same instruction for all those who are His disciples. Jesus says to go into all the world and preach the gospel to every creature. He then says that signs will follow those who believe; in His name will they cast out devils, speak in new tongues, take up serpents, and if they drink any deadly thing it will not hurt them; they shall lay hands on the sick and they shall recover. If we believe, these signs should follow us. In John 14:12-13 Jesus says, "[12]Verily, verily, I say unto you, He that believeth on me, the works that I do shall he do also; and greater works than these shall he do; because I go unto my Father. [13]And whatsoever ye shall ask in my name, that will I do, that the Father may be glorified in the Son." God did not give us His grace for us to sit around and do nothing. God's divine influence upon our hearts should be reflected in our lives by us speaking boldly in Him and that we perform signs and wonders.

* * * * *

2. Romans 12:1-8 [1]I beseech you therefore, brethren, by the mercies of God, that ye present your bodies a living sacrifice, holy, acceptable unto God, which is your reasonable service. [2]And be not conformed to this world: but be ye transformed by the renewing of your mind, that ye may

prove what is that good, and acceptable, and perfect, will of God. ³For I say, through the **grace** given unto me, to every man that is among you, not to think of himself more highly than he ought to think; but to think soberly, according as God hath dealt to every man the measure of faith. ⁴For as we have many members in one body, and all members have not the same office: ⁵So we, being many, are one body in Christ, and every one members one of another. ⁶Having then gifts differing according to the **grace** that is given to us, whether prophecy, let us prophesy according to the proportion of faith; ⁷Or ministry, let us wait on our ministering: or he that teacheth, on teaching; ⁸Or he that exhorteth, on exhortation: he that giveth, let him do it with simplicity; he that ruleth, with diligence; he that sheweth mercy, with cheerfulness.

In this passage of scripture Paul is speaking to the brethren/disciples of Jesus. In verse 5, Paul teaches that though we are many in number, we are one body in Christ. The brethren/disciples make up the body of Christ. As part of the body of Christ, we all have gifts according to the grace that is given to us. God's divine influence upon our hearts will be reflected in our lives as we prophesy, teach, exhort, give, rule, and show mercy. 1 Corinthians 12:1-14 says, "¹Now concerning spiritual gifts, brethren, I would not have you ignorant. ²Ye know that ye were Gentiles, carried away unto these dumb idols, even as ye were led. ³Wherefore I give you to understand, that no man speaking by the Spirit of God calleth Jesus accursed: and that no man can say that Jesus is the Lord, but by the Holy Ghost. ⁴Now there are diversities of gifts, but the same Spirit. ⁵And there are differences of administrations, but the same Lord. ⁶And there are diversities of operations, but it is the same God which worketh all in all. ⁷But the manifestation of the Spirit is given to every man to profit withal. ⁸For to one is given by the Spirit the word of wisdom; to another the word of knowledge by the same Spirit; ⁹To another faith by the same Spirit; to another the gifts of healing by the same Spirit; ¹⁰To another the working of miracles; to another prophecy; to another discerning of spirits; to another divers kinds of tongues; to another the interpretation of tongues: ¹¹But all these worketh that one and the selfsame Spirit, dividing to every man severally as he will. ¹²For as the body is one, and hath many members, and all the members of that one body, being many, are one body: so also is Christ. ¹³For by one Spirit are we all baptized into one body, whether we be Jews or Gentiles, whether we be bond or free; and have been all made to drink into one Spirit. ¹⁴For the body is not one member, but many." God did not give us His grace for us to sit around and do nothing. Verse 7 says, "the manifestation of the Spirit is given to every man to profit withal." It is to profit withal, but this will only happen if we utilize what God has given us.

* * * * *

3. 1 Corinthians 3:5-11 ⁵Who then is Paul, and who is Apollos, but ministers by whom ye believed, even as the Lord gave to every man? ⁶I have planted, Apollos watered; but God gave the increase. ⁷So then neither is he that planteth any thing, neither he that watereth; but God that giveth the increase. ⁸Now he that planteth and he that watereth are one: and every man shall receive his own reward according to his own labour. ⁹For we are labourers together with God: ye are God's husbandry, ye are God's building. ¹⁰According to the **grace** of God which is given unto me, as a wise masterbuilder, I have laid the foundation, and another buildeth thereon. But let every man take heed how he buildeth thereupon. ¹¹For other foundation can no man lay than that is laid, which is Jesus Christ.

In this passage of scripture Paul says that he has laid the foundation as a masterbuilder according to the grace of God that was given to him. It was God's grace that enabled Paul to be a masterbuilder. It was God's grace whereby he was a labourer with God. Matthew 9:35-38 says, "³⁵And Jesus went about all the cities and villages, teaching in their synagogues, and preaching the gospel of the kingdom, and healing every sickness and every disease among the people. ³⁶But when he saw the multitudes, he was moved with compassion on them, because they fainted, and were scattered abroad, as sheep having no shepherd. ³⁷Then saith he unto his disciples, The harvest truly is plenteous, but the labourers are few; ³⁸Pray ye therefore the Lord of the harvest, that he will send forth labourers into his harvest." Jesus went about all the cities and villages, teaching in their synagogues, and preaching the gospel of the kingdom, and healing every sickness and every disease among the people. If we are Jesus' disciples/labourers, then He gave this example for us to follow. The divine influence of God upon our hearts should be reflected in our lives as we teach and preach the gospel, and heal every sickness and disease among the people. Matthew 10:1 says, "And when he had called unto him his twelve disciples, he gave them power against unclean spirits, to cast them out, and to heal all manner of sickness and all manner of disease." As disciples, Jesus has given us power against unclean spirits, to cast them out, and to heal all manner of sickness and all manner of disease. Jesus gave us this power and if we have faith, then we must exercise this power because faith without works is dead. James 2:14-20 says, "[14]What doth it profit, my brethren, though a man say he hath faith, and have not works? can faith save him? [15]If a brother or sister be naked, and destitute of daily food, [16]And one of you say unto them, Depart in peace, be ye warmed and filled; notwithstanding ye give them not those things which are needful to the body; what doth it profit? [17]Even so faith, if it hath not works, is dead, being alone. [18]Yea, a man may say, Thou hast faith, and I have works: shew me thy faith without thy works, and I will shew thee my faith by my works. [19]Thou believest that there is one God; thou doest well: the devils also believe, and tremble. [20]But wilt thou know, O vain man, that faith without works is dead?"

* * * * *

4. 1 Corinthians 15:1-11 [1]Moreover, brethren, I declare unto you the gospel which I preached unto you, which also ye have received, and wherein ye stand; [2]By which also ye are saved, if ye keep in memory what I preached unto you, unless ye have believed in vain. [3]For I delivered unto you first of all that which I also received, how that Christ died for our sins according to the scriptures; [4]And that he was buried, and that he rose again the third day according to the scriptures: [5]And that he was seen of Cephas, then of the twelve: [6]After that, he was seen of above five hundred brethren at once; of whom the greater part remain unto this present, but some are fallen asleep. [7]After that, he was seen of James; then of all the apostles. [8]And last

of all he was seen of me also, as of one born out of due time. [9]For I am the least of the apostles, that am not meet to be called an apostle, because I persecuted the church of God. [10]But by the **grace** of God I am what I am: and his **grace** which was bestowed upon me was not in vain; but I laboured more abundantly than they all: yet not I, but the **grace** of God which was with me. [11]Therefore whether it were I or they, so we preach, and so ye believed.

In this passage of scripture Paul shows us that it was because of the grace of God that was bestowed upon him that he laboured more abundantly than all the other apostles. Matthew 9:35-38 says, "[35]And Jesus went about all the cities and villages, teaching in their synagogues, and preaching the gospel of the kingdom, and healing every sickness and every disease among the people. [36]But when he saw the multitudes, he was moved with compassion on them, because they fainted, and were scattered abroad, as sheep having no shepherd. [37]Then saith he unto his disciples, The harvest truly is plenteous, but the labourers are few; [38]Pray ye therefore the Lord of the harvest, that he will send forth labourers into his harvest." Jesus tells His disciples that the harvest is plenteous (those that need to hear the word and need healing), but the labourers are few. As labourers/disciples, we must teach and preach the gospel of the kingdom and heal every sickness and disease among the people.

Luke 10:1-20 says, "[1]After these things the LORD appointed other seventy also, and sent them two and two before his face into every city and place, whither he himself would come. [2]Therefore said he unto them, The harvest truly is great, but the labourers are few: pray ye therefore the Lord of the harvest, that he would send forth labourers into his harvest. [3]Go your ways: behold, I send you forth as lambs among wolves. [4]Carry neither purse, nor scrip, nor shoes: and salute no man by the way. [5]And into whatsoever house ye enter, first say, Peace be to this house. [6]And if the son of peace be there, your peace shall rest upon it: if not, it shall turn to you again. [7]And in the same house remain, eating and drinking such things as they give: for the labourer is worthy of his hire. Go not from house to house. [8]And into whatsoever city ye enter, and they receive you, eat such things as are set before you: [9]And heal the sick that are therein, and say unto them, The kingdom of God is come nigh unto you. [10]But into whatsoever city ye enter, and they receive you not, go your ways out into the streets of the same, and say, [11]Even the very dust of your city, which cleaveth on us, we do wipe off against you: notwithstanding be ye sure of this, that the kingdom of God is come nigh unto you. [12]But I say unto you, that it shall be more tolerable in that day for Sodom, than for that city. [13]Woe unto thee, Chorazin! woe unto thee, Bethsaida! for if the mighty works had been done in Tyre and Sidon, which have been done in you, they had a great while ago repented, sitting in sackcloth and ashes. [14]But it shall be more tolerable for Tyre and Sidon at the judgment, than for you. [15]And thou, Capernaum, which art exalted to heaven, shalt be thrust down to hell. [16]He that heareth you heareth me; and he that despiseth you despiseth me; and he that despiseth me despiseth him that sent me. [17]And the seventy returned again with joy, saying, Lord, even the devils are subject unto us through thy name. [18]And he said unto them, I beheld Satan as lightning fall from heaven. [19]Behold, I give unto you power to tread on serpents and scorpions, and over all the power of the enemy: and nothing shall by any means hurt you. [20]Notwithstanding in this rejoice not, that the spirits are subject unto you; but rather rejoice, because your names are written in heaven." We see again in Luke 10:1-20 that Jesus instructs His disciples to pray that God would send forth more labourers into His harvest. Immediately after He gives them this instruction, He then tells them to go and perform the ministry. In verse 19 Jesus tells His disciples that he has given them "power to tread on serpents and scorpions, and over all the power of the enemy: and nothing shall by any means hurt you." Today, this power should be reflected in our lives through the divine influence of God upon our hearts.

* * * * *

5. 2 Corinthians 9:1-11 [1]For as touching the ministering to the saints, it is superfluous for me to write to you: [2]For I know the forwardness of your mind, for which I boast of you to them of Macedonia, that Achaia was ready a year ago; and your zeal hath provoked very many. [3]Yet have I sent

the brethren, lest our boasting of you should be in vain in this behalf; that, as I said, ye may be ready: ⁴Lest haply if they of Macedonia come with me, and find you unprepared, we (that we say not, ye) should be ashamed in this same confident boasting. ⁵Therefore I thought it necessary to exhort the brethren, that they would go before unto you, and make up beforehand your bounty, whereof ye had notice before, that the same might be ready, as a matter of bounty, and not as of covetousness. ⁶But this I say, He which soweth sparingly shall reap also sparingly; and he which soweth bountifully shall reap also bountifully. ⁷Every man according as he purposeth in his heart, so let him give; not grudgingly, or of necessity: for God loveth a cheerful giver. ⁸And God is able to make all **grace** abound toward you; that ye, always having all sufficiency in all things, may abound to every good work: ⁹(As it is written, He hath dispersed abroad; he hath given to the poor: his righteousness remaineth for ever. ¹⁰Now he that ministereth seed to the sower both minister bread for your food, and multiply your seed sown, and increase the fruits of your righteousness;) ¹¹Being enriched in every thing to all bountifulness, which causeth through us thanksgiving to God.

In verse 8 of this passage, Paul states that "God is able to make all grace abound toward us, that we will have sufficiency in all things, and may abound to every good work." Through God's grace we will have all sufficiency to abound to every good work. Matthew 6:25-33 says, "²⁵Therefore I say unto you, Take no thought for your life, what ye shall eat, or what ye shall drink; nor yet for your body, what ye shall put on. Is not the life more than meat, and the body than raiment? ²⁶Behold the fowls of the air: for they sow not, neither do they reap, nor gather into barns; yet your heavenly Father feedeth them. Are ye not much better than they? ²⁷Which of you by taking thought can add one cubit unto his stature? ²⁸And why take ye thought for raiment? Consider the lilies of the field, how they grow; they toil not, neither do they spin: ²⁹And yet I say unto you, That even Solomon in all his glory was not arrayed like one of these. ³⁰Wherefore, if God so clothe the grass of the field, which to day is, and to morrow is cast into the oven, shall he not much more clothe you, O ye of little faith? ³¹Therefore take no thought, saying, What shall we eat? or,

What shall we drink? or, Wherewithal shall we be clothed? [32](For after all these things do the Gentiles seek:) for your heavenly Father knoweth that ye have need of all these things. [33]But seek ye first the kingdom of God, and his righteousness; and all these things shall be added unto you." God takes care of the fowls of the air and the lilies of the field, so surely He will take care of His disciples. Through the grace of God, if we seek ye first His kingdom and His righteousness, then all these things (all sufficiency) shall be added unto us. God will supply all that we need in order to do His work for Philippians 4:19 says, "But my God shall supply all your need according to his riches in glory by Christ Jesus."

* * * * *

6. Ephesians 2:2-10 [2]Wherein in time past ye walked according to the course of this world, according to the prince of the power of the air, the spirit that now worketh in the children of disobedience: [3]Among whom also we all had our conversation in times past in the lusts of our flesh, fulfilling the desires of the flesh and of the mind; and were by nature the children of wrath, even as others. [4]But God, who is rich in mercy, for his great love wherewith he loved us, [5]Even when we were dead in sins, hath quickened us together with Christ, (by **grace** ye are saved;) [6]And hath raised us up together, and made us sit together in heavenly places in Christ Jesus: [7]That in the ages to come he might shew the exceeding riches of his **grace** in his kindness toward us through Christ Jesus. [8]For by **grace** are ye saved through faith; and that not of yourselves: it is the gift of God: [9]Not of works, lest any man should boast. [10]For we are his workmanship, created in Christ Jesus unto good works, which God hath before ordained that we should walk in them.

This passage of scripture tells us that we are saved by grace through faith; it is the gift of God and not by our works. Through God's grace we are saved to be His workmanship, created in Christ Jesus unto good works in which we are preordained to walk therein. Matthew 5:14-16 says, "[14]Ye are the light of the world. A city that is set on an hill cannot be hid. [15]Neither do men light a candle, and put it under a bushel, but on a candlestick; and it giveth light unto all that are in the house. [16]Let your light so shine before men, that they may see your good works, and glorify your Father which is in heaven." As disciples, we are the light of the world; we are supposed to let our light shine before men that they may see our good works and glorify our Father in heaven. God gives us grace to do His work so that He may be glorified. We are not supposed to use God's grace as an excuse not to do anything. He does not give us His grace for us just to say that Jesus died on the cross and paid the price so therefore we're justified and there's nothing else for us to do. If we are saved through the divine influence upon our hearts, then it should be reflected in our lives by us working for God through Christ Jesus.

* * * * *

7. Ephesians 4:1-16 [1]I therefore, the prisoner of the Lord, beseech you that ye walk worthy of the vocation wherewith ye are called, [2]With all lowliness and meekness, with longsuffering, forbearing one another in love; [3]Endeavouring to keep the unity of the Spirit in the bond of peace. [4]There is one body, and one Spirit, even as ye are called in one hope of your calling; [5]One Lord, one faith, one baptism, [6]One God and Father of all, who is above all, and through all, and in you all. [7]But unto every one of us is given **grace** according to the measure of the gift of Christ. [8]Wherefore he saith, When he ascended up on high, he led captivity captive, and gave gifts unto men. [9](Now that he ascended, what is it but that he also descended first into the lower parts of the earth? [10]He that descended is the same also that ascended up far above all heavens, that he might fill all things.) [11]And he gave some, apostles; and some, prophets; and some, evangelists; and some, pastors and teachers; [12]For the perfecting of the saints, for the work of the ministry, for the edifying of the body of Christ: [13]Till we all come in the unity of the faith, and of the knowledge of the Son of God, unto a perfect man, unto the measure of the stature of the fulness of Christ: [14]That we henceforth be no more children, tossed to and fro, and carried about with every wind of doctrine, by the sleight of men, and cunning craftiness, whereby they lie in wait to deceive; [15]But speaking the

truth in love, may grow up into him in all things, which is the head, even Christ: ¹⁶From whom the whole body fitly joined together and compacted by that which every joint supplieth, according to the effectual working in the measure of every part, maketh increase of the body unto the edifying of itself in love.

In this passage of scripture, Paul says that all of us (disciples) are given grace according to the measure of the gift of Christ. Jesus gave gifts unto men through His grace so that we may be apostles, prophets, evangelists, pastors, and teachers – not just so we may walk around with a title, but that we perfect the saints, for the work of the ministry, for the edifying of the body of Christ (the church). Again we see the divine influence upon our hearts is reflected in our lives by us working in the ministry and edifying one another. As disciples, this is the reason for us to fellowship together – so that we may edify and uplift one another. We should not fellowship together to have a pity party, but to help one another press on in the name of Jesus so that we may walk as more than conquerors for Romans 8:37 says, "Nay, in all things we are more than conquerors through him that loved us." Because of the grace of God that has been bestowed upon us (disciples), we have a charge to keep. In Romans 12:1 Paul says, "I beseech you therefore, brethren, by the mercies of God, that ye present your bodies a living sacrifice, holy, acceptable unto God, which is your reasonable service." When we present our bodies as a living sacrifice, holy and acceptable unto God, this is just our reasonable service; nothing over and above, just our reasonable service. Each and every day, let us use the grace that God has given us to edify one another for the perfecting of the saints and for the work of the ministry.

* * * * *

8. 2 Thessalonians 1:11-12 ¹¹Wherefore also we pray always for you, that our God would count you worthy of this calling, and fulfil all the good pleasure of his goodness, and the work of faith with power: ¹²That the name of our Lord Jesus Christ may be glorified in you, and ye in him, according to the **grace** of our God and the Lord Jesus Christ.

In this passage of scripture Paul is telling the church of the Thessalonians that he prays God would count them worthy of His calling, and fulfill all the good pleasure of His goodness, and the work of faith with power. Paul is not telling the Thessalonians that they have already made it because of the grace of God. Paul is admonishing them to live their lives so that Jesus may be glorified according to God's grace (the divine influence upon the heart, and its reflection in the life). If we have been given God's grace, then there should be signs of that grace in the life that we live. Are we truly pressing on each day in the name of Jesus or are we trying to use God's grace as justification that Jesus already paid the price and there is nothing that we have to do? In 2 Timothy 4:1-8, Paul tells Timothy, "[1]I charge thee therefore before God, and the Lord Jesus Christ, who shall judge the quick and the dead at his appearing and his kingdom; [2]Preach the word; be instant in season, out of season; reprove, rebuke, exhort with all long suffering and doctrine. [3]For the time will come when they will not endure sound doctrine; but after their own lusts shall they heap to themselves teachers, having itching ears; [4]And they shall turn away their ears from the truth, and shall be turned unto fables. [5]But watch thou in all things, endure afflictions, do the work of an evangelist, make full proof of thy ministry. [6]For I am now ready to be offered, and the time of my departure is at hand. [7]I have fought a good fight, I have finished my course, I have kept the faith: [8]Henceforth there is laid up for me a crown of righteousness, which the Lord, the righteous judge, shall give me at that day: and not to me only, but unto all them also that love his appearing." Paul tells Timothy to preach the word; be instant in season and out of season; to reprove, rebuke, exhort with all long suffering and doctrine. He later goes on to tell him to watch in all things, endure afflictions, do the work of an evangelist, and make full proof of the ministry. As a disciple of the Lord Jesus Christ, we have work to do for Him because of His grace. Paul also mentions that he fought a good fight, he finished his course, and he kept the faith. Paul makes it clear in this passage of scripture that it takes diligence and persistence to carry on the work of the ministry and this is the reflection in the life that should be manifested in us because of the divine influence upon our hearts.

* * * * *

9. 2 Thessalonians 2:13-17 ¹³But we are bound to give thanks alway to God for you, brethren beloved of the Lord, because God hath from the beginning chosen you to salvation through sanctification of the Spirit and belief of the truth: ¹⁴Whereunto he called you by our gospel, to the obtaining of the glory of our Lord Jesus Christ. ¹⁵Therefore, brethren, stand fast, and hold the traditions which ye have been taught, whether by word, or our epistle. ¹⁶Now our Lord Jesus Christ himself, and God, even our Father, which hath loved us, and hath given us everlasting consolation and good hope through **grace**, ¹⁷Comfort your hearts, and stablish you in every good word and work.

In this passage of scripture Paul tells the Thessalonians they should stand fast and hold to the traditions they've been taught in word or epistle ("a written message"). When they do this, they have the assurance that God will give them an everlasting consolation and good hope through grace, comfort their hearts, and establish them in every good word and work. This brings into my remembrance Matthew 28:16-20 which reads, "¹⁶Then the eleven disciples went away into Galilee, into a mountain where Jesus had appointed them. ¹⁷And when they saw him, they worshipped him: but some doubted. ¹⁸And Jesus came and spake unto them, saying, All power is given unto me in heaven and in earth. ¹⁹Go ye therefore, and teach all nations, baptizing them in the name of the Father, and of the Son, and of the Holy Ghost: ²⁰Teaching them to observe all things whatsoever I have commanded you: and, lo, I am with you always, even unto the end of the world. Amen." As we go forth doing the will of God, Jesus gave us a promise that he will be with us always, even to the end of the earth. If the divine influence of God is upon our hearts, then it will be reflected in our lives as we will be established in every good word and work.

Chapter 3:

Grace is given to Minister / Teach

1. Acts 4:29-33 [29]And now, Lord, behold their threatenings: and grant unto thy servants, that with all boldness they may speak thy word, [30]By stretching forth thine hand to heal; and that signs and wonders may be done by the name of thy holy child Jesus. [31]And when they had prayed, the place was shaken where they were assembled together; and they were all filled with the Holy Ghost, and they spake the word of God with boldness. [32]And the multitude of them that believed were of one heart and of one soul: neither said any of them that ought of the things which he possessed was his own; but they had all things common. [33]And with great power gave the apostles witness of the resurrection of the Lord Jesus: and great **grace** was upon them all.

In this passage of scripture we see that the apostles witnessed with great power the resurrection of Jesus and great grace was upon them all. God's grace was upon them as they did the will of God. What's interesting about this power that the apostles had is that it was given to them because they asked God to help them do His will for verses 29-31 read, "[29]And now, Lord, behold their threatenings: and grant unto thy servants, that with all boldness they may speak thy word, [30]By stretching forth thine hand to heal; and that signs and wonders may be done by the name of thy holy child Jesus. [31]And when they had prayed, the place was shaken where they were assembled together; and they were all filled with the Holy Ghost, and they spake the word of God with boldness." The apostles asked for boldness to speak His word and that signs and wonders might be done through them in the name of Jesus. This reminds me of when Solomon prayed to God and asked for wisdom to lead the people in 2 Chronicles 1:7-12, "⁷In that night did God appear unto Solomon, and said unto him, Ask what I shall give thee. ⁸And Solomon said unto God, Thou hast shewed great mercy unto David my father, and hast made me to reign in his stead. ⁹Now, O LORD God, let thy promise unto David my father be established: for thou hast made me king over a people like the dust of the earth in multitude. ¹⁰Give me now wisdom and knowledge, that I may go out and come in before this people: for who can judge this thy people, that is so great? ¹¹And God said to Solomon, Because this was in thine heart, and thou hast not asked riches, wealth, or honour, nor the life of thine enemies, neither yet hast asked long life; but hast asked wisdom and knowledge for thyself, that thou mayest judge my people, over whom I have made thee king: ¹²Wisdom and knowledge is granted unto thee; and I will give thee riches, and wealth, and honour, such as none of the kings have had that have been before thee, neither shall there any after thee have the like."

We must not seek our own will, but the will of God using Jesus as an example in Luke 22:41-43 which says, "⁴¹And he was withdrawn from them about a stone's cast, and kneeled down, and prayed, ⁴²Saying, Father, if thou be willing, remove this cup from me: nevertheless not my will, but thine, be done. ⁴³And there appeared an angel unto him from heaven, strengthening him." As Jesus sought to do God's will, we see that God sent an angel to strengthen Him. What God did for the apostles, Solomon, and Jesus, He will do for us because He is no respecter of persons (Romans 2:11). Acts 10:34-35 says, "³⁴Then Peter opened his mouth, and said, Of a truth I perceive that God is no respecter of persons: ³⁵But in every nation he that feareth him, and worketh righteousness, is accepted with him." If we fear ("revere") God and work righteousness, we will be accepted of Him. If we earnestly ask God to help us to do His will, He will give us the strength and power to do so through His grace.

* * * * *

2. Romans 12:1-8 [1]I beseech you therefore, brethren, by the mercies of God, that ye present your bodies a living sacrifice, holy, acceptable unto God, which is your reasonable service. [2]And be not conformed to this world: but be ye transformed by the renewing of your mind, that ye may prove what is that good, and acceptable, and perfect, will of God. [3]For I say, through the **grace** given unto me, to every man that is among you, not to think of himself more highly than he ought to think; but to think soberly, according as God hath dealt to every man the measure of faith. [4]For as we have many members in one body, and all members have not the same office: [5]So we, being many, are one body in Christ, and every one members one of another. [6]Having then gifts differing according to the **grace** that is given to us, whether prophecy, let us prophesy according to the proportion of faith; [7]Or ministry, let us wait on our ministering: or he that teacheth, on teaching; [8]Or he that exhorteth, on exhortation: he that giveth, let him do it with simplicity; he that ruleth, with diligence; he that sheweth mercy, with cheerfulness.

In verse 3 Paul says, "For I say, through the grace given me ..." Here, Paul is teaching and ministering through the grace given to him by God. In 1 Corinthians 2:1-5, Paul says, "[1]And I, brethren, when I came to you, came not with excellency of speech or of wisdom, declaring unto you the testimony of God. [2]For I determined not to know any thing among you, save Jesus Christ, and him crucified. [3]And I was with you in weakness, and in fear, and in much trembling. [4]And my speech and my preaching was not with enticing words of man's wisdom, but in demonstration of the Spirit and of power: [5]That your faith should not stand in the wisdom of men, but in the power of God." Paul's speech and preaching was not with enticing words of man's wisdom, but in demonstration of the Spirit and of power. The divine influence upon our hearts should likewise be reflected in our lives as we speak and preach with the demonstration of the Spirit and of power. We must truly submit to God and seek to do His will, so His Spirit can work in us.

* * * * *

3. Romans 15:14-16 [14]And I myself also am persuaded of you, my brethren, that ye also are full of goodness, filled with all knowledge, able also to admonish one another. [15]Nevertheless, brethren, I have written the more boldly unto you in some sort, as putting you in mind, because of the **grace** that is given to me of God, [16]That I should be the minister of Jesus Christ to the Gentiles, ministering the gospel of God, that the offering up of the Gentiles might be acceptable, being sanctified by the Holy Ghost.

In this passage of scripture, Paul says it is because of the grace given to him of God, that he is the minister of Jesus Christ to the Gentiles. The divine influence upon his heart was reflected in his life as he ministered Jesus Christ to the Gentiles. If we have the divine influence of God upon our hearts, then it should be reflected in our lives to be ministers of Jesus Christ unto people.

* * * * *

4. Galatians 1:11-17 [11]But I certify you, brethren, that the gospel which was preached of me is not after man. [12]For I neither received it of man, neither was I taught it, but by the revelation of Jesus Christ. [13]For ye have heard of my conversation in time past in the Jews' religion, how that beyond measure I persecuted the church of God, and wasted it: [14]And profited in the Jews' religion above many my equals in mine own nation, being more exceedingly zealous of the traditions of my fathers. [15]But when it pleased God, who separated me from my mother's womb, and called me by his **grace**, [16]To reveal his Son in me, that I might preach him among the heathen; immediately I conferred not with flesh and blood: [17]Neither went I up to Jerusalem to them which were apostles before me; but I went into Arabia, and returned again unto Damascus.

In verses 15-16, Paul says that he was called by God's grace, to reveal His Son in him, so that he might preach to the heathen. Prior to that in verses 11-12, Paul says that he taught through the revelation of Jesus Christ. If we seek to do the will of God, He will speak through us. This is done by His grace. We can look to Jesus' example in John 5:30 as He says, "I can of mine own self do nothing: as I hear, I judge: and my judgment is just;

because I seek not mine own will, but the will of the Father which hath sent me." If Jesus can of His own self do nothing, then how can we? He even tells us in John 15:5, "I am the vine, ye are the branches: He that abideth in me, and I in him, the same bringeth forth much fruit: for without me ye can do nothing." Without Jesus, we can do nothing (spiritually), but we can do all things through Christ which strengthens us (Philippians 4:13). In Matthew 10:18-20 Jesus says, "[18]And ye shall be brought before governors and kings for my sake, for a testimony against them and the Gentiles. [19]But when they deliver you up, take no thought how or what ye shall speak: for it shall be given you in that same hour what ye shall speak. [20]For it is not ye that speak, but the Spirit of your Father which speaketh in you." That's God's grace working in our life. If we seek to do the will of God, the divine influence upon our hearts will be reflected in our lives as He will give us what to speak.

* * * * *

5. Galatians 2:1-9 [1]Then fourteen years after I went up again to Jerusalem with Barnabas, and took Titus with me also. [2]And I went up by revelation, and communicated unto them that gospel which I preach among the Gentiles, but privately to them which were of reputation, lest by any means I should run, or had run, in vain. [3]But neither Titus, who was with me, being a Greek, was compelled to be circumcised: [4]And that because of false brethren unawares brought in, who came in privily to spy out our liberty which we have in Christ Jesus, that they might bring us into bondage: [5]To whom we gave place by subjection, no, not for an hour; that the truth of the gospel might continue with you. [6]But of these who seemed to be somewhat, (whatsoever they were, it maketh no matter to me: God accepteth no man's person:) for they who seemed to be somewhat in conference added nothing to me: [7]But contrariwise, when they saw that the gospel of the uncircumcision was committed unto me, as the gospel of the circumcision was unto Peter; [8](For he that wrought effectually in Peter to the apostleship of the circumcision, the same was mighty in me toward the Gentiles:) [9]And when James, Cephas, and John, who seemed

to be pillars, perceived the **grace** that was given unto me, they gave to me and Barnabas the right hands of fellowship; that we should go unto the heathen, and they unto the circumcision.

Here again, we see the divine influence upon Paul's heart being reflected in his life as he goes out to the heathen to preach the gospel.

* * * * *

6. Ephesians 3:1-12 [1]For this cause I Paul, the prisoner of Jesus Christ for you Gentiles, [2]If ye have heard of the dispensation of the **grace** of God which is given me to you-ward: [3]How that by revelation he made known unto me the mystery; (as I wrote afore in few words, [4]Whereby, when ye read, ye may understand my knowledge in the mystery of Christ) [5]Which in other ages was not made known unto the sons of men, as it is now revealed unto his holy apostles and prophets by the Spirit; [6]That the Gentiles should be fellowheirs, and of the same body, and partakers of his promise in Christ by the gospel: [7]Whereof I was made a minister, according to the gift of the **grace** of God given unto me by the effectual working of his power. [8]Unto me, who am less than the least of all saints, is this **grace** given, that I should preach among the Gentiles the unsearchable riches of Christ; [9]And to make all men see what is the fellowship of the mystery, which from the beginning of the world hath been hid in God, who created all things by Jesus Christ: [10]To the intent that now unto the principalities and powers in heavenly places might be known by the church the manifold wisdom of God, [11]According to the eternal purpose which he purposed in Christ Jesus our Lord: [12]In whom we have boldness and access with confidence by the faith of him.

In this passage of scripture Paul says he was made a minister according to the gift of grace of God given him by the effectual working of His power. Also, he says that it is through this grace given him, that he preaches to the Gentiles the unsearchable riches of Christ... God's divine influence was upon Paul's heart and was reflected in his life as a minister for God. In Luke 17:7-10 Jesus says, "[7]But which of you, having a servant plowing or feeding cattle, will say unto him by and by, when he is come from the field, Go and sit down to meat? [8]And will not rather say unto him, Make ready wherewith I may sup, and gird thyself, and serve me, till I have eaten and drunken; and afterward thou shalt eat and drink? [9]Doth he thank that servant because he did the things that were commanded him? I trow not. [10]So likewise ye, when ye shall have done all those things which are commanded you, say, We are unprofitable servants: we have done that which was our duty to do." Through the grace of God, when we do His will, we should consider ourselves unprofitable servants – we have done that which is our duty to do. We are not seeking any reward in this life, but by doing the will of God, we are laying up our treasures in heaven (Matthew 6:20).

* * * * *

7. 1 Timothy 1:12-14 [12]And I thank Christ Jesus our Lord, who hath enabled me, for that he counted me faithful, putting me into the ministry; [13]Who was before a blasphemer, and a persecutor, and injurious: but I obtained mercy, because I did it ignorantly in unbelief. [14]And the **grace** of our Lord was exceeding abundant with faith and love which is in Christ Jesus.

If God has given us grace, then we must understand what Paul knows – that it was through God's mercy and grace that enabled him and put him into the ministry. God's grace (the divine influence upon the heart and its reflection in the life) is given to us to work in the ministry.

* * * * *

8. 2 Timothy 2:1-2 [1]Thou therefore, my son, be strong in the **grace** that is in Christ Jesus. [2]And the things that thou hast heard of me among many witnesses, the same commit thou to faithful men, who shall be able to teach others also.

Here Paul is telling Timothy to be strong in the grace that is in Christ Jesus and go teach faithful men the gospel so that they may teach others also. The divine influence of God upon our hearts should be reflected in our lives in that we must teach others God's word, so they may learn and go teach others.

* * * * *

9. 1 Peter 4:1-10 ¹Forasmuch then as Christ hath suffered for us in the flesh, arm yourselves likewise with the same mind: for he that hath suffered in the flesh hath ceased from sin; ²That he no longer should live the rest of his time in the flesh to the lusts of men, but to the will of God. ³For the time past of our life may suffice us to have wrought the will of the Gentiles, when we walked in lasciviousness, lusts, excess of wine, revellings, banquetings, and abominable idolatries: ⁴Wherein they think it strange that ye run not with them to the same excess of riot, speaking evil of you: ⁵Who shall give account to him that is ready to judge the quick and the dead. ⁶For for this cause was the gospel preached also to them that are dead, that they might be judged according to men in the flesh, but live according to God in the spirit. ⁷But the end of all things is at hand: be ye therefore sober, and watch unto prayer. ⁸And above all things have fervent charity among yourselves: for charity shall cover the multitude of sins. ⁹Use hospitality one to another without grudging. ¹⁰As every man hath received the gift, even so minister the same one to another, as good stewards of the manifold **grace** of God.

In this passage of scripture we see as every man hath received the gift, we should minister to one another as good stewards of the manifold grace of God. 1 Corinthians 4:1-2 says, "¹Let a man so account of us, as of the ministers of Christ, and stewards of the mysteries of God. ²Moreover it is required in stewards, that a man be found faithful." As ministers of Christ and stewards of the mysteries of God, we must be found faithful. This is why God's grace is given to us. We must not take the gift of God's grace lightly, but we must take on the mind of Christ so that we will be faithful to the end. Philippians 2:5-8 says, "⁵Let this mind be in you, which was also in Christ Jesus: ⁶Who, being in the form of God, thought it not robbery to be equal with God: ⁷But made himself of no reputation, and took upon him the form of a servant, and was made in the likeness of men: ⁸And being found in fashion as a man, he humbled himself, and became obedient unto death, even the death of the cross." John 1:14 says, "And the Word was made flesh, and dwelt among us, (and we beheld his glory, the glory as of the only begotten of the Father,) full of grace and truth." In Philippians 2 we see that Jesus was obedient unto death and in John 1 we see that the Word (Jesus) was full of grace and truth. Let us utilize the gift of God's grace in the same manner – that we will be obedient to the end as good stewards and ministers of Christ. If the divine influence of God is upon our hearts, then it will be reflected in our lives by us being good stewards and ministers of Christ.

Chapter 4:

⌒⋙⌒

Grace is given to be Holy

1. Romans 1:1-7 [1]Paul, a servant of Jesus Christ, called to be an apostle, separated unto the gospel of God, [2](Which he had promised afore by his prophets in the holy scriptures,) [3]Concerning his Son Jesus Christ our Lord, which was made of the seed of David according to the flesh; [4]And declared to be the Son of God with power, according to the spirit of holiness, by the resurrection from the dead: [5]By whom we have received **grace** and apostleship, for obedience to the faith among all nations, for his name: [6]Among whom are ye also the called of Jesus Christ: [7]To all that be in Rome, beloved of God, called to be saints: **Grace** to you and peace from God our Father, and the Lord Jesus Christ.

In this passage of scripture Paul says through Jesus "we have received grace and apostleship, for the obedience to the faith among all nations, for his name …" The divine influence upon our hearts will be reflected in our lives in that we will be obedient to the faith. Again, I will cite Romans 12:1-2 which says, "[1]I beseech you therefore, brethren, by the mercies of God, that ye present your bodies a living sacrifice, holy, acceptable unto God, which is your reasonable service. [2]And be not conformed to this world: but be ye transformed by the renewing of your mind, that ye may prove what is that good, and acceptable, and perfect, will of God." When we present our bodies holy and acceptable to God, this is just our reasonable service. We will accomplish this by renewing our minds daily through the word of God. 2 Corinthians 10:3-6 says, "[3]For though we walk in the flesh, we do not war after the flesh: [4](For the weapons of our warfare are not carnal, but mighty through God to the pulling down of strong holds;) [5]Casting down imaginations, and every high thing that exalteth itself against the knowledge of God, and bringing into captivity every thought to the obedience of Christ; [6]And having in a readiness to revenge all disobedience, when your obedience is fulfilled." We are in a spiritual warfare and Satan is daily trying to bombard our minds with carnal things. If we stay in God's word and meditate on His word, we will win the battle over our minds and walk in obedience to the faith.

* * * * *

2. Ephesians 1:1-12 [1]Paul, an apostle of Jesus Christ by the will of God, to the saints which are at Ephesus, and to the faithful in Christ Jesus: [2]**Grace** be to you, and peace, from God our Father, and from the Lord Jesus Christ. [3]Blessed be the God and Father of our Lord Jesus Christ, who hath blessed us with all spiritual blessings in heavenly places in Christ: [4]According as he hath chosen us in him before the foundation of the world, that we should be holy and without blame before him in love: [5]Having predestinated us unto the adoption of children by Jesus Christ to himself, according to the good pleasure of his will, [6]To the praise of the glory of his **grace**, wherein he hath made us accepted in the beloved. [7]In whom we have redemption through his blood, the forgiveness of sins, according to the riches of his **grace**; [8]Wherein he hath abounded toward us in all wisdom and prudence; [9]Having made known unto us the mystery of his will, according to his good pleasure which he hath purposed in himself: [10]That in the dispensation of the fulness of times he might gather together in one all things in Christ, both which are in heaven, and which are on earth; even in him: [11]In whom also we have obtained an inheritance, being predestinated according to the purpose of him who worketh all things after the counsel of his own will: [12]That we should be to the praise of his glory, who first trusted in Christ.

In verses 3-6 Paul says that God and Jesus "hath blessed us" (Paul, the saints at Ephesus, and the faithful in Christ Jesus [verse 1]) "with all spiritual blessings… according as he hath chosen us before the foundation of the world, that we should be holy and without blame before Him, having predestinated us unto the adoption of children by Jesus Christ to himself, according to the good pleasure of his will to the praise of the glory of His grace, wherein He has made us accepted…" Through the grace of Christ Jesus, He has chosen us (saints/disciples) before the foundation of the world, that we should be holy and without blame before Him. Paul continues in verses 7-8 that "we have redemption through his blood, the forgiveness of sins, according to the riches of His grace; Wherein he hath abounded toward us in all wisdom and prudence; Having made known to us the mystery of his will…" Through the divine influence upon our hearts, Jesus gives us wisdom and prudence and the knowledge of His will. He gives us these attributes so that we can walk in them – so that holiness will be reflected in our lives.

* * * * *

3. 2 Timothy 1:8-11 ⁸Be not thou therefore ashamed of the testimony of our Lord, nor of me his prisoner: but be thou partaker of the afflictions of the gospel according to the power of God; ⁹Who hath saved us, and called us with an holy calling, not according to our works, but according to his own purpose and **grace**, which was given us in Christ Jesus before the world began, ¹⁰But is now made manifest by the appearing of our Saviour Jesus Christ, who hath abolished death, and hath brought life and immortality to light through the gospel: ¹¹Whereunto I am appointed a preacher, and an apostle, and a teacher of the Gentiles.

In this passage of scripture Paul tells Timothy to be a partaker of the afflictions of the gospel according to the power of God, Who saved us and called us with a holy calling according to His own purpose and grace. Hebrew 3:1-2 says, "¹Wherefore, holy brethren, partakers of the heavenly calling, consider the Apostle and High Priest of our profession, Christ Jesus; ²Who was faithful to him that appointed him, as also Moses was faithful in all his house." This passage is telling the holy brethren, partakers of the heavenly calling, to consider or to look to Jesus' example of how He was faithful to God. We see this again in Hebrews 12:1-3 which says, "¹Wherefore seeing we also are compassed about with so great a cloud of witnesses, let us lay aside every weight, and the sin which doth so easily beset us, and let us run with patience the race that is set before us, ²Looking unto Jesus the author and finisher of our faith; who for the joy that was set before him endured the cross, despising the shame, and is set down at the right hand of the throne of God. ³For consider him that endured such contradiction of sinners against himself, lest ye be wearied and faint in your minds." We must run with patience the race that is before us, looking to Jesus the author and finisher of our faith. If we look to Jesus' example, walking holy will be reflected in our lives according to God's divine influence upon our hearts.

* * * * *

4. Titus 2:9-14 ⁹Exhort servants to be obedient unto their own masters, and to please them well in all things; not answering again; ¹⁰Not purloining, but shewing all good fidelity; that they may adorn the doctrine of God our Saviour in all things. ¹¹For the **grace** of God that bringeth salvation hath appeared to all men, ¹²Teaching us that, denying ungodliness and worldly lusts, we should live soberly, righteously, and godly, in this present world; ¹³Looking for that blessed hope, and the glorious appearing of the great God and our Saviour Jesus Christ; ¹⁴Who gave himself for us, that he might redeem us from all iniquity, and purify unto himself a peculiar people, zealous of good works.

The grace of God that brings salvation to all men, teaches us that we should deny ungodliness and worldly lusts, live soberly, righteously, and godly in this present world. In order for us to deny ungodliness, live soberly and righteously in this present world, we must study and meditate on God's word. 2 Timothy 3:12-17 says, "¹²Yea, and all that will live godly in Christ Jesus shall suffer persecution. ¹³But evil men and seducers shall wax worse and worse, deceiving, and being deceived. ¹⁴But continue thou in the things which thou hast learned and hast been assured of, knowing of whom thou hast learned them; [15]And that from a child thou hast known the holy scriptures, which are able to make thee wise unto salvation through faith which is in Christ Jesus. [16]All scripture is given by inspiration of God, and is profitable for doctrine, for reproof, for correction, for instruction in righteousness: [17]That the man of God may be perfect, thoroughly furnished unto all good works." When we study God's word, it will supply us with sound doctrine, reprove us, correct us, and instruct us in righteousness in order that we may be perfect, thoroughly furnished unto all good works. The divine influence of God upon our hearts is reflected in our lives if we deny ungodliness and worldly lusts, live soberly, righteously, and godly in this present world.

* * * * *

5. Hebrews 13:8-9 [8]Jesus Christ the same yesterday, and to day, and for ever. [9]Be not carried about with divers and strange doctrines. For it is a good thing that the heart be established with **grace**; not with meats, which have not profited them that have been occupied therein.

This passage of scripture tells us that Jesus is the same yesterday, today, and forever – He does not change. Isaiah 40:8 says, "The grass withereth, the flower fadeth: but the word of our God shall stand for ever." The passage in Hebrews goes on to say that we should not be carried away with divers and strange doctrines. 2 Timothy 4:2-4 says, "[2]Preach the word; be instant in season, out of season; reprove, rebuke, exhort with all long suffering and doctrine. [3]For the time will come when they will not endure sound doctrine; but after their own lusts shall they heap to themselves teachers, having itching ears; [4]And they shall turn away their ears from the truth, and shall be turned unto fables." In order for us to remain steadfast, it is a good thing for our hearts to be established ("to stabilize") with grace. Is this saying for our hearts to be established with God's unmerited favor? No, it is saying for our hearts to be established with the divine influence of God and it should be reflected in our lives as we are obedient to that influence.

* * * * *

6. 1 Peter 1:3-16 [3]Blessed be the God and Father of our Lord Jesus Christ, which according to his abundant mercy hath begotten us again unto a lively hope by the resurrection of Jesus Christ from the dead, [4]To an inheritance incorruptible, and undefiled, and that fadeth not away, reserved in heaven for you, [5]Who are kept by the power of God through faith unto salvation ready to be revealed in the last time. [6]Wherein ye greatly rejoice, though now for a season, if need be, ye are in heaviness through manifold temptations: [7]That the trial of your faith, being much more precious than of gold that perisheth, though it be tried with fire, might be found unto praise and honour and glory at the appearing of Jesus Christ: [8]Whom having not seen, ye love; in whom, though now ye see him not, yet believing, ye rejoice with joy unspeakable and full of glory: [9]Receiving the end of your faith, even the salvation of your souls. [10]Of which salvation the prophets have enquired and searched diligently, who prophesied of the grace that should come unto you: [11]Searching what, or what manner of time the Spirit of Christ which was in them did signify, when it testified beforehand the sufferings of Christ, and the glory that should follow. [12]Unto whom it was revealed, that not unto themselves, but unto us they did minister the things, which are now reported unto you by them that have preached the gospel unto you with the Holy Ghost sent down from heaven; which things the angels desire to look into. [13]Wherefore gird up the loins of your mind, be sober, and hope to the end for the **grace** that is to be brought unto you at the revelation of Jesus Christ; [14]As obedient children, not fashioning yourselves according to the former lusts in your ignorance: [15]But as he which hath called you is holy, so be ye holy in all manner of conversation; [16]Because it is written, Be ye holy; for I am holy.

Verses 13-16 say, "[13]Wherefore gird up the loins of your mind, be sober, and hope to the end for the grace that is to be brought unto you at the revelation of Jesus Christ; [14]As obedient children, not fashioning yourselves according to the former lusts in your ignorance: [15]But as he which hath called you is holy, so be ye holy in all manner of conversation; [16]Because it is written, Be ye holy; for I am holy." We should gird up our minds to be sober. Philippians 4:8 tells us what we should think on as it says, "Finally, brethren, whatsoever things are true, whatsoever things are honest, whatsoever things are just, whatsoever things are pure, whatsoever things are lovely, whatsoever things are of good report; if there be any virtue, and if there be any praise, think on these things."

As verse 13 continues, it tells us to hope to the end for the grace that is brought unto us at the revelation of Jesus Christ, as obedient children. As He which called us is holy, we should be holy in all manner of conversation ("behavior"). Colossians 3:23 says, "And whatsoever ye do, do it heartily, as to the Lord, and not unto men." We should strive daily to be holy because God is holy. Daily, we must read, study, and meditate on the word of God, fellowship with the saints, and continually be in prayer. The grace of God, the divine influence upon our hearts is reflected in our lives as we live holy.

Chapter 5:

~*~

Grace: Greeting / Salutation to the Church / Saints

In this chapter, we will not go in depth on the passages of scripture. Our main goal with these scriptures is to recognize that the word "grace" was used as a greeting/salutation to the church/saints (disciples) only, and does not apply for the masses of people.

1. Romans 1:1-7 ¹Paul, a servant of Jesus Christ, called to be an apostle, separated unto the gospel of God, ²(Which he had promised afore by his prophets in the holy scriptures,) ³Concerning his Son Jesus Christ our Lord, which was made of the seed of David according to the flesh; ⁴And declared to be the Son of God with power, according to the spirit of holiness, by the resurrection from the dead: ⁵By whom we have received **grace** and apostleship, for obedience to the faith among all nations, for his name: ⁶Among whom are ye also the called of Jesus Christ: ⁷To all that be in Rome, beloved of God, called to be saints: **Grace** to you and peace from God our Father, and the Lord Jesus Christ.

In this passage, Paul says, "Grace to you and peace from God our Father, and the Lord Jesus Christ" to "all that be in Rome, beloved of God, called to be saints." The word "saints" in the Greek is defined as physically pure, morally blameless or religious, and ceremonially consecrated.

* * * * *

2. 1 Corinthians 1:1-3 [1]Paul called to be an apostle of Jesus Christ through the will of God, and Sosthenes our brother, [2]Unto the church of God which is at Corinth, to them that are sanctified in Christ Jesus, called to be saints, with all that in every place call upon the name of Jesus Christ our Lord, both their's and our's: [3]**Grace** be unto you, and peace, from God our Father, and from the Lord Jesus Christ.

In this passage Paul says, "Grace be unto you, and peace, from God our Father, and from the Lord Jesus Christ" to "the church of God which is at Corinth…" The word "church" in the Greek is defined as, "Christian community of members on earth." The word "Christian" in the Greek is defined as, "a follower of Christ." We must be true to ourselves and examine our lives and ask ourselves the question, "Am I a follower of Christ or am I just hiding under the title 'Christian' to make me feel good?" 2 Corinthians 13:5 says, "Examine yourselves, whether ye be in the faith; prove your own selves."

* * * * *

3. 2 Corinthians 1:1-2 [1]Paul, an apostle of Jesus Christ by the will of God, and Timothy our brother, unto the church of God which is at Corinth, with all the saints which are in all Achaia: [2]**Grace** be to you and peace from God our Father, and from the Lord Jesus Christ.

In this passage Paul says, "Grace be to you and peace from God our Father, and from the Lord Jesus Christ" to "the church of God which is at Corinth."

* * * * *

4. Galatians 1:1-5 [1]Paul, an apostle, (not of men, neither by man, but by Jesus Christ, and God the Father, who raised him from the dead;) [2]And all the brethren which are with me, unto the churches of Galatia: [3]**Grace** be to you and peace from God the Father, and from our Lord Jesus Christ, [4]Who gave himself for our sins, that he might deliver us from this present

evil world, according to the will of God and our Father: [5]To whom be glory for ever and ever. Amen.

In this passage of scripture, Paul says, "Grace be to you and peace from God the Father, and from our Lord Jesus Christ" to "the churches of Galatia."

* * * * *

5. Ephesians 1:1-2 [1]Paul, an apostle of Jesus Christ by the will of God, to the saints which are at Ephesus, and to the faithful in Christ Jesus: [2]**Grace** be to you, and peace, from God our Father, and from the Lord Jesus Christ.

In this passage of scripture, Paul says, "Grace be to you, and peace, from God our Father, and from the Lord Jesus Christ" to "the saints which are at Ephesus, and to the faithful in Christ Jesus."

* * * * *

6. Philippians 1:1-2 [1]Paul and Timotheus, the servants of Jesus Christ, to all the saints in Christ Jesus which are at Philippi, with the bishops and deacons: [2]**Grace** be unto you, and peace, from God our Father, and from the Lord Jesus Christ.

In this passage of scripture, Paul says, "Grace be unto you, and peace, from God our Father, and from the Lord Jesus Christ" to "all the saints in Christ Jesus which are at Philippi, with the bishops and deacons."

* * * * *

7. Colossians 1:1-2 [1]Paul, an apostle of Jesus Christ by the will of God, and Timotheus our brother, [2]To the saints and faithful brethren in Christ which are at Colosse: **Grace** be unto you, and peace, from God our Father and the Lord Jesus Christ.

In this passage of scripture, Paul says, "Grace be unto you, and peace, from God our Father and the Lord Jesus Christ" to "the saints and faithful brethren in Christ which are at Colosse."

* * * * *

8. 1 Thessalonians 1:1 ¹Paul, and Silvanus, and Timotheus, unto the church of the Thessalonians which is in God the Father and in the Lord Jesus Christ: **Grace** be unto you, and peace, from God our Father, and the Lord Jesus Christ.

In this passage of scripture, Paul says, "Grace be unto you, and peace, from God our Father, and the Lord Jesus Christ" to "the church of the Thessalonians which is in God the Father and in the Lord Jesus Christ."

* * * * *

9. 2 Thessalonians 1:1-2 ¹Paul, and Silvanus, and Timotheus, unto the church of the Thessalonians in God our Father and the Lord Jesus Christ: ²**Grace** unto you, and peace, from God our Father and the Lord Jesus Christ.

In this passage of scripture, Paul says, "Grace unto you, and peace, from God our Father and the Lord Jesus Christ" to "the church of the Thessalonians in God our Father and the Lord Jesus Christ."

* * * * *

10. 1 Timothy 1:1-2 ¹Paul, an apostle of Jesus Christ by the commandment of God our Saviour, and Lord Jesus Christ, which is our hope; ²Unto Timothy, my own son in the faith: **Grace**, mercy, and peace, from God our Father and Jesus Christ our Lord.

In this passage of scripture, Paul says, "Grace, mercy, and peace, from God our Father and Jesus Christ our Lord" to "Timothy, my own son in the faith." Here when Paul says Timothy is his son in the faith, he is indicating that Timothy is part of his spiritual family, just as Jesus describes His spiritual family in Matthew 12:47-50 which says, "⁴⁷Then one said unto him, Behold, thy mother and thy brethren stand without, desiring to speak with thee. ⁴⁸But he answered and said unto him that told him, Who is my mother? and who are my brethren? ⁴⁹And he stretched forth his hand toward his disciples, and said, Behold my mother and my brethren! [50]For whosoever shall do the will of my Father which is in heaven, the same is my brother, and sister, and mother."

* * * * *

11. 2 Timothy 1:1-2 [1]Paul, an apostle of Jesus Christ by the will of God, according to the promise of life which is in Christ Jesus, [2]To Timothy, my dearly beloved son: **Grace**, mercy, and peace, from God the Father and Christ Jesus our Lord.

In this passage of scripture, Paul says, "Grace, mercy, and peace, from God the Father and Christ Jesus our Lord" to "Timothy, my dearly beloved son."

* * * * *

12. Titus 1:1-4 [1]Paul, a servant of God, and an apostle of Jesus Christ, according to the faith of God's elect, and the acknowledging of the truth which is after godliness; [2]In hope of eternal life, which God, that cannot lie, promised before the world began; [3]But hath in due times manifested his word through preaching, which is committed unto me according to the commandment of God our Saviour; [4]To Titus, mine own son after the common faith: **Grace**, mercy, and peace, from God the Father and the Lord Jesus Christ our Saviour.

In this passage of scripture, Paul says, "Grace, mercy, and peace, from God the Father and the Lord Jesus Christ our Saviour" to "Titus, mine own son after the common faith."

* * * * *

13. Philemon 1-3 [1]Paul, a prisoner of Jesus Christ, and Timothy our brother, unto Philemon our dearly beloved, and fellowlabourer, [2]And to our beloved Apphia, and Archippus our fellowsoldier, and to the church in thy house: [3]**Grace** to you, and peace, from God our Father and the Lord Jesus Christ.

In this passage of scripture, Paul says, "Grace to you, and peace, from God our Father and the Lord Jesus Christ" to "Philemon our dearly beloved, and fellowlabourer, and to our beloved Apphia, and Archippus our fellowsoldier, and to the church in thy house."

* * * * *

14. 1 Peter 1:1-2 ¹Peter, an apostle of Jesus Christ, to the strangers scattered throughout Pontus, Galatia, Cappadocia, Asia, and Bithynia, ²Elect according to the foreknowledge of God the Father, through sanctification of the Spirit, unto obedience and sprinkling of the blood of Jesus Christ: **Grace** unto you, and peace, be multiplied.

In this passage of scripture, Peter says, "Grace unto you, and peace, be multiplied" to "the strangers scattered throughout Pontus, Galatia, Cappadocia, Asia, and Bithynia, Elect according to the foreknowledge of God the Father, through sanctification of the Spirit, unto obedience and sprinkling of the blood of Jesus Christ." "Elect" in the Greek means "select." The strangers that were scattered throughout Pontus, Galatia, Cappadocia, Asia, and Bithynia were the elect of God through sanctification of the Spirit, unto obedience …

* * * * *

15. 2 Peter 1:1-4 ¹Simon Peter, a servant and an apostle of Jesus Christ, to them that have obtained like precious faith with us through the righteousness of God and our Saviour Jesus Christ: ²**Grace** and peace be multiplied unto you through the knowledge of God, and of Jesus our Lord, ³According as his divine power hath given unto us all things that pertain unto life and godliness, through the knowledge of him that hath called us to glory and virtue: ⁴Whereby are given unto us exceeding great and precious promises: that by these ye might be partakers of the divine nature, having escaped the corruption that is in the world through lust.

In this passage of scripture, Peter says, "Grace and peace be multiplied unto you through the knowledge of God, and of Jesus our Lord" to them "that have obtained like precious faith with us through the righteousness of God and our Saviour Jesus Christ."

* * * * *

16. 2 John 1-3 ¹The elder unto the elect lady and her children, whom I love in the truth; and not I only, but also all they that have known the truth; ²For the truth's sake, which dwelleth in us, and shall be with us for ever. ³**Grace** be with you, mercy, and peace, from God the Father, and from the Lord Jesus Christ, the Son of the Father, in truth and love.

In this passage of scripture, the elder says, "Grace be with you, mercy, and peace, from God the Father, and from the Lord Jesus Christ, the Son of the Father" to "the elect lady and her children, whom I love in the truth."

* * * * *

17. Revelation 1:1-6 ¹The Revelation of Jesus Christ, which God gave unto him, to shew unto his servants things which must shortly come to pass; and he sent and signified it by his angel unto his servant John: ²Who bare record of the word of God, and of the testimony of Jesus Christ, and of all things that he saw. ³Blessed is he that readeth, and they that hear the words of this prophecy, and keep those things which are written therein: for the time is at hand. ⁴John to the seven churches which are in Asia: **Grace** be unto you, and peace, from him which is, and which was, and which is to come; and from the seven Spirits which are before his throne; ⁵And from Jesus Christ, who is the faithful witness, and the first begotten of the dead, and the prince of the kings of the earth. Unto him that loved us, and washed us from our sins in his own blood, ⁶And hath made us kings and priests unto God and his Father; to him be glory and dominion for ever and ever. Amen.

In this passage of scripture, John says, "Grace be unto you, and peace, from him which is, and which was, and which is to come; and from the seven Spirits which are before his throne; And from Jesus Christ, who is the faithful witness, and the first begotten of the dead, and the prince of the kings of the earth" to "the seven churches which are in Asia."

Chapter 6:

‿ℳ‿

Grace: Farewell / Benediction to the Church / Saints

In chapter 5 we established the fact that the word "grace" was used to greet the church/saints only and does not apply for the masses of people. In this chapter, we will see that the word "grace" is used as a farewell/benediction to the church/saints. Only the passage of scriptures will be listed.

1. Romans 16:24 The **grace** of our Lord Jesus Christ be with you all. Amen.

* * * * *

2. 1 Corinthians 16:21-24 ²¹The salutation of me Paul with mine own hand. ²²If any man love not the Lord Jesus Christ, let him be Anathema Maranatha. ²³The **grace** of our Lord Jesus Christ be with you. ²⁴My love be with you all in Christ Jesus. Amen.

* * * * *

3. 2 Corinthians 13:11-14 ¹¹Finally, brethren, farewell. Be perfect, be of good comfort, be of one mind, live in peace; and the God of love and peace shall be with you. ¹²Greet one another with an holy kiss. ¹³All the saints

salute you. [14]The **grace** of the Lord Jesus Christ, and the love of God, and the communion of the Holy Ghost, be with you all. Amen.

* * * * *

4. Galatians 6:18 Brethren, the **grace** of our Lord Jesus Christ be with your spirit. Amen.

* * * * *

5. Ephesians 6:21-24 [21]But that ye also may know my affairs, and how I do, Tychicus, a beloved brother and faithful minister in the Lord, shall make known to you all things: [22]Whom I have sent unto you for the same purpose, that ye might know our affairs, and that he might comfort your hearts. [23]Peace be to the brethren, and love with faith, from God the Father and the Lord Jesus Christ. [24]**Grace** be with all them that love our Lord Jesus Christ in sincerity. Amen.

* * * * *

6. Philippians 4:21-23 [21]Salute every saint in Christ Jesus. The brethren which are with me greet you. [22]All the saints salute you, chiefly they that are of Caesar's household. [23]The **grace** of our Lord Jesus Christ be with you all. Amen.

* * * * *

7. Colossians 4:15-18 [15]Salute the brethren which are in Laodicea, and Nymphas, and the church which is in his house. [16]And when this epistle is read among you, cause that it be read also in the church of the Laodiceans; and that ye likewise read the epistle from Laodicea. [17]And say to Archippus, Take heed to the ministry which thou hast received in the Lord, that thou fulfil it. [18]The salutation by the hand of me Paul. Remember my bonds. **Grace** be with you. Amen.

* * * * *

8. 1 Thessalonians 5:25-28 [25]Brethren, pray for us. [26]Greet all the brethren with an holy kiss. [27]I charge you by the Lord that this epistle be read unto all the holy brethren. [28]The **grace** of our Lord Jesus Christ be with you. Amen.

* * * * *

9. 2 Thessalonians 3:17-18 [17]The salutation of Paul with mine own hand, which is the token in every epistle: so I write. [18]The **grace** of our Lord Jesus Christ be with you all. Amen.

* * * * *

10. 1 Timothy 6:20-21 [20]O Timothy, keep that which is committed to thy trust, avoiding profane and vain babblings, and oppositions of science falsely so called: [21]Which some professing have erred concerning the faith. **Grace** be with thee. Amen.

* * * * *

11. 2 Timothy 4:22 The Lord Jesus Christ be with thy spirit. **Grace** be with you. Amen.

* * * * *

12. Titus 3:15 All that are with me salute thee. Greet them that love us in the faith. **Grace** be with you all. Amen.

* * * * *

13. Philemon 25 The **grace** of our Lord Jesus Christ be with your spirit. Amen.

* * * * *

14. Hebrews 13:25 **Grace** be with you all. Amen.

* * * * *

15. 1 Peter 5:12-14 [12]By Silvanus, a faithful brother unto you, as I suppose, I have written briefly, exhorting, and testifying that this is the true **grace** of God wherein ye stand. [13]The church that is at Babylon, elected together with you, saluteth you; and so doth Marcus my son. [14]Greet ye one another with a kiss of charity. Peace be with you all that are in Christ Jesus. Amen.

* * * * *

16. 2 Peter 3:17-18 [17]Ye therefore, beloved, seeing ye know these things before, beware lest ye also, being led away with the error of the wicked, fall from your own stedfastness. [18]But grow in **grace**, and in the knowledge of our Lord and Saviour Jesus Christ. To him be glory both now and for ever. Amen.

* * * * *

17. Revelation 22:21 The **grace** of our Lord Jesus Christ be with you all. Amen.

Chapter 7:

~~~

We shall not continue to Sin because of Grace

Romans 5:18-6:11 [18]Therefore as by the offence of one judgment came upon all men to condemnation; even so by the righteousness of one the free gift came upon all men unto justification of life. [19]For as by one man's disobedience many were made sinners, so by the obedience of one shall many be made righteous. [20]Moreover the law entered, that the offence might abound. But where sin abounded, **grace** did much more abound: [21]That as sin hath reigned unto death, even so might **grace** reign through righteousness unto eternal life by Jesus Christ our Lord. (Chapter 6) [1]What shall we say then? Shall we continue in sin, that **grace** may abound? [2]God forbid. How shall we, that are dead to sin, live any longer therein? [3]Know ye not, that so many of us as were baptized into Jesus Christ were baptized into his death? [4]Therefore we are buried with him by baptism into death: that like as Christ was raised up from the dead by the glory of the Father, even so we also should walk in newness of life. [5]For if we have been planted together in the likeness of his death, we shall be also in the likeness of his resurrection: [6]Knowing this, that our old man is crucified with him, that the body of sin might be destroyed, that henceforth we should not serve sin. [7]For he that is dead is freed from sin. [8]Now if we be dead with Christ, we believe that we shall also live with him: [9]Knowing that Christ being raised from the dead dieth no more; death hath no more dominion over him. ¹⁰For in that he died, he died unto sin once: but in that he liveth, he liveth unto God. ¹¹Likewise reckon ye also yourselves to be dead indeed unto sin, but alive unto God through Jesus Christ our Lord. ¹²Let not sin therefore reign in your mortal body, that ye should obey it in the lusts thereof. ¹³Neither yield ye your members as instruments of unrighteousness unto sin: but yield yourselves unto God, as those that are alive from the dead, and your members as instruments of righteousness unto God. ¹⁴For sin shall not have dominion over you: for ye are not under the law, but under **grace**. ¹⁵What then? shall we sin, because we are not under the law, but under **grace**? God forbid. ¹⁶Know ye not, that to whom ye yield yourselves servants to obey, his servants ye are to whom ye obey; whether of sin unto death, or of obedience unto righteousness? ¹⁷But God be thanked, that ye were the servants of sin, but ye have obeyed from the heart that form of doctrine which was delivered you. ¹⁸Being then made free from sin, ye became the servants of righteousness.

Chapter 6 verse 1 of Romans asks the question, "Shall we continue in sin, that grace may abound?" The answer to that question is in verses 2-4 which read, "²God forbid. How shall we, that are dead to sin, live any longer therein? ³Know ye not, that so many of us as were baptized into Jesus Christ were baptized into his death? ⁴Therefore we are buried with him by baptism into death: that like as Christ was raised up from the dead by the glory of the Father, even so we also should walk in newness of life." Remember "grace" is the divine influence upon the heart and its reflection in the life. The divine influence upon the heart will quicken our spirit so that we will be able to walk in newness of life. In order for this to happen, we must submit to God. James 4:7 says "Submit yourselves therefore to God. Resist the devil, and he will flee from you." Jesus provides us an example of submitting to God and resisting the devil in Matthew 4:1-11. Whenever the devil tempted Jesus, He spoke the word to Satan. Jesus submitted to God, resisted Satan, "then the devil leaveth him…" (Matthew 4:11). This can only happen if we have our mind made up that we are going to do God's will and not our own. In Matthew 26:39, speaking of Jesus the verse says, "And he went a little farther, and fell on his face, and prayed, saying, O my Father, if it be possible, let this cup pass from me: nevertheless not as I will, but as thou wilt." This mindset is not natural and must be developed through daily reading, studying, meditating, sharing God's word with one another, and praying.

Verse 15 asks the question, "shall we sin, because we are not under the law, but under grace?" The answer from verses 15-17 is, "[15]... God forbid. [16]Know ye not, that to whom ye yield yourselves servants to obey, his servants ye are to whom ye obey; whether of sin unto death, or of obedience unto righteousness? [17]But God be thanked, that ye were the servants of sin, but ye have obeyed from the heart that form of doctrine which was delivered you." As saints, they were once servants to sin, but obeyed from the heart (through "grace" - the divine influence upon the heart and its reflection in the life) that form of doctrine which was delivered to them that they now yield themselves servants of obedience unto righteousness. John 8:31-32 says, "[31]Then said Jesus to those Jews which believed on him, If ye continue in my word, then are ye my disciples indeed; [32]And ye shall know the truth, and the truth shall make you free." We will be free from the bondage of sin if we will continue ("stay") in the word of God.

Chapter 8:

⌒*แ*⌒

Grace is given to the Humble

1. James 4:1-7 [1]From whence come wars and fightings among you? come they not hence, even of your lusts that war in your members? [2]Ye lust, and have not: ye kill, and desire to have, and cannot obtain: ye fight and war, yet ye have not, because ye ask not. [3]Ye ask, and receive not, because ye ask amiss, that ye may consume it upon your lusts. [4]Ye adulterers and adulteresses, know ye not that the friendship of the world is enmity with God? whosoever therefore will be a friend of the world is the enemy of God. [5]Do ye think that the scripture saith in vain, The spirit that dwelleth in us lusteth to envy? [6]But he giveth more **grace**. Wherefore he saith, God resisteth the proud, but giveth **grace** unto the humble. [7]Submit yourselves therefore to God. Resist the devil, and he will flee from you.

This passage of scripture is showing us that God gives us more ("larger") grace, in order to combat the lust ("intensely crave possession") to envy ("jealousy"). God gives us more grace when we humble ourselves to Him. When God gives us grace; when He divinely influences our hearts, it is reflected in our lives as we submit to Him and resist the devil. When we do this the devil will flee from us. We must not give in to the lust to envy. When that lust to envy comes upon us, we must rebuke it, bind it, and cast it out in the name of Jesus. Matthew 17:15-21 says, "[15]Lord, have mercy on my son: for he is lunatick, and sore vexed: for ofttimes he falleth into the fire, and oft into the water. [16]And I brought him to thy disciples, and they could not cure him. [17]Then Jesus answered and said, O faithless and perverse generation, how long shall I be with you? how long shall I suffer you? bring him hither to me. [18]And Jesus rebuked the devil; and he departed out of him: and the child was cured from that very hour. [19]Then came the disciples to Jesus apart, and said, Why could not we cast him out? [20]And Jesus said unto them, Because of your unbelief: for verily I say unto you, If ye have faith as a grain of mustard seed, ye shall say unto this mountain, Remove hence to yonder place; and it shall remove; and nothing shall be impossible unto you. [21]Howbeit this kind goeth not out but by prayer and fasting." Matthew 12:24-29 says, "[24]But when the Pharisees heard it, they said, This fellow doth not cast out devils, but by Beelzebub the prince of the devils. [25]And Jesus knew their thoughts, and said unto them, Every kingdom divided against itself is brought to desolation; and every city or house divided against itself shall not stand: [26]And if Satan cast out Satan, he is divided against himself; how shall then his kingdom stand? [27]And if I by Beelzebub cast out devils, by whom do your children cast them out? therefore they shall be your judges. [28]But if I cast out devils by the Spirit of God, then the kingdom of God is come unto you. [29]Or else how can one enter into a strong man's house, and spoil his goods, except he first bind the strong man? and then he will spoil his house." Matthew 18:18 says, "Verily I say unto you, Whatsoever ye shall bind on earth shall be bound in heaven: and whatsoever ye shall loose on earth shall be loosed in heaven." Matthew 8:16 says, "When the even was come, they brought unto him many that were possessed with devils: and he cast out the spirits with his word, and healed all that were sick."

We must not let the lust to envy or any of Satan's devices get into our thought pattern because if we think on anything long enough, we'll start to consider doing it; if we consider doing anything long enough, we will act on it; if we act on anything enough times, it will become a habit; and the repetition of a habit becomes a stronghold. This is why the second an evil thought (anything that goes against God's word) enters into our mind, we must rebuke it, bind it, and cast it out.

* * * * *

2. 1 Peter 5:1-7 [1]The elders which are among you I exhort, who am also an elder, and a witness of the sufferings of Christ, and also a partaker of the glory that shall be revealed: [2]Feed the flock of God which is among you, taking the oversight thereof, not by constraint, but willingly; not for filthy lucre, but of a ready mind; [3]Neither as being lords over God's heritage, but being examples to the flock. [4]And when the chief Shepherd shall appear, ye shall receive a crown of glory that fadeth not away. [5]Likewise, ye younger, submit yourselves unto the elder. Yea, all of you be subject one to another, and be clothed with humility: for God resisteth the proud, and giveth **grace** to the humble. [6]Humble yourselves therefore under the mighty hand of God, that he may exalt you in due time: [7]Casting all your care upon him; for he careth for you.

The word "proud" in the Greek means "haughty." The word "humble" means "depressed" in the Greek. The scripture is not speaking of being depressed in mood, but in thinking of or reliance upon oneself. In John 3:3, John speaking of Jesus said, "He must increase, but I must decrease." In John 15:4-5 Jesus says, "[4]Abide in me, and I in you. As the branch cannot bear fruit of itself, except it abide in the vine; no more can ye, except ye abide in me. [5]I am the vine, ye are the branches: He that abideth in me, and I in him, the same bringeth forth much fruit: for without me ye can do nothing." We must abide ("stay") in Jesus. We must stay in the word of God. Jesus said we can do nothing without Him and Philippians 4:13 also tells us that we can do all things through Christ which strengthens us. If we will submit ourselves to God and seek Him, He will give us grace and He will exalt us. We must not try to exalt ourselves. Luke 14:11 says, "For whosoever exalteth himself shall be abased; and he that humbleth himself shall be exalted." The divine influence of God is upon our hearts and is reflected in our lives as we are obedient to what the Holy Ghost would have for us to do. When this happens, God will exalt us.

Chapter 9:

cM

Believing through Grace

1. Acts 11:19-23 [19]Now they which were scattered abroad upon the persecution that arose about Stephen travelled as far as Phenice, and Cyprus, and Antioch, preaching the word to none but unto the Jews only. [20]And some of them were men of Cyprus and Cyrene, which, when they were come to Antioch, spake unto the Grecians, preaching the LORD Jesus. [21]And the hand of the Lord was with them: and a great number believed, and turned unto the Lord. [22]Then tidings of these things came unto the ears of the church which was in Jerusalem: and they sent forth Barnabas, that he should go as far as Antioch. [23]Who, when he came, and had seen the **grace** of God, was glad, and exhorted them all, that with purpose of heart they would cleave unto the Lord.

Verses 19-21 show us that a great number of the Grecians in Antioch believed and turned unto the Lord because they heard the preaching of the word. When Barnabas came to Antioch, he saw the grace of God. He saw the divine influence upon the heart reflected in the lives of the Grecians as they believed and turned unto the Lord. Romans 10:13-15 says, "[13]For whosoever shall call upon the name of the Lord shall be saved. [14]How then shall they call on him in whom they have not believed? and how shall they believe in him of whom they have not heard? and how shall they hear without a preacher? [15]And how shall they preach, except they be sent? as it is written, How beautiful are the feet of them that preach the gospel of peace, and bring glad tidings of good things!" A person can only believe in Jesus through the preaching of the gospel because it is the gospel that influences one's heart. As disciples, we must preach the word of God so it may influence the heart of the unbeliever and be reflected in their life as they believe.

* * * * *

2. Acts 18:24-28 ²⁴And a certain Jew named Apollos, born at Alexandria, an eloquent man, and mighty in the scriptures, came to Ephesus. ²⁵This man was instructed in the way of the Lord; and being fervent in the spirit, he spake and taught diligently the things of the Lord, knowing only the baptism of John. ²⁶And he began to speak boldly in the synagogue: whom when Aquila and Priscilla had heard, they took him unto them, and expounded unto him the way of God more perfectly. ²⁷And when he was disposed to pass into Achaia, the brethren wrote, exhorting the disciples to receive him: who, when he was come, helped them much which had believed through **grace**: ²⁸For he mightily convinced the Jews, and that publicly, shewing by the scriptures that Jesus was Christ.

Verse 27 of this passage says Apollos "helped them much which had believed through grace." Those who believed, did so through grace – through the preaching of the word of God which was the divine influence upon their heart. Acts 15:7 says, "And when there had been much disputing, Peter rose up, and said unto them, Men and brethren, ye know how that a good while ago God made choice among us, that the Gentiles by my mouth should hear the word of the gospel, and believe." Again, as disciples, we must preach the word of God so it may influence the heart of the unbeliever and be reflected in their life as they believe.

Chapter 10:

Justified by Grace

1. Romans 3:21-26 ²¹But now the righteousness of God without the law is manifested, being witnessed by the law and the prophets; ²²Even the righteousness of God which is by faith of Jesus Christ unto all and upon all them that believe: for there is no difference: ²³For all have sinned, and come short of the glory of God; ²⁴Being justified freely by his **grace** through the redemption that is in Christ Jesus: ²⁵Whom God hath set forth to be a propitiation through faith in his blood, to declare his righteousness for the remission of sins that are past, through the forbearance of God; ²⁶To declare, I say, at this time his righteousness: that he might be just, and the justifier of him which believeth in Jesus.

Verse 24 of this passage of scripture tells us that we are justified ("to render innocent") by His grace through Christ Jesus. Verse 26 tells us that God is the justifier of him which believeth in Jesus. We saw in the previous chapter that it is through God's grace, the divine influence upon our hearts that we believe in Jesus. Now we see that we are justified through believing in Jesus. Acts 13:38-39 says, "³⁸Be it known unto you therefore, men and brethren, that through this man is preached unto you the forgiveness of sins: ³⁹And by him all that believe are justified from all things, from which ye could not be justified by the law of Moses."

* * * * *

2. Titus 3:1-8 ¹Put them in mind to be subject to principalities and powers, to obey magistrates, to be ready to every good work, ²To speak evil of no man, to be no brawlers, but gentle, shewing all meekness unto all men. ³For we ourselves also were sometimes foolish, disobedient, deceived, serving divers lusts and pleasures, living in malice and envy, hateful, and hating one another. ⁴But after that the kindness and love of God our Saviour toward man appeared, ⁵Not by works of righteousness which we have done, but according to his mercy he saved us, by the washing of regeneration, and renewing of the Holy Ghost; ⁶Which he shed on us abundantly through Jesus Christ our Saviour; ⁷That being justified by his **grace**, we should be made heirs according to the hope of eternal life. ⁸This is a faithful saying, and these things I will that thou affirm constantly, that they which have believed in God might be careful to maintain good works. These things are good and profitable unto men.

In verses 6-7 we see that we are justified by grace through Jesus Christ. Paul goes on to tell Titus in verse 8, "This is a faithful saying, and these things I will that thou affirm constantly, that they which have believed in God might be careful to maintain good works. These things are good and profitable unto men." It is through the grace of God that we believe and are justified; and if we believe, we should be careful ("to exercise thought") to maintain ("to practice") good works for this is good and profitable unto men.

James 2:14-26 says, "¹⁴What doth it profit, my brethren, though a man say he hath faith, and have not works? can faith save him? ¹⁵If a brother or sister be naked, and destitute of daily food, ¹⁶And one of you say unto them, Depart in peace, be ye warmed and filled; notwithstanding ye give them not those things which are needful to the body; what doth it profit? ¹⁷Even so faith, if it hath not works, is dead, being alone. ¹⁸Yea, a man may say, Thou hast faith, and I have works: shew me thy faith without thy works, and I will shew thee my faith by my works. ¹⁹Thou believest that there is one God; thou doest well: the devils also believe, and tremble. ²⁰But wilt thou know, O vain man, that faith without works is dead? ²¹Was not

Abraham our father justified by works, when he had offered Isaac his son upon the altar? ²²Seest thou how faith wrought with his works, and by works was faith made perfect? ²³And the scripture was fulfilled which saith, Abraham believed God, and it was imputed unto him for righteousness: and he was called the Friend of God. ²⁴Ye see then how that by works a man is justified, and not by faith only. ²⁵Likewise also was not Rahab the harlot justified by works, when she had received the messengers, and had sent them out another way? ²⁶For as the body without the spirit is dead, so faith without works is dead also." This passage tells us in verse 19 that if we believe, we do well, but the devils also believe and tremble. If we believe, then works should follow. Once again, grace is the divine influence upon the heart and its reflection in the life. When we believe through the divine influence upon our hearts, the fact that we do believe should be reflected in our lives through good works. This is why verse 24 says, "Ye see then how that by works a man is justified, and not by faith only."

Chapter 11:

Continue in the Grace of God

Acts 13:38-43 ³⁸Be it known unto you therefore, men and brethren, that through this man is preached unto you the forgiveness of sins: ³⁹And by him all that believe are justified from all things, from which ye could not be justified by the law of Moses. ⁴⁰Beware therefore, lest that come upon you, which is spoken of in the prophets; ⁴¹Behold, ye despisers, and wonder, and perish: for I work a work in your days, a work which ye shall in no wise believe, though a man declare it unto you. ⁴²And when the Jews were gone out of the synagogue, the Gentiles besought that these words might be preached to them the next sabbath. ⁴³Now when the congregation was broken up, many of the Jews and religious proselytes followed Paul and Barnabas: who, speaking to them, persuaded them to continue in the **grace** of God.

Paul and Barnabas persuaded the Jews and proselytes ("convert to Judaism") to continue in the grace of God – that the divine influence upon their hearts will continue to be reflected in their lives. Ephesians 6:10-18 says, "¹⁰Finally, my brethren, be strong in the Lord, and in the power of his might. ¹¹Put on the whole armour of God, that ye may be able to stand against the wiles of the devil. ¹²For we wrestle not against flesh and blood, but against principalities, against powers, against the rulers of the darkness of this world, against spiritual wickedness in high places. ¹³Wherefore take unto you the whole armour of God, that ye may be able to withstand in the evil day, and having done all, to stand. [14]Stand therefore, having your loins girt about with truth, and having on the breastplate of righteousness; [15]And your feet shod with the preparation of the gospel of peace; [16]Above all, taking the shield of faith, wherewith ye shall be able to quench all the fiery darts of the wicked. [17]And take the helmet of salvation, and the sword of the Spirit, which is the word of God: [18]Praying always with all prayer and supplication in the Spirit, and watching thereunto with all perseverance and supplication for all saints." In order for us to continue in the grace of God, we must put on the whole armor of God so that we can fight off all the attacks of Satan and his demonic forces. We put on the spiritual armor: truth, righteousness, peace, faith, and salvation by daily reading, studying, meditating on God's word, and praying.

Chapter 12:

⌒ℳ⌒

Receive not the Grace of God in Vain

2 Corinthians 6:1-10 [1]We then, as workers together with him, beseech you also that ye receive not the **grace** of God in vain. [2](For he saith, I have heard thee in a time accepted, and in the day of salvation have I succoured thee: behold, now is the accepted time; behold, now is the day of salvation.) [3]Giving no offence in any thing, that the ministry be not blamed: [4]But in all things approving ourselves as the ministers of God, in much patience, in afflictions, in necessities, in distresses, [5]In stripes, in imprisonments, in tumults, in labours, in watchings, in fastings; [6]By pureness, by knowledge, by long suffering, by kindness, by the Holy Ghost, by love unfeigned, [7]By the word of truth, by the power of God, by the armour of righteousness on the right hand and on the left, [8]By honour and dishonour, by evil report and good report: as deceivers, and yet true; [9]As unknown, and yet well known; as dying, and, behold, we live; as chastened, and not killed; [10]As sorrowful, yet alway rejoicing; as poor, yet making many rich; as having nothing, and yet possessing all things.

In verse 2, Paul beseeches the Corinthians not to receive the grace of God in vain. In verse 3 he explains what he means by not receiving the grace of God in vain: giving no offence ("a stumbling, i.e. an occasion of sin") in anything, that the ministry be not blamed. In verse 4 Paul says we should approve ("to exhibit") ourselves as ministers of God. This is how the divine influence upon our hearts should be reflected in our lives. In 1 Corinthians 15:9-10 Paul says, "⁹For I am the least of the apostles, that am not meet to be called an apostle, because I persecuted the church of God. ¹⁰But by the grace of God I am what I am: and his grace which was bestowed upon me was not in vain; but I laboured more abundantly than they all: yet not I, but the grace of God which was with me." Paul says the grace of God that was bestowed upon him was not in vain, but through the grace of God he labored more abundantly than the other apostles. Likewise, we must not let God's influence upon our hearts go in vain. We must submit to the influence in order to keep us from stumbling and it will be reflected in our lives as we approve ourselves as God's ministers.

Chapter 13:

◁yℓ▷

Jesus' Grace is Sufficient

2 Corinthians 12:5-10 [5]Of such an one will I glory: yet of myself I will not glory, but in mine infirmities. [6]For though I would desire to glory, I shall not be a fool; for I will say the truth: but now I forbear, lest any man should think of me above that which he seeth me to be, or that he heareth of me. [7]And lest I should be exalted above measure through the abundance of the revelations, there was given to me a thorn in the flesh, the messenger of Satan to buffet me, lest I should be exalted above measure. [8]For this thing I besought the Lord thrice, that it might depart from me. [9]And he said unto me, My **grace** is sufficient for thee: for my strength is made perfect in weakness. Most gladly therefore will I rather glory in my infirmities, that the power of Christ may rest upon me. [10]Therefore I take pleasure in infirmities, in reproaches, in necessities, in persecutions, in distresses for Christ's sake: for when I am weak, then am I strong.

In this passage of scripture, Paul says a messenger ("an angel") of Satan was sent to buffet ("to wrap with the fist") him. After Paul besought Jesus three times for it to depart from him, Jesus said, "my grace is sufficient for thee." God's grace is sufficient ("satisfactory") because His strength ("miraculous power") is made perfect ("to complete") in weakness ("feebleness"). When we depend on God, this is when His miraculous power will be made complete in us. For this reason we should always stand on Philippians 4:13 which says, "I can do all things through Christ which strengtheneth me." We can do all things through Christ which strengthen us because His divine influence upon our hearts is sufficient enough for us to do His will (reflection in our lives).

Chapter 14:

Saved by Grace

Acts 15:6-11 ⁶And the apostles and elders came together for to consider of this matter. ⁷And when there had been much disputing, Peter rose up, and said unto them, Men and brethren, ye know how that a good while ago God made choice among us, that the Gentiles by my mouth should hear the word of the gospel, and believe. ⁸And God, which knoweth the hearts, bare them witness, giving them the Holy Ghost, even as he did unto us; ⁹And put no difference between us and them, purifying their hearts by faith. ¹⁰Now therefore why tempt ye God, to put a yoke upon the neck of the disciples, which neither our fathers nor we were able to bear? ¹¹But we believe that through the **grace** of the LORD Jesus Christ we shall be saved, even as they.

In verse 11 Peter says, "But we believe through the grace of the Lord Jesus Christ we shall be saved, even as they." Romans 10:8-9 says, "⁸But what saith it? The word is nigh thee, even in thy mouth, and in thy heart: that is, the word of faith, which we preach; ⁹That if thou shalt confess with thy mouth the Lord Jesus, and shalt believe in thine heart that God hath raised him from the dead, thou shalt be saved." It is through the word of faith being preached unto us (the divine influence upon our hearts) whereby we can confess with our mouths the Lord Jesus, and believe in our hearts that God has raised Him from the dead (its reflection in our lives), that we shall be saved.

Chapter 15:

Good Communication Ministers
Grace to the Hearer

Ephesians 4:29 Let no corrupt communication proceed out of your mouth, but that which is good to the use of edifying, that it may minister **grace** unto the hearers.

Our communication should be to edify, that it may minister grace to the hearers – that it will divinely influence the hearer's heart and be reflected in their life. In John 6:63 Jesus says, "It is the spirit that quickeneth; the flesh profiteth nothing: the words that I speak unto you, they are spirit, and they are life." We must speak the word of God to others because His word is spirit and it is life. It is the word of God that will divinely influence the heart of the hearer so that it may be reflected in their life.

Chapter 16:

One's Speech should be with Grace

Colossians 4:1-6 [1]Masters, give unto your servants that which is just and equal; knowing that ye also have a Master in heaven. [2]Continue in prayer, and watch in the same with thanksgiving; [3]Withal praying also for us, that God would open unto us a door of utterance, to speak the mystery of Christ, for which I am also in bonds: [4]That I may make it manifest, as I ought to speak. [5]Walk in wisdom toward them that are without, redeeming the time. [6]Let your speech be always with **grace**, seasoned with salt, that ye may know how ye ought to answer every man.

Verse 6 tells us that our speech should always be with grace – when we are inspired by the divine influence of God upon our hearts, it should be reflected in our lives as we may know how we should answer every man. Matthew 10:17-21 says, "[17]But beware of men: for they will deliver you up to the councils, and they will scourge you in their synagogues; [18]And ye shall be brought before governors and kings for my sake, for a testimony against them and the Gentiles. [19]But when they deliver you up, take no thought how or what ye shall speak: for it shall be given you in that same hour what ye shall speak. [20]For it is not ye that speak, but the Spirit of your Father which speaketh in you. [21]And the brother shall deliver up the brother to death, and the father the child: and the children shall rise up against their parents, and cause them to be put to death." God will give us what to speak through His Spirit – this is the divine influence upon our hearts. John 5:30 says, "I can of mine own self do nothing: as I hear, I judge: and my judgment is just; because I seek not mine own will, but the will of the Father which hath sent me." Just as Jesus did nothing on His own, but judged as He heard from God, we too must not seek our own will, but let the divine influence upon our hearts be reflected in our lives to speak as we hear from God.

Conclusion

As we have seen throughout this book, grace is the divine influence upon the heart, and its reflection in the life. God does not give us grace in order for us to do nothing. God gives us His grace in order for us to perform His perfect will for our lives. His perfect will for our lives will be manifested as we diligently read, study, meditate on His word, pray, and are obedient to what He puts into our hearts.

Conclusion

Printed in Great Britain
by Amazon.co.uk, Ltd.,
Marston Gate.